CONTEMPORARY CANADIAN

LABOUR RELATIONS

JOHN A. WILLES

B.A., M.B.A., LL.M.,
Barrister-At-Law, Associate Professor in
Industrial Relations and Business Law,
Queen's University

McGRAW-HILL RYERSON LIMITED

TORONTO MONTREAL NEW YORK AUCKLAND BOGOTÁ
CAIRO GUATEMALA HAMBURG JOHANNESBURG LISBON
LONDON MADRID MEXICO NEW DELHI PANAMA PARIS
SAN JUAN SÃO PAULO SINGAPORE SYDNEY TOKYO

CONTEMPORARY CANADIAN LABOUR RELATIONS

ISBN 0-07-548766-7

1 2 3 4 5 6 7 8 9 0   D   3 2 1 0 9 8 7 6 5 4

Printed and bound in Canada by John Deyell Company

Care has been taken to trace ownership of copyright material contained in this text. The publishers will gladly take any information that will enable them to rectify any reference or credit in subsequent editions.

CANADIAN CATALOGUING IN PUBLICATION DATA

Willes, John A.
  Contemporary Canadian labour relations

Includes index.
ISBN 0-07-548766-7

1. Industrial relations - Canada.   I. Title.

HD8106.5.W54 1984   331'.0971   C84-098702-1

TABLE OF CONTENTS

CHAPTER ELEVEN
COLLECTIVE BARGAINING IN THE PUBLIC SECTOR 347

PART VII   THE FUTURE FOR LABOUR RELATIONS IN
CANADA 369
CHAPTER TWELVE
THE FUTURE FOR LABOUR RELATIONS: CHALLENGES AND
RESPONSES 371

PREFACE

Contemporary Canadian Labour Relations was written as a general text-book for either a full two-term or a single-term industrial relations course. The text deals with the employment relationship in both a non-union and unionized setting, and examines the collective bargaining relation-ship in its historical context. The information contained in the text is presented for the purpose of providing students with an overview of the labour relations process, rather than the specific law on each topic. While every effort has been made to describe accurately the current legislated policy of the various jurisdictions, laws constantly change, and for any particular situation or province, reference should be made to the appropriate statutes or a practitioner in the field of labour law should be consulted.

In using this text as a single-term course information source, an instructor might consider Chapters 1–4 inclusive to provide the students with the legal nature of the employment, the historical development of trade unions, and the general policy framework. Chapter 5 and the introductory parts of 6–10 may be selected to provide an overview of the certification process, the negotiation of a collective agreement, and the arbitration process. Chapter 11 on public sector bargaining may also be included to complete an introductory course. Chapter 12 might be considered as a wrap-up chapter or left to a second-term course. A full two-term course would utilize all of the text material.

The text includes a number of cases to illustrate each of the various topics covered, and should constitute a sufficient variety of case material for a course taught using the case method. Most of the cases are based upon the author's own work in the labour field, with the names and data changed. The cases are entirely fictional with respect to persons, corporations, and related information, and are presented for discussion purposes.

The preparation of a text on such a broad subject is not an easy task, as it requires a constant assessment of the content as the material is written. One of the greatest difficulties is deciding how much to include on any one topic when so much can be said. In this regard I am indebted to many friends and colleagues, who, ever mindful of the reader, not only restrained me from writing exhaustively about each topic, but provided many helpful suggestions and valuable criticism of the work. In particular, I would like to express my gratitude to my good friend and mentor, Professor Emeritus ''Connie'' Curtis, who, many years ago, introduced me to the fascinating field of labour relations during my student days at Queen's University, and who, since that time has willingly shared with me his vast knowledge and invaluable advice on the subject.

I am indebted to many others as well. Mr. Fred von Veh of Toronto, an experienced labour relations law practitioner, willingly read my entire manuscript and provided me with an evaluation from a management perspective, as did Mr. Bert Rovers, an International Representative of the United Automobile Workers Union, who reviewed my work from the point of view of a union negotiator. My colleagues, Professors Brian W. Downie, Richard L. Jackson, and Frank Collom, read either the entire manuscript or parts thereof, and their comments as educators were most welcome and helpful. Finally, I owe special thanks to my labour relations students at Queen's University, who, during the Fall Term of 1983, patiently laboured through the draft manuscript as it was written, and at the end of the course, provided me with a useful evaluation of the material from a student's perspective.

I would also like to express my thanks to those special people who assisted me in the research and preparation of the manuscript for publication. In this regard I would like to acknowledge the contributions of my research assistant, William Moore, who painstakingly collected the many references referred to in the work, John Starky, who assisted me during the course of my writing of Chapters 1–6, and Nora Perry, who checked references and proofread the galley pages. I am indebted as well to my secretaries, Mrs. Rose Marie Baird and Mrs. Gail LeSarge, for their secretarial help in the typing of parts of the manuscript, and to my wife Fran, who once again, with her usual enthusiasm, undertook the job of administrator of the project, and performed the myriad of duties involved in the preparation of the manuscript for the publisher.

I am grateful as well for the assistance provided by Mr. Henry Klaise, my sponsoring editor, and for the willingness of the entire production group at McGraw-Hill Ryerson Limited to bear with me as I prepared the text.

ABBREVIATIONS

A.C.	Appeal Cases
All E.R.	All England Reports
Am.Dec.	American Decennial Digest
B.C.C.A.	British Columbia Court of Appeal
c.	chapter
C.A.	Court of Appeal
Can. L.R.B.R.	Canadian Labour Relations Board Reports
C.C. (Cox C.C.)	Cox Criminal Cases
C.C.C.	Canadian Criminal Cases
C.C.L.	Canadian Current Law
Ch.	Chancery Reports
CLLC	Canadian Labour Law Cases
C.L.R.B.R.	see Can. L.R.B.R.
D.L.R.	Dominion Law Reports
Edw.	Edward
Geo.	George
L.A.C.	Labour Arbitration Cases
Metc.	Metcalf's Report
N.L.R.B.	National Labour Relations Board
O.L.R.B.	Ontario Labour Relations Board
O.R.	Ontario Reports
O.W.N.	Ontario Weekly Notes
P.C.	Privy Council
R.S.A.	Revised Statutes of Alberta
R.S.B.C.	Revised Statutes of British Columbia
R.S.C.	Revised Statutes of Canada
R.S.M.	Revised Statutes of Manitoba
R.S.N.	Revised Statutes of Newfoundland
R.S.N.B.	Revised Statutes of New Brunswick
R.S.N.S.	Revised Statutes of Nova Scotia
R.S.O.	Revised Statutes of Ontario
R.S.P.E.I.	Revised Statutes of Prince Edward Island
R.S.Q.	Revised Statutes of Quebec
R.S.S.	Revised Statutes of Saskatchewan
s.	section
S.M.	Statutes of Manitoba
ss.	subsection
S.S.	Statutes of Saskatchewan
Stat.	Statute
Vict.	Victoria
W.W.R.	Western Weekly Reports

PART I

INTRODUCTION

CHAPTER ONE

INTRODUCTION TO LABOUR RELATIONS

The Employment Relationship in its simplest form is a relationship between two individuals whereby one person agrees to perform work or services under the direction and control of the other in return for some form of remuneration. From a conceptual point of view the relationship is contractual in nature, with the terms and conditions of employment established through negotiation, but subject to a number of "rules" developed by the courts, and more recently, by statute.

While in theory the two parties negotiate the terms and conditions of the relationship as equals in bargaining power, in practice, this is not always the case. Where employers employ large numbers of employees, the duties of the employee and the terms and conditions of employment are often fixed, and the choice open to the prospective employee is limited to acceptance or rejection of the offered employment. True negotiation of the employment relationship is generally limited to those cases where the employee is a professional or in possession of senior management skills, and is sought out by the employer to play an important role in the operation of the firm, or where the employer operates a small business, and possesses the flexibility to negotiate an agreement with the employee that can be tailored to fit their own respective interests.

One of the principal reasons for the development of labour unions was the perceived lack of individual bargaining power by employees in their dealings with their employer. It was their belief that by banding together as a trade union they could collectively negotiate the conditions of their employment on a more equal footing with their employer. While many employees have organized or joined unions for this purpose, approximately two-thirds of the work force in Canada still works under individually negotiated employment agreements. For this reason, it is only fitting to examine the non-union employment relationship in some depth before turning to the relationship where a labour union plays an important role.

EMPLOYMENT AT COMMON LAW

The individually negotiated employment relationship is usually referred to as a common law contract of employment, in order to distinguish the relationship from the union-negotiated relationship characterized by a collective agreement. In a non-union setting, the employer and the employee are basically free to negotiate the duties that the employee will perform and the remuneration that the employer will pay for the labour, subject to the limitations that the law imposes on the negotiating parties. Some of the limitations are in the form of rules established by judges in employment cases that have found their way to the law courts, and that the judges would apply if a similar case came before them for a decision in the future. These "rules" are part of what is known as the **common law**, and hence, the name given to an employment agreement made subject to such rules is a **common law contract of employment**.

Before examining the common law rules for employment agreements, it is important to note that in addition to the common law (or judge-made law) the legislatures of all provinces and the Parliament of Canada have passed **statutes** that have defined a number of rights and duties for both employers and employees, and any employment relationship that the parties establish within one of the legislative jurisdictions would be subject to their particular rules as well.

The parties to an employment relationship, then, are generally free to establish any mutually agreed upon terms and conditions under which the work will be performed, provided that the terms and conditions do not contravene the requirements of a statute or the common law. These restrictions on the parties are not a new development, however, since the courts and the governments have established such laws in Canada from the days of the early settlers to the present time. Indeed, in England, where many of the Canadian common law rules and statutes have their roots, laws relating to employment go back to at least the early fourteenth century.

The employment relationship is a very old legal relationship, and it is difficult to determine when the first employer engaged the services of an employee in the modern sense. Some characteristics, nevertheless, are apparent. Employment does not include relationships between unfree persons and their masters, since by definition, only free persons may enter into an employment relationship. This is so because the rights and duties of the parties are negotiated. Each person must be free to acquire rights or assume duties and obligations, and each must be free to terminate the employment agreement in accordance with its terms or the laws relating to termination. In a sense, the parties make their own rules to govern their relationship, subject only to the laws of the land.

Employment has always been subject to a certain amount of state control in the form of laws regulating different aspects of the relationship. For example, in England, during the mid-fourteenth century, legislation was enacted which attempted to control the wages and working conditions of employees,[1] and in the latter part of the next century, laws were passed which, among other things, contained regulations that required employers to pay wages only in coin of the realm.[2]

The courts have also treated the employment relationship in a different light from earliest times. While the employment agreement has been considered a form of contract by which the parties may freely establish their own rights and duties (which the courts will enforce), certain long-standing common law rules have remained. One of the most important of these rules relates to the rights of third parties injured by employees while carrying out their employer's business. The general rule here is that the employer is liable for an injury caused to the third party by the employee's negligence or carelessness in the conduct of his duties.

Over the years the courts and the various levels of government have modified the relationship by the imposition of additional duties, or the establishment of special rights for one party or the other, but the basic relationship has remained intact. What many of these laws have attempted to do is eliminate some of the more glaring abuses of employees by thoughtless employers, rather than alter the relationship between the parties. As a result, the employer and employee are essentially free to establish their own rights and duties by way of a contract, subject to certain overriding laws which apply to the relationship. A general overview of these laws is the subject matter of the next part of this chapter.

THE NATURE AND FORM OF THE CONTRACT OF EMPLOYMENT

The agreement which the parties make to establish their employment relationship need not be a formal written document. In fact, in most provinces, it need not be in writing unless it is a contract that is to run for a fixed term of more than one year.[3] The requirement of writing, however, does not mean that a formal written contract must be drawn up for the purpose. To comply with the requirement of writing, the agreement for the fixed term may consist of an exchange of letters, signed by the parties, which sets out the various terms and conditions. This has generally been held to be sufficient to comply with the statute,[4] and in one case, the signed notation in a corporation's minute book was held to be a sufficient memorandum in writing to satisfy the requirement of writing.[5] Apart from this particular instance where there is an obligation to have the agreement documented, the employment contract need not be in writing. Even a long-term agreement where no fixed termination date is mentioned need not be in written form, as a contract of indefinite hiring is treated by the courts as being outside the requirements of the statute[6] unless some other specific legislation imposes such a duty on the parties. The form of the agreement then, except for this one exception, may normally be as formal or informal in terms of writing as the parties may themselves desire; or they may, if they wish, have a verbal agreement as to the nature of their relationship.

Apart from the requirement of form, the employment relationship must fall within the legal definition of "employment" in order for one of the parties to become an employer and the other, an employee. This is due to the fact that other relationships such as that of the agent, independent contractor, and partnership are similar in some respects to the employment relationship, but the legal obligations and the rights of such parties differ from those of the employer and employee in a number of significant ways. The many new and complex relationships developed by modern business have compounded the problem of clearly identifying the employment relationship, and it has been necessary for the courts to devise a number of "tests" to distinguish the one from the many others.

The original test used to distinguish the contract of employment was the basic test of **control**. Historically, the employment relationship was one where the employee, in return for the payment of a wage or other remuneration, agreed to carry out the directions of the employer. In other words, the employer had the right to decide what work the employee was to do, and to direct the manner in which it was to be done. In effect, the employee performed the work under the control of the employer.[7]

This test was adequate for many years, but as other more complex work relationships developed during the recent century, it became evident to the courts that a more elaborate test was necessary to properly identify the employment relationship. As a result, a **fourfold test** was devised to provide a more accurate means of identification of employers and employees. Control still remained an important part of the test, but in addition to the "control" aspect, the courts considered the ownership of tools, the chance of profit, and the risk of loss.[8] This test provided three other factors to consider as guides for the determination of the relationship, and is currently used extensively not only by the courts, but by Labour Relations Boards and other administrative bodies to identify the employment relationship.

As a means of further identification of the employment relationship, the courts have more recently devised an **organization test** that examines the relationship in terms of the activities of the parties with respect to the business itself. According to this test, the relationship is determined by the nature of the services performed. The services are considered to be those of an employee if the work done is an integral part of the other person's normal business, but if the work is not an integral part of the business activity, but only accessory or adjunct to it, then the relationship is not necessarily that of employment.[9]

The tests described are most useful in distinguishing employees from independent contractors and agents. As a general rule, work done by independent contractors is usually adjunct or accessory to an employer's main business activity, but in cases where the independent contractor does not have employees and works exclusively for the one employer, it is often difficult to distinguish him from an employee. This is especially true in the case where the employer exercises a considerable degree of control over the work done by the independent contractor.

Independent contractors, as the name implies, are not employees, but frequently do work for others in return for a fixed payment. A person who hires an independent contractor usually specifies the work to be done, but the manner in which it is performed is normally left with the contractor. Ordinarily, the independent contractor is readily distinguishable from an employee because the work of the contractor is not subject to supervision or direction, but this is not always the case, and it is in such cases that the tests are most useful.

For example, A hires B to clean the windows, doors, lobby, and corridors of his office building. The work requires about forty hours per week of B's time. A will only permit the work to be done after 6 p.m. and on Saturdays, when the normal occupants of the building are not using the building. A requires the halls and lobby to be cleaned daily. Is B an employee, or an independent contractor? The application of the **fourfold test** and the **organization test** may help to answer the question.

The first step is to examine the degree of control exercised by A over B. Does A direct the work to be done and the manner in which it is done by B? Does B work under close supervision by A? Is B free to do the work as he sees fit, provided that the building is always clean? The second step is to examine the ownership of tools. Does A provide the cleaning equipment used by B? The third step is to consider the chance of profit. Who stands to profit from the arrangement? Is A's liability fixed regardless of B's efficiency in performing the service? Is B's chance of profit affected by his performance? The same questions may be asked concerning the risk of loss. Who bears the risk? Must A pay, regardless of B's performance?

The organizational test is also useful here. Suppose A's business is that of insurance. Is B's activity or work an integral part of the business? Is it accessory to it?

While it would be necessary to know more about the relationship between A and B to more precisely determine whether B is an employee of A, if B is not supervised by A, B provides his own cleaning equipment, and receives a fixed amount for his services, regardless of the time required to perform them, the **fourfold test** would tend to indicate that B would not be an employee, but an independent contractor. This would be substantiated by the **organization test**, which would also indicate that B's work is not a normal part of A's insurance business, but accessory or adjunct to it.

The tests may also be used to distinguish employees from sales agents and other kinds of agents. True agents are persons who perform services for their principals where the services are normally dictated by the principal, but the performance of the service is left with the agent. For example, a principal may engage an agent to sell a quantity of goods. Normally the agent is free to seek out a suitable buyer using his own time and methods and to negotiate the sale without consultation with the principal, except perhaps to confirm that the selling price is acceptable. In such a case the agent is clearly not an employee because the principal exercises no control over the agent's activities. However, if the principal sets down detailed controls over the agent's activity and time in the agency agreement, and exercises supervision of the agent's work, again, it is sometimes difficult to distinguish the relationship from that of employment. Where the question is raised, the **fourfold test** and the **organization test** may be used to indicate the nature of the relationship that the parties have established, regardless of how it is described.

THE RIGHTS AND DUTIES OF THE PARTIES

The contract of employment seldom details the particular rights and duties of the employer and employee, but often, simply spells out the initial rate of pay of the employee and the general nature of the work expected in return for the remuneration. This is due in part to the fact that the general rights and duties of both the employer and the employee have been delineated to a marked degree by the common law, and by legislation aimed at specific aspects of the relationship. These laws have been directed at both the work environment and the employment contract, largely for the purposes of protecting the employee's health and safety, and preventing unfair economic treatment of employees by employers.

Throughout the latter part of the nineteenth century and the first part of the twentieth century, most of the laws were directed at the conditions under which work was performed with a view to making the work place a safe and healthy environment for employees. These laws, which were usually described as factory, shop, or mine acts, generally required employers to provide suitable conditions for work, and safe equipment for the employees to operate to reduce the likelihood of injury or illness. By the early twentieth century, the various levels of government were interested not only in the work environment, but also in the terms of employment of the employees. They began to construct a fundamental legislative framework within which the parties were permitted to negotiate the terms of their agreement. Most of these laws took the form of prescribing minimum rights or duties. At the present time, most provinces have in place legislation of this kind which sets out a large number of employment limitations that apply to most employees governing minimum wages payable, maximum hours of work, vacations with pay, holidays, overtime work, and time limits on notice of termination of employment by employees and employers. More recently, considerable attention has been given to discriminatory employment practices. As a general rule, employers are prohibited by law from discriminating against persons on the basis of age, sex, racial origin, or religion, and in some cases, if the person is disabled.

Apart from the limitations imposed by the legislative framework an employer has an obligation to pay an employee the agreed upon remuneration, and provide all necessary information to enable the employee to calculate his or her wages if they are based upon a bonus or piecework earning system. In addition, there is also an implied obligation on the part of the employer to provide the employee with the necessary tools to do the work required, unless by custom of the trade the employee is expected to provide his own tools and equipment for the job. If the employer requires the employee to carry out his duties other than at the employer's place of business, the employer is also usually required to compensate the employee for any travel expense unless custom or the terms of employment dictate otherwise.

The duties imposed on the employee for the most part concern the performance of work. The primary obligation is the duty to obey and carry out promptly all reasonable orders given by the employer, provided that they do not involve a safety hazard, and provided that they involve the performance of duties for which the employee was hired, and is qualified to perform. In addition, the employee is expected to act in the best interests of the employer at all times, and to use the equipment and tools of the employer in a reasonable and careful manner. All information of a confidential or secret nature divulged to the employee must be kept confidential, both during the employment period and after the employee leaves the employ of the employer. Special technical skills learned on the job, nevertheless, may normally be used by the employee if he should find employment elsewhere, but secret processes usually may not. And finally, where an employee professes to possess special skills, he would be expected as an implied term of his employment to perform his work in accordance with the standard required for his skill or profession.

TERMINATION OF EMPLOYMENT

A contract of indefinite hiring normally continues in effect until the employer ceases business, the employee reaches a statutory retirement age, or notice of termination of the contract is given by one of the parties. Written contracts of employment often provide for a specific notice period if either party should desire to terminate the employment relationship. This might be any agreed time period, ranging from one week to a year, with the minimum time period subject to any minimum set by the applicable provincial or federal government legislation. If the agreement does not provide for a notice period, which would normally be the case where the agreement is not in writing, then at common law a party is expected to give **reasonable notice** of termination. Reasonable notice, unfortunately, tends to vary according to a number of factors, and may range from as little as the statutory minimum of a week or two to as much as a year or more. What is "reasonable" takes into consideration the length of service of the employee, the nature of the employer's business, the customs of that trade, the age of the employee, the position held by the employee in the firm, the opportunities for similar employment elsewhere, the qualifications of the employee, any representations made by the employer as to the length of time that the employee would be employed, and more recently, the manner in which the termination is made.

Applying these factors to a case where an employee who was hired for only a short time in an unskilled position with no promise of long-term employment is terminated, the notice required would likely be quite short, probably the statutory minimum. On the other hand, a long service employee, approaching retirement age, employed in a senior management position, who would require considerable time to find a similar position in another firm, would probably be entitled to a notice period of perhaps as long as a year if his contract of employment is to be properly terminated.

Notice need not be given in cases where the employer has grounds for immediate dismissal of the employee because of the employee's actions, but care must be taken by employers in such instances to make certain that the grounds for dismissal are sufficient to warrant such action. As a general rule, the employer may dismiss without notice where the employee is guilty of wilful misconduct or disobedience, or a wilful neglect of duty that has not been condoned by the employer.[10] This would include such actions on the part of the employee as theft of the employer's property, or a wilful refusal to carry out work properly assigned to the employee where there are no mitigating circumstances.

If the employer should dismiss the employee where there are insufficient grounds for so doing, or where inadequate notice of termination is given, the employer may be liable for damages for wrongful dismissal. Should this be the case, the employee would have a duty to seek other employment immediately, in order to mitigate financial loss, then institute legal proceedings for damages. If the employee can establish wrongful dismissal, the damages awarded by the courts would normally be the amount of money that the employee would have received had reasonable notice of termination been given, less any earnings received from other employment obtained during the notice period. If the employer had treated the employee improperly in the course of the dismissal (for example, by improperly accusing an innocent employee of theft in front of other employees), the courts may award the employee additional damages for the injury suffered as a result of the employer's actions.

The federal government, under its *Canada Labour Code*,[11] and several provinces, now provide an alternative for employees who believe that they have been unjustly dismissed by their employers. Labour legislation in these jurisdictions usually provides for a government inspector or officer to investigate a complaint of unjust dismissal, and if a settlement of the dispute cannot be negotiated, for the appointment of an impartial adjudicator to hear the dispute and make an award. Unlike the courts, if an adjudicator should find that the employee was unjustly dismissed, he may order the reinstatement of the employee with compensation as an alternative to a monetary award.

COLLECTIVE BARGAINING

While approximately two out of every three employees are employed under individual or common law contracts of employment, a large number of employees have elected to negotiate their conditions of employment collectively through a labour union. This type of employment agreement differs substantially from the individual contract of employment in the sense that the collective bargaining relationship through which it is negotiated is essentially a creature of statute law, or at least a form of organization and negotiation legitimated by statute.

The events which led to the enactment of collective bargaining legislation began several centuries ago in England, where workmen who were unsatisfied with their employer decided to band together to deal with their problems on a collective rather than individual basis. Among the first groups to band together were craftsmen who not only had a common interest in the protection of their trade from encroachment by the semiskilled, but who were living above the subsistence level. The fact that they lived above the subsistence level was an important impetus for the organization of the craftsmen, since it enabled them to undertake strike action against their employer if their demands or grievances were not satisfied. Because their earnings were in excess of those living at the subsistence level, they not only had cash savings which they could draw from if they found it necessary to withdraw their labour, but they were also in a position to provide assistance to their less fortunate fellow craftsmen in a lengthy strike.

A further important factor which fostered the organization of craftsmen was the difficulty that employers had in replacing craftsmen if they should withdraw their labour in concert. It was clearly difficult, for example, to replace a printer with anyone else but another printer. Consequently, if the printers of a particular employer engaged in a strike, their employer could only replace them with much difficulty, because apart from the scarcity of tradesmen with that skill, a printer was generally hesitant to take the job of a fellow craftsman due to the special community of interest that all members of the craft had for the preservation of their trade.

A final factor that permitted the organization of the craft groups before other unskilled groups was the experience that most craftsmen had in the organization of their fellow workmen. Craftsmen had been members of guilds originally, but with the decline of the guild, craft groups generally formed journeymen's clubs or "benevolent societies" to provide aid in the event of the illness, injury, or death of a fellow member. While these organizations were essentially formed for the purpose of providing financial assistance for the unfortunate craftmen, they also represented an organization through which the craftsmen could discuss their employment problems, and organize collective action.

Benevolent or friendly societies, as they were sometimes called, were not trade unions as such since their purpose was essentially for mutual aid. They did, however, frequently provide an organized base for assisting members of the craft who might be engaged in a labour dispute with their employer. In a sense, they also provided the organizational experience for members, and represented the forerunners of the labour organizations that emerged in the nineteenth century.

Collective action by craftsmen, apart from the lack of a formal organization was not easy. Employers were quick to recognize the threat posed by an organized work force, and were not entirely adverse to using the law to prevent their employees from engaging in strike action or any concerted effort that represented a restraint of trade. Public policy in the eighteenth and nineteenth centuries, as now, prohibited any conspiracy or combination in restraint of trade and, in earlier times, any combination of workmen who refused to work or engaged in a strike for the purpose of obtaining higher wages was considered a combination in restraint of trade. As a result, the courts were used by employers to control collective action by employees, but not to the degree one might expect. Legal action was frequently employed as a threat but seldom instituted for the simple reason that employees found guilty of conspiracy in restraint of trade were imprisoned. An employer with his work force in jail was no better off than if the employees were on strike since replacement of craftstmen was not an easy task, particularly where the employer was obliged to rely on the local skilled labour pool for employees. Consequently, the labour movement in England continued its steady growth throughout the early part of the nineteenth century without a great deal of employer resistance, and it was during this period that the first of the true trade unions made their appearance in many towns and cities.

By the middle of the nineteenth century the development of convenient transportation facilities made communication between the industrial communities possible and set the stage for the formation of large, national labour organizations. The first union to develop a national organization was the Amalgamated Society of Engineers during 1850 to 1851. Most other craft unions formed similar organizations shortly thereafter, and within a relatively short time, large numbers of skilled workmen in England joined local unions affiliated with the national craft bodies.

The national unions played an important part in the development of labour relations in England throughout the last half of the nineteenth century. The new organizations became power centres in the union movement, and not only co-ordinated the activities of the local unions, but controlled the strike funds as well. As a result, the unions established a countervailing force to the power of the employers, at least in so far as skilled employees were concerned.

In the years that followed, the national unions soon discovered that mutual problems of trade unions were best resolved through a concerted effort on the part of all unions, and in 1871 formed the Trades Union Congress (T.U.C.). The principal purpose of this new organization was to provide a forum for the discussion of problems of organized labour, and to act as a lobby for legislation favourable to the interests of the unions and its members. The power remained with the national unions, however, and the Congress continued as a co-ordinating body only.

Due to the efforts of organized labour, the last half of the nineteenth century became a period of considerable reform in the work environment. Apart from this, the most notable victory for organized labour itself was the amendment of the law to legitimize the labour movement. In 1871, the British Parliament amended the criminal law to recognize trade unions as lawful entities, and permitted collective bargaining by employees, provided that their actions were otherwise lawful.[12]

The nineteenth century also saw the migration of many skilled workmen from England to Canada and the United States, and along with their dreams of a better life in the New World, they also carried with them the knowledge and experience of the union movement. As a result, the union movement in both England and North America followed a roughly similar pattern of development. Shoe workers in Philadelphia, Pennsylvania, formed a union as early as 1792, and shipbuilders in Halifax, Nova Scotia, had organized and engaged in strike activity against their employer in the early 1800s. In Ontario, printers in the town of York (now Toronto) formed a union in 1832. Nevertheless, throughout the first half of the nineteenth century the union movement was largely local in nature due to the isolated nature of industrial development. It was not until the latter half of the century that the national (and international) unions emerged, and the modern trade union movement had its beginning.

In Canada, as in England, public policy dictated that all conspiracies or combinations in restraint of trade were unlawful, and this policy included any combination of workmen that acted in concert in their dealings with their employer. In 1872, however, this was changed by an amendment of the *Criminal Code*[13] to exempt workmen and to declare that the labour unions that represented them were not unlawful entities simply because they had organized for the purpose of bargaining collectively with their employers on matters of wages and working conditions. This change in the law permitted the lawful development of the trade union movement in Canada, and in the century that followed, the organization of employees expanded to the point where one in three members of the work force is now a member of a union. The many changes and internal problems that the movement encountered during its growth over the past century are outlined in the next chapter.

REVIEW QUESTIONS

1. *Explain how an employee differs from an independent contractor. What are the characteristics of each contractual relationship?*
2. *Discuss the nature of the tests which the courts have developed to distinguish the employee from other employment relationships.*
3. *How does collective bargaining differ from individual bargaining?*
4. *On what basis was collective bargaining illegal in the past?*
5. *Discuss the rights and duties of an employee under a common law contract of employment.*
6. *How is an employment relationship established?*
7. *Indicate the methods by which an employment relationship might be terminated.*
8. *In what way (or ways) does lawful termination of a contract of employment differ from wrongful dismissal?*
9. *What are the rights and duties of an employee who believes that he has been wrongfully dismissed?*
10. *How does a court arrive at a damage award if wrongful dismissal is established by the employee?*

NOTES

[1]25 Edw. III (1350), Stat. 1. *A Statute of Labourers* was proclaimed by the King some time before, 23 Edw. III (1349), but was not a true Act of Parliament. Parliament was prorogued at the time due to the Black Plague which had ravaged the land and wiped out almost one-third of the adult population, and the Royal Proclamation was an attempt to prevent a rapid rise in wages due to the widespread shortage of workers.

[2]4 Edw. 1V (1464), c. 1, s. 5(14); 17 Edw. IV c. 1, s. 5(13).

[3]*The Statute of Frauds* or similar legislation in many provinces requires contracts for a fixed term of more than one year to be in writing in order to be enforceable. See for example: R.S.O. 1980 c. 481, s. 4; R.S.N.B. 1973 c. S-14, s. 1(e); R.S.N.S. 1967 c. 290, s. 6(e).

[4]*Goldie v. Cross Fertilizer Co.* (1916), 37 D.L.R. 16.

[5]*Connell v. Bay of Quinte Country Club* (1923), 24 O.W.N. 264.

[6]See for example, *Co-operators Insurance Association v. Kearney* (1964), 48 D.L.R. (2d) 1.

[7]See *Harris v. Howes and Chemical Distributors, Ltd.* (1928), [1929] 1 W.W.R. 217.

[8]*City of Montreal v. Montreal Locomotive Works Ltd. et al.* (1946), [1947] 1 D.L.R. 161.

[9]*Mayer v. J. Conrad Lavigne Ltd.* (1979), 27 O.R. (2d) 129.

[10]*Employment Standards Act,* R.S.O. 1980, c. 137, s. 40(3)(c).

[11]*Canada Labour Code,* R.S.C. 1970 c. L-1, s. 61.5 as amended.

[12]See *Criminal Law Amendment Act* (1871), 34 & 35 Vict. c. 32, s. 1; *Trades Union Act* (1871), 34 & 35 Vict. c. 31.

[13]See *Criminal Law Amendment Act* (1872), 35 Vict. c. 31, s. 1; *The Trade Unions Act* (1872), 35 Vict. c. 30.

RECOMMENDED REFERENCES AND SOURCE MATERIAL

Christie, I.M. *Employment Law in Canada,* Toronto, Canada: Butterworth and Co. (Canada) Ltd. (1980).

Willes, J.A. "The Employment Relationship." *Contemporary Canadian Business Law.* Toronto, Canada: McGraw-Hill Ryerson Ltd. (1981), pp. 366–85.

Willes, J.A. *The Employment Relationship and Discharge and Discipline.* Kingston, Canada: Queen's University Industrial Centre (1976).

CASE PROBLEM FOR DISCUSSION
RADIO ACTIVE ORE CASE

Radio Active Ore Company carries on business as a mining company in Northern Ontario, where it operates two mines at the outskirts of a town of 10,000 inhabitants. The community is serviced by a transcontinental railway, a major highway, and an airport. The company employs approximately 2,000 employees in its operations, and in view of the remote location of the town relative to other population centres, the company established a number of recreational facilities for the benefit of its employees and the community in general. These included a large recreational complex, a lakeside park for camping, and an arena.

In addition to these facilities, the company also erected four large apartment buildings for rental use by employees with families. These buildings were necessary in order to provide housing facilities which would not otherwise be available in the community due to the cyclical nature of the mining, and the resulting reluctance on the part of investors to construct rental accommodations in mining towns.

The three apartment buildings, each containing 220 suites were completed in 1980, and opened for occupancy by November of that year.

Before the first tenants moved into the units, the company placed the following "Help Wanted" advertisements in the local newspaper:

JANITORIAL SERVICES REQUIRED
220-UNIT APARTMENT BUILDING
ONE YEAR CONTRACT WITH RENTAL
UNIT PROVIDED AT $80.00/MONTH
LIST OF DUTIES AVAILABLE AT
MINE MANAGER'S OFFICE
WRITTEN APPLICATIONS FOR
THE POSITION WILL BE
RECEIVED UNTIL NOVEMBER 30TH

Jake Kelly submitted an application for the position, and on December 1 received a letter which read:

Dear Mr. Kelly:

This is to confirm that a contract for janitorial services at 8 Mill Road has been released to you at the rate of $1,600.00 per month. In addition, a three-bedroom apartment will be provided at the rate of $80.00 per month, exclusive of hydro charges.

The contract is effective December 1, 1980, for a period of one year, at which time the contract may be renegotiated. The contract may be terminated by either party upon giving thirty (30) days notice at which time the apartment occupied by yourself will be vacated.

The company will pay at the rate of $800.00 on the fifteenth and the last day of the month upon receipt of your bill for services rendered. This should be submitted to Radio Active Ore Company to the attention of the Manager of Mines.

Your duties will include those responsibilities set out on the list of duties provided to you at the time of your application for the position.

This is to state that notwithstanding the rental lease, effective December 1, 1980, you are not an employee, but a janitorial contractor operating under a signed contract.

It is understood by both parties if and when the contract is terminated by either party upon giving thirty (30) days notice, that you will vacate the premises on or before the end of the thirty-day notice period.

The Manager of Mines is responsible for the care and maintenance of the Company's housing and you should keep him informed of all activities at your apartment building.

If the terms and conditions of this agreement as set forth in this letter are acceptable to you, would you please sign one copy and return it to the Company.

Yours very truly,

RADIO ACTIVE ORE COMPANY.

The duties set out in the list of responsibilities for Janitorial Services included the following:

1. Vacuum corridor rugs, stairways, lobby entrances and make certain any marks on walls are cleaned immediately.
2. Keep entrance, lobby, glass, and doors clean at all times.
3. Keep garbage areas clear daily and floors clean at all times.
4. Check fire extinguishers daily, and once a month, date and sign tag attached to extinguishers.
5. Check emergency lights and fire alarm fittings daily.
6. Accept calls from tenants at all hours and deal with their problems.
7. Perform minor maintenance repairs.
8. Contact the Mines Manager in the event major repairs are required or contact repair tradesmen if an emergency arises.
9. Check and clean newly vacated units and prepare for tenancy.
10. Cut, rake, and water lawns as required.
11. Keep lawns, walkways and parking lots clear of debris in summer, and keep all entrances clear of snow and ice in winter so that doors will close properly.
12. Keep all walkways to parking lots clear of snow.
13. Keep a daily log of activities and report regularly to the Manager of Mines.
14. Show new or prospective tenants to apartments and be responsible for keys.
15. Clean laundry rooms daily and check washers and dryers for proper operation.
16. Prepare and submit a weekly report for the Manager of Mines.

Kelly moved into the apartment building and began working as the building janitor. He was essentially on call at all hours, and obliged to deal with tenants' problems at any time during the day or night. He was assisted in his work by his wife and fourteen year old son. If they wished to take a holiday at any time, it was necessary to make arrangements with someone to look after the building during their absence.

Each week, the Manager of Mines would make an inspection tour of each building to check its condition, and to authorize major repair where necessary. The inspection visits lasted from one-half hour to an hour, and were supplemented by semimonthly meetings at the Manager's office when Kelly submitted his reports and picked up the cheques issued in payment for his services.

In November of 1981, Kelly and the Manager of Mines discussed the renewal of his contract, and on December 1, 1981, a new letter was received by Kelly which contained the same information as his 1980 letter, save and except for the monthly payment amount, which was raised to $1,650.00. The agreement was again reviewed as at December 1, 1982, for a further year when Kelly completed the second contract year. The only difference in the third letter of appointment was an increase in the monthly payment rate to $1,700.00 and an increase in his apartment rental to $90.00 per month.

Kelly continued to perform his janitorial duties until May 28, 1983, when he received a registered letter, written under the hand of the Manager of Mines, advising him that the company intended to terminate the agreement which it had with him, effective June 30, 1983. The letter also requested that he vacate the apartment which he occupied by the date specified in the letter for termination of the agreement.

When Kelly received the letter, he immediately contacted the Manager of Mines and enquired as to why he had been terminated as janitor. The manager replied that it was necessary to terminate the contract because several tenants of the building had complained that Kelly was rude and uncooperative when they telephoned him to have minor repairs made in their apartments. The manager further stated that Kelly had been slow at clearing the snow from the walkways to the parking lot during the previous winter, and intimated that the part-time job which Kelly had (as a night security guard at a nearby lumberyard) might be interfering with his janitorial duties at the apartment.

Kelly responded to the manager's accusations by stating that he was unaware of any complaints from tenants concerning the snow on the walkways, and he had always cleared the pathways when each fall of snow had ended. He could recall no instances when he was rude and uncooperative with tenants in the building. The manager, however, was not prepared to accept Kelly's explanation and insisted that he vacate the apartment by June 30, 1983.

CASE DISCUSSION QUESTIONS

1. *Analyze the nature of the relationship between Kelly and Radio Active Ore Company. Is the relationship in fact what the letter states it to be?*
2. *Describe the nature of the relationship in the light of the* **fourfold test** *and the* **organization test**. *If you should reach the conclusion that Kelly is an employee, indicate his rights, if any, at law.*

CHAPTER TWO

THE HISTORY OF THE TRADE UNION MOVEMENT

The trade union movement in Canada and the United States had its origins in England where skilled craftsmen had organized journeymen's clubs or benevolent societies to provide mutual aid and assistance for the less fortunate members of their particular crafts. The benevolent or friendly societies were established by journeymen craftsmen with a threefold purpose. First, to provide sickness and accident benefits for members who were unable to work. Second, to help unemployed members find employment, and third, to assist each other and to support members that had disputes with their employers concerning wages, working conditions, and craft rights.

In the years before the industrial revolution in England, most goods and services were provided by skilled craftsmen who worked alone or with the aid of a few apprentices or journeymen. The capital requirements to establish a business were generally low, as in most cases the craftsman required only a quantity of hand tools and some materials. With the industrial revolution came the introduction of machinery and equipment to produce goods, and the capital requirements for a craftsman to set up his own business became prohibitive. This change in production methods reduced most craftsmen to the ranks of the employed. In addition, the introduction of machinery and mechanized methods of producing goods permitted less skilled persons to produce machine-made goods of a quality comparable to the goods produced by skilled craftsmen. This, in turn, eliminated the need for large numbers of persons who possessed the traditional skills formerly used. The industrial revolution not only eliminated the opportunity for many craftsmen to become independent producers of goods but also eliminated a great many employment opportunities for craftsmen by reducing the requirement for skilled labour. As a result, the need to protect craft skills by those craftsmen who were employed took on a greater importance and became an important goal of the various benevolent societies.

As the industrial revolution progressed, many craft groups saw further erosion of the need for their skills and faced greater competition for jobs from unskilled and semiskilled workers. Now when employers attempted to introduce new technology, the skilled tradesmen followed a course of "mutual support" which led to the first collective action in the form of strikes and work stoppages. Employers tolerated some of this activity but by the end of the eighteenth century collective action by workmen had reached the point in England where employers pressed the government of the day for legislation to restrict the practice of collective bargaining. In 1799 and 1800, the Combination laws[1] were passed by Parliament which prohibited combinations of employees and employers for the purpose of restraint of trade.

The Combination Acts proved to be relatively ineffective in preventing collective action by employees, however, and the number of craft organizations continued to grow during the early part of the nineteenth century. In 1824, the government recognized the ineffectiveness of the Combination laws and passed the *Combination Law Repeal Act*[2] which repealed the statutes that had been passed in 1799 and 1800. This left employers and employees to make whatever agreements they wished with respect to wages and working conditions, provided that they did so by peaceful means. The law continued to prohibit the use of intimidation, coercion, or violence in labour disputes, but permitted employees to negotiate collectively with their employers.

Freedom from the restrictions of the Combination Acts produced a flurry of collective action in the following year and when violence occurred during some of the many strikes for higher wages, the government was once again compelled to act. In 1825, the *Combination Law Repeal Amendment Act*[3] was passed which defined a lawful combination as one which was organized for the purpose of providing benefits to its members and for the purpose of negotiating wages and hours of work only. In an attempt to prohibit violence during strikes, the law proscribed the obstruction of any person at a work place, and made an offence of any act designed to molest a workman or employer.

However, the legislation proved to be relatively ineffective in restricting the formation of combinations of workmen, and the numbers continued to grow. During the first quarter of the century, journeymen's clubs or societies had been largely local because the transportation system in England was poor and travel difficult, but by 1827, the situation had changed somewhat as a result of a decade of road building and improvement of the transportation infrastructure. During this time, many local craft groups attempted to form national craft organizations, albeit with little success.

One of the first groups established was the General Union of Carpenters and Joiners, which formed in 1827. It grew in response to the threat that the general building contractor posed to craftsmen in the building industry. Until the 1820s, building tradesmen such as carpenters, stonemasons and others were engaged by architects for the construction of buildings. However, during the period 1820–1830, general contractors gradually assumed the role of employer of the tradesmen since they took over the responsibility for the actual construction of a building in accordance with the plans prepared by the architect. As the general contractor usually agreed to handle the construction for a fixed price, the subtrades were obliged to negotiate with the contractor rather than the architect or the property owner. This meant that the general contractor frequently attempted to hold down building costs as much as possible to enhance his own profit. To further counteract this action, another union of building trades was formed in 1832: the Operative Builders' Union.

The new union was made up of many individual craft unions associated with construction and was governed by a Builders' Parliament which met twice each year to discuss the concerns of the craft unions. Notwithstanding the fact that the organization was made up of many local and national union organizations, the Operative Builders' Union had little power since the unions which formed the national organization were largely autonomous with diverse interests. Unfortunately, not long after the new organization was formed, the country suffered a period of economic recession and most unions experienced a decline along with business activity in general. Throughout this period, unions also found that employers were pressuring their employees to sign a pledge not to join a union, a type of employment arrangement that United States trade unionists later referred to as a "yellow dog" contract.

By 1840, renewed attempts were made to establish general unions consisting of both skilled and unskilled employees but these were for the most part unsuccessful. Craft unions, nevertheless, did experience a period of steady growth between 1840 and 1850, and trade unionists during this decade began the organization of coal miners in many parts of England. It was not until the beginning of the next decade, however, that the trade union movement formed itself along organizational lines that became the model that modern trade unions would follow.

In 1850–51, the Amalgamated Society of Engineers established a national union of machinists, millwrights, pattern-makers, and engineers that was able to maintain an organization of sufficient strength to withstand periods of economic recession and employer resistance. The new organization consisted of a central office with control over finances and the general activities of the union as a whole. The organization was made up of many locals, each closely tied to the central organization but possessing a certain amount of autonomy over primarily local matters. The organization was characterized by the requirement that high dues be paid by its members, most of which was passed along to the central body to hold as a strike fund to be used for the payment of generous benefits to less fortunate members. The form of organization of the Amalgamated Society of Engineers proved to be so successful that many other craft union groups patterned their national organizations along similar lines. A notable example was the Amalgamated Society of Carpenters and Joiners which formed in 1860.

By 1868, about a quarter of a million tradesmen belonged to labour unions. During that year, an attempt was made to establish a congress where papers could be presented on matters of concern to the unions and where trade union ideas could be publicized. The National Trade Congress in 1868 was the first move in this direction and two years later, a meeting was held in London, England, to form a permanent organization, the Trades Union Congress (T.U.C.). The first meeting of the Congress was held in 1871 and the organization has been in existence since that time.

The first legislative success of the new Congress was reflected in the *Trades Unions Act*[4] of the same year which gave unions legal recognition, protected their funds by way of registration with the registrar of friendly societies[5] and permitted them to use benefit funds to support members on strike. The Act represented a major breakthrough for trade unions in their struggle for legitimacy but did nothing to assist unions in the event of a strike. While the union could not be charged with conspiracy in restraint of trade, the union members could still be charged as a conspiracy to molest an employer in the conduct of his business,[6] or a conspiracy to injure.[7] As a result, the unions to some extent were worse off than before if they engaged in any strike activity that might be viewed as an attempt to persuade other employees or customers to break their contracts with the employer. Moreover, registration of the union under the *Friendly Societies Act* was held by the courts to give the union a legal existence which enabled injured employers or employees to take legal action against the organization itself.[8]

The *Conspiracy and Protection of Property Act*[9] passed a few years later in 1875 permitted union members to engage in acts normally considered to be in restraint of trade, provided that they were not criminal acts. This legislation, in effect permitted lawful strikes. It was not until 1906, however, with the passage of the *Trade Disputes Act*[10] that persons were no longer liable if they persuaded others to go on strike by peaceful means.

By the beginning of the twentieth century, the trade union movement had established a position of legitimacy, and an important role in the area of employer-employee relations. Throughout the period of its development the English trade union movement provided an important training ground for craftsmen who emigrated to the United States and Canada. These craftsmen took with them the ideas of collective bargaining and the methods of organization of the unions themselves. Upon their arrival in North America, their presence gave added impetus to the growth of the labour movement.

THE UNITED STATES TRADE UNION DEVELOPMENT

Journeyman clubs or benevolent societies were formed by skilled tradesmen in the American colonies before the declaration of independence in 1776. Like their English counterparts, they were primarily designed to provide benefits and assistance to less fortunate members. However, the role of the organization was not limited exclusively to benevolent matters in some of the clubs. For example, when printers in Philadelphia, Pennsylvania, engaged in a strike against their employer in 1786, their fellow printers pledged to help support those in dispute with their employer.[11] Thirteen years later, shoemakers in the same city appointed representatives to meet with representatives of the shoe manufacturers to discuss the demands of the workers.[12] Similar union organizations were formed by skilled workers in other large cities during this period but the business recession which followed the early nineteenth century wars in Europe had a serious effect on union growth, and union membership reached a low point by 1820.

The next decade, however, produced considerable interest in union membership as the economy improved and many new unions were formed. Among the many new organizations was the United Tailoresses Union,[13] which was one of the first women's labour organizations. They carried out the first strike in which women alone were involved in 1825 in New York. The decade also saw the first attempts by organized labour to establish multi-union associations to further the common interests of craftsmen. In 1827, the Mechanics' Union of Trade Associations[14] was formed in Philadelphia as a citywide organization of local unions, but as a form of organization, it did not develop beyond the boundaries of the city, nor did it become a common form of organization elsewhere during this period.

An ambitious attempt to form a national labour federation began in 1834 in New York City, where a National Trades Union was organized by a number of craft union leaders. The idea, however, was premature, and the federation dissolved in 1837.[15] Instead, during the next decade, the various skilled trades embarked upon the formation of national trade unions. The shoemakers[16] and printers[17] for example, organized national unions in the period 1835–1840.

The struggle for recognition by organized labour was slow, and very little progress was made during the first half of the nineteenth century. Until 1842, trade unions had a doubtful status in the eyes of the law, but during that year, in the case of *Commonwealth of Massachusetts v. Hunt*,[18] the court ruled that labour unions were lawful organizations. However, they still remained liable as combinations or for conspiracy in restraint of trade should they engage in any such criminal activities against employers.

It was not until the middle of the century that the skilled trades in the United States were able to organize their first permanent national organizations. By this time, as in England, the transportation system had developed to the point where it permitted relatively easy travel and communication between population centres. This in turn enabled the skilled groups in each community to form an organization with a central body capable of controlling and co-ordinating the actions of affiliated groups over a wide area. The first union to successfully establish such a body (one which has endured to the present day) was the Typographical Union,[19] which had its first convention in 1850 and was permanently established by 1852. Many other crafts followed and organized on a national basis, with members of the crafts in the various cities and towns forming "locals" of the national unions.

From this point on, the structure of the various craft unions was set, with other skilled groups such as the Brotherhood of Locomotive Engineers,[20] one of the new skill groups, forming a union in 1863, at the time of the American Civil War. Along with the new national unions, a quite different union was organized near the end of the decade, one which had as its objective to become a society of workers producing their own goods in co-operatives rather than as employees. This organization, known as the Noble Order of the Knights of Labor,[21] was formed as a secret society by Uriah Smith Stephens[22] in 1869.

The general aim of the Knights of Labor was to encourage co-operatives of workers to produce their own goods and to engage in political activity designed to curb the power of the banks. The Knights of Labor were not directly concerned with collective bargaining. The organization itself was established as a three-tiered body with a central group having ultimate authority. Regional bodies under the direction of the central authority were given charge of specific geographic areas. At the bottom of the hierarchy, local associations were organized as either single craft associations or mixed associations. These included all types of skilled and unskilled workers. A regional body normally consisted of a half-dozen or more local associations.

The Knights of Labor grew rapidly as a labour organization and within a decade had in excess of one-half million members. The organization, nevertheless, by its very nature and objectives contained the seeds of its own destruction, and it was not more than a decade before the craftsmen lost interest in the Knights and moved to form their own labour organization. The problem that most craft groups in the Knights of Labor encountered was the conflicting interests that craftsmen had with the unskilled members. The craftsmen had a community of interest which centred around their craft itself, and they were keenly interested in the protection of the craft from encroachment by unskilled workers. This objective was diametrically opposed to the interests of the unskilled, who often wished to engage in craft work without progressing through a lengthy apprenticeship. In addition, skilled groups possessed most of the bargaining power, and had little to gain from affiliation with unskilled workers. As a result, the craft groups soon tired of the Knights and moved to form their own federation in 1881: the Federation of Organized Trades and Labour Unions of the United States and Canada.[23]

The new federation was initially made up of the larger unions and craft groups; among them printers, carpenters, glassworkers, iron and steelworkers, cotton and wool spinners, cigarmakers and lake seamen. The organization became the forerunner of the American Federation of Labor which was formed a few years later, in 1886, when a large number of national unions banded together.[24]

The American Federation of Labor, unlike the Knights of Labor, concentrated on matters related to collective bargaining rather than politics. The AFL directed its efforts towards problems which concerned the national unions in its membership. Under the general direction of Samuel Gompers[25] of the Cigarmakers Union, the federation experienced a slow but steady growth for the remainder of the nineteenth century. By the end of the century, the AFL had approximately 275,000 members.[26] Thereafter, growth became more rapid and membership reached two million by the time the United States entered the First World War. By 1920, membership had doubled to four million.

While many unions of workers were not affiliated with the American Federation of Labor, the majority of unionized workmen, about 80 percent, were members of unions in the federation. As a result of their large size, the structure and patterns of development for many national unions were fixed. Unlike the geographical grouping of all types of workers into one organization as in the pattern of the Knights of Labor, the unions in the AFL possessed greater autonomy. As opposed to the central body of the Knights of Labor, the federation had very little prescriptive authority. The various national unions retained control over their own locals. The federation operated primarily as a forum where common union problems could be discussed and disputes between unions resolved. Through the AFL forum, the goals of organized labour were established and the actions of the national unions in furtherance of these goals were co-ordinated. The Federation as a co-ordinating body dealt with the concerns of organized labour generally, leaving matters of concern to individual trades to be dealt with by the national union responsible.

The decade of the 1920s proved to be a difficult period for the union movement in spite of the best efforts of the American Federation of Labor. The business recession of 1921–22 placed pressure on union members to accept lower wages. This, coupled with a series of unsuccessful strikes in the steel industry and coal mines, had a demoralizing effect on the labour movement. The unions also suffered from the use of strikebreakers by some employers and the formation of many company unions which employers organized to discourage other unions from attempting to organize the workers in their plants. The result was that by the end of the decade the union movement had lost close to one and one-half million members. When the Great Depression followed the stock market crash in 1929, organized labour urged the government to take action to cure the economic ills that plagued the nation and to take steps to protect the rights of workers to unionize.

In response to the demands of organized labour, and in particular to the pressure of the American Federation of Labor, the *Norris-La Guardia Act*[27] was passed in 1932. This Act prohibited employers from using "yellow dog" contracts to prevent employees from joining unions and restricted the availability of injunctions to employers involved in labour disputes. Under the *Norris-La Guardia Act*, the employer could only obtain an injunction if he could show that he would suffer irreparable harm from the union activity which he wished the court to stop, and that he had made all reasonable efforts to settle the dispute prior to his application to the court. The Act was a major breakthrough for the unions, as it removed two important weapons from the employers which had been used frequently against unions to prevent the unionization of plants and to break strikes.

The next year, the employees' right to organize without employer interference was established as a part of the *National Industrial Recovery Act*.[28] Once this right was available at law, many employees in previously unorganized industries formed new unions or joined locals of the many national unions. Much of the organization took place in the mass production industries during this time, and because these plants were largely manned by unskilled workers, the unions which organized them did so on an industrial basis, rather than by craft. This occurred in the rubber, aluminum, automobile and other industries. Since the national unions in the American Federation of Labor were craft unions, the new unions were given separate charters by the Federation.

In spite of the new freedom to organize, all did not go well for organized labour in the 1930s. As a result of the heavy craft orientation of the AFL, a practice was established whereby mass production workers would be organized on an industrial basis as directly chartered locals; then the various craft unions would be allowed to carve out their own groups from the industrial union, leaving only the unskilled and semiskilled workers in the industrial union. Because this practice weakened the bargaining power of the industrial union, their leaders objected to the craft method of organization at the 1935 Convention of the AFL. Their objection, needless to say, fell on deaf ears, as the craft unions voted down the industrial union motions to have the practice stopped.

To counter the practice, a number of the industrial unions in the

AFL, notably the United Mine Workers, the United Textile Workers, the Mine, Mill and Smelter Workers, and a few others formed the Committee for Industrial Organization (CIO) to promote the organization of the mass production industries along industrial, rather than craft lines. The formation of the new organization within the AFL prompted a response from the executive, and the Committee was ordered to stop its activities. The industrial unions, however, refused to do so and in due course were suspended by the federation.

The suspension of the industrial unions produced a predictable response. The industrial unions led by John L. Lewis of the United Mine Workers formed a new federation along lines similar to the AFL, which they called the Congress of Industrial Organizations to preserve their previous acronym, CIO. The new federation then embarked on an active campaign to organize the mass production industries in competition with the AFL unions. What followed was a great rivalry for the right to represent employees in the new industries. By the time that the United States entered the Second World War in 1941, union membership had grown to the point where it exceeded ten million workers.

The growth in membership was not entirely due to the rivalry for members, although this was a contributing factor. What was largely responsible for the rapid unionization of employees was the passage of the *National Labor Relations Act* (the Wagner Act)[29] by the United States Congress in 1935. The new Act, which replaced the provisions of the *National Industrial Recovery Act* pertaining to the right to organize, established a complete frame-work for labour relations on a national basis. The legislation provided for a National Labor Relations Board to oversee the organization of employees by unions, and to establish not only the appropriate unit of employees for collective bargaining purposes, but to determine the union entitled to represent the unit. The Act also required the employer to meet and bargain in good faith with the union certified to represent the employees, and provided penalties for employers who interferred with the organization process, or refused to bargain in good faith. The net effect of the law was to eliminate most of the old obstacles which had lain in the path of employees seeking to organize. This permitted the rapid growth of the union movement, now free from most forms of employer interference.

During the war years 1941–1945, the unionization of industries engaged in war production was encouraged by the War Labor Board, and while strikes were discouraged (some did occur), the bargaining emphasis shifted from wage negotiations to fringe benefits, as wages were controlled. In spite of the limitations on collective bargaining imposed by the war, membership continued to grow at the rate of about one million a year throughout the 1941–1945 period. By 1946, however, the period of relative tranquility for labour relations had ended.

When controls were lifted after the war, industry was plagued by a great many strikes and work stoppages because wages had not kept pace with price increases. Many unfair union tactics also came to light during this time, and it was necessary for the government to again redress the inequities in the area of labour relations. In 1947, the *Labor Management Relations Act* (the Taft-Hartley Act)[30] was passed in spite of strong union opposition. The Act prohibited clauses in collective agreements that would permit unions to require an employer to dismiss an employee expelled from the union for any reason other than for nonpayment of union dues, and also prohibited a number of other unfair union activities such as secondary boycotts, and closed shop clauses in collective agreements.

The next decade saw the end to the rivalry between the AFL and CIO. They managed to resolve their major differences and merged in 1955. The merger, however, did not end the problems for organized labour, as the United States Senate began an investigation of alleged corruption and racketeering in organized labour in 1957. The Senate investigation prompted the newly formed AFL-CIO to initiate its own investigation and clean-up of unions that had permitted criminal elements to control their activities. Unfortunately, the clean-up by the federation was limited to the expulsion of unions that were found to be dominated by criminal elements, and new federal legislation was necessary in addition to action by the criminal law enforcement agencies to end union racketeering.

In 1959, the United States Congress passed the *Labor Management Reporting and Disclosure Act*[31] to eliminate coercive activities such as "hot cargo" clauses (the refusal by unions to handle goods shipped by struck or non-union plants) certain picketing practices of unions, and the secondary boycott activities of unions, where the boycott was an attempt to coerce a company to cease doing business with an employer who had a labour dispute with a union.

For the next two decades, labour relations in the United States continued with a number of significant changes, the most notable being the change in characteristics of union membership. Technological changes since 1960 steadily reduced the demand for blue collar workers in most mass production industries. Unions, in response, organized white collar workers in greater numbers. This in turn, altered the make-up of the AFL-CIO, with the result being a decline in the power and influence of the craft unions, and a new and important role for the white collar and service industry workers in the formulation of policy and the direction which organized labour will take in the future.

THE CANADIAN LABOUR MOVEMENT

Some of the earliest unions in Canada were formed on the east coast by employees in the shipbuilding firms around 1812. A union of printers was established in Quebec City as early as 1827.[32] The first union to remain in existence for any length of time, however, was a union of printers, which was organized in Toronto, Ontario (then the Town of York), in 1832. The union disappeared in 1837, but was revived again in 1844, and has continued since that time, although as a part of an international union.[33]

The early unions were essentially organizations of craftsmen who had emigrated from England and brought with them their past experiences with the union movement. As it was in England at the time, the new organizations were local in outlook and interests, since most communities in the early part of the nineteenth century were relatively isolated due to the primitive state of transportation and communication facilities in the country. As a general rule, the new unions were largely interested in providing sickness and accident benefits for their members rather than collective bargaining because the need for collective bargaining was less important in the small manufacturing businesses of the day. Most employers had only a few employees and produced for a local market. Consequently, most had a good working relationship with their work force. Since the economy was based primarily on agriculture and forest products, the union movement did not take hold until the latter part of the century when the establishment of railroads expanded the market for goods and permitted the development of larger manufacturing firms which served other than local markets.

Railroad building, commencing in the second half of the nineteenth century and continuing through until the time of the First World War in 1914, opened up large areas of the country for agricultural purposes, lumbering, and mining. With this expansion came a great many immigrants who not only settled new lands in Canada, but created a market for manufactured goods. While many of the early settlers were craftsmen from the British Isles, who had brought with them their trade union experience, the greatest influence on the union movement in Canada came from the United States, particularly after the American Civil War. Improved transportation and communications with the United States permitted craftsmen interested in the trade union movement to have frequent contact with one another, and the United States labour movement rapidly became the dominant influence on the direction that the trade union movement would take in Canada.

In 1871, the first council of trade unions was held in Toronto and the Toronto Trades Assembly was formed.[34] Unions in most urban areas formed local councils or assemblies around this time as well. A year later, in 1872, the printers in Toronto went on strike for a nine-hour day and, predictably, the leaders of the strike were charged with conspiracy in restraint of trade. The strike, nevertheless, had an outcome which was beneficial to the trade union movement as a whole. Shortly after the strike, the Government of Canada passed the *Criminal Law Amendment Act*,[35] which exempted trade unions from illegal acts in restraint of trade. In addition, it passed the *Trade Unions Act*,[36] which in effect made trade unions lawful associations.

The new legislation permitted trade unions to organize without fear of criminal action and a large number of craft unions were formed thereafter, either as traditional craft unions, or as a part of the Knights of Labor that had established itself in Canada. This new freedom also enabled the union movement to consider the feasibility of forming a nationwide federation of trade unions and a first attempt at the formation of this type of organization was made in Toronto in 1883. At that meeting, the Knights of Labor and the Toronto Trades and Labour Council formed the Dominion Trades and Labour Congress which ten years later became known as the Trades and Labour Congress (TLC). The Trades and Labour Congress, with some changes in membership affiliation, remained in existence until the middle of the 1950s at which time it merged with a later federation, the Canadian Congress of Labour (CCL; founded in 1940). The merger of the TLC and CCL in 1956 created the present Canadian Labour Congress (CLC).

In spite of its long existence, the Trades and Labour Congress had a difficult time in its attempts to quell internal differences in the labour movement. The first major problem was largely inherited from the American labour movement when the craft unions in the AFL, through their Canadian affiliates, pressured the TLC to expel any union that claimed jurisdiction over a trade group that conflicted with the jurisdiction of a craft union affiliated with the AFL. This move, largely at the behest of craft unions, was designed to oust the Knights of Labor from the TLC, as the Knights frequently organized workers on a local basis regardless of craft.

The proposal placed the Knights of Labor in direct conflict with the jurisdiction of the craft unions and because the AFL affiliated craft unions had managed to establish majority support in the TLC, the motion was carried. The Knights of Labor and other Canadian unions, whose jurisdictions conflicted with those of international unions and AFL affiliates were expelled from the Congress in 1902.[37]

The expelled unions, however, were not prepared to operate without a federation, and later in the same year organized the National Trades and Labour Congress in opposition to the TLC.[38] The new Congress was renamed the Canadian Federation of Labour (CFL) in 1908 and succeeded in bringing into affiliation several large Canadian labour organizations, including the influential Provincial Workmen's Association of Nova Scotia in 1910.[39] From its initial membership of 7,000, the CFL experienced somewhat erratic growth but comprised over 17,000 members by 1923.[40]

The two rival federations did not include all Canadian unions and for many years a number of unions operated outside the umbrella of the TLC and the AFL. Unions of Catholic workers, for example, formed their own federations as early as 1912 in Quebec,[41] and some unions, such as the One Big Union (1919),[42] maintained a separate existence for many years. By 1927, however, the need for a more united voice became apparent and an attempt was made to form a new federation in addition to the TLC and the AFL.

The One Big Union, some Electrical Workers' unions, the Brotherhood of Railway Employees and other unaffiliated unions formed the All Canadian Congress of Labour (ACCL)[43] in 1927, and promptly merged with the Canadian Federation of Labour under the name of the new Canadian Congress. The All Canadian Congress of Labour continued in existence until 1940, at which time the Canadian CIO affiliated unions that had been ousted by the TLC joined the ACCL. At this point the members decided to change the name of the federation and the new organization became known as the Canadian Congress of Labour (CCL).[44]

The final significant change in the Canadian labour movement occurred in 1956 when the Trades and Labour Congress, and the Canadian Congress of Labour merged to form the Canadian Labour Congress(CLC).[45] The new congress became the largest organization of unions in Canada and the dominant voice of organized labour from that date to the present. The internal structure of the Canadian Labour Congress and the national and international unions that consititute its membership are examined in detail in the next chapter.

REVIEW QUESTIONS

1. *To what extent did the transportation system in England and North America inhibit the development of the trade union movement?*

2. *Explain why the Amalgamated Society of Engineers represented the first successful labour organization in England.*

3. *How did the rise of the general contractor affect the union movement?*

4. *What was the significance of the "restraint of trade" laws in a labour relations context?*

5. *In what ways did the philosophy of the Knights of Labor differ from that of the American Federation of Labor?*

6. *Define a "yellow dog" contract, and explain how these were affected by the Norris-La Guardia Act in the United States.*

7. *Describe the changes that the National Labor Relations Act (Wagner Act) made in the area of collective bargaining and the importance of the legislation in the expansion of the trade union movement.*

8. *What was the intent and purpose of the Taft-Hartley Act? The Labor Management Reporting and Disclosure Act?*

9. *Assess the contribution of the British trade union movement on the growth of unionism in Canada.*

10. *Explain how the United States trade union movement became a dominant influence on the development of the Canadian labour movement.*

NOTES

[1]*An Act to Prevent Unlawful Combinations of Workmen* (1799), 39 Geo. III, c. 81; amended (1800) 39 & 40 Geo. III, c. 106.

[2]*Combination Law Repeal Act* (1824), 5 Geo. IV, c. 95.

[3]*Combination Law Repeal Amendment Act* (1825), 6 Geo. IV, c. 129.

[4]*Trades Unions Act* (1871), 34 & 35 Vict., c. 31.

[5]*Friendly Societies Act* (1855), 18 & 19 Vict., c. 63.

[6]See *Regina v. Bunn, Ray, Jones, Wilson and Dilley* (1872), 12 Cox C.C. 316.

[7]See *Quinn v. Leathem*, [1901] A.C. 495.

[8]See *Taff Vale Railway Co. v. The Amalgamated Society of Railway Servants*, [1901] A.C. 426.

[9]*Conspiracy and Protection of Property Act* (1875), 38 & 39 Vict., c. 86, s. 3.

[10]*Trade Disputes Act* (1906), 6 Edw. VII, c. 47.

[11]John R. Commons et al., *History of Labor in the United States*. New York: Augustus M. Kelly, 1966. vol. I, p. 123.

[12]*Ibid.*, vol. I, pp. 121–22.

[13]*Ibid.*, vol. I, p. 156.

[14]*Ibid.*, vol. I, pp. 189–92.

[15]*Ibid.*, vol. I, pp. 424–25, 428.

[16]*Ibid.*, vol. I, p. 441.

[17]*Ibid.*, vol. I, p. 444.

[18]*Commonwealth of Massachusetts v. Hunt* (1842), 45 Mass. (4 Metc.) 111; 38 *Am. Dec* 346.

[19]*Supra*, note 11, vol. I, pp. 620–21.

[20]*Ibid.*, vol. II, pp. 6-1-62. This organization was formed in May, 1863, in Detroit and was known as The Brotherhood of the Footboard. It adopted the name Brotherhood of Locomotive Engineers in 1864.

[21]*Ibid.*, vol. II, p. 197.

[22]*Ibid.*, vol. II, p. 197. Uriah Smith Stephens was born at Cape May, New Jersey, in 1921. He was educated as a Baptist minister but took up tailoring in order to earn a living. A member of a garment cutters union organized in 1862–63, Stephens founded the Knights of Labor in 1869 in an effort to counteract the decline of the earlier union's influence in the industry.

[23]*Ibid.*, vol. II, p. 318.

[24]*Ibid.*, vol. II, pp. 409–10.

[25]*Ibid.*, vol. II, pp. 306–7, 412, 512–14. Samuel Gompers was born in England in 1850. He was elected the first president of the AFL in 1886 and remained so, except for the years 1894–95, until his death in 1924.

[26]*Ibid.*, vol. II, p. 501.

[27]*Norris-La Guardia Act* (1932), *U.S. Statutes at Large*, 72nd Congress, pt. I, pp. 70–73, refer ss. 3, 7.

[28]*National Industrial Recovery Act* (1933), *U.S. Statutes at Large*, 73rd Congress, pt. I, p. 195, s. 7(a). This Act was later held to be unconstitutional. See *Schechter Poultry Corporation et al. v. Ryan et al.* (1935), U.S. Reports, vol. 293, p. 388.

[29]*National Labor Relations Act* (1935), (Wagner Act) U.S. Statutes at Large, 74th Congress, pt. I, p. 449.

[30]*Labor Management Relations Act* (1947) (Taft-Hartley Act) U.S. Statutes at Large, 80th congress, 1st Session, vol. 61, c. 120, p.136.

[31]*Labor Management Reporting and Disclosure Act* (1959), U.S. Statutes at Large, 86th Congress, 1st Session, vol. 73, p. 519.

[32]Eugene A. Forsey, *The Canadian Labour Movement 1812-1902*, Booklet #27 Ottawa: The Canadian Historical Association, 1974. p. 3.
[33]*Ibid.*, p. 4.
[34]*Ibid.*, p. 5. The Toronto Trades Assembly remained in existence until 1878.
[35]*Criminal Law Amendment Act* (1872), 35 Vict., c. 31.
[36]*Trade Unions Act* (1872), 35 Vict., c. 30.
[37]Harold Amos Logan, *Trade Unions in Canada*. Toronto: Macmillan and Co., 1948. pp. 71-73, 368.
[38]*Ibid.*, p. 370.
[39]*Ibid.*, p. 372.
[40]*Ibid.*, p. 373.
[41]*Ibid.*, p. 565.
[42]*Ibid.*, p. 306.
[43]*Ibid.*, p. 381.
[44]*Ibid.*, pp. 386-87.
[45]Stuart Jamieson, *Industrial Relations in Canada*. Toronto: Macmillan of Canada, 1973. pp. 30-31, see also pp.38-39.

RECOMMENDED REFERENCES AND SOURCE MATERIAL

Abella, Irving. *The Canadian Labour Movement 1902-1960*, Booklet #28. Ottawa: The Canadian Historical Association (1975).

Aspinall, A. *Early English Trade Unions*. London: Batchworth Press (1949).

Forsey, Eugene A. *The Canadian Labour Movement 1812-1902*, Booklet #27 Ottawa: The Canadian Historical Association (1974).

Goldenberg, S.B. *Industrial Relations in Quebec, Past and Present*. Kingston, Canada: Queen's University Industrial Relations Centre (1975).

Jamieson, Stuart. *Industrial Relations in Canada*. Toronto: Macmillan of Canada (1973).

Litwack, Leon F. *The American Labour Movement*. Englewood Cliffs, New Jersey: Prentice-Hall Inc. (1962).

Logan, Harold A. *Trade Unions in Canada*. Toronto: Macmillan and Co. (1948).

Pelling, Henry. *A History of British Trade Unionism*. London: Macmillan and Co. (1963).

Rayback, Joseph G. *A History of American Labor*. New York: Macmillan and Co. (1959).

CHAPTER THREE

THE STRUCTURE OF ORGANIZED LABOUR IN CANADA

In its one hundred and sixty-odd year existence organized labour in Canada has developed from a few small scattered groups of craftsmen to a large and complex organization. It comprises many thousands of local unions, several hundred national and international unions, and a number of national labour federations, with a total membership in excess of three million.[1]

For the early part of its existence, organized labour was essentially local in outlook and limited in its sphere of influence. The local union remained the centre of activity for each craft in each community and was concerned with the economic well-being of its own members. Some attempts were made to link up locals of the same craft or skill in the middle of the nineteenth century but the state of transportation and communications at the time effectively made the formation of a national body impossible. As a result, the local union was initially the only union to which the members could look for support and benefits in the event that they suffered some injury or loss, or had a labour dispute with their employer. Since most of the early unions were craft unions, their organization was established on a geographic basis. They consisted of persons engaged in the same craft who worked in a particular town or city. This form of local organization has continued until the present time, especially for craft unions engaged in the construction industry, although each now has a national or international organization as well. In most areas the craft union also has membership in a larger, national federation of labour.

While craft unions still continue to have their local unions organized on a geographic basis, other unions have tended to organize locals on an individual plant basis. This is largely because the community of interest of such union members is single plant or single employer oriented. Consequently, unions such as the steelworkers, auto workers, rubber workers and other similar industrial unions generally establish locals made up of all of the production workers in a single plant. If the community is large, with a number of organized plants, the union might have several or many locals within the same community. Each, however, would be concerned only with the members in its own local, since frequently each plant has a different owner, manufactures a different line of products, and has different labour relations policies and practices. For example, a steelworkers' union might organize one local in a plant of a manufacturer of sheet metal products such as cooking utensils, pails, and tools, and another local might be organized in a plant which manufactures metal cans for food products. Each of the two locals in the city or town would be concerned with its own members and problems. However, if one union had a major problem such as a strike, the other local of the union in the area might provide help to the striking workers in the form of financial aid and support.

Since the support that locals in a given area could provide was generally limited to the resources of the local membership, the local unions were quick to realize that a larger, national organization could be of greater assistance to a local union, since it would be able to draw upon greater resources when required. The national organization would also provide a structure through which the activities of many locals in communities throughout the country could be co-ordinated. When transportation and communication facilities in Canada reached the stage where contact between communities was relatively easy, many unions promptly set up national bodies patterned along the lines of the British Amalgamated Society of Engineers.[2]

The characteristics of such central organizations or national unions were generally similar for all central bodies formed during the last half of the nineteenth century. Little has changed since that time. As a rule, the national union is controlled by a **convention**, made up of delegates from all of the local unions that belong to the central body. The convention is held on a regular basis, usually every two years. Its primary functions usually are to elect the executive of the national union, to establish the policies of the organization, and to deal with important union matters.

The election of the executive has been, and still is, an important activity at each convention. The members elected to the various offices of a national union conduct the business of the union between conventions and generally have a considerable influence over the activities of the organization during the interval. Their actions must conform to the policies set down by the convention, but nevertheless, they do exercise considerable power since most of the union funds, in particular strike funds, are administered by the national union. The ability to provide or withhold financial support is one of the most important powers of the central body. This enables the central organization to exercise a certain amount of control over local unions that might wish to engage in strike activity not sanctioned by the central body.

The principal service that the national executive provides to the local union generally takes the form of expert assistance. They advise the local representatives during their negotiations with employers and assist in resolving grievances and other local problems. The central body also provides training and advice to local union officers and others in the operation of the union local. In addition, the national executive is generally responsible for the organization of new locals. Most of these services are provided through full-time employees of the national union called field representatives or business agents. These union employees generally have responsibility for all the locals in a given area. They travel from one local to another and assist them in their operations. The representatives are also responsible for explaining national union policies to the local union officers and for communicating to the national executive the concerns and attitudes of local union members regarding the policies or decisions of the national executive. In a sense, the field representatives are the communication link between locals and the central body. They are also the principal organizers of new locals and the suppliers of expertise in labour relations matters to the local unions. The ability of national and international union executives to accurately read the mood of the rank and file membership is due in a large measure to the effective communication system which is provided by the field organization in each union.

The organization of the executive of most international unions is characterized by a large number of vice-presidents. While not all unions follow this practice, the constitution of a typical international union will often provide that a vice-president be placed in charge of each area of activity of the central organization.[3] These officers of the union are elected by delegates to the union's national convention. They, along with the President, Secretary, and Treasurer, form the national union executive. As stated earlier, the executive carries on all union business between conventions, and is ultimately responsible for the effective operation of the organization at all times.

The financial support of the national union comes from dues assessments paid by the locals. Members of the locals are obliged to pay dues on a regular basis, usually monthly. Monthly union dues for an individual member may range from a few dollars to well over one hundred dollars depending upon the nature of the union and the benefits that the union provides to its members. On average, union dues paid by the member of a local union would perhaps be the equivalent of one to two hour's wages per month, bearing in mind that considerable variation exists, depending upon the type of union, and the services that it offers to its members.

The number of unions that provide substantial financial benefits to their membership has diminished substantially over the years. This is because many benefits such as sickness and accident insurance, pensions, and death benefits are now provided by employers or government administered plans. Except for some of the craft unions, unions at the present time tend to concern themselves less with the provision of membership benefits of this nature and more with negotiating the provision of benefits by employers through the collective bargaining process. Consequently, the union dues fixed by most unions do not include a benefit component, but rather, cover only the maintenance of the union itself. This includes such expenses and such services as union executive and staff salaries, office rental and the cost of providing union publications and educational services. In many cases, the union is also required to pay a membership fee if it belongs to a labour federation.

As a general rule, most of the union dues paid at the local level are passed on to the international or national union. The local union is usually permitted to retain sufficient funds to maintain the services that it provides at the local level, and usually this includes the cost of providing a local union hall, printing newspapers or news letters, staff salaries and similar expenses. The international or national body normally receives a large part of the local dues and these are used to maintain a strike fund, pay the salaries of central office staff and field representatives, and to fund the educational, research, and other activities conducted at the head office level.

Apart from the economies of scale associated with such centralized organizations, the delivery of services by the national body through its field organization and the central control of services, especially funds, gives the national union the necessary degree of control over local unions to enable it to operate for the benefit of the overall membership. The ability of the national or international executive to control strike funds, permits it to limit financial support to locals where a strike would likely have some chance of achieving the aims of the members. Most central organizations tend to urge locals to avoid unnecessary strikes and ones that are likely to fail, since the union as a whole as well as the local members must bear the resulting economic loss. The central control of funds has an added benefit to the membership in that it enables the international body to audit the finances of the local unions and protect the membership from possible mismanagement.

A final measure through which the national organization may exercise control over the local is the right of the national under its constitution to place a local union under trusteeship if the local officers fail or refuse to conduct local matters in accordance with the central union's constitution and policies. This step is usually only taken by the national or international union where the central organization believes it necessary to protect the local membership and the assets of the local union from mismanagement. Nevertheless, it provides a special check on local union officers in the sense that they are aware that they may be removed from office if they fail to conduct the affairs of the local union in accordance with their prescribed duties under the constitution of the local union.

The organizational structure adopted by trade unionists has proved to be a satisfactory and enduring form of organization for the particular needs of labour. In order to maintain and direct the overall organization in the best interests of the membership in general, a central organization is essential. Thus, local organizations are made responsive not only to the immediate needs of the local membership but to those of the entire body. The two levels of organization in a sense each perform their own roles with a substantial degree of autonomy, yet they constitute a single cohesive unit for the furtherance of the overall goals of the organization and the membership. The success of this form of organization has inhibited the formation of any broader forms of organization, ones that might encompass different industrial or craft groups, as did the early Knights of Labor. Although there has been the formation of federations of trade unions or loosely formed alliances, power remains concentrated in the international or national union executives.

The largest federation of trade unions in Canada is the Canadian Labour Congress (CLC). As at the beginning of 1982, it had in affiliation fifty-three international and twenty-three national organizations, three provincial organizations, and seventy-seven directly chartered locals.[4] The combined membership of all affiliates was slightly more than 2,082,000.[5] The organization of the Congress is similar to that of a large international union, but lacks the power of the typical international because it exercises little direct control over its membership. The power within the organization still rests in the large international and national unions, even though the federation has in excess of two million members.

The Canadian Labour Congress holds a convention every two years, at which time delegates from the locals of unions that make up the federation attend and select the executive officers of the organization. In addition to the election of officers, the convention delegates raise and discuss matters of concern to organized labour, such as government policies, the economic climate, the direction that the union movement should take, and other issues of a similar nature. From these discussions, the policies of the federation are established, and the elected officers charged with the responsibility to carry them out.

As with the larger unions, the executive of the Canadian Labour Congress consists of a President, a Secretary-Treasurer, and many Vice-Presidents.[6] The federation has many Standing Committees and Departments, each concerned with a particular problem or area of activity of organized labour. Among the Standing Committees are groups dealing with the following matters:

AFL-CIO Liaison	**Maritime**
Bank Workers	**Metric Conversion**
Broadcast Unions	**Organization**
Constitution and Structure	**Performing Arts Unions**
Economic Policy	**Political Education**
Education Advisory	**Public Relations**
Farm Implement	**Public Sector**
Grain Handling and	**Retirement**
Transportation	**Social Services**
Health and Safety	**Technology**
Human Rights	**White Collar**
International Affairs	**Women Workers**

In addition to the Standing Committees, the organization executive also has a number of Departments, with the following responsibilities or areas of operation: Education, Research and Legislation, International Affairs, Public Relations, Political Education, Women's Bureau, Government Employees, and Organizational and Chartered Body

Relations. Each Department is generally responsible to an executive vice-president of the federation, and in turn to the convention.

The funds necessary to support the federation are paid by the unions, (as of September 1, 1983), on the basis of $0.43 per member per month.[7] The services provided by the federation in return consist of lobbying the federal government for legislation favourable to organized labour as a whole, education and informational services to members, research on economic and other matters for the union movement, and the provision of procedures for the resolution of interunion disputes. The organization does not maintain strike funds, except for a small fund to support directly chartered locals, nor does it assert any direct influence or control over the international or national unions that form the bulk of its membership. Its principal role is essentially to act as the voice of organized labour, and to operate as a co-ordinating body, rather than a union as such.

Labour relations in Canada is for the most part a provincial matter, with the federal government's jurisdiction limited to those industries or firms of an interprovincial nature such as the railways, airlines, banking, communications, atomic energy, and others which fall within its specific jurisdiction. As a consequence, most business firms are subject to provincial labour laws and policies. To effectively deal with the provincial governments, many of the larger unions also belong to the provincial Federations of Labour, which are also chartered by the Canadian Labour Congress. As with the Canadian Federation of Labour, the provincial federations each act as a research and educational body as well as a lobbyist for organized labour at the provincial government level.

The provincial labour federations are patterned after the national federation, with some variation in structure and services offered to its provincial members. For example, the Ontario Federation of Labour holds an annual convention, at which time the delegates elect a President, Secretary-Treasurer, and fourteen Vice-Presidents. The Ontario provincial federation has only seven Standing Committees, and nine Departments, which reflect its concern with matters of a provincial, rather than national nature. Its principal role is to lobby for legislation favourable to organized labour at the Ontario Government level. In contrast, the Nova Scotia Federation of Labour has eight Vice-Presidents, and only two Standing Committees.[8]

The local organization of labour unions is in the form of district labour councils. These are similar in nature to the early local labour

EXHIBIT 3-1 STRUCTURE OF THE LABOUR MOVEMENT IN CANADA

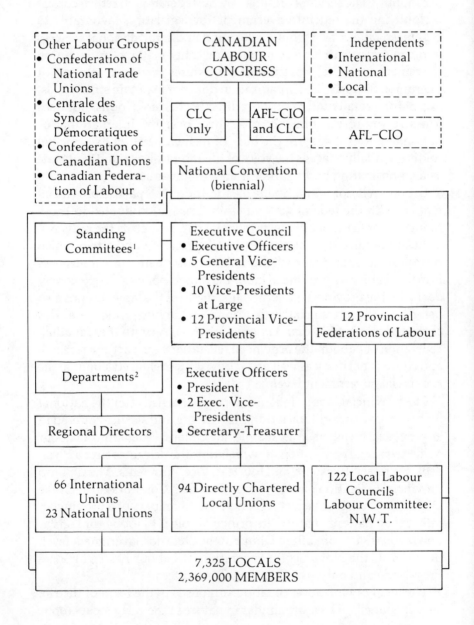

1 Standing Committees		2 Departments
AFL-CIO Liaison	Maritime	Public Relations
Bank Workers	Metric Conversion	International Affairs
Broadcast Unions	Organization	Organization and
Constitution and	Performing Arts	Chartered Body
Structure	Unions	Relations
Economic Policy	Political Education	Research and
Education Advisory	(2)	Legislation
Farm Implement	Public Relations	Government
Grain Handling and	Public Sector	Employees
Transportation	Retirement	Education
Health and Safety	Social Services	Women's Bureau
Human Rights	Technology	Social and
International Affairs	White Collar	Community
	Women Workers	Relations
		Political Education

Reproduced with the permission of Queen's University Industrial Relations Centre.

councils that formed in cities and towns during the nineteenth century, and today they are concerned with many of the same problems. At the present time, one hundred and twenty-three local labour councils are chartered bodies of the Canadian Labour Congress. These organizations, which have as members locals of the unions operating in the community, enable the local unions to undertake concerted action to deal with problems at the municipal level of government, and to play an active role in community affairs.

It is important to note that the Canadian Labour Congress with its many affiliated provincial federations and councils is not the only federation or organization of trade unions in Canada. Many unions belong to other federations, the most common being the Confederation of National Trade Unions, the Canadian Federation of Labour, and the Confederation of Canadian Unions. These organizations tend to be much smaller or regional in membership, and reflect the divergent views and philosophies that characterize the labour movement in Canada. For example, the Confederation des Syndicats Nationaux (C.S.N.) or, in English, the Confederation of National Trade Unions (C.N.T.U.) is a Quebec-based federation. It represented approximately 217,000 Quebec union members in 1982.[9] Formerly the Confédération des travailleurs catholiques du Canada (C.T.C.C.), the C.S.N.

EXHIBIT 3-2 FLOW OF UNION REVENUES AND SERVICES

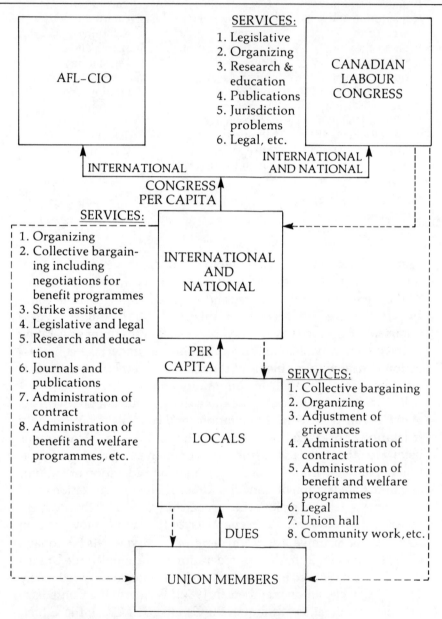

Source: Statistics Canada, Corporations and Labour Unions Returns Act, Part II - Labour Unions. 1981.

adopted its present name in 1960 after several unsuccessful attempts at merger between 1956 and 1959 with the then newly formed Canadian Labour Congress. The largest labour federation in Quebec is, however, a CLC affiliate; the Quebec Federation of Labour (Q.F.L.) which represented approximately 320,000 members in 1982.[10]

THE NATURE OF A UNION

A trade union is a unique organization. Its form of organization is similar to that of any unincorporated club or fraternal organization, yet its purpose and operation bears little resemblance, outwardly at least, to the typical service club found in most communities. This can be explained in part by the historical background of the union movement, as unions were initially illegal organizations if their purpose was to engage in acts in restraint of trade. Consequently, their early legal existence was frequently in the form of a club or benevolent society, to give the organization an outward appearance of legality. The early organizations of tradesmen usually took the form of a journeymen's club or friendly society. The organization was in fact for social purposes in the sense that it provided assistance to needy members, and a place where the members could gather to engage in a variety of lawful social activities. As a result, the club format was adopted as a means of organization, and groups of workmen would conduct their activities within the framework of a club constitution. The constitution of the club would establish the general goals and purposes of the organization, and delineate the duties and responsibilities of the elected officers or executive. Thus the organization, according to its constitution, would be for lawful pursuits and its existence legitimate, at least for all outward appearances. Underlying the constitution, however, would be the unwritten goal of the organization. Generally, this was to promote the welfare of the membership by way of mutual support and action in any dealings carried on between the membership and their employers. These activities were not incorporated in the union's constitution for to do so would render the organization unlawful in its purpose (as a combination in restraint of trade) under earlier laws. Some unions, nevertheless, were formed with a constitution that incorporated "restraint of trade objectives," but these remained secret organizations. However, this left the membership without recourse before the law in the event that a dishonest treasurer absconded with the organization's funds, or the officers of the organization acted contrary to the constitution of the group.

In most of the early cases that came before the courts, the judges of the day consistently applied the laws relating to clubs and fraternal organizations to the early trade unions. On this basis, the union was considered to be the same as any athletic club or voluntary organization and an organization that had no existence at law apart from its individual members.[11] Thus, the early trade union was treated as if it was simply a group of people who had joined together for social purposes or to promote a certain lawful cause or object. The members were considered to be persons "whose conduct in relation to one another is regulated in accordance with the constitution, by-laws, rules and regulations to which they have subscribed."[12]

From the comments made by the judges of the day, a number of observations concerning the legal nature of a union may be made. First, the organization is one which has no legal existence apart from its members. This means that a union has no separate existence as a corporation might have, but consists only of the members that belong to it. Second, the persons who are members of the organization are bound to one another in the organization by an agreement to carry out the objects of the organization. They must act in accordance with the procedures or rules set out in the constitution of the organization to which they ascribe. In other words, the members have agreed with one another to act together to carry out the goals of the organization in accordance with the rules which they have established.

In essence, the courts have determined that the relationship that exists between the members is one of contract. The contract is not a single contract between the individual member and the organization as an entity, but rather, a series of contracts between each member, and every other member of the union. This is known as the **contract theory** of the legal nature of a trade union. Under this theory, if a member of the union fails to comply with the contract or agreement made with the other members of the organization, then he or she has violated the contract and the other contracting parties may then decide that, as a result of the breach of the agreement, they no longer wish to be associated with such a person. If this should be the case, the other members would then treat their contracts with the offending member as being at an end and the member would be expelled from the organization. However, under the contract theory, there is no inherent power in a voluntary association to discipline or expel a member unless the power to do so is set out in the contract and agreed to by each member. Consequently, the parties must establish such a right if they wish to control unruly or disruptive members. This usually takes the form of rules or regulations embodied in the organization's constitution, which is incorporated in the individual contracts between members.

Other theories have been developed by the courts in an effort to explain the relationship between a voluntary association (such as a trade union) and individual members of the organization, but these have been rejected in favour of the contract theory by the Supreme Court of Canada, notwithstanding the fact that the theories were developed and accepted in other jurisdictions quite some time ago.

The earliest theory was the **property rights theory**, which in simplest terms states that every member of an association or club has a right in common with all other members to the assets or property possessed by the organization. On the basis of this theory, if a member is expelled from the organization, he or she is in effect deprived of the right to enjoy the property or to a share of the assets possessed by the association.[13] Interference with a property right entitles the aggrieved party the right to apply to the courts for relief, and in turn, the court will examine the actions of the organization to determine if the organization's interference with the member's property rights was lawful and correct under the terms of the association's constitution and the rules of natural justice.

The property rights can vary depending upon the nature of the organization, but the most common union "property" is in the form of benefits such as the social use of the union hall, welfare benefits, insurance, etc., and the right to obtain employment through the union hiring hall. Property rights nevertheless need not be substantial before the courts will interfere, as in one reported U.S. case, the court accepted the plea of a member of an association where he established that he had been improperly deprived of his share of the assets of an organization where the only assets consisted of a Bible and a wooden gavel.[14]

The property rights theory has not been widely accepted in Canada, due largely to the adoption of the contract theory. However, judges have occasionally adopted the property rights approach to deal with a specific expulsion dispute.[15] The principal advantage of this theory over the contract theory is that it permits the courts to intervene in most expulsion situations, as in almost all cases, the organization has some assets. The main weakness is that it does not permit recourse to the courts where a nonmonetary right is affected, such as disciplinary action that bars a union member from attendance at union meetings or from running for office for a period of time.

A third theory, which currently appears to be gaining some support in the United States and England is the **status theory**. This theory simply states that a person, by virtue of being a member of an association, union, or club acquires a certain "status" which is associated with the membership, and if a person should be improperly deprived of the status, then the wrongful destruction of the status would be actionable at law. This theory was accepted by the Manitoba Court of Appeal in a case concerning a union member improperly expelled from a union,[16] but it was later rejected by the Supreme Court of Canada in favour of the contract theory.

The rejection of the status theory was due for the most part to the fact that the court considered it to be too vague and ill-defined to form a basis for court intervention into the internal affairs of a union. Unlike the contract theory, it provided a basis for intervention only, and the court was still required to examine the organization's constitution to determine the rights of the parties.[17] As a result, the contract theory has become the principal theory to which the courts ascribe to explain the legal nature of the relationship between members of a trade union. On this basis, the union constitution becomes the key element of the contract in any determination of the rights of individual union members.

In practice, most organizations, in addition to the right to expel members, usually provide some mechanism or procedure to deal with members who violate their agreement and this is also frequently set out in the organization's constitution. The usual form that this may take is an administrative procedure whereby the union executive officers call a meeting of the members to hear the complaint against the member who has allegedly violated the rules of the organization. Following the hearing, at which the accused is entitled to appear and explain his or her actions, the members decide by way of a vote if they wish to end their association with the accused, or if the accused should be allowed to remain in the organization, perhaps subject to certain disciplinary action to correct improper behaviour.

The requirement for a hearing and the opportunity that it affords to the parties to present the complaint and the evidence to the membership is essentially an imposition of the common law on the organization. The courts have generally been reluctant to interfere with the internal affairs of private clubs and associations of a similar nature, but because trade unions often are in a position to seriously affect a craftsman's ability to earn a living if expelled from the union, they have been quite prepared to ensure that union members are treated fairly in any proceedings taken against them by others in their union organization. Thus, the courts have always been ready to intervene in the internal affairs of a union if a member could establish to the satisfaction of the court that the organization had denied the member a fair hearing before expulsion.

The concerns of the courts have been largely associated with the fairness of the organizations in their treatment of members. Judges have clearly recognized that the organizations were voluntary associations, and as such, had the obvious right to control the actions of members who acted contrary to the goals of the organizations, or acted in some fashion that was prejudicial to the interests of the other members. The courts looked upon the officers and members of the unions as if they were acting in a judicial or quasi-judicial manner when they conducted expulsion or disciplinary proceedings within their organization, and assumed the authority to review the actions of the organization as if they were domestic tribunals. From a legal point of view this meant that the courts would examine the procedure that the organization followed to discipline or expel a member in terms of "fairness." If the court determined that the procedure offended the rules for **natural justice**, the decision of the organization would be quashed.[18]

The rules or principles of natural justice imposed by public policy require the organization to first give the accused notice of the charges made against him and an opportunity to prepare his case before a hearing is scheduled. The accused must then be given notice of the hearing and the opportunity to appear at the hearing to cross-examine his accusers and present his answers to their charges. Only after the hearing is completed may the members then decide the matter before them.[19] In addition to these basic principles or requirements, the courts have also stated that the union has a duty to act impartially and in good faith in reaching a decision, and that the hearing procedure followed by the union officers must be in accordance with the union constitution. Following these additional requirements, the unions must not raise new charges at the hearing, nor can they avoid the requirement of a hearing by providing in their constitution for the automatic expulsion of union members under specified circumstances.[20]

In an effort to ensure that every member is treated in a fair and equitable manner, many unions have incorporated in their constitutions a hearing procedure that meets the requirements of fairness laid down by the courts. Most unions also provide an appeal procedure whereby a union member who has been disciplined or expelled by the local union membership may appeal to the international union, with power in the international body to reverse the decision of the local if any unfairness existed or if improper procedures were followed at the local level. As a further attempt to act fairly, some unions have carried the appeal procedure one step further and established a public review body which is made up of prominent, independent persons who act as a final appeal tribunal, with power vested in them to reverse or confirm any action taken against a member by either the local or international union. Provision for this type of public review body may be found in the constitutions of unions such as the United Automobile Workers (see exhibit 3-3), the Packinghouse Workers, and the Upholsterers' Union, to name a few.

Where a union has provided an appeal procedure for members who believe that they have been unfairly treated at the local union level, the aggrieved union member may not, as a general rule, ask the court to intervene immediately. The practice of the court is to require that the party exhaust the internal appeal procedures of the union before it will act. However, if the actions of the union executive are such that they have ignored the union constitution or by-laws, or acted beyond their jurisdiction, the court will intervene without requiring the aggrieved member to exhaust the union appeal procedure.[21]

THE RIGHT TO JOIN A UNION

A labour union is considered to be a voluntary organization not unlike typical societies or social organizations such as a local athletic club. As a consequence, the courts in general have taken the position that a person has no lawful right or entitlement to membership. However, the courts have also recognized that a labour union differs from the ordinary social or athletic club in the sense that the union may control a person's opportunity for employment. In particular crafts or firms, the union may establish itself as the supplier of labour to employers through the use of union hiring halls, or by negotiating a collective agreement with employers that requires union membership as a term or condition of employment for all employees. In each of these instances, union membership is of the utmost importance. In the case of the union hiring hall, which is common in the construction

EXHIBIT 3-3   UNITED AUTO WORKERS UAW
APPEAL PROCEDURE

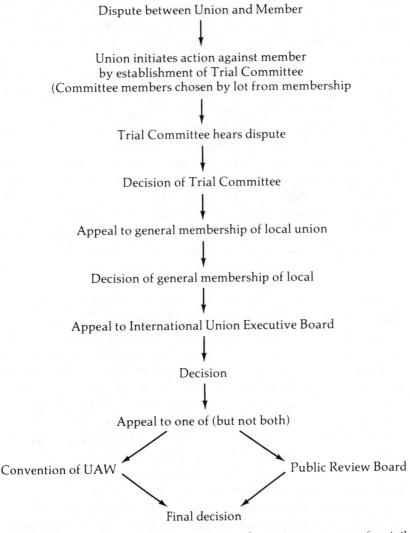

Dispute between Union and Member

Union initiates action against member
by establishment of Trial Committee
(Committee members chosen by lot from membership

Trial Committee hears dispute

Decision of Trial Committee

Appeal to general membership of local union

Decision of general membership of local

Appeal to International Union Executive Board

Decision

Appeal to one of (but not both)

Convention of UAW   Public Review Board

Final decision

A possible final "appeal" to the court exists by commencement of a civil
action by the aggrieved member against the union. This in turn would
open up a new appeal route if grounds for appeal should exist.

field, the union provides qualified craftsmen as and when required by
employers. Persons who do not belong to the union are denied the

opportunity to work, because they seldom can obtain employment except through the union hiring hall, an avenue blocked by the lack of a union membership card. This "closed shop" employment system is much less common outside the construction industry, as employment in most plants and offices tends to be of a more permanent nature, and the need for a hiring hall to supply labour is less important to employers. Nevertheless, in the nonconstruction sector, unions have, in many cases, negotiated collective agreements with employers that require as a term of employment an obligation on all employees to join the union and remain as members. Under these circumstances, continuous membership in the union would be equally as important in order for a person to continue working as an employee. For these reasons the courts have refrained from considering a labour union in exactly the same fashion as a non-union voluntary organization, and have expressed a willingness to examine those instances where membership has been denied to a person by a union, if the denial contains an element of discrimination or arbitrary action on the part of union officers. The courts have also been prepared to provide a remedy where discrimination or arbitrary action is established. For example, in one case[22] a person belonged to a musicians' union for many years, and regularly paid all union dues. Unfortunately, the union member failed to pay his union dues on one occasion, and his name was summarily struck from the union's membership list. The result was catastrophic for the musician because the union had agreements with all employers of musicians in the area, and these agreements provided that they would employ only union members. The ex-member of the union was unable to find any work as a musician and was forced to work as an unskilled labourer in order to earn a living. Finally, he appealed to the courts on the basis that the union secretary who had struck his name from the list had acted in an arbitrary manner. The court agreed and held that the person's membership could not be terminated in such an arbitrary manner without a hearing, and final determination by the union members. In another case[23] where the union constitution provided for the automatic termination of membership for nonpayment of union dues, the court held that automatic forfeiture or expulsion clauses were a denial of natural justice and beyond the powers of a union.

The federal government and the provincial legislatures have also recognized the need to protect persons from possible discriminatory practices on the part of trade unions. Under the various statutes dealing with human rights, discrimination against any person by a trade union on the basis of race, creed, colour, sex, nationality, ancestry or place of origin, is generally prohibited.[24] In addition, most governments in their labour legislation prohibit such discrimination and through their Labour Relations Boards grant unions the right to represent employees only in those instances where the union is prepared to admit as members all of the employees in the particular plant or unit requested.[25]

While all of these limitations on the rights of a union to select its membership prevent discrimination or arbitrary action by union officers against individual members, the right to refuse membership or to expel or suspend a person for legitimate reasons after a full and impartial hearing remains. As with any voluntary organization, the union membership may establish in its constitution the right to bar or expel from membership persons who are not prepared to support or conform to the goals of the organization. This permits the union to enforce its rules and regulations, provided that it does so in a fair and impartial manner.

REVIEW QUESTIONS

1. Explain the role of the **convention** in a trade union context.
2. Describe the nature and activities of a **local** union, and indicate how these activities differ from the activities of a **national** or **international** union.
3. Describe the various methods used by a national union to control its locals.
4. Explain the role of a field representative or business agent in a national or international union.
5. Why did unions form federations? What is the purpose of a federation in the labour movement?
6. What is the legal nature of a union?
7. Briefly describe the **contract theory** of the nature of a trade union.
8. Why is the **constitution** of a union important? How does it affect the individual members?
9. What safeguards have the courts imposed on unions to protect individual members from arbitrary or unfair treatment at the hands of union officers?

NOTES

[1] Statistics Canada 71–202, *Annual Report of the Minister of Supply and Services Canada under the Corporations and Unions Returns Act*, Part II, Labour Unions 1981, Table I.

[2] The British Amalgamated Society of Engineers, Machinists, Smiths, Millwrights and Pattern-Makers, as it was originally called, was founded in 1850–51 in London, England by William Allan and William Newton. Both men were members of an earlier labour organization, The Journeymen Steam Engine Makers, or "Old Mechanics," founded in Manchester in 1826. See Henry Pelling, *A History of British Trade Unionism*, London: Macmillan and Co., 1963. pp. 41–42.

[3] See for example, the constitution of the United Steelworkers of America, the United Automobile Workers, etc.

[4] *Directory of Labour Organizations in Canada 1982*. Ottawa: Supply and Services. p. 163.

[5] *Ibid.*, p. 163.

[6] *Ibid.*, pp. 163–65. Refer also the Constitution of the Canadian Labour Congress, revised May, 1982; article VI.

[7] The Constitution of the Canadian Labour Congress, revised May 1982; article XVII.

[8] The number of standing committees and even departments in the various labour federations will vary from time to time depending upon the current concerns of the membership.

[9] *Supra*, note 4, p. 180.

[10] *Ibid.*, p. 168.

[11] For a review of the law refer *Astgen et al. v. Smith et al.*, [1970] 1 O.R. 129.

[12] *Ibid.*, p. 133.

[13] *Rigby v. Connol* (1880) 14 Ch. D. 482.

[14] Reported in C. W. Summers, "Legal Limitations on Union Discipline" (1951), 64 *Harvard Law Review*. p. 1,049.

[15] See *Lakeman and Barrett et al v. Bruce et al* [1949] 3 D.L.R. 527; [1949] 1 W.W.R. 886 (B.C. C.A.).

[16] *Tunney v. Orchard et al* [1955] 15 W.W.R. (N.S.) 49 (Man. C.A.)

[17] *Orchard et al v. Tunney* (1957) 8 D.L.R. (2d) 273.

[18] See for example, *Bimson v. Johnston et al. representing the Association of Letter Carriers of Canada*, [1957] O.R. 519; affirmed on appeal (1958) 12 D.L.R. (2d) 379.

[19] *Evaskow v. International Brotherhood of Boiler Makers etc., et al.* (1969), 9 D.L.R. (3d) 715.

[20] *Edwards v. Society of Graphical and Allied Trades*, [1970] 3 All E.R. 689.

[21] *Kuzych v. White et al.* [1950], 4 D.L.R. 187.

[22] *Bonsor v. Musicians' Union*, [1955] 3 All E.R. 518.

[23] *Supra*, note 15.

[24] For example, see *Ontario Human Rights Code*, R.S.O. 1980, c. 340, s. 5(1).

[25] See for example, *International Union of Operating Engineers, Local 796* (applicant) *and Metropolitian Life Insurance Company* (respondent), [1967] 67 C L L C 16,026 (O.L.R.B.).

RECOMMENDED REFERENCES AND SOURCE MATERIAL

Brooks, J.H. "Impartial Public Review of Internal Union Disputes: Experiment in Democratic Self Discipline." 22 *Ohio State Law Journal* 64 (1961).

Cox, A. "The Role of Law in Preserving Union Democracy." 72 *Harvard Law Review* 609 (1959).

Estey, M. *The Unions: Structure, Development and Management.* N.Y.: Harcourt, Brace and World Inc. (1967).

Fogel, W. and A. Kleingartner, (eds.) *Contemporary Labor Issues.* Belmont, Calif.: Wadsworth Publishing Co. Inc. (1968).

Stone, A.J. "Wrongful Expulsion From Trade Unions — Judicial Intervention at Anglo-American Law." 34 *Can. Bar Rev.* 1,111 (1956).

Summers, C.W. "Legal Limitations on Union Discipline." 64 *Harvard Law Review* 1049 (1951).

CHAPTER FOUR

THE LEGISLATIVE FRAMEWORK FOR COLLECTIVE BARGAINING

HISTORICAL DEVELOPMENT OF LABOUR LEGISLATION

Apart from statutes designed to regulate or control specific aspects of the employment relationship and the early restraint of trade laws designed to prohibit trade union activity of a collective bargaining nature, until comparatively recent times very little attention was given to the development of a legal framework in which unions could operate. As a result, collective bargaining was conducted in an informal, and in the early years of the nineteenth century, essentially illegal climate. During the latter part of the century, organized labour through the lobbying of the Trades and Labour Congress managed to convince the legislatures of a number of provinces that laws were necessary to control some of the more exploitive practices of employers of the day. Yet apart from laws enacted to improve the work environment in factories and mines, or to protect the wages of wage earners, very little thought was given to some sort of legislative machinery for collective bargaining. By the end of the century, however, the organization of craft workers had reached the stage where the craft unions could demand voluntary recognition from employers, at least during the prosperous years when skilled labour was scarce.

In 1872, trade unions were declared lawful entities by virtue of certain changes in the criminal law embodied in *The Trade Unions Act*,[1] but it was not until the beginning of the twentieth century that unions and the practice of collective bargaining received sufficient public attention to warrant some form of legislative regulation.

A few provinces, nevertheless, did attempt to provide some form of assistance to the parties shortly after the 1872 legislative changes which permitted unions to lawfully represent their members. The Province of Ontario passed *The Trades Arbitration Act* in 1873,[2] which took a voluntary approach to labour disputes. Under this Act, which was essentially a copy of the *English Conciliation Act* of 1867,[3] a framework was established within which conciliation boards and arbitration boards could be organized if employers of craftsmen and the members of a craft so desired. The practice was purely voluntary, and was put in motion by the filing of a memorandum of agreement at the County Registry Office by employers and craftsmen residing in a particular community. The Act did not mention unions, but provided for the organization of workmen and employers on a craft basis, with the understanding, one must assume, that the individual craft groups would be represented by their respective unions in order for the system to operate.

The Act contemplated negotiations between craftsmen and employers on a community basis, with issues (other than wages) that could not be resolved to be presented to a two-man conciliation board called a Board of Reconciliation. This board consisted of one craftsman and one employer. If they could not resolve the dispute, the dispute was submitted to a Board of Arbitration for final resolution.

The procedure applied to all parties who signed the memorandum and could be used to resolve both individual employee-employer disputes and those that affected the group as a whole. However, because the legislation did not give the boards authority to deal with future issues such as wage rates, etc. the legislation was largely ignored by the unions. Employers were also unwilling to use the legislation, for to do so would, in effect, recognize the craft unions as representatives of their employees and constitute tacit acceptance of the collective bargaining process itself. The lack of mutual interest in the resolution of disputes by the procedures provided under the Act was the principal reason for its failure. Had the Act provided for compulsory rather than voluntary arbitration of all disputes, the effect of the legislation would undoubtedly have been quite different. Instead, it provided for the maximum freedom of the individuals involved by leaving the decision with them, an idea wholly in keeping with the laissez-faire attitudes of the day, but unfortunately, an ineffective remedy for the resolution of labour disputes.

A decade and a half later, in 1888, Nova Scotia took a different approach and introduced compulsory conciliation and arbitration by its passage of *The Mines Arbitration Act*[4] to deal with disputes in the mining industry. The Act provided for compulsory conciliation as a first step in the resolution of disputes between employers and employees, during which time working conditions were frozen and the right to strike and the right to lock-out were suspended. The Act provided for compulsory arbitration of disputes that could not be resolved, but the only time a union attempted to use the Act the results were unsatisfactory. The employer challenged the validity of the legislation, and without waiting for the courts to resolve the question, the union abandoned its attempt to have the matter go to arbitration and called a strike instead.

In 1894, some six years after the Nova Scotia experiment was introduced by the legislature of that province, both British Columbia[5] and Ontario[6] passed new legislation to deal with labour disputes. These new statutes, which were generally referred to as trade disputes acts, were based upon Australian laws with one notable difference: both provinces continued to make the process voluntary, which permitted the parties to avoid using it if they so desired. Ontario continued to exclude future wage rates from matters that would fall within the jurisdiction of the boards, thus making the process even less appealing to unions. The voluntary aspect of the legislation once again proved to be the weakness of the laws, with the result that employers and unions did not avail themselves of it in the resolution of their disputes.

The first successful provincial legislation was passed by the Province of Quebec in 1901.[7] The Quebec statute, which was also patterned after the Australian (New South Wales) model did not initially avoid the problems of the Ontario statute, but was later modified to incorporate the essential element of compulsion by requiring the parties to use the procedures set out in the Act if they could not resolve the dispute themselves. As a result of this change, either party, the Mayor of the community, or the Registrar could call for conciliation, and the employer and the union would be required to submit to the process.[8] These changes were early recognition of the public interest aspect of labour disputes and the need to regulate activities of the parties that could have had an adverse impact on the community at large. This legislation signalled a move away from the purely voluntary approach of the previous labour relations legislation in the provinces of Ontario and British Columbia, and a move towards public involvement in labour disputes. Unlike the other provinces, Quebec continued to use its *Trade Disputes' Act*, (with amendments) until 1964, at which time it replaced the law with a new *Labour Code*. The remainder of the provinces tended to ignore labour relations in the first quarter of the twentieth century on the mistaken belief that labour relations was a matter best left with the federal government.

One of the earliest federal statutes that dealt with the collective bargaining process was the *Conciliation Act*[9] of 1900. The Act was not the first Canadian legislation of this nature, but this statute was significant in the sense that the Parliament of Canada recognized the need for some legislative mechanism to resolve labour disputes, particularly with regard to the railways. The *Railway Labour Disputes Act*,[10] which was introduced some three years later, carried over the essential features of the *Conciliation Act* in that it provided for a conciliation committee to be established by the Minister of Labour either on his own initiative, at the request of either party to the dispute, or any municipal government affected. The committee was to consist of a member named by each party to the dispute, with a third party who would be the independent chairman to be selected by the two parties or, on default, by the government.[11]

The conciliation committee had the duty to endeavour to bring about a settlement of the dispute, if possible, by way of conciliation or mediation, and to report its results to the Minister of Labour.[12] If the committee was unsuccessful, the Minister could then establish a similar board as a board of arbitration which would investigate and report its findings to the Minister along with its recommended settlement of the dispute.[13] While the award of the arbitration board was not binding on the parties, the award was nevertheless of persuasive value since the Minister's report was made public.[14] The new legislation was not well received by organized labour and was condemned by the railway unions who perceived it as a threat to their existence. It did nothing to enhance collective bargaining, but simply provided compulsory conciliation and persuasive arbitration as an alternative to the right to strike for dispute resolution. The failure of the legislation to either substitute compulsory arbitration, or fix a complete framework within which meaningful collective bargaining could take place were the principal drawbacks of the Act. Since the legislation did neither, it contributed little to development of collective bargaining law, apart from the legislative recognition of the public interest in labour disputes.

The first significant national legislation followed some years later, when the federal government passed *The Industrial Disputes Investigation Act* in 1907.[15] The Act applied to employers and unions in those industries which could be classified at that time as being "public-utilities," and where some level of intervention in the public interest could be justified. The Act defined "employer" to include any person or corporation which employed ten or more persons in the fields of mining, transportation (including railways and streamships) communications (including telephone and telegraph), and public utilities such as gas, electric, and water power.[16] The Act could also be applied to other parties involved in labour disputes if both sides agreed to be bound by it.[17] The new legislation went much farther than either the *Conciliation Act* or the *Railway Labour Disputes Act*, in that it recognized (albeit indirectly) the right of employees to bargain collectively, and provided a framework within which collective bargaining disputes might be resolved, or at least regulated to a degree. Nevertheless, the Act fell far short of providing a full legislative framework for collective bargaining, since its application was limited to the resolution of disputes arising out of the collective bargaining process. It did nothing to assist the unions in the establishment of collective bargaining rights, nor did it regulate the activities of employers, other than prohibit the use of lock-outs while conciliation took place. What the legislation did, however, was postpone strikes and lock-outs until after a formal attempt had been made to resolve the labour dispute. It also recognized the disruptive effect of labour disputes on the public at large and represented the first broad attempt to minimize the impact of such disputes on the public by postponing strike or lock-out action until the disputes had been investigated by a Board of Conciliation and Investigation. The Act did not prohibit work stoppages, but merely postponed them, provided that the parties followed the conciliation procedure set out in the Act. If they did, the strike or lock-out was still available to them but not until the investigation by the Conciliation Board was completed. If they did not follow the Act, they could do nothing, except of course, settle their dispute without resort to the strike or lock-out.

The *Industrial Disputes Investigation Act* was subject to a certain amount of change over the years, with the more notable changes including a prohibition designed to prevent employers from dismissing employees who had participated in an application for conciliation under the legislation, and a definition of the word "employee" to include employees who engaged in a lawful strike or who were subject to a lock-out by the employer.[18] These amendments represented the first attempts by the government to curb employer abuses of its power to control employees through control over their jobs.

In 1920, the legislation was amended again to expand the definition of "employer" to include a number of employers acting together with a common interest in a labour dispute. The determination of the multiple employer group was left with the Minister of Labour to determine,[19] but was a significant change in that it recognized the fact that labour disputes frequently went beyond the single plant or single employer. It was not, however, until some time later that the concept of the appropriate bargaining unit would emerge, but this change in the legislation represented a short step in that direction. Previously the Act, in an indirect way, did deal with the question since it was essential for the Board of Conciliation to be able to identify the employer and the particular group of employees involved in the labour dispute. This, in effect, was a determination of the group of employees represented by the union, but until the 1920 amendment, the definition was limited to a particular craft group, plant, or single employer. What the amendment did was permit the Minister to give an expanded definition of the group in recognition of the realities of collective bargaining.

The Industrial Disputes Investigation Act remained in force as the single most important collective bargaining legislation in Canada until 1925, at which time its application to purely provincial labour relations matters was brought into question. That year, a labour dispute at the Toronto Electric Commission resulted in an application by the union for conciliation under the Act, but before the process was completed, the Toronto Electric Commission instituted legal proceedings in the Supreme Court to have the application of the legislation to a purely provincial undertaking determined.[20] The case of the Toronto Electric Commissioners v. Snider eventually reached the British Privy Council, which was the highest Court of Appeal at the time, where it was held that labour relations except in those undertakings that fell within the exclusive jurisdiction of the federal government under the British North America Act was a matter of property and civil rights, and was, therefore, a purely provincial matter. The Industrial Disputes Investigation Act as a result, had no application to the Toronto Electric Commission labour dispute in question and provincial labour relations as a whole. Moreover, the decision of the House of Lords shifted most of the responsibility for labour relations matters to the jurisdiction of the provinces, and out of the control of the federal government.

The effect of the decision that The Industrial Disputes Investigation Act was ultra vires the powers of the federal government in respect of provincial employer-employee relations had a profound effect on labour relations in Canada. It brought to an abrupt end any thought of a national labour policy for Canada. It was necessary for the federal government to immediately amend the Act to limit its application to those labour disputes that fell within the federal jurisdiction, such as navigation and shipping, interprovincial railways, canals, telegraph companies, and works declared for the general advantage of Canada. The amendment also provided that the Act would be applicable to disputes that were declared to be in the nature of a national emergency.[21] A final and important provision from the point of view of a national labour policy was one which permitted any province to make the Act applicable to labour disputes that would ordinarily fall within the exclusive jurisdiction of the provinces.

Over the next seven years, all provinces except Prince Edward Island passed legislation to render *The Industrial Disputes Investigation Act* applicable to provincial labour disputes, and it appeared that the Act, now applicable in this fashion to all labour disputes (except those in Prince Edward Island's jurisdiction) would represent the cornerstone of a new uniform national labour policy for the country. However, the temptation by many provinces to assume control over labour relations within their jurisdiction doomed the uniform policy very soon after it was established. Quebec was the first to introduce new legislation to regulate labour relations matters, and while it continued to use *The Industrial Disputes Investigation Act*,[22] it extended the powers of the government to apply private agreements to other firms in specific industries by government decree. By 1937, nearly all of the provinces that had brought labour disputes under the federal Act had either replaced it with their own legislation, or so extended or modified their labour policy that any semblance of the legislation to the embryo national policy that had emerged in the short period which followed the case had virtually disappeared.

The change in attitude may be explained in part by the developments in labour legislation which took place in the United States during the same 1925–1937 period. Prior to 1925 and federally until 1937, the emphasis in Canada had been on a voluntary approach to the resolution of labour disputes. The federal government provided the legislative machinery to assist the parties, but the general policy was one of voluntary use, rather than compulsion, and even then, with a minimum of government interference with the parties. In contrast, the approach that began to emerge in the United States as early as 1926 was one of significant government regulation of labour disputes, and in support of collective bargaining. The first development in this direction in the U.S. was *The Railway Labor Act* of 1926.[23] While the Act was applicable only to the railways, it set down some of the principles of labour relations which were later incorporated in the present labour legislation of that country. The most important of these were the freedom of employees to choose their own representatives without interference by their employer, with the representative so chosen to be the exclusive representative of the employees; the compulsory recognition of the bargaining representative by the employer; and compulsory collective bargaining. These principles later appeared in the *National Industrial Recovery Act* of 1933[24] which extended collective bargaining rights to all major segments of industry engaged in interstate trade, and finally, into *The National Labor Relations Act* (the Wagner Act) of 1935.[25]

The National Labor Relations Act provided for a National Labor Relations Board to administer the legislation and the labour policies applicable to most large industries in the country. Until the passage of the Wagner Act, labour unions were faced with a number of serious obstacles which they were obliged to overcome before meaningful collective bargaining could take place. The first and foremost problem was the problem of organization. Employers during the early part of the 1930s tended to avoid hiring employees who were interested in collective bargaining, and also dismissed others already in their work force that attempted to organize a union in the work place. These actions on the part of employers tended to discourage unionization, particularly in the mass production industries, where the work force was largely unskilled. The matter of organization was of less importance to the craft groups who, historically, had little difficulty organizing because of the community of interest that bound together the craftsmen in each trade.

In addition to the problem of organization, the unions of the day faced enormous difficulties in gaining recognition as the bargaining representative of groups of employees. Employers were generally reluctant to recognize unions because to do so virtually obliged them to bargain collectively with the organization, rather than with their employees on an individual basis. Again, the craft unions seldom had difficulty in this regard, but in general, the union movement found employer refusal to recognize a union as one of the most difficult obstacles to overcome, and one that frequently required strike action to force an employer to do so. On this issue, most unions believed that only government action through some form of compulsion could cure this difficulty.

Attendant with the problem of recognition was the equally serious matter of employer refusal to bargain with the union. Even when a union could demonstrate that it represented a large percentage of the employer's work force, the fact did not guarantee the union the opportunity to negotiate with the employer on behalf of the employee group. Nor did the fact guarantee that the negotiations, if they did take place, would be meaningful. What the unions wanted in this regard was clearly some duty imposed on employers to require them to meet and bargain with them since they had been selected by the employees as their bargaining agent. Again, the union movement saw government action of a compulsory nature as the only route to follow to achieve this end. For unions in the United States, the Wagner Act provided the solution to most of these problems.

The U.S. Act established a complete framework for collective bargaining and expressed a general policy of the government which was to encourage the practice of collective bargaining. The National Labor Relations Board in the U.S. very quickly formulated policies whereby the appropriate bargaining unit of employees for collective bargaining might be determined and the appropriate representative selected. Employers were essentially excluded from the selection process and any discrimination by employers against employees because they were members of a union, or exercised rights under the Act, was penalized. Employer practices such as "black listing" and "yellow dog" contracts were prohibited. Once the bargaining representative of a unit of employees was certified by the National Labor Relations Board, it became the exclusive representative of the employee group. The employer was obliged to meet with the representative and to bargain in good faith with a view to making a collective agreement.

The Wagner Act established a climate in the United States that was favourable to the unionization of the mass production industries. As a result, the industrial unions in that country embarked on a highly successful organizing campaign which produced a dramatic increase in union membership. This had a spill-over effect on labour unions in Canada and many of the international unions that were members of the Trades and Labour Congress urged the Congress to press for Canadian legislation similar to the Wagner Act that existed in the United States. In 1936, the Trades and Labour Congress prepared a draft bill which it presented to the various provincial governments.

Few were prepared to accept the draft as it was presented. Nova Scotia was the first province to pass a new Act patterned along the lines of the union draft but it, too, differed from the proposed bill.[26] It did however, embody many of the proposals, among them the right of employees to form and join trade unions, to bargain collectively with their employer through the union of their choice, and compulsory recognition and bargaining. Refusal to bargain by an employer was subject to penalty under the Act. Alberta, in the same year, passed an *Industrial Conciliation and Arbitration Act*[27] which adopted many of the policies, such as the recognition of trade unions and the freedom of association, but neither the Alberta Act nor the Nova Scotia legislation provided the administrative machinery that was the key to the success of the United States labour law. Other provinces, such as British Columbia,[28] and New Brunswick[29] also modified their laws to provide for compulsory recognition and compulsory bargaining, but refrained from developing a complete framework that included the administrative machinery to supervise bargaining representative selection and the application of the Act in general.

The outbreak of the Second World War in 1939 had a profound effect on labour relations in Canada, and a shift of emphasis from the provincial to the federal level of government. Shortly after Canada entered the conflict, it became apparent that policies were required to deal with labour relations and labour disputes in an economy that had suddenly moved to a war footing. Orders-in-Council issued under the *War Measures Act*, made the *Industrial Disputes Investigation Act* applicable to all labour disputes in war-related industries,[30] but even this did not go far enough, as the Act did not contain the administrative machinery to deal with the recognition problems of unions, nor did it guarantee that essential war work would not be interrupted by strikes or lock-outs. The Act relied very much on persuasion rather than compulsion to resolve labour differences, even though wages were controlled during the war period. What was clearly needed was legislation that contained an element of compulsion to enable unions to negotiate with employers. All of this was found in the Wagner Act, and organized labour throughout the early years of the war urged the federal government to introduce legislation similar to the United States statute as a means of promoting industrial peace.

The federal government, nevertheless, was unwilling to go so far as to adopt the Wagner Act at that time, but in 1941, by Order-in-Council, it streamlined the investigative machinery of the *Industrial*

Disputes Investigation Act by giving the Minister the authority to appoint a commission to investigate any situation where a strike appeared imminent.[31] The commission had the same powers of investigation as a commissioner under the *Inquiries Act*, and could investigate labour disputes and allegations of discrimination. However, the nature of the penalty imposed in cases where coercion or discrimination was found was left with the Minister of Labour to determine. In spite of the expanded investigative powers granted to the commission, the changes did very little to relieve the major problems associated with the organization of employees and recognition of unions by employers. It remained with the provinces to take the first steps in the direction of the Wagner Act before the federal government finally acted.

British Columbia was the first to make changes in its labour legislation in an attempt to give unions in that province some assistance in overcoming employer resistance to collective bargaining. The British Columbia *Industrial Conciliation and Arbitration Amendment Act*,[32] which had been passed some seven years before, was amended to include a requirement that compelled an employer to recognize the union that had the support of a majority of his employees. Special consideration was given to bargaining groups where the employees consisted of both skilled and unskilled, and provision was also made for separate craft bargaining units. The Minister of Labour was charged with the responsibility of confirming the identity of the union chosen by the employees, and he would do so after satisfying himself that the selection (usually following a vote) by the employees had been properly carried out. The Minister could then notify the employer of the name of the union, and the employer was required to meet with the union and bargain in good faith with a view to making a collective agreement.[33] The Minister performed a number of the functions which were performed by the National Labor Relations Board in the United States, but on the whole, the changes fell far short of the Wagner Act in that the British Columbia legislation failed to provide a body to which the union could turn for prompt action. The changes, nevertheless, did represent a move in the direction of the compulsory policies characteristic of the United States approach, and a move away from the voluntary approach found in the Canadian federal legislation.

The Province of Ontario was the first province to embrace the principles of the Wagner Act with the passage of new collective bargaining legislation in 1943,[34] but it, too, took a somewhat different approach with respect to the administrative machinery to implement its policies. The legislation established the right of employees to bargain collectively through the bargaining representative of their choice, and prohibited employer interference with employees during the selection process. It also prohibited discrimination by employers against employees who belonged to or joined unions and provided the administrative machinery for the certification of unions as bargaining representatives. Employers were compelled to bargain in good faith with the union certified as the representative of a particular unit of employees. Unlike the Labor Relations Board approach used in the United States under the Wagner Act, Ontario placed the administration of the Act in the hands of a Labour Court which was established as a part of the Ontario Supreme Court.[35]

The *Collective Bargaining Act* was very broad in its application to employers in Ontario. With the exception of persons engaged in farming, employers of domestic servants, municipalities and the Hydro Electric Power Commission of Ontario, it covered all industries in the province except those which were undertakings that fell within the exclusive jurisdiction of the federal government. The definition of employee under the Act was equally as broad, including all persons except persons employed in a managerial capacity or whose jobs for the employer required them to deal with confidential matters relating to labour relations in the company. Special emphasis was placed on the right of employees to form and join unions without employer interference, and employer discrimination was forbidden in all its forms, including the "yellow dog" contract. The union, however, was not permitted to use strike tactics to gain bargaining rights for any group of employees, and could only acquire the right to be the bargaining representative of employees if the employer voluntarily recognized the union as the exclusive bargaining representative (a rare occurrence, except in the case of craft unions) or if the union was certified as the bargaining representative by the Labour Court.

Under the Act, any organization was permitted to apply to the Labour Court for certification as the bargaining agent of a group of employees, provided that it had collective bargaining as one of its objects, and provided further that it was not dominated or controlled by the employer. Certification was a relatively simple process, which required the bargaining agency to establish that it represented a majority of the employees of an employer in an appropriate unit of the employer's work force (such as a particular craft group). If the court was satisfied that the bargaining agency had majority support, it would certify the agency as the exclusive bargaining representative of the employee group; if not, the court would reject the application. Where two or more unions were each maintaining that they had majority support, or where a group of employees or the employer alleged that a union did not have the support of the majority, the court would usually order the Registrar of the Court to hold a vote of the employees to determine their true wishes. If the vote revealed majority support for a particular bargaining agency, the court would certify that organization as the bargaining representative of the employees. The court also had the power to revoke the certification of a union at any time, if the agency had acquired its bargaining rights through fraud, or at any time after one year if the employees (or in some cases, the employer) could satisfy the court that the particular union should no longer represent the employees.

The effect of certification by the court was to establish the union as the exclusive bargaining representative of the group of employees named in the court order. The employer was then required to meet with the certified bargaining representative and bargain in good faith with a view to making a collective agreement. The Act did not require the parties to reach an agreement, nor did it provide any assistance in the form of conciliation, which were the principal features of the federal *Industrial Disputes Investigation Act*. The Act did, however, give the court the authority to deal with any use of unfair tactics by the parties during negotiations. Apart from this, the parties were left to negotiate the agreement in any manner that they saw fit and were free to strike or lock-out at any time after negotiations broke down.

A unique feature of the legislation was the fact that it conferred upon the court the power to interpret any collective agreement made by the parties. This was in contrast to the arbitration method which was, at that time, the approach taken by the federal government and a number of the provinces. The legislation, unfortunately, did not remain in effect long enough to assess the effectiveness of this particular and different approach to labour dispute resolution. Within less than a year after it had been established, the government of Ontario felt obliged to bring labour relations within the province under the new, War Labour Relations Board which the federal government had established by Order-in-Council P.C. 1003 in early 1944.

In spite of the brief interval in which the *Collective Bargaining Act* applied to labour relations in Ontario, the legislation set the course for government collective bargaining policy in the future. As of 1943, the shift from a voluntary to a compulsory system had been made, and thereafter, the government set for itself an active role in the area of labour relations. The unique feature of a Labour Court, however, was not to appear in the provincial legislation which followed the end of the war, partly because union satisfaction with the War Labour Board during the period from 1944 to the end of hostilities determined the nature of the administrative tribunal that would later be adopted by the provinces. The Labour Court, nevertheless, performed an essential role in the furtherance of collective bargaining in Ontario. Unlike the experience in the United States where employers tended to challenge the authority of the National Labor Relations Board, employers in Ontario were prepared to accept the decisions of the Labour Court as final and authoritative, albeit in some cases, with little enthusiasm.[36]

P.C. 1003,[37] the Order-in-Council of the federal government under the *War Measures Act*, represented the acceptance of the principles of the United States Wagner Act at the federal level, and a departure from the policy of voluntary assistance found in the *Industrial Disputes Investigation Act*. The new Order-in-Council copied in many respects the United States policy and established a complete legislative framework to deal with labour disputes concerning the organization of employees, the recognition of trade unions as bargaining representatives, and compulsory collective bargaining. A National War Labour Board was established in Canada with provincial War Labour Boards appointed in each province where enabling legislation had been passed allowing the board to deal with non-war-related industry.

In many respects P.C. 1003 embodied the essential or major features of the Ontario Act, save and except the concept of a Labour Court, but with the added feature of compulsory arbitration of any disputes that might arise out of the interpretation of a collective agreement once it was in force. The Order also incorporated the compulsory conciliation provisions of the earlier *Industrial Disputes Investigation Act* in order to assist the parties in the negotiation of their collective agreements, and prohibited the strike or lock-out until the process had been completed and a fourteen day waiting period had elapsed. As in the Ontario *Collective Bargaining Act*, the federal Order established the right of employees to form and join labour unions and to engage in their lawful activities. It also protected employees from discriminatory or unfair practices which might be used by employers against them because they had joined a union.

The Order provided for the establishment of a War Labour Relations Board to determine the right of a union to represent a group of employees and to determine the appropriate unit of employees that a union might represent. As with the Ontario legislation and the U.S. Wagner Act, a union certified by the War Labour Board had the exclusive right to represent the employee bargaining unit and the employer was compelled to recognize and bargain with the certified bargaining agency.

The procedure that the Order-in-Council imposed upon the parties if they could not reach an agreement within a reasonable time was compulsory conciliation. After thirty days of negotiations, either party could apply for conciliation, and the Minister of Labour would appoint a conciliation officer to meet with the parties to assist them in their negotiations. The officer had fourteen days in which to meet and report back to the Minister with his findings and a recommendation with regard to the appointment of a Conciliation Board. If the officer believed that a board might be useful, the Minister would appoint a board which consisted of three persons: one who represented the views of labour, one who represented the views of the employer, and a neutral chairman. The selection of the first two was based upon the recommendations of the parties. The neutral chairman was usually chosen on the basis of the recommendation of the two representative parties selected for the board. If they could not agree, the Minister had the power to appoint a chairman of his own choosing.

The conciliation board was expected to continue the work of the conciliation officer and attempt to effect a settlement during a fourteen day period following their appointment. The board was expected to make a report of its findings and recommendations at the end of that time. The Minister was free to release the report to the public after he had forwarded copies to the parties. If an agreement was not reached by the end of the process, no strike or lock-out could take place until a further fourteen days had elapsed after the report of the Conciliation Board had been released to the parties.

The wartime order overcame most of the problems that had plagued organized labour throughout its long struggle to acquire a place in the industrial relations system. The procedures under the Order provided the necessary protection to employees who wished to join and participate in union activity, and protection as well from many of the unfair practices which some employers had previously used to avoid dealing with a bargaining agency. The certification system provided the successful union with a measure of security such that it could neither be ignored by the employer nor summarily displaced by another union. In addition, the compulsory grievance procedure and arbitration requirements for the resolution of disputes once a collective agreement was in place, reduced the need to resort to strikes or lock-outs. Under the wartime order, only in those cases where a collective agreement could not be reached would the parties be allowed to resort to strike or lock-out action, and then, only after the conciliation process. Since wages were not a matter for negotiation during the war years, but subject to strict regulation outside the bargaining process, the new wartime Order was accepted by the labour movement with a minimum of objection. Overall, the Order was accepted by employees as well, and when the war ended, P.C. 1003 became the model for the peacetime labour relations legislation which most provinces introduced.

In 1948, the federal government introduced *The Industrial Relations and Disputes Investigation Act*.[38] This legislation incorporated many of the features of the wartime Order. The new Act, of necessity, had to recognize the realities of the *Snider case* of 1925 and as a result applied only to those undertakings and industries that fell within the jurisdiction of the federal government. It also incorporated a number of significant departures from the provisions of the wartime Order which met with only the limited approval of organized labour. The most important of these were the powers granted to the Labour Relations Board to decertify a union if it no longer represented a majority of the employees in the bargaining unit, the power to declare that a collective agreement made between an employer and an employee-dominated union would not be a bar to an application for certification by any other union. The certification process, the requirement for compulsory conciliation and arbitration, as well as the postponement of strikes and lock-outs (with minor modification) were carried over into the new legislation.

A meeting of Labour Ministers of the provinces with the federal Minister of Labour was held in 1946 in an attempt by the latter to establish uniform collective bargaining legislation by all jurisdictions as far as possible, but the conference failed to achieve this end. Most provinces, nevertheless, did use the wartime Order as a basis for their peacetime legislation but by 1948, when the federal government introduced its *Industrial Relations and Disputes Investigation Act*, most of the provincial governments had formulated their own ideas as to what their legislation should contain. As a result, the postwar system of labour law was less than uniform, but many of the essential features, such as labour relations boards, the certification process, and compulsory negotiation were carried over.

Since 1948, provincial independence has produced even further divergence and, to some extent, even greater involvement by both levels of government in the process of collective bargaining and labour relations in general.

REVIEW QUESTIONS

1. *Explain why the early collective bargaining legislation failed to satisfy the trade unions.*
2. *Assess the effect of the Toronto Electric Commissioners v. Snider case on labour policy in Canada. How did the various legislative jurisdictions deal with this decision?*
3. *Assess the impact and influence on Canadian labour relations of the legislative developments in the United States during the period 1926–1940.*
4. *Outline the problems that a labour union encountered in Canada during the period prior to 1940 if it wished to become a bargaining representative.*
5. *Identify and explain the "tie" between conciliation and the strike/lock-out provisions of the collective bargaining legislation prior to 1940.*
6. *Describe the changes in federal government labour policy that occurred during the war years of 1939–1945.*
7. *Explain the contribution of the Ontario Labour Court to the labour relations scene during its brief period of existence.*
8. *What advantages (if any) did the Labour Relations Board have over the Labour Court in dealing with trade unions?*
9. *Define certification, bargaining unit, conciliation, exclusive bargaining representative.*
10. *Why did all Canadian jurisdictions adopt labour relations legislation that contained the essential features of P.C. 1003 when hostilities ceased?*

NOTES

[1]*The Trade Unions Act*, (1872), 35 Vict. c. 30 (Can.).

[2]*The Trades Arbitration Act*, (1873), 36 Vict. c. 26 (Ont.).
[3]*Councils of Conciliation Act*, (1867), 30 & 31 Vict. c. 105 (U.K.).
[4]*The Mines Arbitration Act*, (1888), 51 Vict. c. 3 (N.S.).
[5]*Labour Conciliation and Arbitration Act*, (1894), 57 Vict. c. 23 (B.C.).
[6]*The Trade Disputes' Act*, (1894), 57 Vict. c. 42 (Ont.).
[7]*The Trade Disputes' Act*, (1901), 1 Ed. VII c. 31 (Que.).
[8]*An Act to Amend The Trades Disputes Act*, (1909), 9 Ed. VII c. 32 (Que.).
[9]*Conciliation Act*, (1900), 63 & 64 Vict. c. 24 (Can.).
[10]*Railway Labour Disputes Act*, (1903), 3 Ed. VII c. 55 (Can.).
[11]*Ibid.*, s. 3.
[12]*Ibid.*, s. 4.
[13]*Ibid.*, s. 5.
[14]*Ibid.*, s. 11.
[15]*The Industrial Disputes Investigation Act*, (1907), 6 & 7 Ed. VII c. 20 (Can.).
[16]*Ibid.*, s. 2(c).
[17]*Ibid.*, s. 56, 62, 63.
[18]*An Act to Amend The Industrial Disputes Investigation Act*, 8 & 9 Geo. V, c. 27 s. 1 (1918).
[19]*An Act to Amend The Industrial Disputes Investigation Act, 1907*, 10 & 11 Geo. V, c. 29 s. 3 (1920).
[20]*Toronto Electric Commissioners v. Snider et al.*, [1925] A.C. 396.
[21]*An Act to Amend The Industrial Disputes Investigation Act, 1907*, 15 & 16 Geo. V, c. 14 s. 2A (1925).
[22]*The Industrial Disputes Investigation Act* (1932), 22 Geo. V, c. 46.
[23]*The Railway Labor Act*, 44 Stat. 577 (1926) U.S.
[24]*National Industrial Recovery Act*, 48 Stat. 195 (1933) U.S. s. 7(a).
[25]*The National Labor Relations Act*, 49 Stat. 449 (1935) U.S.
[26]*The Trade Union Act*, (1937), 1 Geo. VI c. 6 (N.S.).
[27]*The Industrial Conciliation and Arbitration Act* (1938), 3 Geo. VI c. 57 (Alberta).
[28]*Industrial Conciliation and Arbitration Act* (1936), 1 Geo. VI c. 31 (B.C.).
[29]*Labour and Industrial Relations Act*, 2 Geo. VI c. 68 (1938) (N.B.).
[30]*The War Measures Act*, R.S.C. 1927 c. 206, P.C. 3495 (Nov. 9, 1939) and P.C. 1708 (Mar. 10, 1941).
[31]P.C. 4020 (1941).
[32]*Industrial Conciliation and Arbitration Amendment Act* (1943), 7 Geo. VI c. 28 (B.C.).
[33]*Ibid.*, s. 4.
[34]*Collective Bargaining Act, 1943*, 7 Geo. VI c. 4.
[35]*An Act to Amend The Judicature Act* (1943), 7 Geo. VI c. 11.
[36]For a more detailed examination of the Court and the Legislation see Willes, J.A. *The Ontario Labour Court*. Kingston, Ontario: Queen's University Industrial Relations Centre, 1979.
[37]P.C. 1003 (Feb. 17, 1944).
[38]*The Industrial Relations And Disputes Investigation Act* (1948), 11 & 12 Geo. VI c. 54 (Can.).

RECOMMENDED REFERENCES AND SOURCE MATERIAL

Jamieson, S. *Industrial Relations in Canada*. Toronto, Canada: Macmillan of Canada (1973).

Logan, H.A. *Trade Unions in Canada*. Toronto, Canada: Macmillan and Co. (1948).

Willes, J.A. *The Ontario Labour Court*. Kingston, Canada: Queen's University Industrial Relations Centre (1979).

Wood, W.D. and P. Kumar. *The Current Industrial Relations Scene in Canada, 1983*. Kingston, Canada: Queen's University Industrial Relations Centre (1983).

PART II
THE ORGANIZATION PROCESS

CHAPTER FIVE

THE ORGANIZATION PROCESS

THE ORGANIZATION FRAMEWORK

The formation of a union by employees raises the question: why should employees wish to bargain collectively with their employer, rather than bargain on an individual basis? In the distant past, when employers virtually had a free hand in the determination of wage rates, working conditions, and hours of work, it is not difficult to see why employees sought protection through unionization. In the event of a dispute, the individual as a member of an organization would be in a stronger bargaining position with respect to the employer. Today, however, one might wonder if the same motive holds true, particularly in the light of the many federal and provincial laws which fix maximum hours of work, minimum rates for wages, provide for holidays and vacations, and require employers to maintain a safe and healthy work environment. Surprisingly, even more employees are interested in collective bargaining today than in the past, in spite of the many employment safeguards provided by both levels of government.

There are many reasons why employees join unions, but the reasons most often advanced by union members tend to be closely related to their general desire to improve their standard of living, either in a material or social status sense.[1] The improvement of the work environment and greater remuneration for their efforts are the most common motives, but workers frequently join unions for other reasons as well. The opportunity to alter their social status and sense of self-respect are two of the noneconomic reasons that are most often cited as being equally as important as wage increases and improvement of the work place.

For the employee with a desire to improve his or her social status, the union movement provides an alternative to advancement within the business organization itself. The advancement to or through management ranks is often closed to many employees, either by reason of the employee's limited education or management skills, or the limited availability of job openings at the management level. The trade union movement, on the other hand, provides the opportunity for members to participate in the conduct of the affairs of the union if they are successfully elected to one of the many executive offices of the union. Many of the union officers and persons elected as shop stewards or grievance committee members deal with senior management personnel of the employer's organization on a regular basis. Apart from the personal satisfaction that the activity provides to the union member, it also carries with it a special personal status, and usually the respect of fellow employees. In addition, active participation in the conduct of the affairs of the union frequently includes community responsibilities, which in turn, provides the member with the opportunity to enhance his or her status and respect within the community itself. Finally, the structure of the international or national union also provides the opportunity for advancement from the local level to the national level through election or appointment to a position in the central organization. While these opportunities are open to all union members, not all employees are likely to satisfy their desire for respect and status in this manner. Nevertheless, it does provide the opportunity for some, and an alternative to advancement within the employer's organization.

Closely associated with the desire to have the respect of society and one's fellow workers, is the desire on the part of many employees to have the respect of their employer in the work place. Since the employer, in effect, controls employment opportunity, many employees join unions to alter this power of the employer at the bargaining table. Employees frequently feel insecure in a work environment where they must rely on their own resources in their dealings with their employer, and often prefer the support of a strong organization to act on their behalf. Although employees with specialized skills very often see no need for collective bargaining, employees without readily marketable skills frequently find dealing with their employer through an organization of their fellow workers provides a greater sense of security in the negotiation of the terms and conditions of their employment or the resolution of individual grievances.

While employees usually join a union in order to improve their wages or working conditions, the failure of an employer to satisfy individual grievances will sometimes trigger the unionization of the work force. Unresolved grievances tend to breed discontent in a shop or office and unless some clear procedure is available to deal with such matters, or some management person will provide a satisfactory resolution of the problems, employees will frequently turn to a union to gain for them what they feel is just and fair. Enlightened employers with employees who do not belong to a union clearly see the importance of dealing promptly and fairly with both the individual and collective problems of their work force, and encourage employees to bring forward their grievances to a management person for resolution. The designated person in a non-union organization is frequently the Personnel Manager, who must, in effect, be the support person for the employee in any dealings with other management personnel. Such a person must also possess the necessary authority to resolve the complaint in a manner satisfactory to both parties in so far as it is possible. As an alternative to the Personnel Manager, the approach used in some non-union firms, is for the employer to establish a joint employee-management committee to deal with individual grievances and plant problems, and empower the committee to take the necessary action to settle any disputes or difficulties that might be brought to them.

Notwithstanding the most careful attempts by employers to maintain a safe and healthy work environment, and pay employees in a fair and equal manner, employees may nevertheless decide to form a union and bargain collectively. Should they desire to do so, they may either form an independent union of their own, or form a "local" of an existing national or international union. If the employees are craftsmen, particularly in the construction industry, they need only join a local of their particular craft, since craft unions are usually organized on a geographic, rather than individual plant or employer basis. The formation or joining of a union by a group of employees does not automatically mean that they are free to bargain collectively with their employer, however, as the employees must first organize a sufficient number of the work force in an appropriate bargaining unit to satisfy either the employer or a government appointed labour relations board that a majority of the employees in the unit wish to bargain collectively.

THE ORGANIZATION OF EMPLOYEES

The organization of a majority of the employees is perhaps the most difficult activity in the entire collective bargaining process because it is at this stage that the feelings of employees towards unions, both pro and con, surface. It is a time when long-standing friendships between employees are sometimes severed, new ones formed, and persons who had previously given little thought of themselves as leaders suddenly find themselves thrust into that role. It is also a time when the employer must assess his employment policies and consider his own strengths and weaknesses.

The first step in the organization process requires the formation of the organization itself. If it is the desire of the employees to form their own independent union, the founding members must first draw up a constitution for the organization, with collective bargaining as one of its objects. The constitution must also set out the duties and responsibilities of the members and the elected officers, as well as the procedures to be followed to elect the executive officers and to conduct the business of the organization. Once the constitution is adopted and the executive elected, the union or association may then embark on its drive to organize other employees.

Because many employees lack the skill to form a new organization, a frequent approach to the formation of a new union is for a group of employees to contact the field representative (or business agent) of a national or international union of their choice, and request the representative to assist them in establishing a new local of the union. Since the formation of new union locals is a part of an international union representative's job, most representatives are prepared to do this, and help carry out the organization process with the employees as well. Where the union is to be a local of a larger international or national union, the constitution of the new local must generally conform with the requirements for local constitutions as set down by the parent organization. In most cases, the constitution is prepared by the national or international union for adoption by the local membership. Again, once the local is established, the membership drive may then take place to recruit as many employees of the employer as possible.

In a small plant or office, where all of the employees are well known by the organizers of the union, new members are frequently recruited by direct contact, either immediately after work, or by a personal visit to the person's home in the evening or on a weekend. If the work force is large, the union officers or the field representative will frequently set up a meeting at a local hotel, union hall, or auditorium, and invite interested employees to attend. At such a meeting, the purpose and need for a union would be discussed and those in attendance would be urged to join the new organization. Organization meetings would also be held from time to time in an effort to interest as many employees as possible. Between meetings, the membership committee of the new union would continue to meet with employees on an individual basis in an effort to sign them as new members. This is essential in order that the union might acquire the right to be the bargaining agent of the employees.

If a very large percentage of the work force should join the union, and if the employer expresses a willingness to accept collective bargaining, the new union might approach the employer and request **voluntary recognition** of the new union as the **exclusive bargaining representative** of the employees in a particular **bargaining unit**. In most cases, however, this is not done. Instead, the union makes an application to the appropriate labour relations board for certification as the exclusive bargaining representative, if only for the security of having the board issue a certificate to the union.

ELIGIBILITY FOR COLLECTIVE BARGAINING

Collective bargaining at any particular plant, office, or other work place may fall under the jurisdiction of either the federal government or the province in which the employer's operation is located, depending upon the nature of the business or undertaking. During the organization process, the union must therefore determine the proper jurisdiction in order to prepare for certification under the appropriate labour legislation. The present division of powers in Canada gives exclusive jurisdiction to the federal government over labour relations in the following types of industries and activities:

1. *All federal Crown corporations, the formation of which being declared for the general advantage of Canada.*
2. *Industries in the private sector of an interprovincial or nationwide nature such as interprovincial railways and truck transport companies, canals, telegraph, and telephone companies.*
3. *Banks and banking.*
4. *Uranium mining.*
5. *Grain elevators.*
6. *Airports and air transportation.*
7. *Navigation and shipping.*
8. *Interprovincial and international ferry services.*
9. *Radio and television broadcasting stations.*

As a consequence of *The Toronto Electric Commissioners v. Snider*[2] case in 1925, labour relations matters were held to fall within the jurisdiction of the provincial governments, save and except for those activities or undertakings that fall under federal control. As a result, most business firms, other than those noted as falling under federal jurisdiction may be considered to be within the provincial sphere, and the provincial labour legislation applicable. Examples of the general areas where provincial labour laws apply would include employment in the wholesale and retail trade, the service industries (e.g., restaurants, dry cleaners, taxis, and local delivery firms), manufacturing, mining, and the construction field.

One of the advantages to employee groups that call upon a field representative of a national or international union for assistance in the formation of a local union is the fact that the field representatives are generally aware of the jurisdiction under which the particular employer's business would fall, or could determine the appropriate jurisdiction from the union's head office staff. The appropriate jurisdiction is important in the sense that the organization of employees and the application which the union later makes for certification must be in accordance with the procedures laid down in the jurisdiction's labour legislation. Once the proper jurisdiction is determined, the union must follow the rules for that jurisdiction in its organization activity and application for certification.

The first consideration in the organization of employees is for the union to identify the employees eligible for collective bargaining, because not all employees are entitled to bargain collectively. In most provinces the legislation has excluded some types of employees, since the governments in question have felt that collective bargaining rights were not required for those particular employees, or because the employees were subject to other legislation which provided them with collective bargaining rights or other employment protection. Consequently, labour relations statutes vary, containing from few exclusions to many. For example, under the *Canada Labour Code*, no "employees" are denied the right to bargain collectively except those who exercise managerial functions or who are employed in a confidential capacity with respect to labour relations.[3] Similarly, under the British Columbia *Labour Code*, [4] the definition of "employee" excludes persons employed in a managerial capacity and "confidential" employees. Teachers, as defined in the province's *Schools Act* are also excluded. Ontario, specifically excludes from its definition of "employee" persons who are members of the legal, medical, dental, architectural and land surveying professions, as well as persons who exercise managerial functions, and persons employed in a confidential capacity with respect to labour relations. The Ontario legislation also does not apply to persons employed as a domestic in a private home, persons employed in hunting, trapping, agriculture, silvaculture (except municipal employees), or persons employed in horticulture where the employer's primary business is horticulture or agriculture. Members of a police force, full-time firefighters, and teachers (as defined in the legislation which pertains to their particular vocation or profession) are also excluded from collective bargaining under the Ontario *Labour Relations Act*,[5] principally because they are given the right to bargain collectively under other laws that apply specifically to them. Public servants (as a group) are usually subject to special collective bargaining legislation in view of their unique employment relationship with the Crown. Most other provinces exclude certain persons from collective bargaining, with the group usually excluded being one which includes persons who exercise managerial functions and employees employed in a confidential capacity with respect to labour relations. Some professionals are excluded in a few provinces as well, but professional nurses and persons who are employed as professional engineers are usually given the right to bargain collectively, most often as a separate bargaining unit, unless they express a desire to bargain with another unit of employees.

While a great deal of variation exists in Canada with respect to the type of employees who may organize and bargain collectively, the trend has been in the direction of broadening the group of employees eligible for collective bargaining. In the past two decades, most provinces have been moving closer to the position of the *Canada Labour Code* in this respect. In many instances, the definition of "employee" has been broadened to include persons who would not normally be considered employees. Consequently, some independent contractors are permitted to bargain collectively with their "employers" if they can bring themselves within the definition of "dependent contractors" under the labour legislation. Those persons who can meet such a definition, are treated by the labour relations board in much the same fashion as a group of ordinary employees for collective bargaining purposes.

In spite of the exceptions, collective bargaining rights are open to most ordinary employees in all jurisdictions in Canada. As a rule, labour organizers are usually only concerned about the eligibility of persons exercising managerial functions or persons engaged in a confidential capacity with respect to labour relations when they lay out an organizing campaign. Since the former category may include persons in the lower levels of supervision in a plant or office, unions will usually not consider as potential members persons who are foremen or above the rank of foreman in a plant or persons who are departmental supervisors in an office. The decision is sometimes difficult because the authority to determine if a particular person exercises managerial functions falls within the jurisdiction of the labour relations board. Consequently, the eligibility of an employee will not be decided until after the union has made its application for certification as a bargaining agent. At that point, the union can only hope that it will still be in a position to show that it has sufficient support amongst the other employees to acquire bargaining rights if some employees are ruled ineligible.

EMPLOYEE RIGHTS

The right of employees to form and join labour unions came as the result of a long struggle by the labour movement. It now forms a part of the labour legislation in all Canadian jurisdictions. This right is generally couched in terms which provide that no person or organization, including a labour union, may interfere with a person's right to join the trade union of his or her choice and to participate in its lawful activities.[6] Coupled with this right, labour legislation has also outlawed the use of "yellow dog" contracts which employers had used in the past to prevent union membership. This type of contract was one that contained a clause whereby the employee, on penalty of dismissal, promised not to join a union. Any attempt by an employer to restrict the right of an employee by this method would constitute a violation of the labour laws and render the employer subject to a penalty in all jurisdictions.[7] Apart from this, such an agreement would not be enforceable. The use of the "black list," which employers once used as a means of identification of union members for the purpose of refusing them employment has been similarly prohibited under Canadian labour legislation.

While some minor variations in wording exist from province to province and federally, employers are generally prohibited from engaging in the above-noted activities, and from any activity that would have the effect of interfering with an employee's right to join a trade union or engage in its lawful operation. This prohibition would include any attempt by an employer to persuade or coerce an employee by way of threats or promises of any kind, and would also include the refusal to employ a person, or any attempt to induce or persuade a person to cease being a member of a union as well. Apart from the employer's right to express an opinion on the organization of the work force by the union, an employer is not permitted to use any inducement or threat to interfere with the employee's decision to join the union, nor is the employer permitted to interfere in any way with the formation of the union or its activities.

It is important to note, however, that the individual employee's rights under present labour legislation extend beyond the right to join a union. Concurrent with the right to join a union is the right not to join. In this regard union organizers are prohibited under the laws of all jurisdictions from using any force, threats, promises or coercion to gain members, or to retain members in the organization.[8]

A final right of employees that should be noted is the right not to be subject to any form of discrimination in their employment by virtue of their membership in a trade union.[9] On this basis, an employer may not assign work, schedule shifts, or allocate jobs in a manner that discriminates against employees on the basis of union membership. A similar prohibition exists against union discrimination in cases where an employee belongs to a rival or other union. As a general rule, where a union is organizing the employees of an employer for the purpose of acquiring bargaining rights for an employee group, the union must be prepared to accept as members all of the employees in the unit, and represent them fairly and without discrimination. While this is perhaps only a peripheral matter, labour relations boards insist that union membership be open to all employees, regardless of their interest or affiliation with any other labour organization. Where the right of membership is not open to all employees, the union must either amend its constitution to permit "dual membership" or be denied the right to represent the entire group.

UNION RIGHTS AND DUTIES

The right of a trade union to organize employees without interference from the employer is a right established in Canadian labour laws. The laws typically prohibit an employer or anyone acting on the employer's behalf from participating in or interfering with the formation, selection or administration of the union. Nor may the employer contribute financial or other support to the organization. The purpose of this part of the law is twofold. First, it is to protect the union from direct interference by employers through infiltration by pro-management employees. Second, the law attempts to discourage the formation of "company unions" that are not truly independent organizations, but unions that are formed by employers for the purpose of denying legitimate trade unions the right to represent the employees. The importance of this right will be examined in the next part of the text, which deals with eligibility for certification. At this time it is sufficient to note that the union has a right to organize without interference from the employer during the organization process. The reasoning behind this rule is that it is at this time that rival organizations might be formed by an employer, or the temptation for an employer to interfere directly with the union is greatest. While the legislation does nothing to protect a union from competition by other unions for the bargaining rights of any employee group, it does, nevertheless, protect a union from competition from an employer-dominated organization.

The organization of employees by a union usually takes place elsewhere than at the employer's place of business for the obvious reason that the hours which an employee spends on the employer's premises must be devoted to the employer's production demands. The employer's right to the employees' undivided attention to the business is recognized in the various provincial/federal collective bargaining laws by a provision which generally denies union organizers the right to organize employees during regular working hours on the employer's premises, subject to certain exceptions, without the express permission of the employer.[10] This is not normally a problem for union organizers as they are usually in a position to meet with employees after work hours or at a meeting called at a local union hall or hotel for the purpose of soliciting members. However, where the employer's place of business is located in a remote area, as in the case of logging operations or mining camps, a difficult organization problem arises. Often the entire area or community is owned by the employer, and ordinarily the employer has the right to determine who may enter the area. If employers were permitted to exclude union organizers from remote work sites, an employer would, in effect, be in a position to impede or prevent the unionization of employees working at such locations. To avoid this possibility, the right for union organizers to enter a remote work site is generally provided under labour legislation in most provinces where permission of the proper government authority is granted (for example, under Ontario and Quebec labour legislation).[11] Nevertheless, a distinction is made between the right to enter a remote community or camp, and the right to organize during an employee's regular working hours. While the former may be permitted, the latter is not a right of the union. Consequently, the organization of employees is, for the most part, an "after hours" activity.

From a practical point of view, the unionization of the work force of an employer no longer involves union organizers handing out leaflets or union literature at the entrance to a work place, as most of the large plants have long since been organized. The size of the plant or office unionized in recent years is typically small, often with under 100 employees. Due to the small size of the employee group, union organizers will often survey the work force to determine possible union support before attempting to organize the employees. If they find only a small percentage of the employees interested in a union, they will sometimes not proceed further with their organization campaign because of the high cost and relative risk associated with the effort. However, where the union is contacted by a group of interested employees, the union will usually proceed with the organization, using the interested employees to assist them in their job of signing up members in the particular plant or office. Again, the campaign will be carried out in the evenings and on week-ends.

The principal reason for contacting employees outside of working hours, especially in small shops or offices is to avoid direct contact with employees in areas where the employer might view the contact and become aware of the union's actions. Even though the right to organize is protected under labour legislation, employers are seldom enthusiastic about the organization of their work force, and in some cases vent their displeasure in various subtle and not so subtle ways on employees who actively support the union. For this reason, most employees are reluctant to be clearly identified with a union at the early stages of organization, and this reluctance is often cited by unions as one of the greatest deterrents to unionization in the smaller work places.

In a similar vein, when employees are approached by a union organizer, whether a fellow employee or not, they are not obliged to join, and are entitled to refrain from joining a union without fear of harassment or threat. The use of coercion by a union or person acting on behalf of a union constitutes an unfair labour practice under Canadian labour legislation, and is subject to penalty. While experienced union organizers are unlikely to use such tactics in the course of the organization of a work force, overly enthusiastic and inexperienced members have on occasion attempted to sign up fellow workers using threats or harassment. Such action, if reported to a labour relations board, can result in serious difficulties for the union, as a finding that the union had committed such an unfair labour practice may affect its right to represent the particular group of employees that it has organized.

For example, in a firm which a union attempted to organize, canvassers for the union informed a number of employees that the union had agreements with the major firms that purchased goods from their employer and that if they did not join the union, the union would see to it that the other firms would not accept their goods. Ultimately, their employer would be obliged to terminate their employment. When this information was brought to the attention of the labour relations board, the board rejected the union's application for certification.[12]

EMPLOYER RIGHTS AND RESPONSIBILITIES

Some employers in the past used a variety of methods and devices to inhibit attempts by employees to unionize their offices and plants. For this reason, public policy has been concerned with the prohibition of these restrictive methods in an effort to maximize the freedom of employees to join or form trade unions. These restrictions or limitations on the employer have been briefly noted earlier in this chapter to place them in their general context, but they require further development of their application and limits to establish the degree to which they impinge on the employer's rights. These rights, and the right of "free speech," require protection as well. Labour legislation attempts to strike a balance between the right of the employees to organize without interference, and certain equally important rights of the employer. Consequently, while employees are granted the freedom to join unions and to participate in their lawful activities, their freedom is not entirely unfettered, particularly where it conflicts with employer property rights.

Labour legislation specifically prohibits the employer from

refusing to employ or from continuing to employ any person, or from engaging in any form of discrimination against any person because of his or her membership in a trade union. The statutes also prohibit employers from using promises, inducements, threats, or other forms of coercion to prevent employees from joining or remaining members of unions. Nevertheless, the protection given to employees does not prevent employers from exercising their right of "free speech," subject to these parameters, or from exercising their rights as property owners with regard to the use of their premises.

The employer's right as a property owner is essentially the right to control access to the property and the right to control the nature of the activities that take place upon it. Apart from those provinces that permit union representatives to visit employees in remote locations, such as employer-owned logging camps and mining communities, employers as a general rule may, if they so desire, prohibit union representatives from entering on their property for the purpose of organizing their work force. They may further prohibit their own employees from engaging in any form of union activity during regular working hours as well. It is not uncommon for employers to have a general policy of prohibiting any form of solicitation during working hours. If any employee in the face of such a prohibition should engage in the organization of fellow workers instead of working as required, the employer is usually within his or her rights to take steps to end the activity or dismiss the employee. This right exists in the employer as a property right which has been protected by labour legislation notwithstanding that the employer's action interferes with the employees' right to organize. However, it does so by recognizing the fact that the employer has the exclusive right to the employees' time and efforts during working hours. Any union activity in which the employees may wish to engage must take place at times other than when the employees are expected to be working on the shop floor.

The question of whether employees who have joined a union may solicit other employees during lunch breaks and rest periods has not been conclusively decided. In one case[13] where union members had been organizing other employees and distributing union literature during lunch breaks contrary to the employer's orders, the court held that "working hours" included rest periods and lunch breaks. Labour relations boards, however, tend to take a more liberal interpretation of the "no solicitation" provisions of the legislation and have permitted employees to encourage others to join during those intervals when they were not actually working,[14] provided, of course, that the activity did not interfere with the work of other employees or the operation of the employer's business.[15]

In reaching this conclusion, most labour relations boards have attempted to balance the control which the employer is entitled to exercise over activities in the work place with the rights of the employees under the Act. Overall, the labour relations boards have not attempted to deprive the employer of any legal rights, but rather, have obliged the employer to show compelling reasons why employees' rights under the Act should not be exercised during lunch and rest breaks where the employer has a "no solicitation" rule in effect.

The actions of the employer are most carefully scrutinized where the employer has discharged an employee during a union organizing campaign. Employers are not obliged to alter their disciplinary system simply because some of their employees have joined a union, nor are employers obliged to change their practices to accommodate the organizational interests of the employees. However, any disciplinary action taken against employees, particularly if they are active or interested in the union, would be suspect. If an employee should complain to the labour relations board that he or she was dismissed or discriminated against for union activity, the employer must be prepared to satisfy the board that the action taken was not motivated by anti-union feelings, but for legitimate and justifiable disciplinary reasons. The reasons given for the discharge or other action taken by the employer cannot in any way be related to union activity. It must be for entirely unrelated reasons, otherwise the onus of proof will not be met, and the board will find against the employer.[16]

For example, in one case, the employer dismissed an employee for using profane language and making disparaging remarks when discussing the employer. The employee complained to the labour relations board that he had been dismissed because of his support of the union during the previous months when the union was actively organizing the firm's employees. At the hearing, the board concluded that the employee's actions merited dismissal, but discovered that a manager of the employer's firm had attempted to dissuade the employee from joining the union and had intimated that his career might be harmed because of his support of the union. The employer was unable to satisfy the board that the dismissal did not have an element of anti-union motive in it, and as a result, the board ordered the reinstatement of the employee.[17]

Apart from disciplinary action, an employer normally may not use inducements or alter working conditions to discourage union organization of a work force. For example, to withhold wage increases or to promise wage increases on a selective basis in an effort to discourage employees from joining a union may constitute discrimination.[18] However, to alter working conditions in a general manner before a union applies for certification does not necessarily indicate an attempt to discourage employees from joining the union, but where the change in working conditions affects only those employees who are known to be supporters of a union, the employer's actions would be suspect. Similarly, any reduction in the work force that consisted only of union supporters would also leave the employer open to complaints under the labour legislation that the action taken was discriminatory.

A final limitation on the actions of employers which is unique to Saskatchewan at the present time, is related to the use of "spies" by employers to attend and report on union meetings and to observe the actions of union members.[19] While prohibitions against "industrial espionage" have long been a part of Saskatchewan labour legislation, such activity has not been considered to be a serious problem by the remainder of the provinces. It should be noted, however, that in a somewhat similar vein, the province of Manitoba prohibits employers from making any inquiry as to the union membership of any employee during the period prior to certification of the union and thereafter, except for the purpose of complying with any collective agreement in effect.[20]

More recently, this type of activity surfaced in Ontario as a result of a 1983 case which involved persons paid by the employer to infiltrate a union for the purpose of inciting violence and property damage.[21] In response, the Ontario Legislature revised the wording of its statute to prohibit the use of such persons by employers.[22]

In spite of the many limitations imposed upon employers during the period of time when employees are actively engaged in the organization of their fellow employees, the employer's right of free speech remains protected, subject to the limitation that the employer may not use it to make threats, promises, or any inducement to prevent or interfere with the employees' right to form and join a union. The limitations imposed on the range of topics or the subject matter of any speech that an employer might make is clearly limited by this prohibition, but nevertheless, the statute does not preclude any appeal to employees for their loyalty, provided that it is noncoercive.

The concept of "employer free speech" has its roots in the United

States labour relations arena, and in some Canadian jurisdictions has been inserted in their labour relations laws.[23] This concept, however, presents an uncertain path for employers to follow. In one case where the employer expressed a preference for one union over another during a conversation with his employees, the Court of Appeal of Manitoba found that the expression of preference did not constitute illegal interference with the employees or the union. The case turned very much on the fact that the statements contained no coercion or intimidation of the employees, but the finding of the court might well have been otherwise if the facts had been even slightly different.[24] In a somewhat similar situation in Ontario, the labour relations board concluded that the employer had not committed an unfair labour practice when he circulated a letter to all employees requesting them to vote "no" to the unionization of his firm when the representation vote was held.[25] Again, this finding was largely because the employer's letter contained no evidence of intimidation or inducements which might constitute undue influence.

Where some kind of interference is present in the employer's words, the results are often quite different. In a case where the employer indicated that he was prepared to give the employees an opportunity to form an independent union if they voted against the union that had applied for certification, his actions were found to have exceeded his right of "free speech" and constituted an undue influence on his employees.[26] Similarly, in another case, a union had organized clothing workers in a plant that employed a relatively large number of ethnic employees. The employer held a series of meetings with small groups of employees, ostensibly to discuss work-related matters. However, once the formal meeting ended, the management personnel turned the discussion to unions and the possible loss of benefits and jobs if the union was successful. In addition, the employer prepared letters, posters and signs which graphically indicated what the employees might lose if they supported the union. Much of the material, while factual, was intended to illustrate the potential loss that the employees might suffer if the plant was unionized. The Ontario Labour Relations Board, following a review of the employer's actions, concluded that it had been deliberately designed to emphasize the fears that most of the employees held concerning job security, and decided that as a consequence, any vote taken would not reveal the true wishes of the employees.[27]

Once again, the labour legislation with respect to employer and employee rights attempts to strike a balance that will permit both parties to exercise their rights with a minimum of interference from the other. While it has been argued by the proponents of organized labour that the right to organize and join a union is of no concern to the employer, in reality this is not so. Employers are often vitally concerned, and it is imperative that they have the opportunity to express their views on their past performance as employers before their employees make a final decision on the direction that their relationship with the employer will take in the future. The rights of the employer, nevertheless, must be subject to certain limitations in order to protect employees from possible attempts to unduly influence their decision. The balance struck by the courts and the labour relations boards in this regard represents an attempt to give the employer sufficient leeway in the exercise of his or her right of free speech to provide information to enable the employees to make an informed choice between individual and collective bargaining.

REMEDIES FOR INTERFERENCE AND UNFAIR PRACTICES

The employment relationship is a relationship that continues beyond the point of unionization of the work force. Consequently, the nature of the remedies that may be used in labour relations matters must also be quite different from those that are normally applied for ordinary violations of the law. Incarceration of violators, or heavy fines, seldom serve a useful purpose if the effect is to destroy the relationship which the legislature seeks to preserve. For this reason, the remedies most commonly found in the labour sphere tend to be ones that will have the greatest success in curbing the offences while at the same time create a strong incentive to improve the employment climate, particularly if a union has been successful in its bid to represent the employees.

The two most common methods of dealing with interference are prosecution through the courts of the party allegedly at fault and the institution of violation proceedings before a labour relations board. Employers who attempt to dissuade employees from joining a union, or who refuse to employ a person upon the basis of their union membership may be in violation of s.382 of the *Criminal Code*.[28] If found guilty of the offence, they may be punishable on summary conviction. However, employees or unions seldom proceed under the

Criminal Code when an alleged violation has occurred, because the labour legislation in each jurisdiction contains a roughly similar offence to the one that is contained in the Code. Moreover, the range of remedies available under the labour legislation is generally more suited to the end result that the complainant wishes to achieve.

The labour law in most jurisdictions provides a Labour Relations Board with the authority to impose penalties in the form of **monetary compensation** for persons injured as a result of violations of the statute. Labour boards also have the power to order the **reinstatement** of employees dismissed in violation of the no-discrimination provisions, to issue **cease and desist orders** as to prevent further occurrences of violations, and the authority to certify a union as a bargaining representative where the employer has attempted to interfere with the union. Labour relations boards also have the authority to grant injured applicants the consent to prosecute violators of the Act and to revoke the certification of unions that act contrary to certain provisions of the statute.

In addition to the variety of remedial powers at their disposal, labour relations boards tend to provide a less formal forum in which complaints may be heard, and from the point of view of organized labour, a greater perceived appreciation of their problems since labour representatives serve on the board itself. The most important advantage, however, is the fact that the labour relations board will generally attempt to fashion a remedy that is not only fair, but one that will tend to discourage improper activity and foster the development of a proper employment climate. For example, in a case where the employer committed a number of unfair practices during a union organization campaign in an effort to discourage the unionization of its work force, the labour relations board not only certified the union because the board felt that the tactics of the employer prevented the employees from expressing their true wishes, but also required the employer to compensate the union for the extra expense incurred in organizing the employees in the face of the employer's actions.[29] While this result was unusual in the sense that the labour relations board imposed the extra costs of organization upon the employer, it serves to illustrate the flexibility of the remedies from which the board might formulate a fair and equitable remedy when unfair practices occur.

In all cases, however, labour relations boards tend to deal with infractions and violations of labour legislation not in terms of penalties but in terms of remedies. The distinction here being that in the board's view, a penalty serves only to punish the wrongdoer, while a carefully constructed remedy will not only serve the same purpose, but contribute to a better long-term relationship between the parties as well.

REVIEW QUESTIONS

1. *Explain briefly why employees join labour unions.*
2. *What steps do some employers take to satisfy employee problems which could perhaps lead to the formation of a union?*
3. *How is a local union formed?*
4. *What role does the international or national representative of a union frequently play in the formation of a new local?*
5. *Describe a typical membership drive to organize a small manufacturing firm.*
6. *Explain the importance of the proper jurisdiction when a union wishes to apply for certification.*
7. *Why are some employees not included in the groups of employees entitled to bargain collectively? Identify the types of persons most often excluded.*
8. *What are the rights of employees who wish to form a union?*
9. *Describe the organization rights granted to a trade union under collective bargaining legislation.*
10. *Explain the rights and duties of an employer who discovers that a union representative has signed up employees of the firm as members of a new local union.*

NOTES

[1]See E. W. Bakke, C. Kerr, and C. W. Anrod: *Unions, Management, and The Public* Readings and Text, 3rd Ed. N.Y. Harcourt, Brace and World Inc. (1967) p. 85–96 for a complete description of the reasons put forth by employees.

[2]*The Toronto Electric Commissioners v. Snider* [1925] A. C. 396.

[3]*Canada Labour Code* R.S.C. 1970 c. L-1 s. 107 (Can.).

[4]*Labour Code* R.S.B.C. 1979 c. 212 s. 1 (B.C.).

[5]*Labour Relations Act*, R.S.O. 1980 c. 228 s. 1, 2.

[6]See for example: Ontario, *Labour Relations Act*, R.S.O. 1980 c. 228 s. 3; Quebec, *Labour Code*, R.S.Q., 1977 c. C-47 s. 3.; Prince Edward Island, *Labour Act* R.S.P.E.I., 1974 c. L-1 s. 8(1).

[7]See for example, Saskatchewan, *Trade Union Act*, R.S.S. 1978 c. T-17 s.

11(1)(f); Nova Scotia, *Trade Union Act*, R.S.N.S. 1972 c. T-17 s. 51(3)(b).
[8]See for example, Ontario, *Labour Relations Act*, R.S.O. 1980 c. 228 s. 70.
[9]See for example, Ontario, *Labour Relations Act* R.S.O. 1980 c. 228 s. 66(a).
[10]See for example, Ontario, *Labour Relations Act*, R.S.O. 1980 c. 228 s. 71.
[11]See Quebec, *Labour Code* R.S.Q. 1977 c. C-27 s. 8; Ontario, *Labour Relations Act* R.S.O. 1980 c. 228 c. 11.
[12]*U.A.W. and Canadian Fabricated Products Ltd.* (1954) 54 CLLC 17,090.
[13]*Michelin Tires (Canada) Limited and United Rubber Cork, Linoleum and Plastic Workers of America, Local 1028* (1980) 80 CLLC 14,013.
[14]*Seafarer's International Union of Canada and Dome Petroleum Limited et al.* [1978] 1 Can. L.R.B.R. 393 at p. 412.
[15]*Audio Transformer Company Limited and United Electrical, Radio and Machine Workers of America* (1969) O.L.R.B. Mon. Rep. (Nov.) 994.
[16]*Delhi Metal Products Limited.* (1974) O.L.R.B. Mon. Rep. (July); 450; see also *Regina v. Bushnell Communications Ltd. et al.* (1974) 1 O.R. (2d) 442.
[17]*Barrie Typographical Union No. 873 and The Barrie Examiner* (1976) 1 Can L.R.B.R. 291
[18]See for example, Ontario, *Labour Relations Act* R.S.O. 1980 c. 228 s. 66.
[19]Saskatchewan, *The Trade Union Act* R.S.S. 1978 c. T-17 s. 11.
[20]Manitoba, *The Labour Relations Act* S.M. 1972 c. 75 s. 20.
[21]*United Steelworkers of America v. Securicor Investigation and Security Ltd.* 83 CLLC 16,035.
[22]*An Act to Amend the Labour Relations Act* S. O. 1983 c. 42 s. 71(a).
[23]See for example, Ontario, *Labour Relations Act*, R.S.O. 1980 c. 228 s. 64.
[24]*R. V. Malone and Winnipeg Free Press Co. Ltd.* 76 CLLC 14,046 (Manitoba C. A.).
[25]*United Textile Workers of America v. Playtex Ltd.* 73 CLLC 16,086.
[26]*U.A.W. and Wolverine Tube, Division of Calumet & Hecla of Canada Ltd.* 63 CLLC 16,296.
[27]*Amalgamated Clothing and Textile Workers Union Toronto Joint Board and Dylex Limited* 1977 O.L.R.B. Mon. Rep. p. 357 (June).
[28]*Criminal Code* R.S.C. 1970 c. C-34 s. 382.
[29]*United Steelworkers of America and Radio Shack* 1979 O.L.R.B. Rep. (March, July, Dec.)

RECOMMENDED REFERENCES AND SOURCE MATERIAL

Adell, B. "Employer 'Free Speech' in the United States and Canada." 4 *Alberta Law Review* II (1965).

Bakke, E.W., C. Kerr and C.W. Anrod. *Unions, Management and the Public* (3rd Ed.). New York, N.Y.: Harcourt, Brace and World, Inc. (1967).

Christie, I. "The Law of Unfair Labour Practices." *Canadian Industrial Relations: A Book of Readings*. Toronto, Canada: Butterworth and Co. (Canada) Ltd. (1975), p. 71.

Sherman, V.C. "Unionism and the Non-Union Company." *Personnel Journal.* (June 1969), p. 413.

CASE PROBLEM FOR DISCUSSION
CENTRETOWN NEWS CASE

The Centretown News Company carries on business as a newspaper publisher and general printing shop. The firm was founded in 1923 as a general printing business by James Miller, and later merged with the Centretown Press which was established as a weekly newspaper in 1925. The latter was only a marginally successful operation, due to the lack of interest in business management on the part of its founder, Arthur Wilson. The merger brought together the management skills of Miller and the newspaper expertise of Wilson, and the business flourished. Over time, the company moved through the hands of succeeding generations of the two families, with the Miller family maintaining responsibility for the general management of the firm, and the Wilson family the newspaper editorial and publishing aspects of the business.

At the present time, the company publishes a daily newspaper and employs a staff of twenty-four employees, exclusive of members of the two families, who occupy most of the senior management positions in the firm. The employees of the firm are not currently represented by a trade union, but a labour union recently began organizing the employees with a view to making an application for certification as the bargaining agent of the newsroom employees. The employees of the printing plant are not organized, but receive wages and benefits in line with those received by unionized printers in the area.

The union organizing campaign in the newsroom began under most unusual circumstances. A young male member of the Miller family, aged twenty-three, on the completion of his community college journalism and photography program was placed in the position of News photographer, a position in the business traditionally occupied by a member of the Wilson family. All went well for the first few months, but unfortunately, an incident took place that triggered his demotion and the organization of the firm by the union.

Miller Jr. had returned from an assignment on September 8, and in an effort to get a number of pictures into the newspaper that morning had left his camera and equipment in the unlocked company car which he had parked in front of the company offices. On his return to the car, he discovered that his camera and equipment had been stolen. He reported the theft to the managing editor, who informed him that contents stolen from a company car were only insured if they belonged to the firm, and since the camera and equipment belonged to Miller Jr. personally, he would have to suffer the loss for his own carelessness.

The attitude of the managing editor, who was a member of the Wilson family annoyed Miller Jr., and he immediately responded with an angry tirade of words which rather bluntly questioned the sanity and legitimacy of all members of the Wilson family in general, and the managing editor in particular. He then marched from the office and slammed the door. Later that day, Miller Jr. was relieved of his duties in the newsroom, and his employment left with his father, Miller Sr., who was the business manager, to determine. Miller Jr. was eventually assigned to an unskilled position in the printing plant area.

Shortly after his demotion, Miller Jr. contacted a representative of the Newspaper Workers' Union, and offered to help him organize the newsroom at the Centretown News. The union representative was wary of the offer initially, but after listening to Miller Jr.'s story, agreed to organize the employees, provided that Miller would give him a list of the employees names and their home addresses. Miller Jr. agreed. He also joined the union at his meeting with the representative.

During the week that followed, the union representative contacted most of the newsroom employees in an effort to convince them that they should be represented by a union. Many of the employees were interested and signed union cards, and the representative was optimistic that a majority of the newsroom employees would favour collective bargaining. When he had almost exhausted the list of names, he determined that over two-thirds of the employees had joined the union. At this point, however, his campaign ran into difficulty.

One of the last few names on the list was that of Denise Smith, a married daughter of the managing editor, and a name that Miller Jr. had forgotten to delete from the list of employees he had given to the union representative. Denise had said nothing about her relationship in the firm to the union representative when he contacted her and urged her to join the union, but immediately after the representative had left her home, she telephoned her father and informed him of the organizing campaign and that Miller Jr. had apparently instigated the unionization of the firm.

On September 19, the next day, at an emergency meeting of management, members of both the Miller and Wilson families agreed that

Miller Jr. (who was absent from the meeting), should be terminated for his actions in the newsroom on September 8. It was also agreed that the newsroom employees should be called together and the whole story behind the unionization told to them.

At 4:30 that afternoon, the managing editor called together the newsroom employees and at the commencement of the meeting explained that he wished to talk to them about the fact that a union was trying to organize the newspaper part of the business, and that any employee who did not wish to hear what he was about to say could leave. He also stated that he wished to make it very clear to all present that they had the right to organize if they wished to do so, and the company would not interfere in any way with the exercise of their rights. When no one left the room, he explained the incident that took place between Miller Jr. and himself, and how his daughter had been informed by the union representative that the union representative had been called in by Miller Jr. to organize the newsroom. He then explained that the company had tried to treat all employees fairly in the past, and had attempted to pay the best wages and benefits that it could afford, yet remain competitive with the larger metropolitan newspapers sold in the area. He concluded his remarks by saying that he did not personally think that the employees needed a union, but if they decided to have one, the company would respect their wishes. At that point he began to leave the room, but before doing so, told the employees that they were free to leave work for the day since quitting time was only twenty minutes away.

A number of events took place after the managing editor's talk with the employees. The next day, many of the employees approached Denise Smith and told her that they had reconsidered their intention to be represented by a union, and that it was their intention to vote against the union if it applied for certification. Denise said nothing in response to each of these voluntary statements, but thanked each of the employees for their support of her father. On the same day, the union filed its application for certification as the bargaining agent of the newsroom employees, and Miller Jr. filed a complaint with the labour relations board on the basis that he had been dismissed because he was a member of the union and exercising his rights under the *Labour Relations Act*.

Other events took place as a result of the unionization. The next day, September 20, while Miller Jr. entertained an attractive young lady friend at dinner, persons unknown apparently coated the black leather seats of his open sports car with black printer's ink. Miller Jr. and his female friend failed to notice the ink on the seats when they returned to the company parking lot to pick up the car after dinner, and with predictable results, the ink ruined Miller Jr.'s suit, his lady friend's dress, and their friendship.

Thereafter, the time passed quickly and without incident. The labour relations board ordered a representation vote with respect to the union's certification application to determine the wishes of the employees. Only five of the fourteen employees eligible to vote cast ballots. Three voted against the union, and two voted in favour. When the union was notified of the results, it complained to the labour relations board that such a low turn out indicated that the employer must have done something to discourage the employees from voting, and requested the board to certify the union without regard to the results of the vote.

CASE DISCUSSION QUESTIONS

1. Determine the limits of employer "free speech" and evaluate the use of free speech by the employer in this case.
2. Identify any unfair labour practices on the part of the employer and the union. Explain how a labour relations board might deal with them.
3. Assess the actions of Miller Jr. in this case. What factors would a labour relations board consider in dealing with his complaint?
4. Assess the union complaint that the employer interfered with the representation vote.

PART III

THE CERTIFICATION PROCESS

CHAPTER SIX

THE CERTIFICATION PROCESS

INTRODUCTION

The underlying goal of collective bargaining legislation in Canada is to promote stability in labour relations by minimizing the impact of labour disputes on the public as well as on the parties directly involved. Before the introduction of comprehensive labour relations laws and the development of a legal framework within which collective bargaining could take place, the relationship between employers and organized groups of employees was usually determined on the basis of power. This was especially true in the case of union recognition and the establishment of bargaining rights. Employers seldom welcomed the unionization of the work force, and rarely agreed to recognize a union as a bargaining agent unless the union was capable of calling a strike that would have a serious economic impact on the employer's operations. Recognition, consequently, became a test of the economic power of the union and the employer which manifested itself in the strike or lock-out.

Time was generally the deciding factor in the success or failure of the endeavour. If the strike successfully closed down the employer's plant, and the employees had the resources or the will to wait, the employer would eventually accept collective bargaining and recognize the union as the bargaining agent of the employees. If the employer continued to operate, or had the resources to remain closed for a lengthy period of time, the union would give up, and the employees would drift back to work or to other employment. In any event, the strike was the test of strength which determined the direction that employee bargaining would take.

The disruptive effect that recognition strikes had on employers, employees, and the communities in which they lived prompted legislative action to minimize the effects of these activities. The first steps taken in this direction were the efforts made in the early collective bargaining legislation to provide conciliation services to resolve disputes, but the laws proved to be ineffective, due to the fact that the legislation usually did not come into play until after the strike or lockout was in effect. In recognition of this problem, legislation in the United States under the *National Industrial Recovery Act*[1], and a few years later under the Wagner Act, introduced an orderly administrative process to replace the recognition strike as a means of determining union bargaining rights.

The *National Industrial Recovery Act* and the Wagner Act provided for the establishment of a National Labor Relations Board to determine the bargaining rights of unions, with power vested in the board to order the employer to meet and bargain collectively with the union that the board certified as the exclusive bargaining agent of a defined group of the employer's employees. This approach was adopted by the Province of Ontario in 1943 and embodied in its *Collective Bargaining Act*[2]. The Ontario legislation provided that a Labour Court would determine the rights of a labour union to act as a bargaining representative, and outlawed the recognition strike as a means of obtaining collective bargaining rights. A similar practice was established in 1944 by the federal government under its wartime labour regulations[3]. At the end of the Second World War, when labour relations were no longer subject to wartime restrictions, all of the provinces and the federal government introduced collective bargaining legislation which provided for the establishment of labour relations boards to determine the right of trade unions to represent employees, and to prohibit the use of the strike as a means of gaining recognition. This administrative procedure, whereby a union acquires the right to act as the bargaining representative, is a **certification** process, and a union that successfully obtains certification from a labour relations board is granted the exclusive right to represent the employee group defined in the certificate. Once certified, a union is entitled to insist that the employer meet with it and bargain in good faith with a view to making a collective agreement. If the employer refuses to bargain with the union, the labour relations board may order compliance, or impose a penalty on the employer for violation of the Act.

The certification process varies from province to province, but in all jurisdictions the process is voluntary in the sense that a union must apply to the labour relations board for the right to exclusive representation as a bargaining agent, and must meet the requirements laid down in the legislation and by the board before the certificate will be granted. A union need not necessarily be certified to become the bargaining representative of a group of employees, as an employer may still voluntarily recognize the union, as in the past. However, this is unlikely, except in the construction industry, and most unions prefer the security of certification to voluntary recognition, especially if the union does not enjoy strong support among the employees.

Very briefly, the certification process involves four findings by a labour relations board:

1. *The union is a bona fide trade union as defined in the legislation.*
2. *The union has the support of a majority of the employees in a defined bargaining unit.*
3. *The defined unit is a unit of employees deemed appropriate by the labour relations board for collective bargaining.*
4. *The employees in question are not already covered by a collective agreement or represented by a certified union.*

THE "APPROPRIATE UNION"

Not every organization of employees is entitled to certification as a bargaining representative, because labour relations boards will only certify an organization that meets the criteria set down in the statute for a *bona fide* trade union. This is so because the legislators realized that an organization that is employer-dominated, or that discriminates against certain employees should not be entitled to exclusive bargaining rights. Of equal importance is the fact that the organization itself must have, as one of its purposes, collective bargaining on behalf of its members. Consequently, to prevent employee social clubs, or similar employee associations from acting as bargaining representatives, the legislation in all provinces provides a definition of a trade union which sets out the general nature of the organization. The Ontario *Labour Relations Act*, for example, defines a trade union as "an organization formed for purposes that include the regulation of relations between employees and employers and includes a provincial, national, or international trade union and a certified council of trade unions."[4] *The Canada Labour Code* provides a slightly different definition by stating that a "trade union means any organization of employees, or any branch or local thereof, the purposes of which include the regulation of relations between employers and employees."[5] These definitions are typical of those found in collective bargaining statutes in that they require the organization to satisfy the labour relations board that one of the purposes of the organization is collective bargaining.

As a general rule, most unions or associations have no difficulty in meeting this legislative requirement because the organization is usually established for the specific purpose of regulating the relationship between the employer and the employees. Nevertheless, some care is necessary in drafting the constitution of the union to ensure that the organization is viable and capable of assuming the duties imposed upon it by the statutes. Labour relations boards are generally satisfied if the constitution provides for elected officers with authority to carry out the obligations of the organization and serve the interests of the members as required by the statute, provided that it meets the definition of a trade union. Inquiry into the internal affairs of the organization seldom goes beyond this point, on the basis that the employees' interests are safeguarded by the provisions of the acts which permit the employees to terminate the bargaining rights of the union if a majority of the employees wish to do so.[6]

Labour relations boards have, on occasion, taken a close look at organizations where some doubt exists as to their viability as a union. For example, in an Ontario case, in a certification application by a local of an international union, an employees' association objected to the application on the basis that it represented the employees in question. The labour relations board was then called upon to determine if the employees' association was a *bona fide* trade union. The association had a constitution that had been adopted some twelve years before, but which had not been adhered to for many years. The organization had no membership requirements, and all employees were free to nominate and vote for a candidate who would represent their respective department. The departmental representatives so elected would in turn choose the president of the organization from among their group. The group also selected a negotiating committee from their members, and this group would meet with the employer to discuss working conditions. Written collective agreements had been made with the employer for a number of years, and in each case, the agreement was ratified by a vote of the employees. The labour relations board, following a review of the activities of the organization decided that the failure of the organization to have membership requirements and a membership fee to establish a contractual commitment between the organization and its members did not create an organization, and the "association" consequently, was not a trade union within the meaning of the act.[7] The decision of the board in this case was based upon the common law principles governing the legal nature of a trade union covered in chapter 3 of the text, and illustrates the importance of a constitution and membership commitment to the organization if it wishes to be treated as a trade union. A New Brunswick Court of Appeal, in a different situation, reached a similar conclusion when it defined a trade union as a body with a constitution and properly elected officers.[8]

In all cases, the "legal existence" of the organization is an important requirement for certification. Consequently, when a union applies for certification it must prove that it was properly constituted before the date of its application for certification, and it must also prove that those employees who joined the organization did so after the constitution was adopted. In some cases, an exception to this rule arises where the organization is a local of an existing international union. Some labour relations boards (notably Ontario) have ruled that a person who joins a local has, in effect, joined the international union, and any question as to the adoption of the local constitution/membership timing is irrelevant since the international union was in existence at the time that the membership card was written. It is sometimes difficult to accept this reasoning in view of the fact that it is the local union that applies for certification, but where the organization of the employees is done by representatives of the international and the new local is chartered later, the employees who join, in effect join the international union at the time and their membership is in an existing union. Since the board permits unions to consist of employees of more than one employer, it sees no difficulty in the members of the international forming a part of the new local after it is established.

Apart from this minimum standard, the union must meet a number of other requirements stipulated in the labour legislation for the particular jurisdiction where it seeks to represent employees. In Ontario, a union must satisfy the labour relations board that as an organization it does not discriminate against any person or persons because of their race, creed, colour, nationality, ancestry, place of origin, sex or age,[9] for the labour relations board is not permitted to certify any organization that discriminates in this fashion. Newfoundland and New Brunswick have similar provisions in their statutes, but other provinces have taken a slightly different approach to the problem. For example, British Columbia denies certification to any union which violates its *Human Rights Code*.[10] While discrimination instances are relatively rare, they do occasionally occur. In an Ontario case, a union that restricted membership to Canadian citizens was denied certification by the labour relations board on the basis that such a restriction discriminated against some persons on the basis of their nationality.[11] The labour relations boards of other jurisdictions have made similar decisions where the union discriminated against native Indians and persons of particular nationalities.

Labour relations boards also require an applicant union to satisfy the board that it will open its membership to all of the employees that it wishes to represent.[12] This requirement is usually not a problem for most unions, but occasionally the constitution of a craft union will limit the eligibility for membership to those persons who are journeymen or apprentices of the particular skill or trade. Where such a restriction exists, the board will expect the union to prove that in practice it does not restrict its membership, and that it is prepared to represent all of the employees, regardless of membership eligibility. If the union fails to discharge this onus, its application for certification will be rejected.[13]

A final qualification which a trade union must meet is its independent status *vis-à-vis* the employer. Labour legislation in all jurisdictions denies certification rights to any organization that is either directly or indirectly dominated by the employer, and this includes organizations that are supported financially by the employer as well. The *Canada Labour Code*, for example, states that "where the board is satisfied that a trade union is so dominated or influenced by an employer that the fitness of the trade union to represent the employees of the employer for the purpose of collective bargaining is impaired ... the board shall not certify the trade union as the bargaining agent ...."[14] The Ontario *Labour Relations Act* is more specific in that it denies certification to any organization if the employer "has participated in its formation or administration or has contributed financial or other support to it."[15]

The purpose of this prohibition is obvious, as the legislation is directed at the "company-dominated" union which employers in the past organized in an attempt to exclude national and international unions. Truly independent, nonaffiliated unions and employee associations, however, are sometimes challenged by international or national unions on the basis that they are employer-dominated, simply because they do not wish to belong to a labour federation, or refuse to be associated with other unions. Sometimes employer domination is raised to justify raiding by the larger union, but in other cases, the independent union, because it usually enjoys a good working relationship with the employer, has inadvertently received some form of financial or other support which renders it suspect under the provisions of the labour legislation.

In most jurisdictions, either the labour relations statute or board policy permits the employer to provide a certified union with space on the company premises for meetings (such as use of the employees' cafeteria) or to compensate employees who are union officers for work time lost while engaging in certain types of union business (for example, attending grievance meetings or negotiation sessions), but apart from these minor concessions, any employer participation, financial, or other support would likely leave the union open to complaints of employer domination. These privileges, of course, would be limited to a point in time after the union has established a bargaining relationship with the employer, as such a concession granted to an independent association engaged in a competition with an international union for certification rights would render the independent organization suspect. Similarly, any assistance provided by the employer, such as granting the independent organization the right to recruit members during working hours while denying the same right to the other union would constitute support or domination, as would any agreement between the employer and the independent union whereby the employer provided the union with the services of the company lawyer, or compensated the association for legal expenses incurred in opposing the certification application. Finally, any direct management involvement in the union, for example by way of pro-management supervisory staff participation, would probably disqualify the organization as a *bona fide* trade union, and deny it certification.

MAJORITY SUPPORT AND MAJORITY RULE

The certification of a trade union introduces collective bargaining to the employment relationship and effectively ends the right of the individual employee to negotiate separate terms and conditions of employment with the employer. In a collective bargaining relationship, the terms and conditions of employment are negotiated by the bargaining representative, and the employees are bound by the agreement reached by the employer and the union, although in most cases the union membership is given the opportunity to ratify the agreement made by the union negotiating committee. The individual employee, then, is restricted to a role of casting votes in favour of or against the agreement along with other interested employees, and the decision of the majority of those casting a vote governs the acceptance or rejection of the agreement. Because the individual employee's role in the establishment of the terms and conditions of the employment relationship is reduced from that of a principal negotiator to that of a single voter in a ratification vote, the legislators who framed the collective bargaining legislation in each jurisdiction have attempted to balance the rights of the employees who wish to bargain as individuals with the desires of those employees who may wish to bargain collectively through a trade union. This balance was accomplished by permitting collective bargaining to take place only where a majority of the employees signify their desire to bargain in a collective manner. The rights of the employees then, are determined on the basis of "majority rule." The development of the concept, however, was not an easy task in view of the serious impact that majority rule has on the rights of the individual, and was only accepted after a lengthy trial period, during which time the question of minority rights vs. majority rule was vigorously debated.

In labour relations, the principle of majority rule is closely coupled with the concept of the bargaining unit, the latter being, by definition, a group of employees determined by a government appointed board to be appropriate for the purpose of collective bargaining through an exclusive bargaining representative. The bargaining unit concept is unique to labour relations in North America and represents the basis upon which collective bargaining rights are determined. Majority rule is essentially the method employed by labour relations boards to determine the wishes of the employees in the particular unit once it is defined.

The principle of "majority rule" in collective bargaining was first formulated in a case involving railway workers shortly after the passage of the *Transportation Act* in the United States in 1920. In that case, the International Association of Machinists and the Atchinson, Topeka, and Santa Fe Railway (and others) were involved in a collective bargaining dispute that was brought before the Railway Labor Board for determination. The Board decided that the agreement reached between the railway and the majority of the class or craft affected should be binding on the rest of the employees in that class or craft, subject to the right of the minority to present grievances to their employer either in person or through their chosen representatives.

The case injected the principle of majority rule into collective bargaining, but it was not until a decade later that the question of majority rule and minority rights became the concern of employee and employer alike.

The passing of the *National Industrial Recovery Act* in 1933 established the right of employees to bargain through a representative of their choice by requiring the employer to recognize and bargain with the representative chosen by them. What the legislation failed to do, however, was indicate whether each employee had the right to select his or her own representative, or whether the representative selected by the majority of the employees would represent the entire unit of employees in collective bargaining with their employer. When faced with this problem in a representation case a short time later, the National Labor Relations Board decided that the representative chosen by the majority of the employees in the bargaining unit should be the exclusive bargaining agent of all of the employees in the unit.

In the interval following the board's decision in this case and the passage of the *National Labor Relations Act* in 1935, the relative merits of minority rights and majority rule were debated, with most employers and those favouring protection of the rights of the minority on one side, and the American Federation of Labor, and those supporting the principle of majority rule on the other.

The major arguments advanced against the principle of majority rule concerned the rights of the individual. Majority rule prevented an employee from dealing directly with his employer on any matter concerning his employment, and if he wished to present a grievance to his employer, he could only do so through a bargaining agent he might not wish to have as his representative. This principle, it was argued, also represented a serious threat to the individual employee's right to work. An exclusive bargaining agent, by virtue of its right to represent all of the employees of the employer, could pressure the employer into accepting the closed shop, or union shop, which would, in effect, require every employee in the bargaining unit to become a member of the union, whether he wished to do so or not. Additionally, the closed shop agreement would have the effect of barring a new employee from employment unless he was a member of the union.

The arguments advanced in support of "majority rule" were based on the effect such a rule would have on the collective bargaining relationship. In addition to being the most democratic method of determining the representative of a group of employees, it was argued that it was the only way in which the superior bargaining power of the employer could be matched by the employees. To use any other system of employee representation, whereby the bargaining unit could be divided into smaller units, would be playing into the hands of employers who held to the theory of divide and conquer as a means of keeping the employees' bargaining power as weak as possible.

A further argument in support of majority rule suggested that there was no reason to believe that the bargaining agent elected by the majority of the employees would be less effective than the individual employee, or a small group of employees bargaining alone. The individual or small group is usually only in a position to accept or reject an employer's offer unless they exercise a special skill that could seriously disrupt the operations of the plant if the skill was withdrawn. A union representing the whole of the employer's work force would normally be at least as effective as the individual bargaining alone, and would, in all probability, be much more effective.

The trade unions themselves pointed out that any responsible union would be sensitive to the wishes of the minority, and if it failed to be, it could be voted out in the same manner as it was voted in. In addition to this argument, it was suggested that there were certain advantages that would presumably accrue to employers as a result of a single union representing all of the employees of the employer. A union that was the exclusive representative of the employees would be better able to control radical elements in the bargaining unit, and thereby reduce the possible risk of work stoppages that might otherwise be caused by small groups in key positions in an effort to enforce unreasonable demands on the employer. An exclusive bargaining agent would similarly be in a position to maintain wage demands at reasonable levels, by suppressing the unrealistic wage demands of special groups in the bargaining unit.

Whether these arguments were given further consideration by the National Labor Relations Board is doubtful, as the board embraced the principle of exclusive representation and majority rule in the cases that followed its first decision, even to the point of certifying a "company" union that had been elected by the majority of the employees in the bargaining unit. By 1935, when *The National Labor Relations Act* was passed, the principle of representation by an exclusive bargaining agent elected by a majority of the employees was firmly established, and embodied in the Act.

Canadian labour legislation related to the determination of the bargaining unit and the principle of majority rule in the selection of the exclusive bargaining agent of the employees in the unit did not appear until close to a decade after the first important North American collective bargaining legislation, the *National Industrial Recovery Act*, was passed in the United States. In 1943, the Province of Ontario passed the *Collective Bargaining Act*, embodying the concept of the bargaining unit, and in the cases brought before the court, the principle of "majority rule" was established.

A year later, when federal control of labour relations was instituted under the *War Measures Act*, P.C. 1003 adopted the concept of the bargaining unit and the principle of majority rule. The Order-in-Council remained in force long enough to set a pattern for collective bargaining throughout Canada when the provinces entered the field with their own legislation after the war. As a result, the provincial legislatures in the preparation of postwar collective bargaining legislation adopted the concept of a bargaining unit defined by a government-appointed board, and the principle of exclusive representation of the unit by the bargaining agent chosen by the majority of the employees in the unit. The passage of the various labour relations statutes made these concepts a characteristic of collective bargaining in Canada. It also raised a further, and perhaps more significant problem as well: the determination of an appropriate unit for collective bargaining.

THE BARGAINING UNIT

THE IMPORTANCE OF THE "APPROPRIATE" UNIT

The concept of the bargaining unit and the determination of the appropriate unit for collective bargaining have had an immense impact on the collective bargaining relationship, and on the course of labour relations in North America.

The concept of the bargaining unit in itself has radically altered the contract of employment, for it requires the replacement of freely bargained individual contracts with collective agreements negotiated by a bargaining representative chosen by a majority of the employees in the bargaining unit.

The application of the bargaining unit concept to the employer-employee relationship requires a definition of the bounds of a unit for collective bargaining, and the failure to define an appropriate unit can seriously affect the collective bargaining that follows. The definition of an appropriate bargaining unit then, is probably one of the most important determinations made in collective bargaining, and undoubtedly one which has far-reaching effects not only on the parties to collective bargaining, but on the public as well.

On the surface, the determination of the appropriate unit for collective bargaining appears deceptively simple: the appropriate bargaining unit is one that consists of a group of employees with common interests, excluding only those employees, or groups of employees, that are not entitled to be in the unit by virtue of the labour legislation. This, however, is not the case, as the determination of the "appropriateness" of the unit must take into consideration many factors that are not apparent on a cursory examination. The size and composition of the unit must be considered in the light of the effect that it will have on the individual employee, special groups of employees, the union, the employer, the nature of the bargaining, and the relative bargaining strength of the parties. It must also be considered in the light of the resulting effect the activities of these parties will have on the public. The determination of the appropriate bargaining unit then, is something more than the mere grouping of employees to increase their bargaining power, for it is a decision that extends far beyond a limitation on the freedom of the individual to bargain on his own behalf with his employer.

The concept of the bargaining unit represented by an exclusive bargaining representative chosen by the majority of the employees in the unit precludes the coexistence of other bargaining relationships. If an employee is included in the bargaining unit, his right to negotiate his own contract of employment with his employer disappears, and he must accept the contract negotiated on his behalf by the bargaining representative chosen by the majority of the employees. If he is not included in the bargaining unit, he is left to his own resources to negotiate the best bargain he can with his employer, which, all too frequently, consists of a decision to accept or reject the offer made to him by his employer.

Since the principal purpose of collective bargaining is to provide employees with additional bargaining strength to offset the superior bargaining power of the employer, the size of the unit, and its composition will have a considerable bearing on the effectiveness of the bargaining of the parties. Unless the employees possess an important skill, or are engaged in a strategic activity in the employer's plant, such that the withdrawal of their labour will exert tremendous pressure on their employer, in most cases the bargaining strength of a unit of employees will probably be proportional to the size of the unit *vis-à-vis* the employer's total work force. The determination of the unit, consequently, will determine to some extent the relative bargaining power of the parties to collective bargaining. Too small a unit may not provide the employees in the unit with sufficient bargaining power to offset the employer's bargaining strength, and may leave the employees little better off than if they bargained individually with their employer. Too large a bargaining unit may upset the relative bargaining strength of the parties to such an extent that an irresponsible union could seriously interfere with the employer's efficient operation of his business.

The impact of the bargaining unit concept, and the determination of the appropriate unit for collective bargaining falls on the employer as well, for its size and composition may determine the nature of the collective bargaining that follows the determination of the unit. If an appropriate unit is determined to be one consisting of the production employees at only one of many of an employer's several plants, a strike called by the employees in the unit may not affect the employer's operations to any extent, because production could be transferred to one of the other plants during the term of the strike, and there would be very little shift in the relative bargaining power of the two groups. An employer-wide unit, including all of the production employees at all of the employer's plants would be another matter, as a unit of this size would place considerable bargaining power in the hands of the employees, and a strike called by the employees could effectively close down the employer's entire operation. This type of unit is not without disadvantages, however, for union problems frequently increase in proportion to the size of the unit. A large bargaining unit not only increases the possibility of divergent interests, personality conflicts, and inter- and intra-plant problems dividing the employees, but increases the difficulty of managing and financing a strike.

Craft groups are vitally concerned in the determination of the appropriate unit for collective bargaining, because they form a group with interests that differ from those of most other production employees. These groups are often key employees, and possess, as a group, bargaining power disproportionate to their size if they are permitted to form a bargaining unit, for a strike called by a craft unit to support its demands may effectively close down the employer's entire operation, while the cost of settling would not appreciably increase the employer's labour cost, if the group is small. The ability of a craft group to attain these benefits will frequently depend upon whether they are permitted to form their own unit, or whether they are included in a larger unit of employees, as a majority of the employees in a larger unit may not be prepared to pay the price of a strike to obtain benefits that would be received only by a minority in the bargaining unit.

The determination of the size and composition of the bargaining unit also affects the union, for the inclusion of anti-union groups in the bargaining unit can present the union with many difficulties. At certification, if such a group of employees is included in the bargaining unit, it can mean the possible defeat of the union on a representation vote, yet if the group is not included, it would leave the door open for other unions to come in and organize these employees, with a resulting fragmentation of the work force, and a corresponding reduction in group strength in collective bargaining.

The size of the unit will also have a considerable effect on the security of the union. An employer-wide bargaining unit of an employer with plants scattered across the country, or a multi-employer unit, is probably one of the best safeguards a union may have against raiding by another union, due to the difficulty of organizing a majority of such a large group of employees to displace the incumbent union. Conversely, a small unit, located in a single plant would provide a union with very little protection from raiding, due to the relative ease by which another union might organize the employees of the unit for the purpose of displacement of the incumbent. The size and composition of the bargaining unit, therefore, in addition to determining the relative bargaining power of the employees, has a considerable effect on the protection available to the union representing them.

By no means the least important group affected by the determination of the appropriate unit for collective bargaining is the public. Collective bargaining has frequently been described as an activity that is limited to the parties involved in the bargaining, but this is not always the case. Collective bargaining, and in particular, industry-wide bargaining, can seriously affect the public in many ways. The determination of an industry-wide unit, whether on a regional or national basis, must be weighed in terms of not only employee benefit, but of the public interest, as this type of unit poses a potential problem to the public if the parties to the bargaining should act irresponsibly. Detriment to the public is not limited to cases of collusion between unions and employers, for the public can be seriously affected where an industry-wide unit exists in a monopoly service. The effects of a strike or lock-out in this type of industry can cause considerable inconvenience or harm to the public, and raises the question of whether labour monopolies should not be subjected to controls similar to those imposed on business monopolies.

THE POLICIES AND PRESSURES AFFECTING THE BARGAINING UNIT

The authority to determine the appropriate bargaining unit in all Canadian jurisdictions is vested in their respective labour relations boards, subject to a number of statutory limitations or guides. Legislation at both the federal and provincial levels usually limits the size of the bargaining unit in other than the construction industry to a plant unit, employer unit, or a subdivision thereof, which would include a craft or technical unit, but in some instances multiple employer units are permitted. Because the labour relations boards have been delegated the task of determining the appropriate unit for collective bargaining, the pronouncements of the boards, and their interpretation of the statutory determinants of the bargaining unit have had an important effect on the size and kind of bargaining units organized, and to some extent, on the character of the units that eventually develop in any given bargaining situation.

Legislative intent and labour board policy are not the only factors that determine the nature of the bargaining unit that ultimately exists, however, because the size and composition of the bargaining unit are subject to a number of pressures that emanate from the labour market itself. These pressures tend to determine the size of the bargaining unit initially requested by the parties, or the size of the unit that may develop gradually after the board has determined a bargaining unit that is not the most appropriate for the particular employer-employee relationship. The importance of these pressures on the bargaining unit and the effect they have on the determination of the appropriate unit have been recognized by the legislatures and partially embodied in the labour legislation. In addition, the labour relations boards have attempted to assess these pressures when faced with the task of determining the size and composition of an appropriate bargaining unit.

Neil W. Chamberlain, a noted authority on labour relations, observed that the bargaining unit is subject to certain pressures that tend to determine a unit that is appropriate for bargaining, at least in the eyes of the parties. He noted that there is pressure from the labour market area to expand the size of the bargaining unit until it takes in the entire area from which the employer draws his work force, and pressure from the product market area to expand the size of the unit to include all of the employees in the market area, so that the inefficient employer will not be in a position to compete on the basis of lower wages. The point at which these pressures generally cease to affect the unit is reached when the labour market area and the product market area coincide.

The major factors making up the pressure which tends to expand the size of the bargaining unit generally arise from changes in technology. These changes have been responsible, either directly or indirectly, for the expansion of the labour and the product market areas, and the growth of corporations and unions. For example, changes in technology frequently reduce the demand for skilled workers, and increase the demand for semiskilled workers, and this in turn tends to expand the unit size to include semiskilled workers in a unit that originally contained only skilled employees. Where the technological changes have required the development of new skills, these new skills are frequently included with the older craft group, and the unit enlarged to include those employees exercising the newer skills.

Unrelated technological change can also affect the size of the bargaining unit. For example, changes in transportation have permitted employers to draw their labour force from a much larger area, and this in turn has resulted in a larger labour market area, with the consequent pressure by labour to expand the bargaining unit to include the larger area. A similar enlargement of the product market area has been made possible by technological changes not only in the area of transportation, but in communications as well. And finally, changes in technology have been responsible for the growth of large corporations and the consequent growth of unions, for the growth or increased power of one party has increased the tendency on the part of the other, weaker, party to increase the size of the bargaining unit until the power of the other has been balanced.

A further factor that tends to enlarge the size of the bargaining unit is the desire on the part of the parties to deal with the policy-making body of either the employer or the union. Since local unions in many cases lack the authority to make binding agreements without the approval of the international, or are unable to alter the agreement demands without the authority of the international, there is a desire on the part of employers to deal with the body that has the authority to negotiate a binding agreement. The result of this desire has been a trend to negotiation between the employer and the international union where an employer has many plants that are widespread geographically, all represented by a single union. The use of standard contract clauses has also encouraged the formation of larger units, and the multi-plant unit in particular.

A desire on the part of the union to deal with the policy-making body of an employer has had a similar effect on the size of the unit. It has often resulted in a change from bargaining with powerless plant representatives of the employer to the central policy-making body of the employer that has the authority to negotiate and accept or reject the union demands.

Not all of the pressures on the bargaining unit tend to expand the size of the unit, for there are many powerful pressures exerted which tend to restrict, or reduce the size of the unit. Many of the factors or pressures that tend to limit the size of the bargaining unit are associated with craft groups. Because craft groups are particularly interested in the skills they exercise, they tend to zealously protect their work from groups of unskilled or semiskilled workers, and this in turn, tends to restrict the size of the unit to those employees who exercise a particular skill to the exclusion of all others.

The desire to restrict the bargaining unit to craft workers is also due to the awareness of the fact that a group of workers exercising a key skill in an employer's plant may be able to obtain greater benefits as a smaller group than as a part of a larger unit. An employer is usually less reluctant to grant a wage or benefit increase to a small group, particularly where the increase may only result in a negligible increase in his total labour cost. This advantage, coupled with the fact that the group may be capable of exercising economic pressure disproportionate to its size, often provides a craft group with benefits it would not normally be able to obtain in a larger unit. This advantage available to a craft group tends to restrict the size of the unit to craft workers, as their advantage would diminish as the size of the unit increases.

The desire to remain separate and apart from a larger unit is not limited only to craft workers, although craft groups do so because they are most interested in protecting their skills, and seem to have interests different from those of the rest of the work force of an employer. Many identifiable minority groups of employees resist merger with larger units because they feel that their particular needs and interests may be submerged by the interests of the majority, or perhaps ignored by a majority that does not appreciate their problems. Minority groups that exist as separate bargaining units are often reluctant to merge with a larger unit, particularly where they enjoy a favourable relationship with their employer, and the larger unit does not. This pressure to limit the size of the unit is sometimes found in the area of multi-employer bargaining. A single employer and an employee unit enjoying a satisfactory collective bargaining relationship may resist multi-employer bargaining, and the resulting larger bargaining unit, if the union-management relationship in the larger unit has been subject to considerable turmoil and tension.

Employers are often reluctant to join in multi-employer bargaining if there is a possibility that the resulting collective agreement will be such that the employer cannot achieve those bargaining policies that are in the best interests of his own particular company. This reluctance on the part of employers to join other employers in multi-employer bargaining tends to restrict the development of multi-employer bargaining units. Unions may also feel that this method of bargaining would not be in their best interests, and may avoid pressing for a multi-employer unit, preferring the smaller, single-employer unit if the larger unit might affect a good working relationship with the single employer.

The size of the unit itself may be a factor limiting further expansion, as negotiations tend to become impersonal and are generally handled by professionals when the unit becomes large. This type of bargaining often becomes less responsive to the needs of individuals and groups in the bargaining unit, and may prevent the employees, and in some cases, the individual employer, from taking an active role, or expressing a view on important conditions or matters of employment.

Wide geographic separation of plants may also limit the size of the bargaining unit. A lack of community of interest between employee groups, particularly where they are represented by local unions that have considerable autonomy, may tend to keep the units separate. There is usually little incentive to merge units where each plant serves a local product market area, and the local is already the exclusive representative of the employer's employees in that area.

The limited jurisdiction of the labour relations boards in Canada would appear to be a further factor limiting the size of the bargaining unit. Provincial labour relations boards may not determine a bargaining unit that exceeds the boundaries of the province, and consequently, cannot find an employer-wide unit appropriate if the employer has plants located outside the province. With the exception of the Canada Labour Relations Board that may find nationwide units appropriate for the employees of those employers within its jurisdiction, the labour relations boards are confined to provincewide units at best. Where bargaining units that exceed the limits of a province do form, they do so on a voluntary basis, as a result of agreement between the parties, rather than by board determination.

These pressures undoubtedly affect the size and composition of the bargaining unit proposed by the parties in an application for certification, and it is necessary for the board in each case to determine the appropriateness of the unit in the light of these pressures. The board, however, must first examine the kinds of employees employed by an employer in order to determine whether or not certain employees are entitled to bargain collectively and be included in an appropriate bargaining unit under the labour legislation.

FACTORS CONSIDERED BY LABOUR RELATIONS BOARDS IN THE DETERMINATION OF THE APPROPRIATE BARGAINING UNIT

Labour relations boards are frequently faced with the difficult task of determining appropriate bargaining units that will provide employees with effective bargaining power, yet protect minority groups that have interests which differ substantially from the interests of the majority of the employees.

Only a few of the provinces have provided even the slightest direction to their labour relations boards in the determination of the appropriate bargaining unit. In these provinces, the statutes are generally concerned with the appropriate unit for identifiable groups such as professional employees or craft groups, but fail to provide guidance with respect to other basic factors that enter into the decision.

The factors considered by labour relations boards may be roughly categorized into six basic groups for examination in terms of their use as determinants of the appropriate bargaining unit. Broadly speaking, these six groups would be:

1. *History of collective bargaining.*
2. *Traditional methods of organization.*

3. *Common working conditions.*
4. *Common supervision and integration of production processes.*
5. *Similarity of work or common skills.*
6. *The wishes of the parties.*

Community of interest is present in each of these groups, as the fundamental reason for employee organization is to permit groups with similar employment problems and interests to bargain collectively with their employer. The history of bargaining, and traditional methods of organization are factors that generally denote unit formations or methods of formation of employees with common interests that have proved to be successful in the past. Similarity of work or common skills, common working conditions, common supervision, and integration of the production processes are all factors that usually indicate a community of interest of the employees involved. Finally, the wishes of the parties, at least in so far as the employees are concerned, is probably one of the most reliable indicators of community of interest, for employees with common interests will generally propose a bargaining unit based on this factor. The employees themselves are probably the best judges of the size of the group that has a community of interest in matters concerning their employment.

HISTORY OF BARGAINING

The history of bargaining is frequently considered by labour relations boards in the determination of the appropriate bargaining unit. This history is considered to mean the type of bargaining that has taken place in an employer's plant prior to the case before the board. In this sense, it is distinct from the history of bargaining of the union, which is generally described as the traditional method of organization.

The consideration of the history of bargaining in terms of the success or failure of the previously defined bargaining unit represents a conservative approach to bargaining unit determination. Where emphasis is placed on the importance of past bargaining by the employees, the tendency is to preserve the existing bargaining unit, even though the presence of the issue before the board on a second occasion may be an indication that the previously determined unit was unsuccessful or inappropriate. Stability in labour relations is one of the fundamental aims of the legislation, and labour relations boards must consider whether the determination of a bargaining unit will promote industrial peace or be a disruptive force.

The history of bargaining favours the existing bargaining unit and maintenance of the status quo, as the fact that the incumbent union has achieved a bargaining relationship with the employer gives the appearance of stability in labour relations. The danger inherent in placing great weight on the history of bargaining in bargaining unit determination is that too much emphasis on this factor might result in a "peace at any price" policy, which may in turn, result in inefficiency or intra-union difficulties.

Labour relations boards are undoubtedly aware of the emphasis that should be placed on the history of bargaining as a factor in bargaining unit determination, and generally consider it in conjunction with such other factors as the nature of the industry, and the organizational practices in that industry.

TRADITIONAL METHODS OF ORGANIZATION IN THE INDUSTRY

Labour relations boards frequently consider the traditional methods of organization in an industry as an important factor in bargaining unit determination. In some industries, such as the construction industry, traditional patterns of bargaining were established prior to the introduction of collective bargaining machinery by the federal and provincial governments, and labour relations boards have attempted to recognize this in determining appropriate bargaining units.

In the construction industry, where the traditional method of organization is along craft lines, the boards have considered this to be a dominant factor in unit determination. This attitude of the labour relations boards, however, is based to some extent on legislative direction, for the laws of many of the provinces have embodied directions in their statutes whereby craft union rights to separate bargaining units must be respected.

For example, in the *Kent Tile and Marble Co. Ltd* case,[16] the Ontario Labour Relations Board determined the bargaining unit on the basis of the traditional methods of organization in an industry. The chairman of the board stated: "In the construction industry, where organization has traditionally been carried on on a craft basis, it is our opinion that great weight must be given to craft interests. It is not without significance in this connection that the Legislature must have had in mind the jurisdictional claims of certain trade unions when it set up machinery for dealing with jurisdictional disputes. Although the section is not confined to the construction industry, surely a Board such as this should take cognizance of the well known fact that it is in the construction industry where most disputes concerning jurisdiction arise."

The chairman of the board in this case clearly indicated that the board's respect for the traditional methods of organization in an industry in bargaining unit determination is to avoid possible conflict between unions over craft jurisdiction. The board, in effect, considers this factor as a means of ensuring industrial peace and stability, rather than as an indicator of the community of interest of the employees, although the traditional methods of organization are generally based on the latter.

Bargaining units based on the traditional methods of organization in an industry undoubtedly minimize the possibility of conflict, but it should be noted that this factor is generally carefully considered, as the slavish adherence to craft units could result in the formation of rigid bargaining patterns in industries where technological change in some situations has rendered the traditional unit unsuited to the needs of the employees.

COMMON WORKING CONDITIONS

Common working conditions are generally considered by labour relations boards to be indicative of common interests, and consequently a factor in the determination of the bargaining unit. Where employees are required to work together under similar conditions, such as in the same plant, with common supervision, the problems they may have with their employer are often similar as well. This is particularly true of employees working in a plant where production is based on an assembly line process, and where all work is geared to the production line, or where the employer operates a number of establishments in the same area.

For example, in an Ontario case[17] which concerned an application for certification of all of the employees employed at the retail outlets of an employer in a large metropolitan city, the Ontario Labour Relations Board found a multi-location bargaining unit appropriate where the employees at each location worked under the same conditions. The decision as to the nature of the bargaining unit was based upon the similarity of working conditions at each location: the stores were apparently very much alike, carried similar lines of goods, operated for the same hours, with the employees at each store performing substantially the same kind of work.

It is a basic purpose of collective bargaining to provide a means whereby employees may negotiate not only their wages, but the conditions under which they are required to work. The definition of the bargaining unit usually groups together employees that work under similar conditions, in order that they may bargain with their employer concerning these conditions. The weight given to common working conditions as a factor in the determination of the appropriate bargaining unit is something else again, however, as many groups of employees may be required to work under similar working conditions, but their needs and interests may vary a great deal. An examination of a modern production plant may reveal office, technical, and professional employees working under substantially the same conditions as unskilled, semiskilled, and skilled employees, yet the needs and interests of each of these groups may differ, and grouping on the basis of similar working conditions would fail to consider other special and important interests of each of these groups.

Considered alone, common working conditions as the determinant of the bargaining unit would be dangerous from the point of view of the interests of the parties, but as a basic consideration, to be used in conjunction with other factors, such as the wishes of the employees, or similarity of skills, this factor provides a labour relations board with an extremely useful tool for unit determination.

THE INTEGRATED NATURE OF THE EMPLOYER'S OPERATIONS

Like common working conditions, labour relations boards frequently consider the integrated nature of the employer's business and lines of supervision in the determination of the appropriate bargaining unit. Integrated processes, such as the assembly line, where all production employees are subject to the operation of the line and usually work under a common supervisor may indicate the limits of a group of employees that have common bargaining interests. The degree of integration of an employer's operation may also be considered in relation to multi-location bargaining units as well. Similar activities carried on at a number of the employer's establishments, together with frequent interchange of personnel, and central control of the entire operation, foster a community of interest on the part of the employees at all of the locations. Where this is the case, the labour relations boards often consider these factors as evidence of the suitability of the multi-location or system-wide bargaining unit.

In cases involving banks, communication, trucking companies, and similar establishments with branches or offices in many locations, the Canada Labour Relations Board frequently considers nationwide, regional or multi-location bargaining units appropriate because the employees at each establishment perform similar functions, move frequently from location to location, work under very similar working conditions, and are usually subject to a centralized control of establishments that in themselves would be too small to form units capable of effective bargaining.

Emphasis on the integrated nature of the employer's business to the exclusion of all other factors would probably mean that the only appropriate bargaining unit in many cases would be employer-wide units, and this would pose serious problems in so far as the spread of collective bargaining and the principle of self-determination are concerned. The organization of employees spread over a wide area would represent a formidable task for a union, and would consequently make the certification and representation of employees much more difficult. It would also have the effect of denying employees at any one establishment of the employer the right to choose their own bargaining representative. To offset the possibility of undue emphasis being placed on the integrated nature of the employer's business in the determination of the bargaining unit, labour relations boards frequently consider other factors such as the traditional methods of organization in the industry, or the wishes of the parties. These factors generally counterbalance the tendency to find only the larger unit appropriate.

SIMILARITY OF SKILLS

The similarity of skills is an important factor considered by labour relation boards in bargaining unit determination. The exercise of a common skill in itself is not an appropriate determinant of the bargaining unit, but the exercise of a particular skill generally denotes craftsmen that have served an apprenticeship to learn the skill, and this usually identifies employees that have separate and distinct interests. For this reason, similarity of skill warrants consideration as a factor that shapes the bargaining unit.

The attitude of the craft employees toward their work sets them apart from unskilled and semiskilled employees, for the skilled craftsman, unlike the unskilled or semiskilled employee, usually has a less personal relationship with his employer. His interests are usually centred around his trade or skill, and because encroachment on this skill by unskilled or semiskilled workers would mean a loss of status, the protection of this skill is of primary importance. It is this special interest in his craft and its protection that sets the craftsman apart from his fellow workers.

The consideration of the special interests of identifiable employee groups in the determination of the bargaining unit assumes that the similarity of skills distinguishes a group of employees that do in fact possess different interests. The difference in interests, however, may not be sufficient to warrant a separate bargaining unit. For example, in an Ontario case, the Ontario Labour Relations Board came to the conclusion in considering an application by stationary engineers to sever from an industrial unit that the special interests of the craft group had been properly represented by the incumbent union for many years, and the mere fact that the craft group exercised a particular skill was not a sufficient reason to warrant their severance from the larger bargaining unit.

Because the interests of separate craft groups may not differ appreciably from the interests of a larger group of employees, similarity of skill considered alone would be inappropriate as the determinant bargaining unit. Consequently, similarity of skills as a factor is usually considered in conjunction with an examination of the interests of the employee unit or other factors by labour relations boards.

THE WISHES OF THE PARTIES

Labour relations boards in Canada are especially cognizant of the wishes of the employer, the union, and the employees in the determination of the bargaining unit. Most labour relations boards are usually prepared to accept a bargaining unit determined or agreed upon by the parties as appropriate, provided that it does not conflict with any policy of the board with respect to appropriateness, and provided it is made up of employees as defined in their labour relations legislation. The boards, however, are not prepared to allow the parties complete discretion in determining the unit they feel is best suited to their needs, for to do so would be a failure on the part of the boards to carry out their duty under the statute, which is to determine the appropriate unit for collective bargaining.

The problem facing a labour relations board is compounded by the fact that the parties may, by agreement, alter the bargaining unit after certification, and after initial determination by the board. The wishes of the parties, as a result, are usually given considerable weight in the determination of the appropriateness of the unit in the first instance, although units proposed by the parties that run contrary to board policy are vigorously opposed.

Provision has been made in labour legislation to permit a labour relations board, if it so desires, to make such enquiries as it deems necessary to determine the size and composition of a bargaining unit that would be appropriate for collective bargaining. In Ontario, the *Labour Relations Act* specifically permits the labour relations board to hold a vote, which in effect provides the employees with an opportunity to engage in a certain amount of self-determination of the bargaining unit. The board is not bound by the results of such a vote, but the voting constituencies are determined by the board, and in view of this fact, there would seem to be no good reason why the board should not accept the results of the balloting as an appropriate determination of the bargaining unit.

This method of self-determination would appear to be an adoption of a method originally employed by the National Labor Relations Board in the United States. During the first few years following the passage of the Wagner Act, the board in the United States attempted to solve the problem of determination of the appropriate bargaining unit by allowing the employees to express their wishes as to the type of bargaining unit they desired by means of a vote. This method, which became known as the "Globe Rule," was developed in the *Globe Machine and Stamping Co.* case.[18] In this case, the board was faced with the question of deciding whether a craft group or an industrial unit would be appropriate when the reasons for the establishment of a separate craft unit as opposed to its inclusion in an industrial unit were equally compelling. To solve the problem, the Board decided to hold separate elections to allow self-determination on the part of the craft group.

Although this method of determining the bargaining unit was usually applied in cases involving craft exclusion or severance from larger industrial units, it was also used by the National Labor Relations Board in cases where different groups of employees were involved in the certification proceedings. The validity of the Globe Rule as a method of determining the bargaining unit came before the courts in a later case involving department store employees where the board had ordered a vote involving seven voting constituencies to determine the appropriate bargaining unit or units. When the matter was reviewed by the court, the court held that the board was obliged to establish a bargaining unit prior to the vote, and that its failure to do so was an improper delegation of its authority to the employees by allowing them to select the appropriate unit. The board abandoned the Globe Rule method of determination of the bargaining unit for a number of years following this decision, but later returned to it, using it only as a means of determining the *wishes* of the employees, rather than the bargaining unit.

Some Canadian jurisdictions adopted the Globe Rule, and used it in cases where the wishes of the employees with respect to their inclusion or exclusion from the bargaining unit was important. The Ontario Labour Court used the Globe election in 1944, when it was required to decide whether office employees should be included in a bargaining unit of production and maintenance employees, and the Saskatchewan Labour Relations Board employed this method to determine the wishes of professional employees with respect to their inclusion or exclusion from a bargaining unit consisting of other employees.

The Ontario Labour Relations Board has the authority to use a vote to determine the wishes of the employees with respect to the appropriateness of the bargaining unit, but this should not be taken to mean that other boards attach less weight to the wishes of the parties as to the appropriateness of the unit, for all jurisdictions will allow interested parties to make representations to the board as to the make-up of the unit.

The Ontario Labour Relations Board has frequently indicated that it considers the wishes of the parties with respect to the make-up of the bargaining unit to be a very important factor in its determination of the bargaining unit. In one of the earliest cases[19] requiring the board to consider the appropriateness of a bargaining unit, the board was not prepared to find a proposed bargaining unit appropriate unless an identifiable group of employees clearly expressed the desire to bargain as a part of a larger unit. This same concern for the wishes of the parties is also found in a number of other cases,[20] all of which seem to be based on the principle that a bargaining unit acceptable to the employees, the union, and the employer will promote industrial peace and stability in labour relations.

The policy of the Ontario Labour Relations Board with respect to part-time employees is probably another example of the regard shown for the wishes of the parties. Where an employer employs persons working less than twenty-four hours per week, the board will generally include these employees in the bargaining unit unless an objection is raised by one of the parties to their inclusion. If either of the parties objects to part-time employees being included in the unit, the board will generally exclude them.

One of the basic difficulties with giving considerable weight to the wishes of the employees, or the applicant union, is that the unit desired may not necessarily be most appropriate for collective bargaining. It is necessary for the labour relations boards to distinguish between the genuine desire of employees for a particular bargaining unit that they feel would be most suited to collective bargaining with their employer, and the desire of some employees or a union for collective bargaining that could only be satisfied by creating a gerrymandered unit in which they would have a majority. A rather striking example of this situation may be found in a Saskatchewan case[21] where the union requested a bargaining unit that consisted of only those departments of the company where it felt it had majority support, while the employer argued that a single unit, including all of the employees would be the appropriate bargaining unit. From the reported decision there would appear to be no good reason for the unit requested by the union, as it included a variety of departments that could not conceivably be considered as forming a distinguishable unit. The only apparent reason seemed to be that the unit requested would give the union the necessary majority to be certified as the bargaining agent.

Labour relations boards, fortunately, try to distinguish between cases where an identifiable group of employees wish to bargain separately, and cases where the bargaining unit has been selected by the union on the basis of the extent of its organization of the employees. While they are prepared at times to define bargaining units that consist of identifiable groups of employees in an employer's organization, they usually do not consider bargaining units based on the extent of organization of the union as appropriate. Where the bargaining unit has been determined on the basis of the extent of organization of the employees by the union, the interests of the employer and the rest of the employees are usually carefully considered.

In addition to these basic factors, labour relations boards consider many other factors in relation to appropriate bargaining units for specific kinds of employees, and particular industries. The boards have consistently refused to set down rigid rules with respect to the appropriateness of these bargaining units, but it is possible to determine, with some degree of certainty, the policies of the boards with respect to these specific and identifiable groups of employees, by examining the board decisions relating to their bargaining units.

Labour relations boards will give serious consideration to the wishes of the parties as to the make-up of a bargaining unit, but over time, most boards have established certain policies which have led to the determination of particular units for collective bargaining. Certain identifiable employee groups are normally considered by labour relations boards to have a sufficient community of interest to warrant placement in a separate bargaining unit. The most common of these are as follows:

OFFICE EMPLOYEES

Most labour relations boards consider office employees as a separate and distinct group, and rarely mix them with production groups. The reason for this separation is largely historical, for in the past, office employees worked different hours, under different working conditions, and were salaried rather than hourly paid employees. In addition, they were usually separated from the plant employees, were subject to different supervision, and enjoyed privileges (such as better opportunities for advancement, etc.) not open to the hourly rated employees. Many of these reasons for separation have disappeared as a result of changes in the work place, but labour relations boards continue to hold that separate units for office employees are appropriate, and indeed, office employees generally desire a separate bargaining unit, rather than a mixed office-plant unit. This is borne out by the fact that even though separate office and plant bargaining units may merge into a single unit after certification (if represented by the same union), merger rarely takes place.

PROFESSIONAL EMPLOYEES

Collective bargaining by professional employees is a relatively recent change on the labour relations scene. However, with the organization of public sector employees and collective bargaining by teachers, nurses and other professional employees, professional employees in large industrial firms have concluded that their interests may be better served by bargaining collectively with their employer. Most jurisdictions permit all professional employees to bargain collectively, but some provinces, such as Ontario and Prince Edward Island exclude some professionals such as physicians, dentists, land surveyors, lawyers, and architects from their labour relations legislation. Where professionals are permitted to bargain collectively, labour relations boards will usually establish a separate unit of professional employees, or include them with office employees only if a majority of the professionals signify that they wish to bargain collectively as a part of the office group.

TECHNICAL EMPLOYEES

Technical employees are generally persons with special skills such as chemists, time and motion study specialists, materials analysts, and other technicians who usually work in a support capacity in a firm. Their work is often associated with new product development, quality control, or work efficiency improvement in either a laboratory or shop environment. Technical employees are frequently included with office employees as a part of an "office and technical" unit, and seldom included in a plant unit because their work is often concerned with production methods and other activities that might affect the wages or efficiency of production employees. Occasionally, where large numbers of professional and technical employees work together, the two groups may be included in a single unit if the professional employees wish to bargain with the technical group.

SECURITY GUARDS

Security guards usually bargain separately from other employees of an employer, and in Ontario must not only form a separate bargaining unit, but be represented by a union that represents only security guards. The reasoning behind this separation is that security guards have a duty to their employer which includes the control of the employer's premises and the protection of plant property. This duty includes a surveillance of other employees, and to avoid any possible conflict of interest, the security guards are usually placed in a separate bargaining unit where they are represented by a separate union. "Watchmen" on the other hand, are treated differently by labour relations boards, and are usually included in a bargaining unit with other employees since their duty is only to "watch" rather than exercise disciplinary authority over other employees.[22]

CRAFT EMPLOYEES

Craft employees in the construction industry generally constitute appropriate bargaining units since the units are generally described on a geographic basis. In the manufacturing sector however, craft employees are usually included with other production and maintenance employees in a plant bargaining unit. However, where a craft union can establish that the particular craft which it usually represents has a history of a separate bargaining, labour relations boards will normally establish a craft unit as a separate unit. This is an attempt to balance the rights of employees with special interests with the public policy goals of industrial stability which tend to favour all inclusive employee units in industrial plants. To avoid the fragmentation of larger plant units, labour relations boards seldom allow craft unions to carve out their particular crafts from established all-employee plant units if the craft groups are adequately represented by the incumbent industrial union.

PART-TIME EMPLOYEES

Many business firms, particularly those engaged in service activities employ persons on a part-time basis to augment their full-time employee work force. These employees are not excluded from collective bargaining and will usually be included in the same bargaining unit as the full-time employees unless the employer or the union have good reasons to exclude them. Where part-time employees are not included in a bargaining unit with full-time employees, they are often organized and may form a separate unit of their own for collective bargaining purposes.

PLANT CLERICAL EMPLOYEES

Plant clerical employees are those persons engaged in office clerical work in a plant setting. Plant clericals are usually support personnel for plant foremen and supervisors, or persons who perform clerical work exclusively in connection with the production process. They work under the same conditions as plant employees, and frequently have the same supervision. Plant clericals are usually included in a plant unit with other production employees, but occasionally they will be excluded if the employees, the union, and the employer do not wish to have clerical employees in the bargaining unit. However, labour relations boards are normally reluctant to do so, as the exclusion would leave the clericals as a 'tag end' unit which could later be organized by another union. Plant clericals may be included with office employees if the office staff are organized at a later date, and some of the plant clericals are signed up by the union at the time of the office certification application.

WORKING FOREMEN

Persons who exercise managerial functions are excluded from collective bargaining, but some lower level supervisory personnel who possess no authority to discharge or discipline other employees may be entitled to bargain collectively. These persons will only be included where the labour relations board finds that the work that the employees do is essentially to manage products rather than people. Working foremen generally fall into this class, and will be included in a bargaining unit with other production and maintenance employees.

CERTIFICATION PROCEDURE

While the requirements for certification vary to some extent from province to province, most provinces have established procedures that are basically similar. In all provinces, certification proceedings commence with a written application for certification by the trade union. The application sets out some of the information that the labour relations board requires to determine the identity of the employer, the *bona fides* of the union, the appropriateness of the bargaining unit, and the number of employees affected. On the receipt of the application for certification, the labour relations board then notifies the employer of the application, and requires the employer to post notices of the application throughout the premises where the employees work to inform them of the union's actions. The employer is usually required to provide the board with information as well, and this information usually takes the form of a list of all employees employed on the date of the union's application, and specimen signatures of each employee to enable the board to compare the membership records of the union with the employer's work force.

Posted notices are designed to inform all employees of the union's application for certification in order that employees opposed to the union may take steps to object, and also to notify any other union that is actively organizing the employees of their competitor's application. In the case of the latter, a competing union must quickly notify the labour relations board of its own organization activities in order that the board may consider its claim to representation as well as that of the applicant. In addition, the posted notice will notify the employees, the employer and any other union of the procedure that they must follow if they wish to object to the union's application for certification. The notice will also indicate the date upon which the hearing will be held, and the place where all interested parties may attend to have their objections heard. The notice, then, refers to two dates: the date by which written objections must be filed, (usually referred to as a **terminal date**) and a **hearing date**, when the board will hear the case.

Employees and competing unions are permitted to actively campaign against the certification of the applicant union following the posting of the notice, and the employer may exercise his "right of free speech" within the limits imposed by the legislation. However, the employer may not alter working conditions or the benefits paid to employees after the application for certification is made except for legitimate business reasons, and provided that the proposed change is not one which may be interpreted as an attempt to influence the employees.

The purpose of the hearing is to enable the labour relations board to hear evidence from both the employer and the union (as well as other interested parties) as to the appropriate bargaining unit, and to determine if the union has the support of a majority of the employees in the particular unit. The procedure followed in most jurisdictions is one whereby the board compares the evidence of membership submitted by the union with the employment records submitted by the employer to ascertain the number of employees in the bargaining unit that have joined the union.

Some provinces, such as Ontario and New Brunswick require the union to submit proof that the employees who it claims are members have made some modest monetary sacrifice to join the union as firm evidence of their desire to bargain collectively. This usually takes the form of a money payment of at least one dollar, which the employees must personally pay to the union as a membership fee. The failure to pay this sum personally, or any irregularity in the payment, such as where the union organizer pays the amount on behalf of some employees, will usually render the membership records of the union suspect.

Where the membership evidence is "borderline" in the sense that it is in the 45–55 percent range, the labour relations board will hold a representation vote to determine the degree of support that the union actually has in the bargaining unit. In some jurisdictions, such as Ontario, the board is required to hold a vote where the evidence falls within this range, and in others, the percentages may vary, with a vote held in Saskatchewan where the support is as low as 25 percent. The range in Quebec is 35–50 percent, and in New Brunswick, 40–60 percent, with most others falling somewhere in between. Where some employees challenge the union membership, or where a competing union contends that it has strong or majority support as well, a labour relations board will hold a representation vote to determine the true wishes of the employees. In Ontario, electioneering is usually prohibited in the seventy-two hour period before a representation vote is scheduled to take place.

As a rule, where two unions are in competition for bargaining rights, the union that receives a majority of the votes cast in its favour is treated as the union with majority support, and if no other union is competing with the applicant union, if a majority of those employees who cast their ballots vote in favour of the union, the union will be considered to have majority support. This would be the case in most provinces, even where less than a majority of the employees cast ballots, as labour relations boards normally consider employees who do not vote as being neutral on the question.

Where only one union applies for certification and the union membership evidence indicates that the union has substantial majority support amongst the employees, a labour relations board will usually certify the union without a vote. Some boards, such as those in Ontario and British Columbia, have a similar power to certify without a vote where the employer or others have committed unfair practices which would lead the board to believe that a vote would not reveal the true wishes of the employees.

Prehearing votes may be held by labour relations boards in a number of provinces where such a vote is requested by the union in its application for certification. A prehearing vote takes place shortly after the application for certification is made, and may be used where the union believes that another union is also organizing the employees, or where the union feels that the employer or a group of anti-union employees may act to discourage support for collective bargaining. Where a prehearing vote is permitted, the labour relations board determines a voting constituency which generally resembles the bargaining unit, holds the vote, then seals the ballot box until after the hearing is held. The ballots are then counted, and majority support determined. If the board concludes, after hearing the evidence, that the union has at least the minimum support required to entitle it to a representation vote, the results of the prehearing vote will be treated as indicative of union support, and will be used to determine the union's fate.

If the membership evidence indicates that the union has less than the percentage required to have a representation vote held, or if a vote is held and the union does not receive a majority of the votes cast in its favour, the application for certification will be dismissed. To prevent repeated applications for certification, labour relations boards will often prohibit a further application by the union for a period of time. This may vary depending upon the nature or magnitude of the union's error, but is often fixed at six months unless the deficiency is of a minor nature, in which the case the board may permit a new application to be made earlier or perhaps at any time.

CERTIFICATION PROCEDURES IN THE CONSTRUCTION INDUSTRY

The certification procedure in the construction industry differs from that of industry in general due to the nature of the industry. Historically, craft unions organized on a geographic basis in an effort to establish uniform wages and working conditions for their members. The unions also operated and continue to operate hiring halls in order to facilitate the employment of their members in an industry where work for each employer is essentially for a limited period of time. Unlike the general manufacturing sector, the construction industry is characterized by a demand for many different crafts, each for a period of time to perform an essential part of the construction of a specific building or work. For example, heavy equipment operators are required for the excavation of ground for the foundation of a building; cement workers and reinforcing steel workers, along with block layers perform the work of laying the foundation of the building; steelworkers erect the structure of the building; while plumbers, electricians, and sheet metal workers install the various services; brick layers, carpenters, roofers, and various other trades each perform their part of the construction work for the construction until the building is completed. As the work of each trade is finished, the employees in that trade either move on to another building, or find themselves unemployed until hired by another building contractor in the construction of another building project. During the course of a year a skilled tradesperson may be employed on many construction sites, and by many employers, often in many places in a given geographic area, since work must necessarily be performed where the building or undertaking is located.

Initially, labour legislation in most provinces did not deal with the unique aspects of collective bargaining in the construction industry. This was due in part to the fact that the industrial and commercial sectors of the construction industry were largely organized around the hiring hall, with the unions in each craft recognized on a voluntary basis by the employers. Additionally, as a countervailing force to the unions which were in a virtual monopoly position, employers in many areas had established employers' organizations or associations, and negotiated with the unions through them. The collective agreements that were made covered given geographic areas, and included the projects undertaken by the employers in those areas.

For those employers who did not voluntarily recognize the unions, the certification procedure in most provinces was unsuitable. What the union was required to do was essentially sign up employees at a project site, then apply to the labour relations board in the usual manner for certification. Except for very large projects, the time delay meant that the work of the craft was usually drawing to a close by the time that the union was in a position to give notice to the employer to bargain. The procedures under the Act were clearly not designed with the construction industry in mind, but when the problem was recognized, most provinces established specific procedures for certification in that industry.

The province of Quebec was the first province to deal with the special problems of the construction industry, and as early as 1934 provided a legislative mechanism whereby the terms and conditions of employment in the construction industry could be uniformly applied to employers and employees in given areas. The remainder of the provinces did not turn their attention to the industry in any serious way until unrest in the construction field in the 1960s prompted action on the part of the various legislatures.

Except for the province of Manitoba, most provinces provided a streamlined procedure to enable unions to obtain bargaining rights, and this was later expanded to a system whereby bargaining would be established on a regional or provincewide basis between each craft and the employers in the area. These changes obliged employers to form associations for the purpose of collective bargaining, and over time, permitted the bargaining to expand to larger bargaining areas. The approach taken by most provinces has been to retain existing certification procedures, but accept applications for certification on an area or geographic basis without regard to the build-up of the work force, a method that would enable a union to become the bargaining agent regardless of employee numbers, for all projects of the employer in the particular area.[23]

In most provinces, the trend in the construction industry has been to collective bargaining between unions or councils of trade unions and employers' associations, with the collective agreements applicable to large geographic areas. The residential segment of the industry, however, has been to some extent untouched by these changes in some provinces, due to the existence of many small contractors, and the large numbers of non-union employees in that segment of the industry. Apart from the residential construction part of the industry, however, unions and employers' associations have generally accepted the developments that have dictated larger geographic bargaining units and the establishment of accredited or certified bargaining agents to represent both employers and employees on a regional or province-wide basis.

BARS TO CERTIFICATION

In addition to the requirement that the organization which applies for certification must be a *bona fide* trade union with the support of a majority of the employees in the bargaining unit, the time when the union applies for certification may also be an important determinant if the employees are already represented. Collective bargaining legislation permits a union to apply for certification at any time if no other union has been certified or recognized as a bargaining agent for the employee unit, but where another union has been certified, or a collective agreement is in effect, labour relations boards may only accept applications for certification at specific times. The reasoning behind this restriction is that public policy dictates industrial stability as one of the principal goals of the process, and to allow unions to raid one another at any time would defeat the purpose of the legislation. Consequently, the legislation attempts to balance industrial stability with the right of employees to replace their bargaining agent by permitting the displacement of an incumbent union only at certain times during the collective bargaining process, and only after a specific time has elapsed following the certification of the incumbent union. The timeliness of the application takes on special significance where a union wishes to raid an incumbent, or where the employees wish to take steps to terminate collective bargaining with their employer. Additionally, a union which has made an unsuccessful attempt to gain certification may be barred from bringing another application for certification for a period of time, particularly if the previous application was dismissed on the basis of falsification of membership evidence or the commission of unfair practices during the organization process. As a general rule, labour relations boards will impose a six-months interval between applications, but this may be varied according to the circumstances. Ontario, for example, under its *Labour Relations Act* permits the board to impose a waiting period of up to ten months between applications.[24]

A further bar to certification would arise where the union, either before or after making an application for certification, engages in a recognition strike or work stoppage. The purpose of the certification process is to eliminate the disruptive problems of recognition by replacing the recognition strike or work stoppage with an administrative procedure, and to permit unions to continue to use the recognition strike would defeat one of the principal goals of the legislation itself. As a consequence, labour relations boards will generally dismiss the application for certification by a union that engages in a recognition strike, or withhold certification rights until the work stoppage has ended.[25]

DISPLACEMENT AND THE TERMINATION OF BARGAINING RIGHTS

In most provinces and federally, an existing collective agreement (or incumbent union) represents a bar to certification by any other union for the obvious reason that labour legislation permits only one union at any one time to be the exclusive representative of a bargaining unit. However, as previously noted, the legislation also recognizes the fact that some mechanism must exist to allow employees, and in some cases the employer, to take steps to terminate the bargaining rights of a union that has failed to properly represent the employees, or has performed its role in some unsatisfactory manner. The termination of bargaining rights may occur in five ways:

1. *Termination where the incumbent union acquired its bargaining rights by way of fraud.*
2. *The abandonment of bargaining rights by a union, and voluntary notice to the labour relations board that the union no longer wishes to represent the employee unit.*
3. *The termination of bargaining rights for a failure to bargain.*
4. *The displacement of an incumbent union by another union that wishes to represent the employees.*
5. *The cessation of business by the employer.*

The question of fraud or any attempt to mislead the labour relations board in certification proceedings is a serious matter, and subject to penalty under the labour relations statutes of most jurisdictions.

Apart from any penalty provided for a violation of the law, some provinces provide in their legislation that any fraud discovered after a union has been certified will result in the loss of bargaining rights for the union, and the termination of any collective agreement made by the union and the employer. As a consequence, most unions will take steps to ensure that the evidence submitted to the labour relations board is accurate and not designed to mislead, as employers, other competing unions, or employees who oppose the union will generally inform the board of any irregularities that they discover in the application for certification.

Of the remaining four methods, the abandonment of bargaining rights by a union creates the least amount of procedural difficulty for the employer and the employees, but is one that rarely occurs. Normally a union that applies for certification will carry on with its role as a bargaining representative if it is certified by a labour relations board. Nevertheless, if the union, once certified, should desire not to represent the particular bargaining unit, it may inform the board that it no longer wishes to represent the employees and request that its rights be terminated. A more likely approach, however, would be for the employer or a group of employees to apply to the labour relations board for the termination of the bargaining rights of a union that has failed to exercise its rights following certification. In Ontario, for example, if a union fails to give the employer notice to bargain within a period of sixty days following certification, either the employer or the employees may apply to the labour relations board for a declaration that the union no longer represents the employees.[26] If the union then signifies that it wishes to abandon its bargaining rights, the board will so declare, otherwise the board will hear from all parties before making a decision.

The purpose of this provision is to prevent a union from "sleeping on its rights" to the inconvenience and detriment of both the employer and the employees, but it is not intended as a means by which the employer might take advantage of a legal technicality where the union is slow in asserting its rights for legitimate reasons. For example, in an Ontario case[27], the union which had been certified failed to give notice to bargain to the employer during the sixty-day period specified in the statute, and on the expiry of the time, the employer immediately moved to terminate the union's bargaining rights for a failure to bargain. The union had given notice to bargain a few days after the expiry of the sixty-day period, and was able to satisfy the board by way of evidence that it continued to enjoy the support of a majority of the employees in the bargaining unit. Conversely, the employer was unable to show any loss or damage as a result of the delay. The board then dismissed the employer's application on the basis that it was not the intention of the provisions to permit an employer to take advantage of delay on the part of the union to terminate bargaining rights where a reasonable excuse for the delay existed, but to protect employers from loss or damage which might result from the union's failure to exercise its rights. However, in similar cases where the union failed to give notice to bargain because it had lost the support of a majority of the employees following its certification, the board has held a vote of the employees to determine if the union's rights should be terminated.[28]

Where the employees themselves decide that they wish to bargain collectively through another union, or do not wish to have a union represent them, special procedures must be followed. To replace the incumbent union, the new union must not only proceed by way of an application for certification, but it must do so at an appropriate time. This is so because in the interest of industrial stability, labour legislation permits the replacement of an incumbent union only at specific times after the union has been certified. What labour legislation attempts to do in this regard is give a newly certified union time to negotiate a collective agreement, and if it is successful, protect it from displacement by the employees during the life of the agreement. However, if the union attempts to thwart displacement by a long-term collective agreement, "open seasons" are usually provided by the legislation in each jurisdiction to allow applications for certification by other unions, or applications for termination by employees at specific times during the term of the agreement.

The time or times when displacement or termination applications will be entertained by labour relations boards is subject to a certain amount of variation, since each province has its own view on the timeliness of such applications. Nevertheless, the pattern is similar in each jurisdiction. Using Ontario as an example once again, a newly certified union has essentially one year to negotiate a collective agreement,[29] during which time it is safe from displacement by another union and free from attempts by employees to terminate its relationship as a bargaining agent except in the case of failure to pursue its bargaining rights. However, this period may be extended when conciliation or mediation has been requested, or where a lawful strike or lock-out has taken place, as the act provides that no application for certification or termination may be made until thirty days after the release of the report of the conciliation board or mediator (or thirty days after the Minister of Labour advices the parties that no board will be appointed). The period is extended from thirty days to six months when the mediator or conciliation board reports that the differences between the parties have been settled, with the time period calculated from the date that the report is released by the Minister of Labour.

In the case of a lawful strike or lock-out, no application for certification by another union, and no application for termination by the employees may be made until six months after the commencement of the strike or lock-out, or seven months after the release of the conciliation board report or the Minister notifies the parties that no board will be appointed, whichever occurs first.[30] These time limits may extend the one-year period depending upon when the strike commences, or when the conciliation procedure is requested by the parties. This is to allow the incumbent union time to perform its duties free from harassment or pressures from both outside organizations and from within its own ranks, as a newly certified union often has difficulty negotiating its first collective agreement.

In Ontario, where a collective agreement has been negotiated, an application for certification or termination of bargaining rights may only be made during the last two months of operation of the collective agreement, provided that conciliation has not been requested by the incumbent union.[31] If the collective agreement is for a term of more than three years, the "open season" for an application for certification or termination would be during the thirty-fifth and thirty-sixth months, and the last two months of each year which the agreement runs beyond the three years in addition to the last two months of its operation.[32] Collective agreements that contain automatic renewal clauses would have "open seasons" during the last two months of each year that the agreement operates or is renewed.[33]

Provided that the application is made at an appropriate time, the procedure which the labour relations board follows is similar in many respects for both an application for certification and for the termination of bargaining rights. Where a labour union wishes to displace an incumbent union, it must meet all the requirements that would ordinarily be imposed upon any union that applies for certification: it must establish that it is a *bona fide* trade union, having the support of a majority of the employees, and that the application is timely. The labour relations board is free to make such inquiries as it deems appropriate in its assessment of the evidence presented, and will usually hold a representation vote of the employees to determine their wishes where the incumbent union challenges the application for displacement. If the vote reveals that a majority of the employees wish to be represented by the applicant union, the board will certify the new bargaining agent, and in most provinces any collective agreement in existence between the prior bargaining agent and the employer will cease to operate as of the date that the incumbent is displaced.[34] It should be noted, however, that in some jurisdictions (for example, in British Columbia and Manitoba) the collective agreement does not cease to operate, and the new union may be obliged to perform the duties imposed upon the union until the existing agreement expires.[35]

In the case of an application by the employees for the termination of the bargaining rights of the incumbent, the Ontario Labour Relations Board is obliged to hold a vote where the board finds that not less than 45 percent of the employees in the bargaining unit at the time of the application voluntarily signified in writing that they did not wish to be represented by the incumbent union. If on taking a vote, a majority of the ballots are cast in opposition to the union, the labour relations board will declare that the union no longer represents the employees in the bargaining unit.[36] The effect of the declaration is that the union's right to represent the employees immediately ceases, and any collective agreement would also cease to operate, leaving the individual employees free to negotiate their own employment relationships with their employer.

A final method of termination of bargaining rights is the termination of employment by cessation of business of the employer. If an employer permanently closes down a business, the result is an end to the bargaining relationship between the employer, the union, and the employees. With certain exceptions, such as in the construction industry, where some employers tend to operate only part of the year, or where the business is sold, bargaining rights of a certified union will come to an end when the employees end their employment relationship.

In the construction industry, where employees seldom have a permanent and continuous employment relationship with one employer, the temporary cessation of business does not end the relationship which the employer has with the union when the employer terminates all employees. Instead, the relationship continues even though there are no employees, and the collective agreement which the union negotiates will apply to the employees when the employer hires a work force for the next construction project. It is only when the relationship is terminated by the labour relations board or when the employer permanently closes his business that the union relationship ends.

SUCCESSOR RIGHTS

The sale of a business by an employer does not necessarily end the bargaining rights of a union that is the bargaining agent of the employees. In cases where the business is sold as a "going concern" to a buyer, in most provinces the buyer or purchaser of the business is the **successor** to the seller, and may be bound by any collective agreement in existence until a labour relations board otherwise declares. If no collective agreement exists, the employer will be obliged to meet and bargain with the union. For example, in Ontario, a purchaser is deemed to be a successor employer until otherwise declared by the labour relations board, and in effect, inherits the union and the collective agreement along with the purchased business.[37]

Labour relations boards as a general rule will only refuse the union's right to represent the employees where the nature of the purchaser's business is inherently different from that of the seller, where only some of the assets are acquired, or where the work force will be merged with another work force already represented by a labour union. Where the two work forces are merged, the labour relations board is obliged to determine which union should represent the mixed employee group. This is often a very difficult decision for a board to make, but some of the factors considered by the labour relations board in arriving at a decision will include the relative sizes of the two employee groups, the nature of the work done previously by the two groups of employees, and the types of unions involved.

REVIEW QUESTIONS

1. *Explain the purpose of the certification process from the public policy point of view. How does this differ from a union's view of the process?*
2. *Describe the use of "majority rule" in the certification process. Why was it adopted?*
3. *What safeguards have been included in labour legislation to protect individual employee rights?*
4. *Explain the importance of the size of the bargaining unit in labour relations. What factors are considered in this determination?*

5. *Under what circumstances might a labour relations board reject an application for certification from a union?*
6. *Briefly describe the importance of a representation vote in the determination of bargaining rights. When might a union ask for a prehearing vote in a jurisdiction that permits such a vote to be taken?*
7   *How does a labour relations board decide that a trade union is "eligible" for collective bargaining purposes?*
8. *Under what circumstances would a labour relations board terminate a certified union's bargaining rights?*
9. *Under what circumstances would a union acquire "successor" rights?*
10. *Explain how collective bargaining in the construction industry differs from collective bargaining in general manufacturing.*

NOTES

[1]*National Industrial Recovery Act*, 48 Stat. 195 (1933) U.S.

[2]*Collective Bargaining Act*, 1943 7 Geo. VI c. 11 (Ont.).

[3]Order-in-Council P.C. 1003 (Feb. 17, 1944).

[4]*Labour Relations Act*, R.S.O. 1980 c. 228 s. 1.

[5]*Canada Labour Code* R.S.C. 1970 C.L-1 s. 107(1).

[6]See for example, *Canadian Union of Bank Employees and Canada Trustco Mortgage Company*. [1977]. 1 Can L.R.B.R. 125 (O.L.R.B.).

[7]*Tridon Limited and United Electrical, Radio and Machine Workers of America* [1974] O.L.R.B. Rep 16.

[8]*The King v. The Labour Relations Board v. Ex parte Gorton-Pew* (New Brunswick) Ltd. [1952] 52 CLLC 15,038.

[9]*Labour Relations Act*, R.S.O. 1980 c. 228 s. 13.

[10]*Labour Code* R.S.B.C. 1979 c. 212 s. 50.

[11]*Ottawa Mailers Union Local 60 and The Journal Publishing Company of Ottawa, Limited*. [1970] O.L.R.B. Mon. Rep. 925.

[12]*London Assoc. of Painting and Decorating and Journeymen and Gaymer and Outram* (London) [1954] 54 CLLC para 17,073.

[13]See for example, *Campbell/Mail O Matic Employees Association and Campbell Reproductions Limited* [1971] O.L.R.B. Rep. 134.

[14]*Canada Labour Code* R.S.C. 1970 c. L-1 s. 134(1).

[15]*Labour Relations Act*, R.S.O. 1980 c. 228 s. 13.

[16]*United Brotherhood of Carpenters and Joiners of America and Kent Tile and Marble Co. Ltd.* 61 CLLC 16,204.

[17]*United Rubber, Cork, Linoleum and Plastic Workers of America and The Goodyear Service Stores* 65 CLLC 16,018.

[18]*Globe Machine and Stamping Co.* (1937) 3 N.L.R.B. 294.

[19]*United Automobile Workers, Local 426 and Corbin Lock Co. of Canada Ltd.* 46 CLLC 16,406.

[20]See for example, *Kent Tile and Marble Co. Ltd.* 61 CLLC 16,204; *Sheraton Brock Hotel Ltd.* 61 CLLC 16,205.

[21]*Simpson-Sears Limited and Department Store Organizing Committee, Local 1004* 56 CLLC 15,291.

[22]*International Hod Carriers, Building and Common Labourers Union and George A. Crain & Sons Ltd.* 63 CLLC 16,043.

[23]See for example, Ontario, *Labour Relations Act* R.S.O. 1980 c. 228 s.119.

[24]*Labour Relations Act* R.S.O. 1980 c. 228 s. 103(2) (i).

[25]See for example, *Radio Lunch and Mine Mill & Smelter Workers Local 902* [1950] 50 CLLC 17,012.

[26]*Labour Relations Act* R.S.O. 1980 c. 228 s. 59(1).

[27]*Dominion Stores Limited and General Workers, Local 800* [1956] 56 CLLC 18,047.

[28]*Moyer Sand (1965) Limited and United Steelworkers of America* [1966] O.L.R.B. Mon. Rep. 913.

[29]*Labour Relations Act* R.S.O. 1980 c. 228 s. 57(1).

[30]*Ibid.*, s. 61.

[31]*Ibid.*, s. 57(2)(a).

[32]*Ibid.*, s. 57(2)(b).

[33]*Ibid.*, s. 57(2)(c).

[34]*Ibid.*, s. 56.

[35]See for example, *Labour Code* R.S.B.C. 1979 c. 212 s. 46(c).

[36]*Labour Relations Act*, R.S.O. 1980 c. 228 s. 57(4).

[37]*Ibid.*, s. 63.

RECOMMENDED REFERENCES AND SOURCE MATERIAL

Finkelman, J. *The Ontario Labour Relations Board and Natural Justice.* Kingston, Canada: Queen's University Industrial Relations Centre (1965).

Herman, E.E. *The Determination of the Appropriate Bargaining Unit by Labour Relations Boards in Canada.* Ottawa, Canada: Canada Department of Labour, 1966.

Jones, D.L. "Self-Determination v. Stability of Labor Relations." 58 *Michigan Law Review* 313 (1960).

Reed, G.W. *White Collar Bargaining Units Under the Ontario Labour Relations Act.* Kingston, Canada: Queen's University Industrial Relations Centre (1969).

Rose, G. "Minority Rights v. Majority Rule." 37 *American Bar Association Journal* 195 (1951).

Willes, J.A. *The Craft Bargaining Unit Ontario and U.S. Experience.* Kingston, Canada: Queen's University Industrial Relations Centre (1971).

CASE PROBLEMS FOR DISCUSSION
HARRISON INDUSTRIES CASE (A)

Harrison Industries is a limited company operating two plants locally with a combined payroll of approximately 235 people (see appendix B). The company manufactures a variety of sheet metal parts and castings for the domestic and industrial heating industry.

The company was established in 1906 as a stove foundry, and operated as such until 1940, when the company obtained a number of contracts to produce castings for war-related products. After World War II, the company produced a line of oil-fired home heating units and furnaces to take advantage of the house building boom that occurred in the late 1940s and 1950s. By 1955, however, the company had dropped its own line of heating units, and had become a supplier of parts to other manufacturers in the heating field.

The foundry operations are still carried out in the original plant at 3525 Concession Road. The production facilities were updated in a major way on two occasions: initially in 1948, and more recently, in 1978. Minor machinery and equipment replacements have been made on a regular basis to avoid obsolescence.

The company acquired the assets of Smithson Steel Fabricating in 1973. The Smithson Steel company had carried on business at 3510 Concession Road for many years, producing steel stampings, grill work, and sheet metal parts for the heating industry. The company had also been a major supplier of parts for furnaces manufactured by Harrison Industries in the post–World War II period. When the president and principal shareholder of Smithson Steel decided to retire in 1973, Harrison Industries purchased the production facilities of the company, and using the building leased from the vendor, designated the sheet metal fabricating establishment as plant #2.

The foundry at 3525 Concession Road, and the metal fabricating plant at 3510 Concession Road operated as separate plants from 1973 until 1981, with a minimum of interchange of personnel at the production level. In 1981, some office work was consolidated when a new office and metal fabricating plant was constructed on Harrison Park Drive in a suburban industrial park, about six miles from the foundry operation.

The new office and plant building was to some extent an unplanned expansion of the company. Some years before the construction of the new plant, Mr. Harrison had acquired a block of land at the outskirts of the city, with a view to developing it as an industrial park. Very little work had been done on the development when a fire at the 3510 Concession Road plant caused some structural damage to the building, and made a move to new premises necessary. A new building had to be acquired immediately, and the decision was made to build in the new industrial park. A new building was promptly constructed, and the plant, complete with updated machinery was ready for production in less than six months.

The new building contained space for the general office staff, and the company moved the Accounting and Payroll Departments to the new location. The "office" work remaining at each plant was for the most part clerical work of a general nature associated with the production end of the business. Each plant retained a payroll clerk in its plant to make up the necessary records for payroll purposes, but all payroll work was handled from the main office.

At the time of the move to the new location, the company hired Mr. James Owen as Personnel Manager. Prior to the new appointment, employment matters had been left in the hands of the plant managers, who, in consultation with department supervisors, handled hiring, and employment problems. Layoffs, rehiring, and dismissals usually fell within the responsibility of the department supervisors or the foremen. The new personnel manager was expected to assume some of these duties.

Employee problems of a general nature were generally channelled through the Harrison Industries' Employees' Association that had been established in the foundry in 1938. The Employees' Association had operated in a very informal way over the years to deal with working conditions, wages, and other matters in the foundry, and had developed an excellent working relationship with management.

Under the constitution of the association, membership was open to all production and maintenance employees in the plant on payment of annual dues of $1.00. Because the dues were low, most of the employees had joined the association, and remained members. For collective bargaining purposes, the constitution provided that the employees in each department elect a representative to the Bargaining Committee of the association, and the Bargaining Committee so elected was required to bring all employee grievances and employment matters to the attention of management.

Each year, the elected representatives of the Employees' Association met with Mr. Harrison, the president of the company, and discussed wages and benefits for the employees. The meetings were usually little more than a formality, because Mr. Harrison had generally paid wages equal to those paid in most unionized plants in the area, and wage increases were usually given to the employees when the organized work forces in the area received their wage settlements.

When Harrison Industries acquired the metal fabricating plant in 1973, the 100 employees in the new operation were not interested in joining the Employees' Association, and no efforts were made by the association to include the new employee groups in the election of representatives to the Bargaining Committee. The association did, however, discuss wages and benefits for sheet metal employees each year at its regular meeting with Harrison, and received his assurance that wages in the metal fabricating plant would be established in line with those in similar unionized plants in the area.

Shortly after joining the company, Mr. Owen, who had assumed responsibility for the settlement of employee grievances, was told by an employee that many of the employees were unhappy with the procedure used by the foremen in some departments for layoffs and rehiring. Apparently, some of the foremen were not following Mr. Harrison's long established practice of keeping on the longest service employees capable of doing necessary work in the plant, but were, instead, selecting employees for layoff on a job basis. This meant, in a number of cases, that a long-service employee was terminated because no work was available for the employee on the particular type of machine used for the work, even though the employee was skilled in the operation of other machines operated by less senior employees, who were retained.

Owen did nothing about the problem until some months later when a number of long-service employees from two metal fabricating departments came to see him, and complained of the practice that had been reported to him earlier. Owen promised to do something to correct the problem, and immediately called a meeting of departmental supervisors and foremen. He discussed the problem with them, and following the meeting, posted a notice on all plant notice boards to the effect that Mr. Harrison's long-established practice would be formally adopted by the company. Henceforth, all layoffs of employees would be on a departmental seniority basis, provided that the longer-service employees could do the work available.

A few weeks later, Raymond Anderson, an employee with two years (less a week) service was terminated in accordance with the new seniority policy. Anderson had been employed as a material handler in the Stamping Department for close to two years, but now had the lowest seniority of the employees in the Shipping Department at plant #2, as a result of a move that he requested in June of 1982.

Anderson was particularly unhappy about the new layoff procedure established in the company, and complained bitterly to Owen, the Personnel Manager, when his foreman refused to consider his company service record in determining the reduction of staff in the Shipping Department. The basis of his complaint was that he would not have asked for a transfer to the Shipping Department had he known that his seniority elsewhere in the plant would not be considered in the event of a layoff.

Owen said that he could do nothing to settle the grievance, and the layoff was allowed to stand.

Anderson was rehired three weeks later. He appeared to be pleased that he was called back to work, but the foreman in the Shipping Department noted a distinct change in his attitude towards his work and the company following his return. The foreman observed that Anderson was no longer the jovial person that he was before his layoff. Instead, he had become a rather serious person, discussing company policy frequently with his fellow employees both on the job, and during his lunch break.

The foreman was not particularly concerned about Anderson's changed attitude initially, but a few days later he was shocked to hear from an employee in another deparment that Anderson had been "talking union" to his work-mates, and had already convinced a number of them that they should have a union to protect their jobs. The foreman immediately made a number of discreet enquiries to determine the reasons why Anderson had suddenly acquired an interest in unions, and discovered that Anderson had met some members of the Heating Equipment Workers' Union during his layoff, and they had convinced him that their union would have protected him if the plant had been unionized.

During the latter part of August, 1982, Anderson met with James Allen, the Business Agent of the Heating Equipment Workers' Union, on several occasions, and discussed the organization of Harrison Industries' employees. The union was willing to organize the plant, and Anderson provided the union with the names and addresses of a large number of the production employees working at the Harrison Park Drive plant. Anderson also obtained an employee list for plant #1 from Vic Carrazzo, the president of the Employees' Association, on the pretext that he wished to determine employee interest in establishing an interplant bowling league. He passed the list of employees to the union the next day.

On August 23, 1982, the union invited the employees of Harrison Industries to an organizational meeting at a local hotel, and seventy-two employees attended. Allen, and Anderson, who by this time had become a union member, explained the benefits of joining the union to the employees.

After the meeting, fifty-two employees signed membership cards. Most of the employees that had signed membership cards paid the required $1.00, but two employees borrowed $1.00 from Anderson for initiation fees, made no arrangements to repay the money, and in fact did not repay him the money loaned. Anderson personally paid the membership fees for five employees on the strength of their promises to repay him, and all loans were repaid, but not until the period between September 13 and September 20, 1982. Three employees paid nothing, but in the confusion at the end of the meeting, received receipts from Anderson acknowledging payment of the initiation fee.

During the next few days, Anderson managed to sign up as union members two additional employees in the Shipping Department, bringing the total number of signed memberships to fifty-four.

At this point in time, Anderson became concerned about the lack of interest in the union at the foundry (plant #1), and met a number of foundry employees at 3525 Concession Road shortly after 5:00 p.m. on August 26, 1982. He urged the employees to join the union on the basis that membership in the union would cost them at least double the present fee after the union was certified, and when they did not appear to be interested, he said that if they did not join before certification, he would see to it that they would not be permitted to join afterwards. He intimated that this would mean that they would lose their jobs if the union negotiated a union shop agreement. Three employees signed membership cards as a result of Anderson's parking lot discussion, bringing the total number of members at plant #1 to four.

On September 1, 1982, Anderson met another employee at a local restaurant, and urged him to join the union, because "most of the employees had done so." When the employee demurred, Anderson suggested that it might be necessary to "beat some sense into his thick skull" if he did not join the union. The employee, to avoid the embarrassment of a scene in the restaurant, signed a membership card, and paid $1.00 to Anderson.

On September 2, 1982, Anderson delivered the signed membership cards and duplicate receipts to Allen without revealing the discrepancies or the circumstances under which the memberships were obtained.

A few days later, the foreman in the Shipping Department once again gave Anderson notice that his services would be terminated due to a lack of work. On this occasion, the foreman indicated that it might be some time before the company rehired again, since construction for the year was drawing to a close, and demand for the company's sheet metal products would probably not pick up until some time early in 1983. The termination notice was to take effect in two weeks' time.

The union, which had now been established as Local 313 of the Heating Equipment Workers' Union, filed an application for certification with the Labour Relations Board on September 2, 1982, requesting certification as the bargaining representative of all of the production and maintenance employees of Harrison Industries engaged at its plant at 12 Harrison Park Drive, save and except supervisors, persons above the rank of supervisors, office staff, and sales staff.

The application for certification was mailed to the registrar of the Labour Relations Board along with the necessary supporting documents, and was received on September 5, 1982. On September 6, 1982, the registrar served Local 313 with a notice fixing the terminal date for the application at September 13, 1982, and the hearing date at September 20, 1982. The company, on the same date was served with a notice of application for certification, the documentation, and forms, as required under the *Rules of Procedure* and the *Labour Relations Act*.

On September 7, 1982, Mr. Harrison met with the company's lawyer to discuss the organization campaign of Local 313, and the application for certification that the union had made to the Labour Relations Board. Following the discussion, the lawyer prepared and sent to the registrar copies of the company reply, schedules of employees, and company documents containing specimen signatures of the employees. In its reply, the company submitted that the appropriate bargaining unit should include the production and maintenance employees at both company plants. The union was notified of the company's reply on September 9, 1982.

Mr. Harrison arranged to have the notices posted in the Harrison Park Drive Plant as directed by the registrar, in order that all of the employees would be aware of the union's application for certification. He then turned the matter over to Owen to deal with, and suggested that Owen seek the advice of the company's lawyer before making any employment changes.

On September 8, 1982, Owen contacted Vic Carrazzo, and suggested that the Employees' Association should really be the bargaining representative of the employees at both plants, since it had done so in an informal way for many years. He also indicated that he would personally prefer negotiating with the Employees Association rather than the Heating Equipment Workers' Union. When Carrazzo enquired as to the procedure for certification, Owen advised him to sign up as many members as he could at the Harrison Park Drive Plant. Owen also suggested that he would permit Carrazzo to hold a meeting in the plant cafeteria, if Carrazzo wished to do so.

At Owen's suggestion, a notice of the meeting was prepared by Carrazzo and posted on the notice boards at the Harrison Park Drive Plant advising the employees that Carrazzo would speak to them on behalf of the Employees' Association at 12 noon, the following day, in the plant cafeteria.

Fifty employees were present in the cafeteria to hear Carrazzo speak. Carrazzo described the history and operation of the Employees' Association to the group of employees and urged them to consider the Association as an alternative to the Heating Equipment Workers' Union. After his speech, Carrazzo answered questions raised by some of the employees, and then accepted applications for membership from those interested in the association. He collected $1.00 from each applicant and provided receipts for the money so paid. Thirty-eight employees, including two working foremen, joined the association.

On September 9, 1982, the Harrison Industries' Employees' Association filed an Intervention with the Registrar of the Labour Relations Board in accordance with the *Labour Relations Act* and the *Rules of Procedure*. Carrazzo also informed the Registrar of the methods used by Anderson to obtain memberships in Local 313 and the failure of certain employees to pay the required membership fee to the union.

On September 12, 1982, the local union was notified by the registrar of the application for certification made by the Employees' Association. The local union then filed with the registrar a list of allegations concerning the legitimacy of the association as a representative of the employees, and an objection concerning the methods used to sign up members at the Harrison Park Plant.

While the Employees' Association was actively organizing in competition with the Heating Equipment Workers' Union, a group of long-service employees at the Harrison Park Plant decided to oppose the organization campaign. On September 9, 1982, the employees John MacGregor, Joseph Lewicki, Albert Swale, and Albert Blenkhorn, visited Harrison at his office. They requested his advice as to how they might oppose a union coming into the plant. They informed Harrison that many of the employees did not want to be represented by a union, and that some of the employees that had signed membership cards did so only because Anderson was a friend.

Harrison told the employees that his lawyer had informed him that the *Labour Relations Act* prohibited him from advising employees in this matter and that he could not assist them in any way. He confessed to the employees that he was deeply hurt by the actions of Anderson because he felt he had done his best in the past to treat all employees as fairly as possible. Harrison stated he could not understand why some of the employees felt that they needed a union in the plant.

The four employees left Mr. Harrison's office, and following a short discussion, decided to engage the services of a lawyer to help them with procedural matters as set out in the *Labour Relations Act*. MacGregor telephoned a local lawyer and arranged an appointment for 1:00 p.m. the next day. He then asked his foreman for permission to reschedule his lunch break from 12:00–1:00 p.m. to 1:00–2:00 p.m. in order that he might meet with his lawyer but he did not indicate the purpose of his visit. The foreman granted MacGregor's request, and assured him that he would not lose time or wages if he returned late from lunch.

MacGregor met with his lawyer at 1:00 p.m., and explained the organization of the plant and the desire of a group of employees to oppose the application for certification by Local 313. The lawyer prepared a statement of desire to be signed by employees opposing the union and advised MacGregor of the procedure he should follow.

MacGregor returned to work at 1:45 p.m. and contrary to his lawyer's instructions proceeded to obtain the signatures of employees on the statement of desire during working hours. MacGregor obtained a total of twenty-two signatures of employees opposing the union, including six employees who were claimed by the union as members of Local 313.

MacGregor mailed the statement of desire to the Registrar of the Labour Relations Board on September 9, 1982, using the company mail facilities and in an envelope bearing the company's return address which he had obtained from an office secretary.

On September 13, 1982, the registrar notified all parties of receipt by the board of the employees' statement of desire.

On September 19, 1982, the day before the hearing, Owen, at the request of two foremen from Plant #2, hired a new employee for material handling work and transferred an existing long-service employee to the Shipping Department to temporarily fill the vacancy created by the termination of Anderson.

Owen, in his interview of the new employee, explained the union's attempt to organize the plant and its application for certification. He expressed the hope that the new employee would not be interested in joining the union. When the employee stated that he was not interested in unions, Owen replied, "Good. Your chance for promotion will probably be much better if your loyalty is only to the company."

On September 20, 1982, the Harrison Industries case came before the Labour Relations Board for determination.

HARRISON INDUSTRIES CASE (A)

APPENDIX A

Machine operators were normally classified as semiskilled and operated a variety of equipment. Employees experienced at operating only one machine were usually the lowest paid in the semiskilled category, while operators capable of operating many different machines received wages close to those paid to skilled employees.

Semiskilled employees operate equipment designed to cut and bend sheet metal, as well as equipment used to drill holes and stamp parts. Operators of lift-trucks were classed as semiskilled. Skilled employees were those employees that were qualified as journeymen in recognized trades, such as: pattern-makers, tool and die makers, machinists, draftsmen, stationary engineers, electricians, and welders.

Maintenance employees were generally skilled employees. Unskilled employees were normally employed as material handlers, packers, yard workers, plant cleaners, and helpers assigned to skilled employees.

HARRISON INDUSTRIES CASE (A)

APPENDIX B
BREAKDOWN OF THE WORK FORCE AT HARRISON INDUSTRIES
Plant #1

Foremen and above the rank of foreman	6
Working foremen	1
Plant clerical*	1

Payroll clerk   1
Skilled employees   42
Semiskilled employees   33
Unskilled employees   24
plant clericals classified as semiskilled employees.

Plant #2
Foremen and above the rank of foreman   5
Working foremen   2
Plant clerical*   1
Payroll clerk   1
Skilled employees   34
Semiskilled employees   40
Unskilled employees   35
plant clerical employees classified as semiskilled.

CASE DISCUSSION QUESTIONS
HARRISON INDUSTRIES CASE (A)

1. *Determine the procedure for certification under the Labour Relations Act.*
2. *Determine the factors considered by the Labour Relations Board in the establishment of an appropriate bargaining unit.*
3. *Determine the limits on the employer's right of "free speech."*
4. *Identify unfair labour practices on the part of the employer or union. How will the Labour Relations Board probably deal with them?*
5. *Assess Anderson's organizing methods.*
6. *Determine the underlying factors that produced the general interest in collective bargaining. What steps could (or should) management have taken to deal with the problem before organization began?*
7. *Analyze the meeting held on August 23, 1982.*
8. *Assess the actions of Owen in the case.*
9. *What obstacles would the Employees' Association likely encounter in its application for certification as an Intervener?*
10. *Assess the chances of success of Local 313 on its application for certification.*

EXHIBIT 6-1   HARRISON INDUSTRIES CASE (A) APPENDIX C

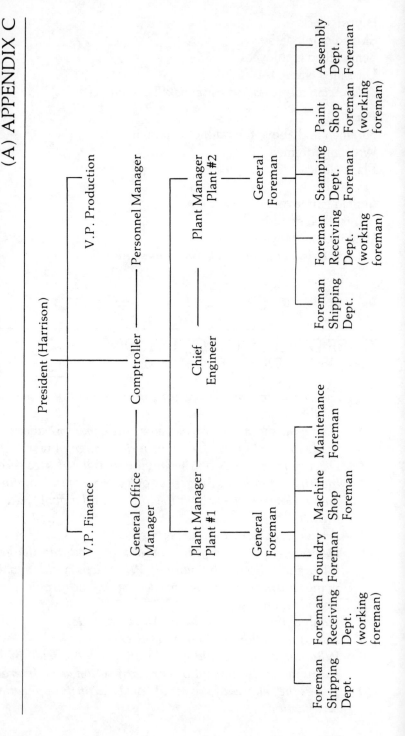

HARRISON INDUSTRIES CASE (B)

Raymond Anderson's last day of work in the Shipping Department was Friday, September 16, 1982. During the two weeks prior to that date, he had casually looked for a temporary job that would carry him through the winter, but very little work was available. The jobs open were generally taken by better qualified people and Anderson resigned himself to a long period of unemployment.

On Wednesday, September 21, 1982, Anderson attended at the local employment office and then spent the rest of the day with Allen at the union hall where they discussed the Harrison Industries' case that had been heard the previous day by the Labour Relations Board. As Anderson was about to leave the hall, a friend and fellow union member who was employed in the Receiving Department of Harrison Industries entered. He informed Anderson and Allen that he had heard by way of plant gossip that an employee who had been working in the Stamping Department was now working at Anderson's old job in the Shipping Department.

The news surprised both Anderson and Allen. Work in the Shipping Department had been slow for some weeks before Anderson's termination, and Anderson had felt certain that the staff reduction in the department was legitimate and necessary. Allen, on the other hand, had suspected the foreman of using a slack period as an excuse to get rid of Anderson and the news of the transfer of the new employee to Anderson's old job confirmed in his mind this previous suspicion. Allen suggested that Anderson file a complaint with the Labour Relations Board and Anderson, with some reluctance, agreed to do so.

On September 22, 1982 the Labour Relations Board received Anderson's complaint that he had been unfairly terminated by Harrison Industries.

On September 22, 1982, several friends of Anderson (who were also union members), met with Owen to protest the hiring of a new employee while Anderson was available for work. Owen received the two employees in his office and listened patiently to their complaint. He then told them that he was not in a position to make changes except at the request of the foreman or supervisor. He indicated that the foreman of the Shipping Department had been unhappy with Anderson's performance following his first layoff and that he (the foreman) required an energetic and willing worker in his department, in order to maintain morale. Owen concluded his assessment by saying that Anderson really didn't get along well with other employees in the Shipping Department and that his recent attempts to persuade other employees to join the union had resulted in complaints by his workmates that he was annoying them on the job with his union sales pitch.

As the employees left his office, Owen suggested that they contact the Shipping Department foreman if they wished to confirm what he had said about Anderson's performance on the job.

Anderson's two friends didn't intend to take the matter as far as the foreman but as they left work that afternoon they met him as he was leaving the plant and walked with him to the parking lot. They explained their problem to the foreman and when they asked him if Owen's assessment of Anderson was correct he confirmed that it was. "In fact," the foreman stated, "during the last week that Anderson was here, he annoyed Lewicki so much with his union talk that Lewicki locked him in the back of one of the trucks leaving the plant. Anderson couldn't get the driver's attention to let him out until the driver stopped for a coffee."

As they parted company at the parking lot, one of Anderson's friends asked the foreman if he disciplined Lewicki for locking Anderson in the truck. The foreman replied that he had done so. He had warned Lewicki that he would send him home for the day if the incident was repeated.

Allen was also gathering information on September 22 to support Anderson's complaint to the Labour Relations Board. That evening he telephoned William Lockyer, a union member who worked in the Stamping Department, and asked him if he had seen a new employee doing material handling work in his department. Lockyer told Allen that he thought that a new employee had been brought in on a temporary basis to fill a vacancy created when a regular employee moved to the Shipping Department. After further questioning regarding the new employee's potential as a union member, Lockyer replied that the new employee seemed to be unwilling to join the union until his job was of a more permanent nature.

Allen informed Lockyer that Anderson had filed a complaint with the board and that the union would insist that he be reinstated in his old job. To this comment Lockyer responded, "I hope you don't mean the Stamping Department when you say "his old job." Frankly, we were pleased to see Anderson move to Shipping. He's a nice guy, but when he gets interested in anything, all he does is talk about it for eight hours a day. If the company puts him back here, he would drive us nuts. He would talk union all the time. Most of the guys would probably burn their union cards or maybe go on strike until he was moved out."

Allen thanked Lockyer for his information, then hung up the telephone. It was time to provide the international office with his assessment of the situation developing at Harrison Industries.

CASE DISCUSSION QUESTIONS
HARRISON INDUSTRIES CASE (B)

1. *Assess the validity of Anderson's complaint.*
2. *Assess the validity of defences that might be raised by the company.*
3. *Outline the procedure that will likely be followed to deal with the complaint.*
4. *If the complaint is not resolved in the course of proceedings, what factors will the Labour Relations Board consider in reaching a decision?*
5. *Using previous decisions of the board as a guide, render a decision on the complaint of Anderson. Give reasons.*

HARRISON INDUSTRIES CASE (C)

The failure of local 313 to attain bargaining rights at Harrison Industries in 1982 did not end the union's organizing campaign. Raymond Anderson, reinstated by the company and placed in his old job in the Shipping Department, continued to "talk union" to other employees during his lunch hours. James Allen of the union personally assumed responsibility for the preparation of a new membership drive to organize the employees at the Harrison Park Drive Plant.

Owen became aware of the union's new drive to organize Plant #2 some months after Anderson had been reinstated. While Mr. Harrison was on vacation and without his knowledge, Owen decided to reduce the effectiveness of the union's propaganda with a propaganda sheet of his own. The new publication was entitled, "The Harrison Industries Newsletter."

The newsletter was described as "an employees' information letter" that would keep the work force informed of company progress and provide a means by which employees could put forward ideas or discuss problems in the plant. Employees were invited to send in suggestions that would improve production and to use the newsletter to bring forward plant problems that had not been resolved to their satisfaction. Owen's intention was to publish the newsletter monthly.

The first issue of the newsletter contained a few short write-ups of proposed production changes in the plant and a brief report of the company's competitive position in the market. It also contained a reprint of a newspaper article that described the financial difficulties of a major competitor of Harrison Industries which intended to close down as a result of a lengthy strike at its plant. The article also cited the problems of the families of the striking employees.

Mr. Harrison became aware of the newsletter on his return from vacation and when he discovered that the first issue had already been circulated he decided to let Owen continue its publication. He warned Owen, however, to restrict the newsletter to matters that concerned the employees of Harrison Industries, and to refrain from publishing articles such as the one dealing with the strike at their competitor's plant.

Before the second issue was prepared for publication Owen received the following submissions:

1. A letter from Anderson reporting that the strike had been settled at Harrison Industries' competitor's plant and that the union had won a substantial wage increase, a generous pension plan, and two additional holidays with pay. The letter did not elaborate on the cost of the strike nor did it indicate the amount of the wage increase. Anderson requested that the letter be printed as a response to the article in the first issue.

2. A letter from Joseph Lewicki stating that certain employees in the plant were circulating union information sheets and signing up members on company time. His letter concluded with the opinion that this practice should be stopped by management and that, in his view, employees engaging in this activity on company time should be dismissed.

3. A letter from Allen announcing a "Union Information Meeting" to be held at a local hotel and inviting all employees of Harrison Industries to attend.

Owen decided to publish a notice to employees prohibiting any union activity on the premises during working hours and included in it dismissal as a penalty. Copies of the notice were also posted on all plant bulletin boards.

Owen rejected Allen's letter for publication and informed him that the newsletter was only open to employees of Harrison Industries.

Owen included Anderson's letter in the second issue of the newsletter but in a parallel column set out a comparison of the benefits obtained by the competitor with the wages paid by Harrison Industries to show that Harrison Industries still paid wage rates equal to its competition.

On August 8, 1983, Anderson and another employee were working on the loading ramp of the Shipping Department and, while the foreman observed them, Anderson stopped work and took some papers from his pocket. Anderson talked to his fellow worker for several minutes, apparently discussing the papers, then handed the material to the employee.

A few minutes later, the foreman asked the employee what he and Anderson had been taking about. The employee replied that Anderson had been trying to convince him that he should join the union. The employee gave his foreman the papers which Anderson had given him and the foreman discovered that they consisted of a union application form and a copy of the union constitution for Local 313.

On the advice of Owen and the plant manager, the foreman dismissed Anderson later that afternoon for violation of company rules.

On August 9, 1983, Anderson filed a complaint with the Labour Relations Board alleging that he had been unfairly terminated by Harrison Industries.

A new membership drive was conducted by Allen in August of 1983 and met with a favourable response by the employees of Plant #2. As a result of careful recruitment of members, proper documentation of memberships, and the payment of membership fees, an application for certification by the union in September of 1983 proved to be successful. The union was certified as the bargaining agent of the production and maintenance employees at Plant #2 of Harrison Industries on September 26, 1983.

During the union's organizing campaign, a change also took place in the management organization of Harrison Industries. James Owen resigned as Personnel Manager, and William Hamilton, a recent university graduate with two years' experience in the Personnel Department of a large pulp and paper company, joined the firm as his successor.

CASE DISCUSSION QUESTIONS
HARRISON INDUSTRIES CASE (C)

1. *What are the implications of Owen's use of the newsletter? What limitations are imposed on its use with respect to the employer's right of free speech?*

2. *Assess Anderson's activities during working hours.*
3. *Evaluate the action taken by the foreman with respect to Anderson.*
4. *What problems should Hamilton deal with first in his new position? What should his long-run goals be in the personnel area?*
5. *What demands will the union likely make on Harrison Industries? How would these demands be determined or formulated?*
6. *How should the company prepare for collective bargaining?*
7. *In view of the past relations between the company and the union, what type of bargaining might take place?*

PART IV
THE NEGOTIATION PROCESS

CHAPTER SEVEN

THE NEGOTIATION PROCESS

THE LEGAL FRAMEWORK

The negotiation process is a process whereby the employer and a trade union that represents a defined group of employees determine the terms and conditions of employment which will govern the employment relationship for a specific period of time. The process begins at a point when a certified trade union gives the employer notice in writing of its desire to bargain, or when the employer voluntarily recognizes the union as the exclusive bargaining agent of a unit of employees, and agrees in writing to bargain collectively with it. Once the process is underway, it proceeds according to the prescribed timetable and conditions set out in the collective bargaining legislation.

Some provinces dictate that the bargaining must be conducted "*in good faith* with a view to making a collective agreement." Except for certain clauses which the law requires the parties to include in the written agreement, the subject matter is left entirely in the hands of the employer and the union. If the parties reach an agreement, the process ends; if they do not, public policy in most jurisdictions requires the parties to proceed through a state-imposed process of third party assistance that may take the form of conciliation, mediation, or arbitration of their unresolved differences. The nature of the assistance will depend in part upon the wishes of the parties and the employer's particular industry or service. In the private sector, with the exception of Saskatchewan, third party assistance is generally in the form of conciliation or mediation of the dispute, while in the public sector, all three forms of assistance are provided, and in some cases arbitration will be obligatory, if mediation or conciliation fails to resolve their differences. However, collective bargaining legislation which has general application in each province usually provides for interest arbitration as a voluntary route which the parties themselves are free to follow if they so desire. Compulsory arbitration as a means of establishing a collective agreement when ordinary negotiations fail is normally found in special legislation which applies to the negotiation process in specific types of industry or the service sectors such as hospitals, fire protection, and similar essential services. Collective bargaining as it relates to employees and unions in these areas of employment are examined in a subsequent chapter of the text; but for the present, it should be noted that collective bargaining legislation generally prescribes some form of third party assistance during the negotiation process in an effort to reduce or postpone the use of economic force as a weapon in the course of the bargaining.

The legal framework in which the bargaining takes place and in which the third party assistance is provided is subject to a certain amount of provincial variation, but the overall format (with the exception of Saskatchewan) is much the same: the parties must meet and bargain. If they fail to resolve their differences by way of negotiation, then they must call for third party assistance as specified in the labour legislation. The strike or lock-out is postponed throughout the negotiation and third party assistance phases of the bargaining, and only when the parties have exhausted the third party assistance procedures are they permitted to take economic action to force an agreement. The entire procedure takes place within a legislated time-frame that attempts to postpone disruptive action for a period of time sufficient to allow third parties to work effectively with the parties. The detailed steps in the procedure are typically[1] as follows:

1. *Written notice to bargain is given by the union to the employer.*
2. *The employer must meet with the union within fifteen days after receipt of the notice, or at a later date agreed upon by the parties.*
3. *At the meeting, and the subsequent meetings, the parties are obliged to bargain (in good faith) with a view to making a collective agreement.*
4. *Any collective agreement made by the parties must be in writing, and most jurisdictions require the agreement to contain a clause whereby the employer recognizes the union as the exclusive bargaining representative of the employees in the bargaining unit, a clause whereby the parties agree that there will be no strikes or lock-outs while the agreement is in operation, and a clause which provides for the resolution of any disputes arising out of the agreement by way of binding arbitration.[2] In addi-*

tion to these required clauses, the agreement must identify the parties, and specify the period of time that it will remain in effect. If the parties fail to specify the term, it is deemed to be one year.

5. In Ontario, if the parties cannot reach an agreement, either party may apply to the Minister of Labour for the province or a designated official for the appointment of a conciliation officer to assist them in the resolution of their differences. The conciliation officer usually has fourteen days to meet with the parties and report back to the Minister, and provision is made to allow the conciliation officer additional time, if he or she believes that the parties are close to agreement.

6. If the conciliation officer reports that the parties have not reached an agreement, the Minister of Labour may appoint a conciliation board as a further body to assist the parties. The board is a representative board, and both the employer and the union are requested to appoint a member. The two persons so appointed select a third party to be the chairman, but if they cannot agree, the Minister of Labour may appoint the third member to the board. The board then arranges a meeting with the parties to hear their respective arguments on the matters in dispute, and must report to the Minister, usually within thirty days of the date of its first meeting with the parties. Again, provision is made for the extension of the thirty-day period if the additional time might produce an agreement.

7. As an alternative to conciliation, the parties may decide to name a mediator to assist them in the resolution of their differences. The selection of a mediator at any time during the conciliation process terminates the conciliation, and substitutes mediation. The mediator selected by the parties then has the thirty-day time period that is usually granted to a conciliation board to work with the parties and help them settle the issues in dispute. Within the time specified, the mediator reports to the Minister in much the same manner as the Chairman of the conciliation board in order that the Minister will be aware of the outcome of the mediation.

8. On the receipt of the report of the conciliation board, or mediator, the Minister is expected to take steps to release it immediately. However, if he should decide not to appoint a conciliation board, notice of the decision must be promptly given to the parties, as the release of the report or the notice of the

decision not to appoint a conciliation board determines the time when the parties may resort to strike or lock-out action.

9. *A full seven-day period is provided for the parties to review and discuss the report of the conciliation board before any strike or lock-out action may take place. If the Minister should decide not to appoint a conciliation board, then the parties are obliged to wait fourteen clear days before a strike or lock-out may commence. In Ontario, the parties must, in effect, wait sixteen days following the release of the notice to permit the full fourteen day waiting period to expire, as the report is deemed to be released on the second day after it is mailed to the parties.*

10. *Where employees have engaged in strike action and the strike has continued for a very long period of time (six months or more), in some provinces the legislation provides for a vote of the employees on the final offer made by the employer, and if the offer is accepted by a majority of the employees, the terms of the offer would form the collective agreement, and end the strike.[3] In some jurisdictions, provision is also made for the submission of any outstanding issues to voluntary binding arbitration. Under this procedure, an arbitration hearing would be held and the decision of the arbitrator would establish the collective agreement.[4]*

Once a collective agreement is in effect, changes in the existing agreement on its expiry, or the negotiation of a new agreement follows a similar procedure. Most collective agreements provide for the renegotiation of the agreement on written notice, usually several months, and in some cases as early as six months prior to the expiry date of the agreement to allow ample time for the parties to meet and negotiate what they believe to be necessary changes in the existing document. Labour legislation in most jurisdictions provides that notice to bargain for a revised agreement may be given by either party at any time during the last two or three months before the existing agreement expires, or at an earlier date if the collective agreement so provides. Notice in writing given within the time period specified in the collective agreement or statute has the effect of initiating the negotiation process set out in the statute, and once the written notice is received by either the employer or the union, the party in receipt of the notice must arrange to meet with the other party within the time-frame specified in the legislation, and bargain with a view to making a new agreement. The entire process of negotiation, conciliation or mediation then comes into play as if the negotiations were for a first agreement, and no strike or lock-out may take place until the process is exhausted.

THE THEORETICAL FRAMEWORK

Some economists treat labour (from a theoretical point of view) as a commodity in much the same fashion as they consider goods: something that may be bought and sold. The seller of the labour is the employee, and the buyer is the employer. The selling price is determined through negotiation between the parties, with the seller anxious to sell at the highest possible price, and the buyer equally as anxious to buy at the lowest price. In this theoretical situation, the minimum price at which a person will sell his or her labour would be at a point where the trade-off between work and leisure would just favour work over doing nothing, or making some alternate use of time such as tending a garden, hunting, fishing or bartering services for necessary goods. In modern society, this theoretical minimum would probably be somewhere around the point where the wages offered by the employer were slightly greater than the welfare payments provided by the government. Both of these price minima represent an oversimplification of the true situation, as many other factors enter into the determination of the minimum price at which a person will sell his or her labour. The minimum wage fixed by government legislation, for example, represents a "floor price" which an employer must pay, and this amount may exceed the welfare payment available in the particular jurisdiction where the employer and employee reside.

In addition, many other factors enter into the decision which determines the minimum acceptable price for a person's labour. These factors would include the availability of alternative job opportunities, the need for funds, the conditions under which the work would be performed, and nonmonetary benefits associated with the work itself, such as social status, social contacts, and personal satisfaction. Consequently, the desire to work or to obtain the benefits provided by employment constitute an important part of wage determination by persons who wish to sell their labour.

In contrast, the employer, as a buyer of services, is presumed to be anxious to purchase the labour at the lowest possible price. While in most instances this price is subject to a minimum fixed by statute, many other factors also come into play in the determination of the price that an employer is prepared to pay for the employee's services. These factors would include the need to retain skilled employees and the cost of training new employees, the wages paid by other employees competing for the same services, the importance of labour cost as a component of the employer's product, and the ability of the employer to pass along wage costs to the buyers of the firm's products. Apart from these factors would be the many social considerations of the employer such as the desire on the part of the employer to share profits and benefits with the employees for their efforts. The price, nonetheless, is subject to a maximum above which the employer will not hire employees. This point would be where the employer could not profitably operate the particular business because of the high price demanded by the employees for their labour.

In general terms, the price at which labour will be bought and sold between employees and employers will fall between the minimum wage, and the point at which it would no longer be profitable for an employer to hire employees to operate the business. Within this range the buyer and seller negotiate a price for the labour acceptable to both parties. In a non-union setting, these negotiations are carried on between the employer and the individual employee as principals.

The insertion of a labour union in the negotiation process radically changes the method of determination of the price of labour, since the negotiations no longer take place between individual employees and the employer. Individual considerations are replaced by the collective desires of all of the employees, and in addition, those of the union. In particular, the union must prove its worth by obtaining from the employer benefits which the employee would perceive as being unobtainable on an individual basis or through another union. Consequently, for its own preservation as a bargaining agent, the union must normally negotiate a wage level for employees that exceeds the minimum wage fixed by the state, and which also exceeds that which the employees might obtain through individual negotiation.

The forms of organization of modern business have also introduced other determinants of the wage rate that would not be present in the individual employer-employee relationship. In most larger businesses, the corporate form of organization has largely replaced the individual owners with a professional management team that is expected to carry on the business in an efficient and profitable manner. The shareholders of the corporation through a board of directors establish general policy guidelines for the managers, but the shareholders seldom play an active part in the operation of the business. The management team, as a result, must negotiate a price for labour which would enable the firm to remain not only competitive, but profitable; otherwise it will be replaced by the owners of the business. This pressure on the employer negotiators, as with the union, introduces a further determinant of the wage rate which will exert a downward pressure on the price that the firm would be prepared to pay to some point in the range that will maintain the firm in a competitive and profitable position in the market.

All of these factors tend to narrow the range in which an acceptable price for labour may fall, and negotiations between unions and management generally produce an agreed rate which will be located somewhere between the wage rates where the employees or the employer would replace the union or management. For example, if the minimum wage in a province is $4.00/hour and the wage rate which the employees negotiated on an individual basis was $8.00/hour average, the union would be expected to obtain for the employees something in excess of $8.00/hour. From the employer's side, if the firm would no longer be profitable when the wage rate exceeded, say $12.00/hour, the management of the firm would be obliged to hold wage rates to some point below $12.00/hour and perhaps below $10.00/hour if the business was to be considered profitable from the point of view of the existing shareholders and potential investors. The management must, therefore, resist wage demands in excess of $10.00/hour to satisfy the shareholders. While initial offers or demands may fall outside these limits, the final negotiation range will normally fall between $8.00 and $10.00, and in theory will be settled at a point where the negotiators would be prepared to accept a compromise wage rate rather than resort to the uncertainty of a strike or lock-out to achieve a rate outside this narrow range.

This theoretical setting is subject to a number of very important variables, the relative bargaining power of the parties being one of the most important determinants of where the final rate will be fixed. One of the principal reasons why employees form or join unions has always been the desire to increase their bargaining power *vis-à-vis* that of their employer. In terms of pure power, the employer in an individual bargaining relationship is essentially "all powerful," since in theory at least, he would control the opportunity for employment. In reality, this is not so, because in many instances the employer must have the services of the employee in order to function, and where the employee possesses a special skill which is not readily available in the area, the employee may very well be able to bargain from a position of considerable strength. However, individual employees with only ordinary skills to offer the employer seldom find themselves in this position. Collective negotiation with the employer, therefore, with the resulting enhancement of their bargaining power generally represents an attractive alternative to individual bargaining. The amount of power which a group of employees will possess through a trade union will generally be determined by their ability as a group to affect the operation of the employers' business if they should withdraw their services. This will vary depending upon such factors as the seasonal nature of the employers' business, the ability of the employer to operate with only the services of supervisory staff, or the ability of the employer to shift production elsewhere during a strike. For example, in a highly automated plant such as a refinery or hydroelectric facility, the number of employees required to operate the equipment would be relatively small. Any withdrawal of their services would perhaps not be of serious concern to the employer if supervisory staff could continue to maintain the equipment and keep it functioning. The bargaining power of the employees in these circumstances would be relatively low, as their ability to impose a significant economic burden on the employer's business would be slight. The ability of the employer to operate at or near full capacity with only slight inconvenience for a lengthy period of time would render the strike ineffective as a bargaining tool.

DETERMINANTS OF BARGAINING POWER

The bargaining power of employees is generally based upon a number of factors, the most important being the organization of the employer's production facilities. If the employer has many plants in different areas, each represented by a different union, and self-sufficient in the sense that production is not dependent upon an uninterrupted flow of goods from other employer-owned plants, a strike at any one facility will not necessarily affect the firm's business. Conversely, if the plants are interdependent, and a strike at one could affect the entire operation, the employer's bargaining power would be lower, since a strike at any one plant would have an enormous impact on the employer's business unless he stockpiled inventory to allow the remaining plants to operate during the strike.

A large inventory of goods on hand will also enhance the bargaining power of the employer, even where the employer has only a single plant operation. Basically, the larger the inventory, the longer the strike which the employer could endure before the lost production would have a financial impact on the business. Similarly, if the employer's business is seasonal in nature (such as a fresh vegetable processing plant) the threat of a strike after the production season ends would have little or no effect on the employer's operation unless, of course, the union could prevent the movement of goods from inventory by picket lines.

The nature of an employer's business may also be a factor in the determination of the bargaining power which he might possess. If the industry is highly competitive, and the product essentially undifferentiated, any interruption in the business by a lengthy strike might result in the permanent loss of customers. For example, in the trucking industry, the shutdown of one firm by a strike will cause its customers to shift to competing companies, and at the end of the strike the customers may not return. In this case, the competitive nature of the industry would tend to be a factor that would lessen or weaken the bargaining power of the employer, and conversely enhance the power of the union.

The bargaining power of the union is determined in part by its ability to support a lengthy strike. The size of its strike fund, or its ability to enlist the financial support of other unions are generally the governing factors in this regard, but the timing aspect is also important. To call a strike in the employer's off-season, or while a seasonal business is shutdown would ensure a lengthy strike as there would be little incentive on the employer's part to settle the dispute during the time interval. Both of these factors therefore determine the bargaining power of the union.

The nature of the issues that are the subject of the disagreement are also important. Employees are usually in strong support of those issues such as wage increases, vacation pay, and hours of work that affect them personally, but are often only mildly interested in such matters as union security clauses and issues of interest to only a small number of employees. The degree of commitment to the cause is consequently an important factor in the determination of the union's bargaining power. Commitment of the rank and file is also closely coupled with the ability of the strikers to effectively shut down the employer's operations through picketing. In this respect the union's bargaining power is largely the converse of that of the employer. Where the strike has only a limited impact on the employer's overall operations, the union's bargaining power will be low, but if it is in a position to shut down a key plant successfully, its bargaining power will be high for the reasons set out previously.

Some years ago, Neil Chamberlain, a noted U.S. labour expert, examined the nature of the bargaining power that the parties to collective bargaining possessed and determined that the bargaining power of one party was essentially a ratio of the perceived cost of the other party disagreeing over the cost of agreeing with the proposed terms.[5] He concluded that bargaining power could be expressed in terms of the willingness of a party to agree or disagree with proposed terms of a collective agreement, and that the bargaining power which, say, a union possessed, would be determined by the perceived cost which the employer would have if he agreed or disagreed with the proposal. If the cost of disagreeing with the union's proposal was extremely high, and the cost of agreeing with the proposal was low, the union's bargaining power would be substantial. However, if the cost of agreeing was high and the cost of disagreeing low, such as in the example given above where the employer could continue to operate at full capacity, then the union's bargaining power would also be low, as any exercise of the power would not inflict any serious cost or economic injury on the employer's business. The use of a strike by the union under these circumstances would unlikely be effective, and unless other factors come into play, the settlement that the parties would finally reach would probably be closer to the terms that the employer would propose for the collective agreement, since the employer's bargaining power would be much greater than that possessed by the employees.

To consider bargaining power alone, however, would be to oversimplify the negotiation process. While each of the parties will generally make efforts to enhance its bargaining power as it is perceived by the other party through such activities as the manipulation of agreement expiry dates (to have them fall at times when a strike or lock-out would have the greatest impact on the other) or through stockpiling inventory, or building large strike funds, the power sometimes cannot be used. For example, in the North American automobile industry, recent, strong competition from foreign manufacturers prevented the unions from exercising their bargaining power in order that some manufacturers might survive, even though the reorganization of the employer's production facilities would mean the loss of many jobs. Until that point in time, union bargaining power was generally used on a selective basis in the industry, but in all cases the use was to establish what was essentially a uniform wage rate. Because the large car market was North American, the costs of disagreeing with the union were not regarded as high by the employers, since the increased labour costs could readily be passed along to the consumer. Foreign competition in the latter part of the 1970s, however, changed consumer demand from the large to small motor vehicles, and the industry suddenly found itself in a competitive situation where it could no longer pass along higher wage costs. At the same time it faced a costly reorganization of manufacturing facilities. The employers were not in a strong bargaining position at this point, but the unions could not exercise their power for fear that it might precipitate even greater layoffs in the industry.

It should be noted that political power may be used to limit or curb the exercise of bargaining power as witnessed in the public sector by the imposition in 1982–83 of the "6 and 5" wage ceilings for all federal public sector employees to halt the inflationary spiral of wages and prices. The effect of this exercise of political power was to eliminate collective bargaining on wage matters by the public service unions, the principal area of negotiation where bargaining power was used. Moral suasion of others is another means by which a party might reduce the bargaining power of a strong opponent and enhance that of the weaker party. In the case of unions, a union with relatively low bargaining power *vis-à-vis* that of the employer may be able to convince other union members employed by the employer to respect their picket lines if they should call a strike, and in so doing, effectively close down the employer's plant, even though the employer might otherwise have been able to operate. Similarly, where a large and powerful union negotiates with many small, economically weak employers, the employers may agree amongst themselves that as a group they will shut down their operations if the union should call a strike at any one firm, and in this fashion attempt to balance the union's power.

Some observers of the bargaining process have attempted to explain the effect of the use of power in the determination of wages and other benefits. J.R. Hicks, an English economist, viewed the establishment of wage rates by way of a model which depicted the settlement in terms of union and employer perceptions of the length of time that a strike might take to achieve a particular result. He suggested that the demands of the union might be depicted on a chart at the highest rate it might possibly expect then gradually decrease in the light of its view of the length of time that a strike might be required to achieve the rate in question. When plotted on a chart, he described this path as the union's **resistance curve**. Similarly, he suggested that the employer would initially wish to pay the lowest wage possible, but would be prepared to raise the rate in terms of the length of time that he would be obliged to close down operations to achieve the particular rate. Hicks described this curve as the employer's **concession curve**. When the employer's concession curve and the union resistance curve are plotted on a time/rate chart, the two curves might appear as follows:

EXHIBIT 7-1

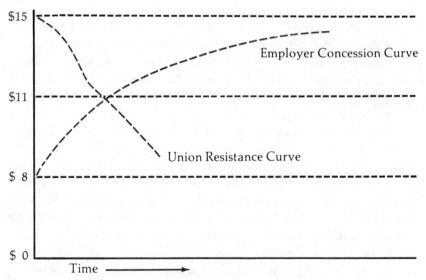

Diagram adapted from: J.R. Hicks, *The Theory of Wages* (2nd ed.) London, Eng.: MacMillan & Co. Ltd. (1963).

Using the chart as an example, if the union's initial demand is $15/hour for wages, the union will reduce the demand if it believes that a lengthy strike would be necessary to achieve that rate (i.e., where the employer's concession curve would reach that rate). As the chart indicates, the length of the strike required to achieve a $15 wage rate would be long indeed as the employer's concession curve tends to flatten as the time increases, and the achievement of the particular rate might not be possible.

On the other hand, the union's resistance curve tends to move in a downward direction at a much steeper rate because of the cost of a lengthy strike to the union and the employees. If the employer accurately knows the path that this curve will follow, he may determine the length of time that the employees will remain on strike before they will be prepared to accept his initial wage offer of $8/hour. This is clearly a much shorter time than the time interval for a strike that the union must endure to gain its initial demand of $15/hour. Hicks suggests that the wage rate at which the parties will likely agree will be where the two curves intersect, in this case at $11/hour.

Hicks bases his model on the assumption that both parties have a full and accurate picture of the time-frame and the path that each curve will follow if a strike should occur. Unfortunately, this is rarely the case, as each party operates on incomplete information and knowledge of the opponent's position. It should also be noted that the path that each curve may follow can and does change during the course of negotiations. For example, if the employer should receive a large "rush order" for goods during the bargaining, it may be imperative that he avoid a strike to meet his commitments. Similarly, if the union should receive a pledge of financial support for its strike fund from another union, the slope of its resistance curve would also change. Hick's theory has been subject to considerable criticism, but nevertheless, the theory does tend to depict the respective bargaining power of each party in a general way, bearing in mind the inaccuracy which is imposed by the lack of information that exists in the conventional bargaining situation.

BARGAINING THEORY

The negotiation process is essentially a continuous process which has as a starting point the time when the parties begin their preparation for the negotiation sessions. For the union, this prenegotiation phase or stage consists of union meetings called for the purpose of determining the various demands which the members wish to have included on the list of items for discussion and further research by the union prior to the finalization of its proposals for negotiation. These demands are usually examined by a committee which will investigate the feasibility of each item and determine if it should be included. Occasionally, a union may present management with a list that includes virtually all of the proposals of the membership, knowing full well that many will be rejected by the employer. The benefit of this approach to the union is that the important demands of the union can be obscured and thus preserved, while the less important or unreasonable demands may be later used as a trade-off to the employer to give some semblance of a co-operative attitude at the bargaining table. The added advantage is that the presentation will satisfy the rank and file that their particular concerns were brought to the attention of their employer by the union.

The prenegotiation stage of the process also includes the research and accumulation of data to support the demands of the union at the bargaining table, since each must be justified by the union if it expects to convince the employer that the demand should be included in the agreement. The final step in the process involves the selection of a union bargaining team or negotiating committee that will conduct the negotiations for the union. This group may vary in size, but usually includes some members of the local union executive, representatives from major departments or special skilled groups in the employer's business, and often a field representative from the international union.

Preparation for bargaining by the employer (where the parties are negotiating their first collective agreement) will usually consist of an analysis of the employer's competitive position in the market, and the determination of the proposals and monetary limits which might be included in a collective agreement, yet permit the firm to remain competitive. A considerable amount of research will be carried out to assemble data on all likely bargaining demands that the union might bring forward, and also to support any demands that the firm might wish to bring forward itself. In addition, the employer bargaining team will be selected well in advance of the first meeting with the union. It will normally include a chief negotiator (who might be employed for the purpose if the firm does not have an experienced negotiator in the ranks of senior management), management representatives from the finance area, and perhaps others from areas of the firm, depending upon the type of bargaining unit. If the bargaining unit is a plant unit, the plant manager, and perhaps management personnel from production or engineering departments might be included. Usually someone from the personnel or human resources area of the firm is involved if the chief negotiator is brought in from the outside, otherwise the chief negotiator is generally from the Personnel/Labour Relations Department, and usually its director or manager. The management committee, once formed, generally conducts an assessment of the union committee if its composition is known, in an effort to determine the key decision makers in the group, and to identify the various bargaining interests of each member. Such an assessment is often useful later in the negotiations when the trade-off of demands takes place, and it is useful as well to know which items are of importance to the individual members of the union committee.

While all of this activity takes place in the prenegotiation stage of the bargaining, the most important overall action taken is the preparation of the list of demands or proposals which the union will present to management at the first negotiation session. The list is often long, and will include essentially three types of proposals:

1. *Those which are of critical or utmost importance, which must be resolved during the negotiations.*
2. *Those which are also important, but which represent some of the long-run goals of the union. The purpose of their introduction at the initial negotiations is essentially to introduce the proposals for future negotiations when they will be the central issues at the bargaining table. While they may be either dropped or traded-off during the first negotiations, they serve notice to the employer of the nature of the bargaining proposals that may surface in the future.*
3. *The third group is often composed of a great many of the remaining proposals put forward by individual rank and file members. These issues, which generally have a low priority, serve the useful purpose of representing employee concerns which the process will bring to the attention of management by way of the bargaining table. In most cases they are recognized by the employer as low priority matters that the union will not seriously pursue. They are usually dropped or withdrawn early on in the negotiations, but nevertheless enable the union to satisfy its membership by bringing them forward, and at the same time shift the responsibility for their rejection to management.*

The negotiation process moves into its second phase or stage when the actual negotiation sessions begin. At the first meeting initial bargaining positions are normally taken on the long list of proposals. These are typically extreme on those issues that will require much discussion and compromise, such as wages and similar cost-related proposals, but to mask true positions on key demands, the initial positions taken on some issues are often close to the expected settlement range.

Initial positions are usually expressed in lengthy speeches and posturing which tends to give the impression that the party's position is firm and unmoveable, and to the uninitiated, may give the impression that the differences between the two sides are unreconcilable. In reality, the posturing and the strong arguments serve to express not only the degree of commitment that the party has to a position, but the general range in which settlement might be expected. An experienced negotiator may use such opening settlements to convey this information to his counterpart, while at the same time appear to discredit all counterargument rigorously.

The presentation of initial demands and the accompanying argument and posturing are normally followed rather quickly by a certain amount of probing and exploration of the opponent's positions to determine where compromise might take place. Considerable skill is required in order to conduct this type of maneuver properly, as the negotiator must do so without revealing his own position in the process, and not until satisfied that he has properly determined the willingness of his opponent to move from an initial demand. This phase of the process is characterized by exhaustive discussion of each issue while each party searches for those bits and pieces of information that represent clues as to the possible range where compromise may take place. Unimportant demands or proposals are often dropped or withdrawn during this stage of the negotiations as the parties tend to narrow their area of concentration to the issues that have been determined to be the most important.

When the key issues have been identified and thoroughly discussed, the negotiations reach the critical stage, for it is at this point where final positions must be taken. It is also at this time when the possibility of a strike or lock-out looms large in the minds of the negotiators. Skill in the presentation of final positions on the issues often determines the success or failure of the negotiations at this stage, and it is here that third party assistance such as mediation often proves to be useful if the parties somehow fail to find common ground. If they should succeed in reaching a settlement, however, the process does not end. It moves to the postnegotiation phase or stage, where the terms and conditions agreed upon during the negotiation sessions are reduced to writing in language acceptable to both parties. This final stage is generally short, but nevertheless important, as the use of ambiguous language in the preparation of the collective agreement may lead to interpretation problems during the time that the agreement is in effect. Consequently, both parties at this point generally strive for clear language in the writing of agreement clauses of special or particular interest to them. Occasionally, where the parties agree in principle, but cannot agree on the precise wording, the clause may be deliberately left ambiguous for interpretation later. However, what happens more often is that each has considered the clause clear by way of his or her own interpretation, when in fact the wording is unclear due to the fact that two distinct interpretations may be taken from the wording of the clause. Because such circumstances can only lead to disputes at a later time, the negotiation of the proper wording should be treated as an important part of the bargaining process.

The negotiation process, and in particular, the bargaining aspect of the process, has been the subject of much scrutiny by a number of theoreticians in different disciplines. Neil Chamberlain, J. Pen,[6] Carl M. Stevens,[7] and D. B. Mabry[8] examined the process as economists. Thomas C. Schelling[9] investigated it as a game theorist, and Richard E. Walton and Robert B. McKersie[10] analyzed the procedure as behavioural theorists. The result of these many and varied investigations has been a mix of theories as diverse as the disciplinary backgrounds of the investigators themselves.

As noted earlier, Neil Chamberlain examined the bargaining process in terms of the perceived costs of agreeing and disagreeing with an opponent at the bargaining table. Pen, in turn, took the Chamberlain model and developed it in a different way. Pen reasoned that the parties to negotiations constantly assess the proposals made during the negotiation process in terms of values and costs, where each proposal has a value established for it and an attendant cost if the other party refuses to accept the proposal. He suggests that the parties engage in a variety of bargaining tactics and strategies to convince their opponents that the proposals made have a high cost if rejected, and either a relatively low cost, or a high value, if accepted. By this theory, bargaining tactics and strategies are utilized to alter the perceived costs and values associated with the proposals in an effort to gain acceptance of those proposals which will have the highest value and least cost to the proposer. In effect, the parties use the tactics in an attempt to maximize their power to satisfy their needs.

Carl M. Stevens borrowed from psychological theory in the formulation of his theory on the negotiation process, and utilized a conflict/choice model as its basis. He suggests that each of the parties at the bargaining table is faced with two essentially negative choices which each attempts to avoid: to accept a proposal on their opponent's terms, or to demand acceptance on their own terms, and pay the cost of the strike or lock-out that would likely result. Stevens argues that the parties will attempt to avoid these extremes through negotiation where compromise is sought using bargaining tactics and strategies. The process is used to seek and exchange information in an effort to determine where the area of compromise might lie, and the tactics or strategies are used (as in Pen's theory) to influence or alter the opponent's perceptions of proposals. Unlike Pen, however, Stevens suggests that the strategies are used to enhance the unattractiveness of the opponent's proposals, and to enhance the attractiveness of the alternative.

For example, an employer is faced with two unacceptable choices at the bargaining table. One is the wage demand of the union, which, if accepted, would perhaps render the firm unprofitable or non-competitive in the market. The other is the cost of the strike that would likely occur if the employer insists that the wages remain unchanged. To avoid these, the employer will seek to reduce the union's wage demands by using tactics or adopting a strategy that attempts to alter the union's perception of the cost of achieving its goal.

Similarly, the union is faced with two equally unattractive choices: accept the existing wage rate (which might result in displacement of the union, or at least its executive) or insist on its entire wage demand, probably resulting in a lengthy strike (or lock-out) which in the end might fail. To avoid these two extremes, the union will also attempt to alter the employer's perception of its position.

Since the strategies of each of the parties are designed to move their opponents away from their unacceptable extremes, the bargaining process, and in particular the information exchanged in the process, tends to move both to a compromise position.

Where these positions overlap or meet, a settlement results. Stevens suggests that in terms of his model this point occurs when each party's desire to avoid each of the alternatives has moved to an equilibrium point between the two. In chart form, Steven's model for the employer would be as on page 193.

According to the Stevens model, lines A and B represent **avoidance gradients**. The solid vertical lines represent the strength of the desire to avoid the particular alternatives. From the chart, the avoidance gradients slope downwards to indicate that the further away from the alternative the party moves, the strength to avoid it decreases. The slope is determined by the strength of the desire to avoid the one alternative as opposed to the other. The point of intersection of the two avoidance gradients lines is the **equilibrium point (E)**, where the strength of the desire to avoid one alternative is equal to the strength

EXHIBIT 7-2

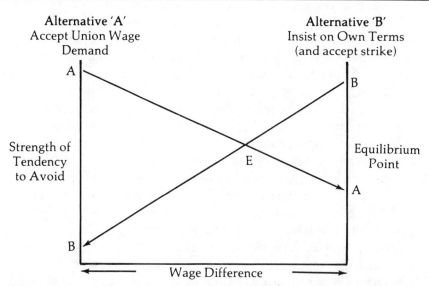

SOURCE: Carl M. Stevens. *Strategy and Collective Bargaining Negotiation.* N.Y.: McGraw-Hill Book Company Inc. (1963) p. 15. Westport, Connecticut: Greenwood Press (1978). Copyright © by Carl M. Stevens.

of the desire to avoid the other. Any move away from point E towards either alternative would increase the strength of the tendency or desire to avoid that alternative, and produce a move by the employer back to the equilibrium point. A similar model may be developed for the union.

Agreement on the particular issue would theoretically occur when the equilibrium points for the employer and the union on their respective charts overlap. In practice, however, agreement will only occur when the two parties realize that overlap has occurred, something which does not always happen in the negotiation process due to inaccurate information, a lack of communication, or inaccurate perceptions of the true state of affairs.

A few years after Stevens developed his avoidance model, D. B. Mabry developed a different theory of bargaining whereby he considered the process to be one of "trade-offs," where the parties attempt to trade off penalties for rewards, with each using bargaining tactics in an effort to maximize their gain and minimize their penalties. As with both Pen and Stevens, Mabry sees the use of bargaining tactics and strategies as the primary means by which the perception of the opponent is altered. In Mabry's case, however, the tactics and strategies are used to alter the opponent's perception of any penalties or rewards which are the subject of trade-offs used to arrive at a settlement. Since the settlement in effect is conceived in terms of **net gains** by the parties, the strategies and tactics are used to convince opponents that the net gain in one proposal is such that other potential settlements would be less likely to produce an equivalent positive gain.

Thomas Schelling examined the bargaining process in terms of game theory, and hypothesized that much of the activity which constitutes collective bargaining concerns the distribution of limited resources between the employer and the employees, with the result that bargaining is distributional, and tends to be a "win-lose" or zero-sum game. The attitude of the parties consequently tends to be adversarial, and the tactics and strategies adopted tend to be directed to achieving goals which are often in conflict. He also examined the use of bargaining power and its use in the negotiation process. Schelling observed that bargaining power is not always synonomous with strength as it is ordinarily known, since power can only be used effectively when the adversary is aware of its existence, and comprehends the threat of its use. Schelling also suggests that bargaining power has a strong relationship to commitment, and that bargaining tactics and strategies may be used to convince an opponent that one is bound to a particular commitment in order to induce the opponent to move closer to the commitment.

In essence, his theory is that where one party is able to convince the other that he or she is so committed to a position or course of action (that the opponent finds more distasteful than conceding) and that no amount of persuasion will move the party from the commitment, then the opponent will move to accept the position or course of action rather than suffer the consequences that would flow from the commitment. The party with the bargaining power in this type of situation is considered to be the party prepared to make the commitment if that party can convince the other negotiating party that the only possible course of action open is to accept the position stated in the commitment.

The principal weakness exhibited by the bargaining theories which researchers have proposed is the inability of these theories to bring together the many facets of collective bargaining into a single "package." While some viewed the process from their position as economic theorists, Schelling explained the actions of the parties in terms of game theory. He perhaps set the stage for the behaviouralists with his examination of the process, for it was not long afterwards that the bargaining process became the subject of scrutiny in terms of the behaviour of the parties.

The actions of the negotiators at the bargaining table and the goals that they seek to achieve were the subject of investigation from a behavioural perspective by researchers Richard Walton and Robert McKersie, and from their observations they determined that the negotiation process involved essentially four identifiable types of activity. These were: distributive bargaining, integrative bargaining, attitudinal structuring, and intraorganizational bargaining. **Distributive bargaining** was identified as a type of bargaining activity concerned with a win-lose or gain-loss outcome, a typical example being the negotiation of monetary issues such as wages. With distributive bargaining, a wage increase was a financial loss for the employer since the wage increase would decrease the profits which he might otherwise have enjoyed. It is essentially a zero-sum game activity, and represents the area of bargaining characterized by much posturing, extreme initial positions on issues, and careful narrowing of the gap between positions in an effort to acquire or retain the largest part of the sum possible, yet still reach a settlement.

Integrative bargaining was the second type of bargaining identified, and may be defined as bargaining which is of a problem-solving nature, where the objective is of a mutual benefit to both parties. In this type of bargaining, the ultimate goal is not in conflict, but the parties may not initially agree on the method of determination or the extent of its application. For example, both the union and management may agree with the principle of job protection for the most senior employees, but the union may wish to use strict seniority as the means of achieving this end. The employer, on the other hand, may agree with the principle, but be concerned that the most senior employees also possess the ability to do the work required if a staff reduction should take place. The type of bargaining about this issue is generally in the form of joint problem solving where the solution sought is one which will satisfy the concerns of both the union and the employer in achieving the goal which they have set out for themselves. In contrast to distributive bargaining, integrative bargaining is usually involved with nonmonetary issues.

Attitudinal structuring as a bargaining process is concerned with changing the basic relationship that exists between the parties. Its goal is to establish a harmonious relationship between the parties, where each has a full appreciation of the problems or needs of the parties to the bargaining. This type of activity might be engaged in by an employer where the union fails to realize the serious nature of an employer's competitive position in an industry. In such a case, the employer is obliged to impress upon the union the need for the union to moderate its demands if the firm is to survive, and to seek ways of making the firm more competitive before the union demands may be met. It is essentially an educational process by which each of the parties attempts to instill in the other an understanding and appreciation of the problems which must be considered at the bargaining table and in the overall relationship.

Intraorganizational bargaining differs from the other three types of bargaining in that it takes place between the chief negotiator of a bargaining team and the organization which the negotiator represents. Most organizations, whether union or employer wish to obtain through the bargaining process much more than their chief negotiator knows that he can realistically deliver. Consequently, intraorganizational bargaining occurs when the chief negotiator realizes that it is necessary to have a reappraisal of the organization's proposals in the light of his assessment of the opponent's position on unresolved issues, and the likelihood of success at the bargaining table. In this type of bargaining, the chief negotiator must convince the organization that his assessment of the opponent's position is correct, and that the best possible settlement that can be achieved would be one which would include revised proposals or demands on the part of the organization. As a general rule in this situation, the chief negotiator will only be successful if he can convince the organization that he has succeeded in obtaining the best bargain possible from his opponent on the issues in question.

In addition to the identification of the four major types of bargaining activity, Walton and McKersie also adopted the terminology first coined by Benjamin Selekman to classify the bargaining relationships which the parties tend to develop.[11] These relationships range along a spectrum from extreme conflict to co-operation in the extreme, depending upon the attitude of the parties towards each other.

At the one end of the spectrum, the relationship is characterized by **conflict**. The employer accepts the union only because the law has directed that the union must be recognized as the exclusive bargaining representative of the employees, and that he must bargain with it. The parties generally dislike each other, and during the negotiation process distrust each other's motives. The bargaining is usually rough and anxious, and best described in terms of victory or defeat when issues are eventually conceded by either side. An example of the relationship might be one in which an anti-union employer is pitted against a doctrinaire socialist-oriented union, where each would be delighted to destroy the other's organization.

A somewhat less antagonistic relationship was described by the researchers as one of **containment-aggression**. In this relationship the employer and the union have accepted each other in the sense that the law has required them to do so. Each, however, is intent upon limiting the power of the other in the bargaining relationship, and the activities of each party are treated with suspicion. The employer and the union tolerate each other, but tend to resolve their disputes only through the threat or use of bargaining power.

A third type of relationship was identified as being less aggressive, and one of **accommodation**. In this case the parties are prepared to accept each other and recognize the legitimacy of the role which each plays. Because the parties have no ideological objection to the existence of the other, the type of bargaining tends to be neutral and directed more in terms of protection of their respective interests and concerns, rather than aggressive containment. Both the employer and the union tend to pursue their own goals rather than actively interfere with the other's organization, and remain content with a relatively formal bargaining relationship.

A stage beyond the accommodation relationship was characterized as one of **co-operation**, where the actions of the parties are generally based upon the full acceptance of each other as integral parts of the firm, and where the two organizations believe that mutual concerns are best resolved in a co-operative manner. The employer and the union tend to be supportive of each other's organization, and collective bargaining is usually conducted in a friendly and constructive atmosphere.

Co-operation in the extreme is the dominant characteristic of the final type of relationship identified by Walton and McKersie. In this instance, co-operation has become **collusive**, and the goals which the parties pursue tend to be exploitive of either the public or some other third party. Each exhibits complete trust in the other's actions, and collective bargaining is conducted in a relatively friendly fashion. Because the union and the employer are engaged in improper or perhaps illegal activity, they are obliged to be supportive of each other's organization. For example, in one community in the United States, a union and an employer who manufactured a line of goods used in the construction industry embarked on a scheme whereby the union required all of the building contractors in the area to purchase the employer's line of products exclusively. The employer acquired a virtual monopoly because the union represented the employees of all of the contractors in the particular trade, and the union could support its part of the bargain through its members, who would refuse to work with any other products. The employer could fix his prices without concern for competition, but in turn, was expected to share some of this wealth with his employees and the union. The agreement between the union and the employer was clearly illegal, and a result of the collusive relationship which the parties had developed.

BARGAINING TACTICS

Skilled negotiators employ a wide variety of tactics during the course of collective bargaining in an effort to achieve a collective agreement which will contain terms and conditions of employment as close as possible to those desired by their principals. Complete success is seldom achieved by negotiators, but negotiating tactics, when skillfully employed, often enable negotiators to come close to their objectives. In the case of distributive bargaining issues such as wages or benefits, the usual approach for the union is to establish an initial demand that is greater than the amount which the union might expect to get in anticipation of the counterarguments and lower offers that the employer might propose during the bargaining. As a general rule, the experienced negotiator will establish a **target rate** which he or she hopes to achieve by the end of the bargaining, then fix an initial demand in excess of this amount to allow for compromise, and to disguise the actual rate sought. The effect of this approach is to hide the target rate from the opponent, and to enable the negotiator to attempt settlement at something greater than this amount if the opponent can be convinced that a greater amount is reasonable. Some care must be taken in the determination of the initial demand, however, because it must appear to be an amount that can be justified by argument. If it is not, then the opponent will recognize the demand as excessive, and label it **blue sky bargaining**. Skilled negotiators expect initial union demands to be inflated to a degree, and in the case of wages, employers generally expect a downward movement or retreat from the union's initial position over the course of the negotiations, but the danger inherent in a demand that is recognized and labelled as "blue sky" is that the employer will perhaps expect the downward movement on the part of the union negotiator to be greater than what the union might anticipate. If the employer determines the union's minimum acceptable rate or **resistance point** to be lower than that which the union has fixed, an agreement will not usually be reached unless the employer can be convinced that he must revise his assessment of what the union's final position on wages actually is. While initial positions taken by unions are usually in the nature of blue sky bargaining, an experienced negotiator generally fixes the initial demand at an amount that is defensible in order to camouflage the amount below which the union is unwilling to move except under extreme pressure, such as an actual strike or lock-out.

Conversely, employers normally establish their opening or initial offers to the union very close to the existing wage rates or benefits which the employees enjoy at the time the bargaining begins. Employers may, of course, introduce new demands as a part of their initial bargaining position, and in times of economic difficulty may propose wage reductions or the elimination of some cost-related benefits enjoyed by the employees. Under normal circumstances, however, this is not done, and the employer's initial position is usually the status quo with perhaps some proposals to broaden or enhance management's rights. As a consequence, employers are generally interested in establishing a new collective agreement with wages and benefits as close as possible to the existing agreement, leaving the union with the obligation to convince them that the old terms and conditions of employment should be changed. To maintain this onus on the union, negotiators for the employer employ the tactic of demanding that the union justify any change in the existing agreement rather than consider a new draft agreement which the union might wish to use as a basis for discussion. This tactic is known as **bargaining from a position**, and has the advantage of requiring the opponent to offer compelling and convincing arguments for movement from the document so chosen. The tactic may of course be used by unions as well where they wish to shift the onus to the employer, but as a rule, most union negotiators have resigned themselves to the fact that they must justify their demands for change.

Current labour relations theorists characterize the practice of movement by the parties from initial demands (or offers) towards their final position or resistance points as a **commitment tactic**. Commitment tactics are designed to convey to the opponent that the negotiator is firmly committed to a particular objective or position on the assumption that a strong commitment, perhaps including the threat of the use of a strike or lock-out to achieve the objective, will convince the opponent that some concession must be made on his or her part to avoid the inevitable resolution of the dispute by way of bargaining power. Commitment tactics are characterized by arguments that put great stress on the importance of the demand, often to the point where the negotiator links his own personal integrity to the acquisition of the objective. It may also be recognized in cases where the union negotiators have raised the expectations of the union members to the point where a failure to achieve a certain goal will precipitate a strike. More often, the tactic is recognized by the presence of a person at the bargaining table whose prestige within the organization is closely related to the particular demand.

The danger associated with commitment tactics is the lack of flexibility which a commitment imposes upon the negotiator. As a rule, once committed to a particular position, movement away from the position is foreclosed without "losing face" or credibility. As a result, experienced negotiators will often use **countercommitment tactics** to prevent an opponent from taking an irrevocable stance on an issue. One of the most common countercommitment tactics used is the structuring of the agenda for meetings in such a way that issues may not be repeatedly raised to permit the repetition of arguments on each. By the arrangement of the agenda for each meeting to include new topics, and to limit discussion to only those topics on the agenda, the opportunity for a negotiator to raise and discuss bargaining positions on particular issues is restricted. Ground rules established by the parties, such as a prohibition on individual press releases or comment to the media during negotiations (which tends to fix positions) or a rule allowing for changes in position on any issue at any time prior to the finalization of the agreement will also provide a certain amount of flexibility and enable persons to retreat from a position without affecting their reputation. These serve to limit the effects of commitment on the negotiators.

Because negotiators must appear to be committed (to some degree at least) to their initial positions, a number of "understandings" or "conventions" have developed over time between negotiators which facilitate the movement away from initial and intermediate positions taken on issues during the course of bargaining. As a rule, movement does not take place until an issue has been thoroughly dealt with, and occasionally this does not occur until all issues have been discussed, and the parties realize that they must make some effort to settle their differences. The desire to make a first concession is often signalled by a statement that expresses a degree of flexibility, but commitment to a broader goal than the particular issue or proposal in question, and invites a similar response. An experienced negotiator will identify such a signal, and will often respond by the expression of an equal degree of flexibility and a request that the opponent speculate as to how his or her position might change if some aspect of the broader issue was altered or revised. For example, a union negotiator might indicate in the course of discussion that the union is concerned about the overall improvement of the employees' wage levels and welfare benefits, but recognizes that the firm must remain competitive to survive as well. This comment might be followed by reference to the benefits package provided by a competitor of the employer, and the suggestion that the union can see no reason why the firm cannot provide at least the equivalent. Such a statement might be taken as a signal to the employer, and the employer response might then be that the union must realize that its wage demand would have to be closer to that of the competitor before the employer could consider anything like the benefit package provided by the competitor. The employer's response in this instance conveys two messages:

1. *It provides the opportunity for the union to revise downward its initial wage proposal.*
2. *It suggests that the employer is prepared to discuss changes in the firm's benefits with some consideration for the proposals of the union based upon the competitor's package.*

Similar signals may be given by other actions of negotiators as well. A proposed **trade-off** of proposals may sometimes be presented whereby one negotiator suggests that he would be prepared to drop a particular proposal if a proposal of his opponent was also dropped or modified. The purpose of this type of comment is to elicit a response which the proposer believes from the attitude of the opponent will be positive, and which will move both parties to their final positions on the two issues. Again, considerable skill is required in "reading" the signals of the other party in order to assess the likelihood of acceptance of the proposal, and only negotiators who have developed an awareness and sensitivity to the verbal and nonverbal communications at the bargaining table successfully utilize these skills.

Other forms of oblique communication may indicate that a negotiator has changed from one position to a point approximating that of the other party. This may occur where the negotiator has firmly rejected a proposal on a number of occasions, and then, when the matter is raised again, says nothing. Silence in this instance may indicate a willingness to concede the issue if the silence on the issue is followed by a suggestion that the parties consider some other issue which is expressed to be of greater concern. Quite often, the raising of the new issue is a signal that the issue previously discussed will be conceded if the parties can work out a satisfactory settlement of the new issue. This signal is based upon the negotiating convention that a concession on an issue by one party will normally be followed by some concession on the part of the other, although the concession need not necessarily be of the same magnitude. The experienced negotiator will rarely take this approach unless the discussion of all issues has reached the stage where there is some likelihood that the opponent is prepared to move on the new issue raised, and that the move will be either close to, or at the perceived acceptable settlement point.

Most negotiators also follow the convention of alternative movement from bargaining positions, and where one party has made a concession, convention dictates a move of equivalent significance on the part of the other. This involves accurate record keeping of moves on the part of the negotiators, with the first move on any issue usually initiated by the party that has given itself the greatest bargaining leeway on the issue. For example, if the union's initial wage proposal represents a "blue sky" demand, it would be expected to make the first move from its position. The negotiator for the employer would consequently watch for signals that indicated that the union was prepared to make a downward movement of its demand, and provide the opportunity for the union negotiator to make a graceful retreat from his initial position. In return of course, the employer would be expected to make some meaningful move on the same or some other issue as a response. In this fashion, the negotiators gradually move closer to their **final positions** or **resistance points** on each issue.

The process whereby the parties move from initial proposals to final positions may take the form of **gradual commitment** or **early final commitment**. With the former, as the words indicate, a negotiator gradually moves from the initial demand position towards the final position while attempting to determine through the course of negotiation where the opponent's final position might be. For example, if the union during the course of the bargaining decides that the employer's resistance point for a wage rate is greater than the union's final position, the union's commitment will gradually move downward to that point without going beyond it. This is one of the particular advantages of the tactic. Early final commitment on the other hand requires a considerable amount of knowledge of the opponent's final position and an accurate assessment of the likelihood of acceptance of the negotiator's own position by the opponent before the move is made. In the case of early final commitment, once the move is made, a retreat may only be made with considerable difficulty, and with some loss of credibility on the part of the negotiator. Consequently, the particular issue upon which early final commitment is made must either be one which the negotiator is instructed to make by his principal, or one which has a favourable chance of acceptance by the opponent, perhaps through the trade-off of some other proposal.

Of the two forms of commitment, on most issues, negotiators tend to make a gradual commitment, because there is a great deal of uncertainty in the process and a gradual commitment permits the negotiator to gain additional knowledge of the opponent's resistance point or final position on each issue. As information is acquired, however, the form of commitment strategy of the negotiator may change, since the negotiator may move to early final commitment once the opponent's final position is determined with some degree of accuracy. Walton and McKersie have observed this phenomenon, and suggest that the number of moves that a negotiator makes before taking a final commitment position is generally determined by the amount of knowledge that the negotiator has concerning the opponent's final position. In their view, the greater the knowledge of the opponent's final position, the fewer the moves that the negotiator will make before taking a final position.[12]

Other bargaining tactics in addition to blue sky bargaining may be used to camouflage the objectives of a party. In an effort to achieve a particular demand, one party or the other may bring forward other proposals, fully aware that the proposals would be unacceptable, but for the purpose of later trading off the proposals for the particular demand which they are anxious to obtain. Proposals designed to be traded during negotiations are often given considerable attention during the discussion stage, and their importance inflated. A strong apparent commitment is often attached to the demand, but skilled negotiators are usually careful to provide for some flexibility to permit a later trade-off without a loss of face or credibility. For the tactic to be successful, the build-up of the importance must be carefully orchestrated, and the eventual trade-off engineered with equal care, for discovery of the tactic by the opponent would not only nullify all efforts, but render other proposals suspect as well. The demand is sometimes raised in conjunction with a proposal which the negotiator wishes to have the opponent accept in the fervent hope that the opponent will see the two proposals as alternatives, and suggest acceptance of the one if the negotiator will drop the other. Since the "trading-horse" is the least acceptable of the two alternatives to the opponent, the opponent may express a willingness to accept the desired proposal in an effort to get what appears to be an unacceptable and troublesome issue off the agenda. The tactic is seldom used by parties where a good bargaining relationship exists, since the tactic is essentially opportunistic in nature. It is most likely to be employed by a party where the relationship is characterized by a containment/ aggressive attitude towards collective bargaining.

All bargaining tactics are not designed to achieve acceptance of a particular bargaining demand. Many tactics are employed by skilled negotiators to facilitate the negotiation process or to effect settlement when the parties are close to agreement. Some tactics such as taking control of the bargaining by establishing the agenda, or bargaining from a particular position may be used for both purposes, since they involve a certain amount of manipulation of the subject matter or control over the other party's actions. However, a skilled negotiator will often employ these methods to prevent an opponent from taking an inflexible position on an issue. For example, in an effort to establish a suitable climate for negotiation at the bargaining table, an experienced negotiator may suggest that once the initial position of each of the parties on the issues has been established that they deal with the least contentious nonmonetary issues first, and leave the monetary and more difficult issues until a later time. By dealing with issues such as a seniority system, where both parties can work together to devise a system that will be fair and equitable for both the employer and the employees, an atmosphere of co-operation or trust may be established before the more contentious issues are considered. The use of these tactics in this fashion often is a reflection of the skill of the negotiator.

Other tactics are frequently used by negotiators in particular instances. The recess or caucus is usually employed by negotiators where the parties have reached an impasse on an issue. A recess for a short time may enable the parties to reconvene for the discussion of another, less contentious matter, and thereby keep the negotiations moving. The recess may also be used for a party caucus where a proposal is made which calls for a concession in return and the implications of the proposal must be discussed in private. A break of this nature permits brief discussion of the proposal and an appropriate response to be formulated by the negotiator on the basis of input from the entire negotiating committee.

Joint **subcommittees** may also be used as a means of facilitating settlement of some issues. Important issues such as wages are unlikely to be turned over to a subcommittee to consider, but some issues upon which the parties have reached agreement in principle may be given to a joint committee made up of a few members from each bargaining committee for further discussion. Such a committee would be expected to work out the remaining minor differences, and report back to the parties at a later date with a draft proposal for consideration by the full negotiating teams. The preparation of a proposal on seniority which would provide for the orderly layoff of employees in accordance with length of service, yet enable the employer to retain persons with required skills, might be an example of the type of matter referred to a committee of this type.

Two further bargaining tactics should also be recognized. These are the **proposal** and the **package deal**. As noted, the proposal often takes the form of trade-off of two positions and while couched in different words, essentially says: "If you do _____, we are prepared to do _____." The object of the proposal in most cases is to resolve an issue (or two) by a proposition that is usually acceptable to both parties. The package deal on the other hand is usually a more extensive proposal which is generally made at or near the end of negotiations, and where the parties are close to, but have not reached agreement on a number of issues which are usually monetary in nature. The most common type of package deal is a proposal by the employer to provide an increase in wages and benefits on a global basis, coupled with the suggestion that the union might break the amount down in terms of wage or benefit increases in any way that it might wish. The offer is usually the final position of the employer, and it would be presented in that light to the union for a response. The advantage of this type of proposal, is that it provides some flexibility for the union if it is convinced that it can get nothing more from the employer without resorting to a strike. The package can be tailored to fit the union's final position on wages and each of the benefit proposals, then be taken back to the union membership for approval on the basis that the package represents the best bargain obtainable, but is one which may be adjusted to fit the union priorities if the members so desire. The disadvantage of the package deal to the union is that its acceptance shifts the responsibility to the union for dealing with any internal dispute over whether the money should be applied to wages or benefits.

Another tactic which is sometimes useful for a skilled negotiator is the use of "**off the record**" sessions between the two chief negotiators. These are occasionally employed by negotiators where it is necessary to inform the other party of difficult internal problems affecting settlement, and to seek ways and means of resolving the problems. For example, the parties may be prepared to agree on most of the issues, but a particular member of the union negotiating committee may be unwilling to have the union settle the major issues unless the employer agrees to permit the union to put union notices on plant bulletin boards. The employer may have refused the proposal initially, unaware of the importance of the proposal to a key member of the union negotiating team. On being advised of this in a private conversation between the two chief negotiators, the chief negotiator for the employer may indicate that the employer would not oppose the posting of notices if the notices were first examined by management to confirm that they pertained only to union business. They might then work out an arrangement whereby the issue would be raised again at the bargaining table and dealt with on that basis, provided that the chief negotiator for the union obtained the acceptance of the remaining proposals by the particular member of the union committee. Such a meeting must not represent a regular occurrence, otherwise it will create problems between the bargaining teams and their respective chief negotiators, but meetings which have the appearance of a chance encounter between chief negotiators may be arranged where it is essential that important information on a problem which could not be raised at the bargaining table be brought to the attention of the opponent. How this tactic and those previously noted are employed during the course of the negotiation process reflect the skill and ability of the negotiator. Experienced negotiators are usually perceptive and sensitive individuals with a highly developed sense of timing in their dealings with others. Bargaining tactics simply represent some of the tools of their trade.

THE DUTY TO BARGAIN IN GOOD FAITH

Collective bargaining legislation in all provinces and under the *Canada Labour Code* provides that an employer must meet and bargain with the certified or recognized bargaining agent of the employees. In five provinces,[13] the parties also have a duty to "bargain in good faith" with a view to making or concluding a collective agreement. As a general rule, a failure to comply with this duty would constitute an unfair labour practice, and expose the activity to labour relations board scrutiny and penalty if the complaint is valid.

The concept of bargaining in good faith was introduced to the labour relations scene in the United States' *National Labor Relations Act* (the Wagner Act) in 1935, and in the years that followed, the U.S. National Labor Relations Board gradually formulated what might be considered the ground rules for good-faith bargaining. Until very recently, Canadian labour relations boards have not been concerned with the negotiation process to any major degree, and consequently, were not called upon to direct much attention to this type of complaint. However, with changes in labour legislation during the past decade, Canadian boards have acquired substantial powers to provide relief in cases of unfair practices, and their remedial powers now enable them to effectively deal with the matter where a complaint of bad-faith bargaining is filed.

The duty to bargain collectively does not require the parties to reach an agreement, nor does it require either party to accept any of the offers or demands of the other. The basic duty to bargain simply involves the obligation to meet and discuss the proposals that each party would like to see in the collective agreement. The duty also involves an obligation to respond to the proposals put forth, but this need not require an exhaustive justification of the position taken. A "no" in many cases would constitute a satisfactory response, but in most cases a brief explanation of why a proposal is unacceptable would be sufficient. If a party should revise a rejected proposal, the duty would of course, oblige the other party to hear the change and respond to it. The duty to bargain would not normally extend beyond this minimum. The duty to bargain in good faith, however, adds a different dimension to this basic duty.

The duty to bargain in good faith is a part of what is essentially a twofold obligation in the sense that the good-faith requirement is coupled with words to the effect that the parties must make "every effort" or "reasonable efforts" to make an agreement. The basic duty to bargain is fulfilled where the parties meet and discuss each others' proposals, but the duty to bargain in good faith requires what might be considered a *bona fide* intention to conclude a collective agreement.[14] It includes something more than attendance at bargaining sessions and engaging in meaningless discussion without the genuine desire to reach an agreement. Bad-faith bargaining for example, may reflect a refusal on the part of the employer to accept the union as the bargaining representative of the employees after the union has been certified. In the case of a union, bad-faith bargaining may be insistence on the settlement of a single issue (such as wages) before any other issues would be discussed, or a demand that the employer discriminate in its employment practices by limiting its employment of particular ethnic groups.

As a general rule, labour relations boards are loathe to establish minimums for good-faith bargaining because they are reluctant to interfere with the bargaining process. Each party to the bargaining approaches the bargaining table with clear-cut goals or objectives and with the intention of reaching a settlement as close as possible to its most favourable position. To do so, initial stances or proposals are frequently excessive or appear unreasonable, but constitute an overall part of the strategy adopted in the particular circumstances. These strategies often represent effective methods of reaching an agreement. To restrict the parties to only "reasonable proposals" would effectively destroy much of the flexibility that is essential for successful collective bargaining, and place the labour relations board in the position of an active participant and arbiter of the reasonableness of each proposal in the process itself. For this reason, the boards have been reluctant to do much more than proclaim those activities that clearly damage the process as "bad faith." In addition to the examples previously cited, the failure to disclose relevant information known only to one party may be treated as bad faith,[15] and to deliberately provide false information in an attempt to mislead a party has been similarly considered by labour relations boards.[16] Apart from those actions and activities that are designed to destroy the bargaining process itself, tactics such as a constant reversal of positions upon which the parties have tentatively agreed, if a part of an overall plan to render the bargaining a nullity, would also be suspect as bad-faith bargaining.

What labour relations boards are essentially trying to do in their enforcement of good faith bargaining is to not interfere with the subject matter of the bargaining, nor the legitimate bargaining tactics which may be employed by the parties, but to preserve the relationship itself. As a consequence, only those activities that would have the effect of rendering the bargaining process meaningless, or interfere with the internal operations of one of the parties, such as the employer by-passing the union and negotiating directly with the employees, would appear to be bad faith. Any violation of the Act, such as the refusal to meet and bargain, would of course also be treated in a similar vein, as would any demand by one party that the other engage in an activity that would violate the Act or any other law.

An example of the difficulties which arise in assessing the extent of the requirement of good-faith bargaining was the early-final-commitment tactic practiced at the General Electric Company in the United States following the appointment of Lemuel Boulware as its Industrial Relations Director. In essence, the stance of Mr. Boulware was to open the negotiations by providing the union with what was essentially the final employer offer on all issues. He then made it clear that he was not prepared to change the offer unless the union could provide compelling reasons for the company to do so. In all cases, the final offer was fair and reasonable, and represented what the company would normally have established as its final position regardless of the type of bargaining followed. This was coupled with a constant stream of communications to the employees by letter and posted notices of the company offer and of the negotiations as they proceeded. The authorities in the United States considered the practice to be one which had the effect of destroying the role of the union in the negotiation process due to the constant direct contact between the employer and the employees. The tactic of making a final offer at the outset of the proceedings (which has since become known as Boulwarism) in itself may, however, be employed as a legitimate stance in bargaining, and indeed the General Electric Company in the U.S. continued to follow the practice in its negotiations after adverse U.S. National Labor Relations Board and Court rulings denied it the right to by-pass the unions by its communications system. From the point of view of good-faith bargaining, there would appear to be nothing objectionable about this approach in most Canadian jurisdictions, provided that the employer did not attempt to pressure the union to accept the proposal by way of constant employer communication with the work force urging acceptance of the employer's final offer.

Apart from the enforcement of good-faith bargaining by the labour relations boards, the compulsory third party procedures which the legislation imposes upon the parties no doubt limits the number of instances where bad-faith bargaining might occur. Conciliation officers in the course of their duty can and occasionally do urge recalcitrant parties to modify their attitudes at the bargaining table in an effort to have the parties make a reasonable effort to conclude a collective agreement, and where bad-faith bargaining is believed to exist, the officer may suggest to the Minister of Labour that a conciliation board be established to report on the bargaining.

REVIEW QUESTIONS

1. Outline the legal framework within which collective bargaining takes place between an employer and a certified bargaining representative. What is the significance of the time limits imposed following the completion of third party assistance?

2. Describe briefly Walton and McKersie's analysis of the bargaining process with respect to the different types of bargaining that takes place. What types do not occur between the employer and the union?

3. Define the following terms: contract zone, resistance point, trading horse, blue sky bargaining, proposal, union resistance curve, employer concession curve.

4. Explain why skilled negotiators tend to use a gradual commitment approach for issues such as wages.

5. To what extent does the duty to bargain in good faith affect the bargaining strategy and bargaining tactics which might be used by employers?

6. Are labour unions subject to a duty to bargain in good faith?

7. To what extent does bargaining power determine the outcome of collective agreement negotiations?

8. Describe the different kinds of relationships which may develop between unions and employers. What steps might be taken to change the relationship by the parties?

9. Assess the importance of "communication" in the negotiation process.

10. Explain briefly the contribution of Neil Chamberlain to negotiation theory.

NOTES

[1]Using the time limits and steps as set out in the Ontario legislation.

[2]Except in Saskatchewan, where the parties are not specifically obliged to have an arbitration clause in their agreement. However, a 1983 amendment to the *Trade Union Act* when proclaimed in force would prohibit the use of strikes or lock-outs during the life of the collective agreement. See S.S. 1983, c. 81, s. 13.

[3]See Saskatchewan, the *Trade Union Act*, R.S.S. 1978, c. T-17 as amended by S.S. 1983, c. 81, s. 13.

[4]See for example, Ontario, *Labour Relations Act*, R.S.O. 1980, c. 228, s. 38.

[5]See Chamberlain, N.W., and D. E. Cullen. *The Labor Sector*. (2nd Ed.) New York: McGraw-Hill Book Company, 1971, pp. 227, 231-32.

[6]Pen, J. "A General Theory of Bargaining." *American Economic Review* (March, 1952).

[7]Stevens, C. M. *Strategy and Collective Bargaining Negotiation*. New York: McGraw-Hill Book Co. Inc. (1963).

[8]Mabry, D. B. "The Pure Theory of Bargaining." 18 *Industrial and Labor Relations Review*. 479 (July, 1965).

[9]Schelling, T. C. *The Strategy of Conflict* N.Y.: The Oxford University Press. 1963.

[10]Walton, R.E., and R. B. McKersie, *A Behavioral Theory of Labor Negotiations*, New York: McGraw-Hill Inc., 1965.

[11]See Selekman, B.M., Fuller, S.H., Kennedy, T., and J. M. Baitsell. *Problems in Labor Relations*. (3rd Ed.) New York: McGraw-Hill Book Company. 1964. pp. 5-8. The five bargaining relationships adopted and redefined are described in detail in *A Behavioral Theory of Labor Negotiations* Supra, footnote 10, pp. 185-90.

[12]*Supra*, footnote 10 p. 123.

[13]British Columbia, R.S.B.C. 1979, c. 212, s. 6; Manitoba, S.M. 1972, c. 75, s. 53; Ontario, R.S.O., 1980, c. 228, s. 15; Newfoundland, S.N., 1977, c. 64, s. 71; Saskatchewan, R.S.S., 1979, c. T-17, s. 2(b).

[14]See *Canadian Association of Industrial, Mechanical and Allied Workers and Noranda Metal Industries Limited* [1975] 1 Can. L.R.B.R. 145 at pp. 158-162 (B.C.L.R.B.).

[15]*United Electrical, Radio and Machine Workers of America v. DeVilbiss (Canada) Limited* (1976) 76 CLLC 16,009 (OLRB).

[16]*The United Steelworkers of America, Local 4487 and Inglis Limited* [1977] 1 C.L.R.B.R. 408 (OLRB).

CHAPTER EIGHT

THIRD PARTY ASSISTANCE IN THE NEGOTIATION PROCESS

INTRODUCTION

Early collective bargaining legislation in Canada was for the most part designed to assist employers and unions embroiled in labour disputes. The statutes usually provided some form of conciliation or mediation of a voluntary nature, but did not establish a framework for collective bargaining that included compulsory third party assistance. Over time, voluntary assistance in the form of a conciliation procedure gradually gave way to assistance which tended to be more compulsory than voluntary, as typified by the federal government's *Industrial Disputes Investigation Act*, but it was not until near the middle of the twentieth century that compulsory third party assistance (when necessary) became an integral part of the overall collective bargaining process. This occurred with the imposition of the *War Measures Act*, and Order-in-Council P.C. 1003 in 1944.

Government intervention in the collective bargaining process since then has become a characteristic of labour relations in Canada. Depending upon the particular industry or service, it may take the form of conciliation, mediation, or some form of arbitration. Except for essential public services, compulsory arbitration is not used as a means of resolving collective bargaining disputes in Canada, but in a number of provinces voluntary arbitration is available if the parties so desire. The principal forms which third party assistance may take usually are conciliation and mediation.

CONCILIATION

From a basic, definitive point of view, conciliation and mediation have the same role to play in the collective bargaining process. Both have the same objective: to help the parties resolve their differences and make a collective agreement. In each case an individual who is a neutral person meets with the parties and assists them in their search for solutions to their problems. The conciliation process in most jurisdictions is a two-stage process. The first stage involves a government employee from the Ministry of Labour (or a person appointed by the Minister) meeting with the parties. The person sent to conciliate is chosen by the Ministry, and is obliged to report back to the Ministry within a given period of time on his or her success or failure to resolve the differences. The second stage involves a decision by the Minister to appoint a conciliation board.

The use of conciliation boards has declined substantially since the two-tier conciliation system was first adopted in compulsory form in P.C. 1003. Most provinces have gradually moved away from the conciliation board stage on the basis that it seldom brings about a settlement. Its use in some provinces (such as Ontario) would appear to be limited to the rare instance where the Minister believes that a board may move the parties closer to agreement, but in most negotiations the process is limited to the first stage.

While compulsory, the conciliation process does not come into play unless the parties reach an impasse in their negotiations. If they reach an agreement, they obviously have no need of conciliation, but when they cannot agree, they must use the conciliation process before they are permitted to engage in strike or lock-out activity. Economic action, consequently, is postponed until the conciliation process has been completed.

The procedure followed in most jurisdictions is to require either party to collective bargaining negotiations to request the appointment of a conciliation officer when negotiations reach a stalemate. The request is usually made to the Minister of Labour, and upon receipt of the request, a ministerial employee will usually be sent out to meet with the parties, and using his or her conciliation skills, endeavour to bring about a change in the positions taken by the parties on the issues in dispute. A number of sessions are usually held by the conciliator, as the conciliator normally must meet with the parties and report to the Minister of Labour within a fixed period of time. The time allowed is usually fourteen days, but in most provinces, provision is made for an extension of time if the conciliator believes that the parties are close to agreement.

Conciliation as a subprocess in the broader negotiation process can play a useful role in the resolution of differences at the bargaining table. To be effective, however, the conciliator must employ many of the methods used by a skilled mediator in order to move the bargaining parties into what is known as the "contract zone." Properly conducted, the conciliation process will be productive in the sense that it will require the parties to establish priorities in the demands which they have made at the bargaining table. A skilled conciliator will often elicit this information at the outset of conciliation, in order that his or her efforts might be concentrated on moving the parties into more flexible positions on the important issues. This is particularly important where one of the bargaining parties has made a firm commitment to a position, and cannot move from it without losing credibility in the eyes of the other party. Because the conciliation officer can meet with each party separately, it is often possible to make proposals which will allow a negotiator to move from an entrenched position to a more flexible position without losing face, something which would unlikely occur where the parties are dealing with each other on a direct basis at the bargaining table.

The fact that the conciliation procedure takes time is often an advantage in the bargaining process. When a request is made for conciliation, the parties have usually reached an impasse, and frequently to the point where strong words have been exchanged. The time interval sometimes provides a useful break in negotiations which the parties may need to assess their positions and consider the impact of economic action on the relationship. In a very real sense it provides a "cooling off period" during which time the conciliation officer may be successful in obtaining agreement by the parties on many issues.

A further advantage of the conciliation process, which only applies to conciliation boards, is the pressure that the board report may exert on the parties. Conciliation boards are expected to arrange a hearing or "sitting" at which time the parties present their problems and arguments to the board. The board is usually given a period of time (thirty days in Ontario) following its first sitting to report to the Minister of Labour. The report will be a response to the directive and terms of reference given to it, and will contain recommendations to the parties on the issues in dispute. Knowledge that the board will make recommendations is often important, and may have a moderating effect on demands, as the report of the board will also be made public.

The conciliation process, nevertheless, is not without some disadvantages, and what are often considered advantages by one party may very well be seen as disadvantages by another. For example, the time required for the process to be completed may be viewed as a "cooling off period," but for negotiators who experience a genuine breakdown in negotiations, the conciliation procedure becomes a slow and time-consuming process which the parties must endure before economic pressure can be brought into play. This is particularly the case where a conciliation board is appointed, as the time-frame for the appointment of a board, and for the board to hold its hearings and make its report may run to several months. Where the process is viewed as a waste of time, the prevailing attitude often makes the role of the conciliation officer an impossible one, and his efforts doomed to failure.

The bargaining strategies of the parties may also affect the conciliation process. Since the strike or lock-out is postponed until the conciliation process has been completed and a time interval expired, negotiators who are not prepared to get down to serious negotiations until the strike deadline is at hand believe that the process is an impediment to the bargaining process. To overcome this tactic, some critics of the process suggest that conciliation should take place at an earlier point in the bargaining process to prevent the parties from making what appear to be early final commitments on the issues under negotiation. The most serious criticism of the process, however, is generally directed at the use of conciliation boards, and the recommendations that they are expected to make.

The principal difficulty with the conciliation board is related to its make-up. The board is a representative board. Each party is entitled to appoint a member, and the two parties chosen select an impartial third party who becomes the chairman of the board. This creates an anomaly of sorts, as the legislation invites partisan appointment, but requires the persons appointed to swear an oath of impartiality. Clearly the two persons appointed by the parties to the dispute will each have a strong bias towards the bargaining positions of their respective parties, and only the chairman will likely be completely unbiased. The reports and recommendations of the boards generally reflect these biases, and the reports more often than not are majority reports only. As a consequence, conciliation boards are seldom appointed in most jurisdictions, and then only when the circumstances would appear to be such that the board would serve a useful role. In most provinces today, conciliation has essentially become a one-stage process, with the conciliation board used only in rare instances. While the reasons cited account for the move away from conciliation as a means of dispute settlement, the development of a trend in favour of mediation has also affected the use of the conciliation board.

MEDIATION

Mediation and conciliation are very much alike where a conciliator has the respect and confidence of the negotiating parties, as the role which a skilled conciliator plays in the process is essentially the same as that of the mediator. Both are interested in helping the parties resolve their differences and make a collective agreement. Mediators may be either government employees or independent persons, but in most cases they are selected by the parties. In contrast, conciliators are usually government employees of the Ministry of Labour who are assigned to the particular dispute in accordance with the requirements of the labour legislation of the jurisdiction.

Mediation also differs in the sense that it may be employed in a preventative manner by the parties. Some unions and employers have found that mediation services early on in negotiations, at a point in time well before commitments are made, tend to keep negotiations running smoothly, and prevent some of the difficulties which arise when final commitments are made prematurely in the bargaining sessions. This form of mediation often resolves many of the issues of minor importance at an early stage in the process, leaving only the more difficult issues to be resolved as the agreement expiry date approaches. Additionally, disputes over the facts as they apply to the major issues are often clarified by this process. In spite of these advantages, however, mediation tends to be used by the parties at the "eleventh hour" in the bargaining process, and often after a strike or lock-out is underway.

While the objectives of the mediator and the conciliator are the same, in some jurisdictions the voluntary aspect of mediation (as opposed to compulsory conciliation) often represents a plus in favour of mediation, as the parties do not view mediation as a process imposed upon them. The mediator is present at their pleasure, and while the mediator is essentially a disinterested, nonpartisan participant in the negotiations, he (or she) is there with a genuine interest in assisting the parties in the resolution of their differences. To be effective in this role, however, the mediator must not only have the respect and confidence of the parties, but must be sensitive, innovative, and a guardian of the trust placed in him by each of the parties when they reveal to him confidential information concerning their bargaining positions.

Apart from the essential requirement that a mediator must be honest and impartial in his dealings with the parties throughout the mediation process, a mediator must exhibit other essential qualities as well.

One of the important qualities that is identifiable in a good mediator is an imaginative and logical mind, capable of rapid assimilation and assessment of information. Coupled with this quality would be the ability to listen, and to respond both verbally and in writing in a clear and articulate manner. Additionally, the emotional make-up of the person is usually characterized by patience and understanding, and the ability to put others at ease, even at those times when the parties have reached the emotion-charged stages of the bargaining process. These qualities will be possessed by most experienced mediators to varying degrees, as no two mediators are obviously alike. The manner in which they display and employ these different abilities contribute to their effectiveness in performing their roles as facilitators in the resolution of labour disputes.

Thomas A. Kochan[1] has suggested that mediation is essentially a three-stage process, and while some overlap exists between the identifiable stages in the activities carried out by the mediator, each stage requires its own distinct form of action on the part of the mediator. The first or initial stage is where the mediator determines the issues in dispute and establishes his or her own credibility as a mediator. If the mediator has been selected by the parties, the credibility of the mediator is usually not in question; the latter task is only important where the mediator is not already acquainted with the chief negotiators. It is, nevertheless, an important aspect of the mediator's task at the first stage of the process, as a failure to establish the confidence and trust of the parties will have a negative effect on the proceedings.

At the first meeting with the parties, the issues in dispute are often presented to the mediator in much the same manner as the issues were first presented at the initial negotiation meeting between the parties. The presentation is often made emotionally and with considerable posturing and castigation of opponents for their inflexibility. Most mediators will listen patiently while the parties set out their positions, all the while sifting through the arguments to determine the areas where some common ground might be found for discussion. The response of the mediator at this stage usually takes the form of gentle questioning in an effort to further explore the issues and any underlying issues which must also be addressed in the negotiations. The initial stage is essentially an information gathering process for the mediator, although at this stage the mediator, when sufficiently informed of the problems, may begin moving the parties in a direction where he believes they must move to effect a settlement.

As a rule, the mediator at this stage will also outline some of the "ground rules" which the parties will be expected to follow. These may include the holding of joint and separate sessions with the parties as the mediator sees fit, holding private meetings with the chief negotiators for each side, either jointly or privately, and the freedom to spend time with one group that may substantially exceed the time spent with the other. The mediator might also require the parties to agree that the time-frame shall be as determined by him, and that he will determine when the process will end. In addition to these time-related rules, the mediator might also note that the parties must not release information to the news media during the mediation process, except through the mediator.

Once the mediator has established the trust of the negotiators and acquired an understanding of the issues in dispute, the process moves to the second stage. The information-gathering process continues into the second stage, but when the mediator believes that his assessment of the moves that the parties are prepared to make is correct, he will begin the process of probing for possible compromises in the direction that he feels a settlement might be. At this stage the mediator will also extract from the parties the relative order of importance of issues which are unresolved, again, as a part of the information-gathering process, but also to clarify in the minds of each bargaining team the priorities that are attached to each of the issues at the bargaining table.

Mediators often play a relatively passive role during the early part of the second stage of the process while carrying out the exchange of proposals between the parties, or suggesting the first compromises that the parties might make. As a general rule, the mediator will attempt to keep both parties from making a final commitment to a position at this stage of the process, but will elicit information on each particular demand and use it to suggest to one opponent where a move on the opponent's own part might be favourably received. All of this not only involves the carrying of information back and forth between the parties, but filtering it along the way. At this stage, the mediator has also determined with some degree of accuracy the "bottom line" of each party on each issue. This information is never revealed without express permission, but is used in the formulation of proposals or compromises by the mediator designed to move both parties in the direction of an acceptable settlement.

The final phase or stage in the mediation process begins when the mediator aggressively pushes the parties towards settlement. The stage is frequently characterized by the mediator playing an active role in the negotiations. This would include the suggestion of compromise solutions and the creation of a climate of urgency in the negotiations in order to pressure the parties into the final decision-making process. In some cases, the mediator must convince both parties that they must adjust their expectations if they wish to avoid a strike or lock-out, and occasionally, the mediator may meet privately with the chief negotiators to urge them to convince the remainder of their bargaining teams that settlement may only be effected if a compromise or package is accepted. What the mediator must do at this stage is convince the negotiators that they have extracted the best deal possible from their opponent short of a strike or lock-out, and that no better deal can be had from further bargaining.

The effectiveness of the mediator during the third stage of the process is largely dependent upon the ability of the mediator to create compromise ideas that would be acceptable in the eyes of the parties, and capable of translation into solutions for the problems faced by the parties. Lowest priority issues are frequently disposed of in this manner first, and the more contentious matters resolved as the process proceeds to its conclusion. In the end, the success or failure of the mediation is often dependent upon not only the "reading" of the dispute by the mediator, but upon the timing of the mediator's actions, as a settlement may only occur when the parties are satisfied that to prolong the process will achieve nothing more in terms of the agreement. The timing of the mediator's final proposals to coincide with this point in the process is often a reflection of the skill and expertise of the mediator as much as it is the desire of the parties for an agreement.

While considerable variation exists, the mediation procedure that many mediators follow is to hold a short meeting with both negotiating teams at the bargaining table to determine the nature of their problems and the issues in dispute, then separate the two parties by sending them to their separate rooms, which are usually located in the same hotel. The mediator will then meet with each group separately to determine the importance that each party attaches to individual demands, and to establish some order of the priority that must be given to each issue. In the case of wages and benefits, the mediator will attempt to determine the "bottom line" and the flexibility of the negotiators on these issues. A mediator who has the trust and confidence of the parties will often be told exactly what the minimum acceptable wage rate or other benefit rate will be, on the understanding that the amount will not be revealed to the opponent except at the appropriate time, and then only in a very oblique manner.

Mediation generally follows a pattern of separate discussion with the employer and union negotiating teams as the mediator works back and forth between the two sides with proposals and suggestions for settlement. Occasionally, the mediator might call together the chief negotiators of each team for a private meeting in his own hotel room to obtain their views on some of his ideas or thoughts concerning the proceedings. Throughout the meetings however, he will attempt to clarify issues by resolving disputes over facts, or clear up misconceptions as to the positions of a party on particular issues.

Skilled mediators are usually aware of the bargaining tactics used by negotiators, and generally devise methods whereby such tactics may be circumvented and the real issues isolated. In addition, the mediator will normally determine and assess the political pressures that are exerted on the bargaining teams, and particularly on the chief negotiators by their respective principals. In many cases, union negotiators are obliged to present and take strong stands on issues at the bargaining table because the issues were proposed by factions within the union, and mediators must be aware of the importance that must be given to these issues during the negotiations by the union chief negotiators, even though the issues may very well be unobtainable. Similarly, management negotiators may be obliged to appear unreasonable on a particular benefit demand in order to satisfy the shareholders that every effort was made to resist the union on the issue. A mediator must appreciate the position of the negotiators on these matters and devise ways and means of dealing with such issues without creating the impression that the negotiators failed to carry out their mandate.

To perform their role, mediators have developed a variety of different tactics of their own to facilitate agreement by the parties. For example, one mediator is reported to sometimes select a disagreeable and uncomfortable setting in which to hold joint sessions, then keep the parties together in such quarters while they work out their differences. The incentive to settle in this case is increased by the desire of the parties to escape from the uncomfortable surroundings as soon as possible. The success of this device is naturally based upon the timing of its use, and the mediator must know the parties in advance, and the likelihood of settlement before it may be employed. A somewhat similar method is for the mediator to schedule continuous or "around the clock" negotiations as the deadline for a strike or lockout approaches. Again, timing of this tactic is important, as the parties must be under some pressure to settle, and the negotiators must be at the stage where the mediator senses that a settlement might be reached if the negotiators are pushed to the point of exhaustion. Because both of these tactics tend to be physical as well as psychological in their application (they are both pressure tactics in a very real sense) the mediator must not only know the limits to which the parties are likely to go in their concessions, but sense that pressure of this type will in all likelihood produce a settlement. If the parties are so far apart on some major issue (such as wages) that the final positions of each fall outside the contract zone, tactics of this type would be useless.

The most important tool that a mediator has is the control over the flow of information between the parties once the process begins. If the parties are separated, the mediator becomes the communication link, and can control not only the messages, but the content itself. This allows the mediator to block moves by either party to a final position on an issue, to sift out and exclude meaningless proposals, and to refuse to convey a "take it or leave it" type of ultimatum.

The control over the flow of information to the media is often controlled by a mediator as well. A prohibition by the mediator on any contact with the media will confine the parties to the bargaining table, and prevent them from negotiating or performing for the public. In this manner the negotiations are likely to be more meaningful since they need not take into consideration public reaction until the process is concluded.

As a facilitator in the negotiation process, a mediator is obliged to devise a number of strategies to keep the process moving closer to the settlement stage. First and foremost the mediator must be able to identify the problems that the parties have, then assist them in finding solutions. Negotiators will often meet an argument with a counter-argument on the method of resolving a problem, which will result in no movement except in opposite directions. A mediator can redirect the parties by asking questions related to the more fundamental issue of why each party believes the problem must be resolved in a particular way, and perhaps point them both in the direction of an alternate solution that might be mutually acceptable.

A practice followed by experienced negotiators as well as mediators is to determine which issues in dispute would be most easily resolved, and place them at the top of the list for discussion. The purpose of this approach is to enable the parties to resolve some of their problems in a relatively short time, and thereby create a climate of co-operation before the more difficult issues are brought forward.

As a means of settlement, mediators may sometimes present pro-posals that they believe are acceptable to both parties as **ideas for discussion**. Such proposals are generally made during the late second and third stages of the process when the mediator begins to take an active rather than passive role in the negotiations. While the mediator may not actively argue the proposal, questioning of the stance of the party on an idea is frequently used to pressure acceptance, as the mediator has usually determined from his discussion with the parties that the idea would probably be acceptable if proposed.

In the final stages of the mediation process, stronger pressure tactics are sometimes used to effect a settlement. Sometimes a mediator will emphasize the cost of a strike or lock-out to bring forcefully to the attention of a recalcitrant party the cost to his principal or organiza-tion of a failure to reach an agreement. Other mediators may blame a chief negotiator for the failure to reach a settlement on an issue as a means of pressuring the negotiator into taking a more flexible and co-operative stance on the next issue that the mediator intends to raise. All of those tactics are designed to create a climate for settlement by clarifying the issues and exerting a pressure on the parties for settle-ment. The effectiveness of the strategy is often a measure of the skill and experience of the mediator, but it is important to note that all the methods used by mediators are employed with the same objective or goal in mind: the resolution of the differences between the negotiating parties. In this sense, the mediator performs the broader public interest function of promoting industrial peace and stability in labour relations.

MEDIATION BOARDS

Mediators in some provinces (such as Ontario) are given the powers of a conciliation board under the labour legislation, but the power granted to the board to hold hearings, investigate issues, and examine witnesses is seldom required by a mediator, and in a very real sense is alien to the process. As a result, mediation boards are rarely used in the private sector. Collective bargaining in the public sector differs to some extent, and under the *Public Service Staff Relations Act*[2] pro-vision is made for the establishment of a conciliation board which has a function somewhat similar to that of a mediator in collective bar-gaining disputes which fall under the legislation. The board is expected to make recommendations, and consequently, the representative nature of the board assures careful consideration of the proposals from each party by the board. The appointment of fact finders under some public sector legislation, such as teachers' collective bargaining legislation serves the same purpose, although the fact finding process is usually limited to a determination of the facts and the formulation of recommendations.

Apart from those segments of the public sector where board recommendations serve a useful purpose in the bargaining process, the use of conciliation or mediation boards has found little favour elsewhere on the collective bargaining scene. This may be due to the fact that the formal nature of the board does not permit it to engage in the practices that single mediators employ to bring about agreement between the parties. Its use, therefore, may be limited to those bargaining relationships where recommendations are important.

ARBITRATION

The growth of collective bargaining in the public sector created a need for some mechanism to resolve disputes in those sections of the public service where the strike or lock-out would create a hardship or have a serious effect on the public at large. Essential services such as police, fire protection and hospitals consequently could not be treated under collective bargaining legislation in the same manner as private sector services where a strike or lock-out would seldom have more than a localized and minimal impact on the public generally. Early collective bargaining legislation, therefore, excluded essential service employees such as firefighters, police officers, hospital employees, and other persons engaged in duties which involved the protection of the public. In most jurisdictions, the right to bargain collectively was extended to persons in these groups under special legislation, but the use of strikes or lock-outs was prohibited. Instead, final and binding arbitration by an arbitration board which consisted of union and employer nominees and an independent chairman was substituted.

Arbitration boards established for the purpose of resolving issues upon which the parties cannot agree determine the **interests** of the parties, and differ from ordinary arbitration boards which have the responsibility to decide grievances and matters pertaining to the **rights** of the parties. Arbitration boards that finalize collective agreements are accordingly called **interest arbitration boards**. Interest arbitration may also be used in some provinces by unions and employers on a voluntary basis if they wish to avail themselves of the process, and agree in writing to be bound by the arbitrator's decision. The use of this method on a voluntary basis, however, would appear to be rare, as the parties usually prefer to use the strike or lock-out when conciliation or mediation fails to resolve their differences. Employers and unions in the designated essential services have no choice in the matter since they are prohibited from using strike or lock-out action to force their demands.

While some variation exists in the arbitration process, the process generally comes into play after some other form of third party assistance has failed to resolve the differences between the parties. In most cases, the parties, with the assistance of the conciliator or mediator, have settled many of the issues at least on a tentative basis, and only those unresolved issues remaining are brought to arbitration. Once appointed under the legislation, the arbitration board will fix a date for a hearing, at which time the employer and the union will present briefs to the board related to the issues in dispute, and file with the board data that supports their respective positions. The board will then hold **executive sessions**, which are private meetings of the board members to discuss the issues and prepare an award. As a rule, the award is justified by reasons formulated at these meetings, and the written decision of the board is later submitted to the parties. In cases where the board members cannot reach a unanimous agreement on the issues, the decision of the majority governs. The award of the board finalizes the collective agreement, and the terms and issues awarded by the board become a part of the collective agreement. No appeal to the courts is permitted from the decision of the board, and unless the board has acted in an unfair or biased manner, or has exceeded its jurisdiction, the award may not be quashed by way of judicial review.

Arbitration as a method of resolving interest disputes has not found a great deal of favour amongst employers and unions, the principal reason being that the parties prefer to make their own agreement, and both sides are prepared to resort to the strike or lock-out as a final means of resolving their differences. In the public sector, in those areas of the public service that are essential or of a safety nature, a substitute must, of course, be used in lieu of the strike or lock-out to prevent injury to the public. The use of arbitration in many provinces has generally been limited to only these public services however, because of employer and union resistance to the process.

The most common objection to arbitration as a method of dispute resolution is the fact that the decision is made by an outside body. While arbitration boards make every effort to arrive at a reasonable decision, the employer and the union must, nevertheless, live with the decision, and it is often difficult for the parties to work under an agreement that is not made by them. Proponents of the compulsory arbitration of interest disputes acknowledge this weakness of the process, but argue that the fear of the unknown associated with arbitration serves to encourage settlement of the disputes by the parties themselves rather than place their fate in the hands of a third party.

RECENT TRENDS AND INNOVATIVE APPROACHES TO DISPUTE RESOLUTION

MEDIATION-ARBITRATION (MED-ARB)

Mediation-arbitration, as the name signifies, constitutes a blending of the two processes, and is generally applied as a two-step process to resolve collective bargaining disputes. The process begins with the appointment of a mediator, who attempts to resolve the differences between the parties using the various mediation techniques available. Issues not resolved during the course of the mediation are settled by the mediator, who then acts as an arbitrator to decide the outstanding issues at the point when the parties reach an impasse.

Med-Arb is occasionally used as a voluntary process in the private sector by employers and unions prepared to try innovative approaches to dispute resolution, and occasionally the process is used for some public sector interest disputes, but again on a voluntary basis. In Ontario, teachers and school boards have occasionally requested this type of assistance from the Education Relations Commission in an effort to resolve collective bargaining disputes during the negotiation process, but in general, little interest has been expressed in the approach. At the present time, this form of third party assistance would appear to be useful only in the public sector. Private sector unions and employers have largely ignored or rejected the approach as a means of dispute resolution.

FINAL OFFER SELECTION

Final offer selection is not unlike arbitration, but the process differs in one important aspect. The arbitrator's decision is limited to the selection of the final offer of one party or the other, without modification or alteration in any manner. The use of this method is provided in public sector collective bargaining legislation in some jurisdictions, the Ontario *School Boards and Teachers Collective Negotiations Act*[3] being a notable example.

Under this Act the procedure is voluntary, but where the parties have agreed to refer any matter remaining in dispute to a **selector**, the Education Relations Commission (which administers the legislation) requires the parties to agree in writing that they will not withdraw from the process once it is instituted, and that they will be bound by the decision. The parties may arrange for a selector of their choice to act in the matter, or the Commission will appoint a selector at their request. Once appointed, the selector is given a joint statement by the school board and the teachers' organization which sets out the matters in dispute, and the matters agreed upon. Within fifteen days, each party must provide the selector with the party's final offer and a statement in support of the offer. The documentation provided by each party is also exchanged in order that the parties are aware of the final offer and supporting statements which each has made. Each party has ten days following receipt of the documents to provide the selector with a reply, and the selector again provides each of the parties with their opponent's response. The selector then holds a hearing, at which time the parties may present any final statements on the final offers. The selector is required to make a selection of one of the final offers within fifteen days after the conclusion of the hearing, and the final offer selected together with the remaining issues which have been previously agreed upon by the parties becomes the collective agreement.

As in the case of interest arbitration, final offer selection has been utilized as a method of dispute resolution largely in the public sector. Unlike interest arbitration, however, its use has been made available as a voluntary process, and usually as an alternative to some other procedure. As a method of dispute resolution, it is worthy of consideration by the parties where only one or two issues remain, and where the parties have final offers which are not far apart. It would also have merit where each party could live with the final offer of their opponent, but would perhaps prefer the decision to be made by a third party for political reasons.

WHEN NEGOTIATIONS FAIL TO RESOLVE DIFFERENCES: THE STRIKE AND LOCK-OUT

There are times when the negotiation process does not produce a collective agreement, and the parties are obliged to use power to resolve their differences. If the unalterable expectations of the employer and the union on an important issue such as wages do not overlap or meet, regardless of the skill of the negotiators or the third parties, the only solution may be the strike or lock-out. A strike, by definition, is a simultaneous cessation of work or refusal to work by a group of employees, and in some jurisdictions, any concerted effort by employees to restrict output is also deemed to be a strike.[4] A lock-out, on the other hand occurs when the employer refuses the entry of the employees to the work place. In both instances, the action occurs as a result of a labour dispute between the parties.

In an effort to promote industrial stability, public policy in Canada prohibits the use of strikes and lock-outs while a collective agreement is in effect, and during the negotiation process. Only after third party assistance has failed to resolve the differences between the employer and the union is the strike or lock-out permitted. In most cases, a "waiting period" is also imposed following compulsory conciliation or mediation before the use of the strike or lock-out becomes lawful.[5]

As a result of labour legislation, strikes may be classified in terms of their legal nature. A strike may be either lawful or unlawful. A lawful strike is a strike that is properly called by a labour union in accordance with the time-frame specified in the applicable labour legislation. For example, in Ontario, a lawful strike would be a strike called after a collective agreement had expired, and after the parties had negotiated, proceeded through the compulsory conciliation process to the point where the conciliation board report was released, and seven clear days had elapsed, or fourteen clear days had elapsed after the Minister of Labour had notified the parties that no conciliation board would be appointed. A strike at any other time would be unlawful.

Unlawful strikes are strikes that are called by labour unions at times other than when a strike is permitted under the labour legislation. An unlawful strike would include a **wildcat strike**, which is a strike that is not called by the union, but a spontaneous refusal to work by the employees, if the refusal occurs at a time when strikes are prohibited. Because unlawful strikes are actionable either at law or under provincial labour legislation, union leaders must take care not to associate themselves with the unlawful activity, otherwise they may implicate the union. In most cases, the labour legislation provides that a union must not call, authorize, or support an unlawful strike, and if an unlawful strike should occur, the actions of the union officers and officials are usually subject to scrutiny. As a general rule, any act of a union officer that is done within the scope of his authority is deemed to be an act of the union, and if the union officer appears to be encouraging or assisting other employees in unlawful strike action, the union may be held responsible.

For example, in Ontario, if a group of employees engage in a wildcat strike while a collective agreement is in effect, the employer might decide to discipline the employees or complain to the labour relations board. If the employer is in a position to establish that union officials actively encouraged and supported the wildcat strike, the labour relations board might hold the union responsible, and issue a declaration that the union engaged in an unlawful strike. Any loss suffered by the employer might then be recovered from the union under the process provided in the collective agreement for violations, since every collective agreement must provide that no strikes or lock-outs occur while the agreement is in effect.

Employees who engage in unlawful strikes do so at their peril, and in violation of their employment relationship. Employers are free to discipline or discharge employees that participate in such strikes, but the right to discharge or discipline does not apply to lawful strikes. If a strike is lawful, the employees do not cease to be employees when they refuse to work, nor does the employer have the right to take any form of action against them for doing so. However, strikes that continue for a very long time might result in replacement of the work force by the employer, and the strike will be lost. Should this happen, in a number of provinces, striking employees are entitled to reinstatement in the work force, provided that they return to work within the period of time specified in the provincial labour legislation, otherwise they are considered to have lost the right to demand employment.

Apart from the limited right to reinstatement, striking employees have no rights against the employer if the strike fails. The strike, like the lock-out, is a tool which the parties use when negotiation fails to resolve their differences. The strike and lock-out represent the exercise of power, the weapon of final resort in the process. Unless events occur during the course of a strike or lock-out that alter the positions of the parties and bring about a settlement, the failure of a strike will signal the end of collective bargaining for the employees. In most cases, however, the parties will continue to meet while a strike or lock-out is in process, and the pressures exerted by the work stoppage will often encourage compromise and a lowering of expectations. In most jurisdictions, third party assistance in the form of mediation is also available if the negotiating parties require the help of a neutral person during the strike or lock-out. While expensive for all parties concerned, most strikes or lock-outs serve a useful purpose if they have the effect of pressuring the parties into an agreement.

The control over the actions of the parties during a strike or lock-out has been the subject of some regulation by government, but only to the extent that the public be protected. In some provinces, however, labour legislation has gone further, and attempted to limit the ability of employers to operate during a lawful strike by prohibiting the use of strikebreakers or the employment of a new work force. In Quebec, for example, an employer is prohibited from employing other employees to replace employees on a lawful strike.[6] British Columbia does not restrict employers to the same degree, but prohibits the use of professional strikebreakers.[7] Three other provinces[8] in addition to British Columbia deal with strikes and lock-outs in their labour legislation, but only to the extent of the legality of the event itself. Each of these provinces and the federal government have empowered its labour relations board to issue "cease and desist" orders if the board is convinced that an illegal strike or lock-out has taken place. Most provinces, however, leave the parties to their own resources if they wish to follow the strike or lock-out route to resolve their differences. Disruptive action as a result of a strike or lock-out is only controlled where it results in injury to property or the public at large, and then only through the application of the civil or criminal law by the courts.

With respect to lock-outs by the employers, it is important to note that a lock-out that is timely and for the purpose of establishing a collective agreement on terms acceptable to the employer is a lawful exercise of the employer's rights under labour legislation. It may not be used, however, for the purpose of avoiding collective bargaining when an agreement is in effect, or for the purpose of preventing employees from exercising their rights under the applicable labour legislation. For example, in a case where an employer announced the intention to split his operations into six separate entities and locate each one outside the geographic bargaining unit area for the purpose of avoiding the collective agreement, the labour relations board held that the change was not for legitimate business reasons but to force the employees to accept altered conditions of employment. The announced move was considered to be an unlawful lock-out within the meaning of the Act.[9] The ruling of the labour relations board in this case underscored the motive of the employer in reaching its decision, and emphasized that employers are free to move their operations for legitimate business reasons at any time while a collective agreement is in effect. Such a move, therefore, would only be an unlawful lock-out where the admitted motive was to require the employees to either accept inferior terms and conditions of employment to those that were negotiated in their collective agreement or face the loss of their jobs in the immediate area.

PICKETING
One of the more difficult problems associated with the lawful strike or lock-out is the control of dangerous or destructive activity that may occur on the "picket line." Picketing, very broadly defined, involves the physical presence of persons at or near the premises of another for the purpose of conveying information, or for the purpose of persuading other persons to do or refrain from doing certain acts. This type of activity may be lawful or unlawful, depending upon when, where, and how it is carried out.

Lawful picketing in a labour dispute as a general rule may only be carried out during a lawful strike. For example, the picketing of an employer's premises while a collective agreement is in effect, if done for the purpose of injuring the employer would entitle the employer to a restraining order to stop the activity. The labour legislation in most provinces does not deal with picketing as a strike or lock-out activity, and resort must be had to the common law and *Criminal Code* to determine the type of activity that constitutes lawful picketing. Surprisingly, the criminal law provisions that deal with picketing do not refer to the activity directly, but instead, establish the unlawful aspect of the activity as "watching and besetting."

The Criminal Code provides that a person is guilty of an offence if the person wrongfully and without lawful authority watches or besets a dwelling, house or place where a person works, carries on business, or happens to be, if the watching or besetting is done for the purpose of compelling the person to abstain from doing something that the person has a right to do, or conversely, to do something that the person has a right to abstain from doing. The law, however, does not apply to a person who approaches any place for the purpose of obtaining or communicating information in a peaceful manner, and it is under this exemption from the law of "watching and besetting" that lawful picketing may take place. From a criminal-law point of view, then, lawful picketing is limited to the peaceful communication of information, and any activity that goes beyond this may constitute an unlawful act.

Labour unions and employees do not necessarily hold this narrow view as the sole purpose of picketing. While the peaceful dissemination of information is the primary purpose of picketing, in their opinion it is also to display the solidarity of the employees in their strike, and to persuade others to place their support behind the strike action. Pickets hope to persuade other nonstriking employees and suppliers of goods to refrain from crossing the picket line in order to exert greater economic pressure on the employer. It is only when these activities take on a violent tone, or result in unlawful activity by some individuals that picketing is likely to be restrained by the courts.

The most common problem that might arise during a strike is associated with pickets blocking the entrance to the employer's plant or place of business. The obstruction of the entrance is normally considered to be a wrongful act since it deprives the employer and others of the right to enter or leave the premises without interference. It often leads to charges against striking employees who deliberately create an obstruction to prevent entry, particularly if they use force to prevent access or if they make any threatening gesture towards the person attempting to enter or leave the property.[10]

While a union will normally set up and supervise the picket lines established during a lawful strike, the union itself is not vicariously liable for the individual acts of its members while they perform picket line duty. For example, a striking employee that assaults an employee who attempts to cross a picket line would have committed an unlawful assault, but the union would not be responsible. The victim of the assault would be obliged to bring charges against the perpetrator of the assault. However, violence on a picket line may result in a court order limiting the number of pickets, if a court of law can be convinced by the employer that a reduction in the number of pickets would be necessary to avoid future violence or unlawful acts. The courts (or labour relations board in some provinces) will not normally interfere with picketing that is peaceful, nor will it restrict the number of pickets unless it is satisfied that the employer has made all reasonable efforts (including the use of the police) to avoid damage and incidents, and that those efforts were unsuccessful. Even **mass picketing**, with large numbers of persons occupying a confined space will not be limited unless the police are unable to control the crowd.

The remedies available for injuries suffered by persons affected by unlawful picketing are known as civil remedies, and include the right to compensation for tortious injury and the right to have the activity which resulted in the injury terminated. Damage to property without lawful excuse is a tort (a civil "wrong"), as is trespass to property, nuisance, and defamation. Where any of these torts are proven in a court of law against the person responsible for the act, the court will usually compensate the injured party for the loss suffered.

Where the employer is the party who suffers the injury, more often than not the employer may simply wish to have the conditions that produced the injury controlled or curtailed. If the damage or injury occurred as a result of mass picketing, and the police were unable to control the activity or appear unable to prevent further damage, the employer may be able to convince the court that an **injunction** prohibiting the picketing, or perhaps reducing the number of pickets to a few persons at each entrance to the plant would end the damage or injury. An injunction issued by the court must be obeyed by all persons named in it, and a failure to obey the terms of the order would constitute contempt of court. The willingness of the court to issue injunctions in labour disputes, however, tends to vary to some extent depending upon the attitude of the courts in each province towards picket line violence, and to some extent upon the alternatives available to the employer under the provincial labour legislation. In most cases, however, the courts will expect the employer to take steps to avoid picket line problems, and to use the police to avoid difficulties before resorting to a request for injunctive relief.

Mass picketing has a potential for **intimidation** if it is used as a means of denying employees, suppliers, or customers access to the employer's premises, but mass picketing in itself is not unlawful, and as long as free access is permitted, and the pickets do not threaten or interfere with persons seeking entry or exit, the practice is unlikely to be restrained.[11] Intimidation, however, may include veiled threats, such as requiring a person to obtain a picket line "pass" from the union hall to pass through the picket line. This type of obligation may amount to intimidation if the procedure to be followed is one by which a person must attend at the union hall and identify himself as an anti-union employee in order to obtain a pass.

Picketing may also constitute a **nuisance** if the pickets block the employer's entrance, or it may be considered as **trespass** if it takes place on private property. Picketing normally takes place on public property such as a street or sidewalk, but occasionally, businesses involved in labour disputes are located on private lands, such as a shopping centre. Where a third party is the property owner, and the picketing affects the property owner's enjoyment of the property, or where the trespass causes injury, either financial or otherwise, the pickets may be excluded by a court order. For example, if an employer who leases a store in a shopping centre has a labour dispute with his employees, and the employees engage in a lawful strike, picketing of the employer's premises in order to be effective would have to take place in front of his shop. The picketing, however, would be on premises which belong to the owner of the shopping centre, and would also interfere with other persons who leased shops in the centre. Under such circumstances, the owner of the shopping centre might have the right to exclude the pickets on the basis of trespass, if control has been retained over the right of access to the premises.

Third parties may also be injured in the course of picketing, and if the picketing is designed to injure the third party in an effort to exert pressure on the employer, the third party may have the right to recover damages from the pickets, and/or have the picketing prohibited. Suppliers and purchasers of goods from an employer involved in a labour dispute represent the two groups most often affected. If a union decides to picket the premises of an independent purchaser, for example, the purpose of the pickets may be to induce the purchaser not to buy from the employer, or if the purchaser is obliged to buy goods under a contract, it may constitute an attempt to induce the purchaser to breach the contract. If the pickets cause any monetary loss or damage to the employer's customer, the customer may take action against the pickets for the loss suffered, and for an injunction to stop the picketing. Picketing of persons not directly involved in the labour dispute is known as **secondary picketing**. Except in cases where the supplier or purchaser is involved in the labour dispute (such as a subsidiary of the employer which has carried on the business during the strike), secondary picketing may not take place except at the risk of legal action. The justification for this stance by the courts is that the labour dispute should be confined to the parties involved, and parties not directly connected with the dispute should be protected by the law.

In cases where an employer has collective agreements with unions covering different bargaining units, a strike lawfully called by one union does not mean that all employees must engage in the strike, nor does it mean that all employees must respect the picket lines. Unless the other collective agreements that are in effect at the time provide that the employees covered by the agreements may honour the picket lines of the striking employees, a lawful strike called by one union does not permit the remaining employees to support the work stoppage, because to do so would constitute a violation of their own collective agreements with their employer. Similarly, a striking union must not attempt to prevent nonstriking employees from entering the employer's plant or premises if they wish to do so, or if they must do so under their own collective agreements. Interference with nonstriking employees by threats or actual violence would entitle the victims to lay charges against their assailants and perhaps entitle the employer to have the picketing itself restricted.

The right to picket is essentially the right to disseminate information concerning the labour dispute that the employees have with their employer. In this regard, the employees are under an obligation to provide accurate information to the public concerning the employer. The employees may believe that the employer, in their opinion, is unfair or unreasonable by refusing to agree with their demands, but their picket signs must not be defamatory. Consequently, if a picket carries a picket sign which states that "our employer is a rat," the employer must in fact be one (an unlikely biological transformation) if the striker wishes to avoid an action for **defamation**.

In spite of the publicity given by the media to the occasional violent confrontation on a picket line, most picketing is conducted in a peaceful manner and without incident. Much of the credit is due to the unions who instruct those responsible for the picketing in the proper ways and means to perform their roles. The various rules of law that apply to unlawful activity on the picket line are not designed to shift the balance of power to one side or the other, but rather to control those activities which in any circumstances away from the picket line would be equally unlawful.

REVIEW QUESTIONS

1. *Describe some of the advantages of mediation and conciliation.*
2. *Describe the various stages that have been observed to occur in many mediation proceedings. Do these always occur?*
3. *How does mediation differ from conciliation? From "Med-Arb"?*
4. *Why do most employees and unions reject interest arbitration as a means of settling their differences?*
5. *Under what circumstances might a lawful strike or lock-out occur?*
6. *Outline the nature of lawful picketing, and describe some of the activities that might take place on a picket line that would not be lawful. What remedies are available in these instances?*
7. *Define the following terms: secondary picketing, injunction, lock-out, wildcat strike, compulsory conciliation.*

8. Assess "final offer selection" as a means of resolving differences. Why is it seldom used in the private sector?
9. Why do mediators frequently prohibit the negotiators from making statements to the media during the mediation process?
10. Explain public policy with respect to strikes and lock-outs.

NOTES

[1]Kochan, T.A., *Collective Bargaining and Industrial Relations*, Homewood, Illinois: Richard D. Irwin Inc. 1980, pp. 279–82.
[2]*Public Service Staff Relations Act*, R.S.C. 1970, c. P-35, s. 78.
[3]*School Board and Teachers Collective Negotiations Act*, R.S.O. 1980, c. 464, Part V, s. 37-49.
[4]See for example, *Ontario Labour Relations Act*, R.S.O. 1980, c. 228, s. 1(1)(o).
[5]*Ibid.*, s. 72.
[6]Quebec, *Labour Code*, R.S.Q. 1977, c. C-27, s. 109.1 as amended by S.Q. 1982, c. 37, s. 2.
[7]British Columbia, *Labour Code* R.S.B.C. 1979, c. 212, s. 3(3)(d).
[8]Alberta, Nova Scotia, and Ontario.
[9]*Retail, Wholesale and Department Store Union, Local 461 and Humpty Dumpty Foods Limited*, [1977] 2 Can. L.R.B.R. 248 (O.L.R.B.).
[10]See for example, *Rex v. Carruthers* (1946) 86 C.C.C. 247.
[11]See for example, *SCM (Canada) Ltd. v. Motley et al.* [1967] 2 O.R. 323.

RECOMMENDED REFERENCES AND SOURCE MATERIAL

Adell, B. *The Duty to Bargain in Good Faith*. Kingston, Canada: Queen's University Industrial Relations Centre (1980).
Chamberlain, N.W. and D.E. Cullen. *The Labor Sector*. (2nd Ed.) N.Y.: McGraw-Hill Book Co. (1971).
Healey, J.J. (Ed.) *Creative Collective Bargaining*. Englewood Cliffs, N.J.: Prentice-Hall Inc. (1965).
Hicks, J.R. *The Theory of Wages*. (2nd Ed.) London, Eng: MacMillan & Co. Ltd. (1963).
Hutchison, J. *Management Under Strike Conditions*. N.Y.: Holt, Reinhart and Winston, Inc. (1966).
Kochan, T.A. *Collective Bargaining and Industrial Relations*. Homewood, Ill.: Richard D. Irwin Inc. (1980).
Mabry, D.B. "The Pure Theory of Bargaining." 18 *Industrial and Labor Relations Review* 479 (July 1965).
MacIntyre, W. "Industrial Rights and the Collective Bargaining Process." 40 *Saskatchewan Law Review* 269 (1974–76).
Monat, J.S. "Determination of Bargaining Power." 50 *Personnel Journal* (July 1971) 513.

Pen, J. "A General Theory of Bargaining." *American Economic Review* (March 1952).

Richardson, R.C. *Collective Bargaining by Objectives.* Englewood Cliffs, N.J.: Prentice Hall Inc. (1977).

Schelling, T.C. *The Strategy of Conflict.* N.Y.: The Oxford University Press 1963.

Sloan, A.A. and F. Witney. *Labor Relations* (4th Ed.) Englewood Cliffs, N.J.: Prentice Hall Inc. (1981).

Stevens, C.M. *Strategy and Collective Bargaining Negotiation.* New York: McGraw-Hill Book Co. Inc. (1963).

Walton, R.E. and R.B. McKersie. *A Behavioral Theory of Labor Negotiations.* New York: McGraw-Hill Book Company (1965).

CASE PROBLEMS FOR DISCUSSION
HARRISON INDUSTRIES CASE (D)

William Hamilton assumed the duties of Personnel Manager on September 15, 1983, and following the certification of the Heating Equipment Workers' Union on September 26, 1983, was placed in charge of labour relations by Mr. Harrison.

Hamilton met with Harrison on October 6, 1983, to discuss the notice to bargain that had been received by the company several days before. Harrison and Hamilton discussed both the union certification, and the establishment of an employer negotiating team. At the end of the meeting, Hamilton drafted a response to the union's notice to bargain stating that the employer was prepared to meet with the union on October 16, 1983. The letter was subsequently delivered to James Allen at the local union hall.

A few days after the company's letter had been received by the union, Hamilton telephoned Allen to discuss arrangements for the first meeting of the negotiating teams. When Hamilton described some of the meeting room facilities at the local hotels in an unfavourable light, Allen gave Hamilton the impression that the union would have no objection to using the employer's facilities if a suitable place could be arranged for the meeting. Hamilton accepted, then suggested that a meeting room on the premises might be preferable and offered to explore the possibility of using the company board room.

The company board room was a relatively large, well-lit, and well-appointed room located in a corner of the building where office noise was at a minimum. It contained a large table that would permit a number of people to sit at each end with a sufficient number of places along each side to seat the company and union representatives. Hamilton felt that the spokesperson for each group and one or two of the chief negotiators from each team could occupy the seats at the ends of the table and had the seating arranged accordingly.

Hamilton invited Allen to inspect the facilities and requested that he bring along a list of the names of the persons who would constitute the union negotiating team when he attended at the office. Later that afternoon, Allen examined the facilities, then demurred on the room arrangements. While he was satisfied that the facilities would be comfortable and convenient, he informed Hamilton that on reflection he believed that the meeting room facilities in a nearby hotel would perhaps be a more appropriate setting in which to negotiate a first agreement. Hamilton reluctantly accepted Allen's request for a change of location, and proceeded to make room arrangements for the first bargaining session.

On October 12, 1983, Hamilton met with Mr. Harrison and the company negotiating team. The group consisted of Hamilton, the personnel manager, as the chairman or chief spokesman, his assistant, the plant manager of plant #2, the vice-president of production, the vice-president of finance, and the chief engineer. At the meeting, Hamilton explained to the group that it was his practice to deal with the union and to answer all comments directed to the company negotiators. He would redirect questions to other members of the team for answers, where necessary. He urged them all to avoid any show of emotion in making responses, regardless of how absurd the questions might seem. Hamilton then went on to provide the group with a brief assessment of each member of the union group. His notes read as follows:

James Allen, the Union Business Agent and Organizer of the union at the plant. An experienced negotiator with an answer for every typical management response to a union demand. Allen's experience is limited to the sheet metal field and the heating industry in particular. He is not unaware of developments and trends in other industries.

Raymond Anderson, President of Local 313. Inexperienced in labour relations and recently dismissed by this company for violation of company rules. Anderson is likely to be a difficult individual to deal with by the company as a result of recent unpleasant encounters with management.

Stan Blakeley, Secretary of Local 313. A press operator in the plant, age fifty-six. An employee of the company since 1963 and employed by Smithson Steel Fabricating for ten years before that date. A good employee. From shop talk, his main concern seems to be inflation and the effect it might have on his pension.

Alex Sutak, Material Handler and Lift Truck Operator. Age twenty-six; married with two small children. Employed by the company since 1978. A friendly, willing worker with a sense of humour. Building his own house in a small rural community about ten miles from the plant.

Marie Laurin, Operates a small press in the plant. Employed since 1982. A serious employee with few outside interests. She supports an invalid mother and is assisting her brother financially with his university education. She did not appear to have any interest whatsoever in the union prior to certification.

Bart Haley, Shop Steward in the Shipping Department. Forty-two years of age; employed since 1974. A pleasant, friendly employee who enjoys hunting and fishing. He has been warned on occasion to refrain from extending his week-ends to three days simply because the fishing was good. Ultra-conservative in his political thinking. Operates a sporting goods and fishing tackle repair business in his spare time.

Hamilton used the balance of the meeting to discuss the company's present position on wages and benefits, and to speculate on the demands that the union would likely make. The current benefits provided by the company were as follows:

Wages: Unskilled employees received an average hourly rate of $7.50 and skilled employees, including the maintenance department, received an average of $9.85. Semiskilled employees received on average an hourly rate of $8.40. Some variation existed in wage rates within each group depending upon skill and length of service. For example, skilled employees' wages ranged from $8.90 to a maximum of $10.50. Wages up to this point in time were largely established by the foreman's evaluation of the employee with length of service playing an important factor in the determination.

Vacations: Following a practiced custom since the acquisition of the fabricating plant in 1963, the plant closed down for two weeks in late August. All employees, regardless of length of service, received their average earnings for the two week period.

Holidays: All employees received as paid holidays: New Year's Day, Good Friday, Easter Monday, Victoria Day, Dominion Day, Labour Day, Thanksgiving Day, Christmas Day, and Boxing Day.

Pension The company provided a pension for employees on attaining age sixty-five, based upon a formula which gave a monthly amount equal to number of years service, times best hourly wage rate times two. For example, an employee with thirty-five years service earning $8.50/hour would receive a monthly pension of $35 \times \$8.50 \times 2 = \$595.99$. In addition, employees would receive the standard Canada Pension. Deductions of CPP were made from each employee, but the company plan was paid for solely by the company.

Health and Related Benefits: The company maintained a group health insurance plan under the provincial system. Fifty percent of the workers' premiums were paid by the company. The company also provided an optional term life insurance which was available to employees at an annual cost of $5.40 per $1000.00 of coverage (up to three times annual earnings maximum).

Working Conditions: Employees currently work an eight hour day with an unpaid lunch period of one hour. Paid morning and afternoon breaks of ten minutes were included in the eight hours of work. Each department had a time clock and employees "punch out and in" to record work time. Employees are allowed seven minutes if late at "punch in" time but tardiness beyond seven minutes would result in loss of pay. Employees working on equipment are provided with safety glasses and wear gloves when necessary.

Employees who arrive late for work more than twice in any one month receive a reprimand from the foreman. Late arrival, however, is seldom a problem, and employees are normally already at work at the official start of the work day.

The company maintains a lunch room where employees may purchase lunches or coffee. The canteen is operated on a contract basis with an outside catering firm. The staff of the canteen are employees of the outside firm but subject to the "rules" laid down in the contract that relate to hours that the canteen remains open, cleaning of the premises, prices to be charged for food, etc. Under the contract, the employees of the canteen are subject to all plant work rules while on the premises.

The procedure in the event of layoff, although unwritten in the past, was to the effect that the longest service employees would be retained if they could do the necessary work. This was later changed to a written policy whereby layoff would be on a departmental basis with employees having longer service being kept on in the event of layoff provided they could do the work available. As a result of the Anderson affair, this policy was further modified to protect employees transferred from one department to another by allowing such employees to retain up to two years seniority upon transfer.

Layoffs represent an annual occurrence in the firm, since the company serves a market that tends to be somewhat seasonal. Usually the work force was reduced in the fall of each year by about 25 percent for a period of about four months. The firm in the past followed a practice of calling back employees in the reverse order of layoff. If an employee whose name was first on the list could not be reached by the person recalling staff, the caller would move on to the next name on the list, until all previous employees had been contacted. New employees would then be hired to fill any remaining vacancies.

The service records of the employees of Plant #2 are as follows:

Service (Plant #2)	Skilled	Unskilled	Semiskilled
under 60 days	-	1	1
over 60 days and under 1 year	1	2	3
over 1 year and under 2 years	3	7	6
over 2 years and under 5 years	5	9	8
over 5 years and under 10 years	10	7	8
over 10 years and under 15 years	8	5	9
over 15 years and under 20 years	3	3	3
over 20 years and under 25 years	3	1	2
over 25 years	1	-	1

The skilled work force is 90 percent male, and the unskilled and semiskilled work force 70 percent male. Eighty percent of the employees are married. The above seniority list does not include the payroll clerk (five years of service), the five foremen, or the two working foremen, the latter employees having nine years and seven years service each.

CASE DISCUSSION QUESTIONS
HARRISON INDUSTRIES CASE (D)

1. *Evaluate Hamilton's actions with respect to the selection of the "negotiation setting."*
2. *Assess Hamilton's selection of the company negotiating team.*
3. *Why did he restrict the response to union questions to himself? What purpose is served by this practice?*
4. *Why might Hamilton be interested in the make-up of the union negotiating team?*
5. *What additional research, and what additional information will Hamilton require before the first bargaining session?*
6. *Suggest an approach to bargaining which Hamilton might follow.*

COLLECTIVE BARGAINING SIMULATION

Harrison Industries cases "A" through "D" provide information not only for analysis and discussion purposes, but also for a background to a collective bargaining simulation. The Harrison Industries "E" case which follows provides additional basic information that a union and/or employer would require in order to negotiate a collective agreement. But, as with a "real world" situation, each party to the negotiations must do a considerable amount of research in preparation for the bargaining sessions to reach a satisfactory collective agreement.

As a simulation, members of a group may assume the roles of employer and union negotiating teams, and be assigned the task of negotiating a suitable first collective agreement for Harrison Industries. The teams may consist of two to six members each, and should undertake the assignment in the same manner as any union officer or employer in today's business environment.

The case is structured to permit Harrison Industries to be situated in the community where the bargaining teams are located, and the economic and employment conditions of the particular area may be applied to the company for bargaining purposes. The labour legislation of the province should govern the negotiations and the collective agreement. As a rough guide, the simulation may be conducted in three segments:

1. **The preparation for bargaining.** *This would include research into area wage rates, industry wage rates, the area labour market, area and industry benefits and working conditions, statutory regulations as to hours of work, vacations and holidays. Some consideration might be given to consultation with local unions and employers in similar industries in the area to determine this and other relevant information. The research data so obtained would form the basis for the formulation of initial union demands and the bargaining strategies of the teams. The instructor or simulation leader might require that a research report be submitted by each team before the second stage begins.*

2. **The bargaining sessions.** *The negotiation of the agreement is usually completed in three to four bargaining sessions of two to three hours each, with the first session typically short, usually less than one hour. Some time should be allowed between each session for further research and reflection. Teams which do not reach an agreement by the end of the last scheduled session are deemed to have failed, and the employees either on strike or locked-out.*

3. **The post-negotiation stage.** *On the completion of negotiations, each pair of bargaining teams prepare their written collective agreement as a joint exercise, then prepare a separate analysis of*

their own goals, strategies, and justification for acceptance of the provisions of the collective agreement which they negotiated. Any bargaining team which failed to reach an agreement would be obliged to justify the strike or lock-out that resulted from their failure to do so. All events leading to the strike or lock-out should be analyzed as well.

The bargaining analysis may be used for seminar discussion purposes by the participants in the simulation, or graded as a class assignment by the instructor or simulation leader.

HARRISON INDUSTRIES CASE (E)

Harrison Industries currently sells about 60 percent of its output of sheet metal parts to other heating equipment manufacturers, 15 percent to hardware and industrial supply outlets and the remaining 25 percent to a large industrial customer under a five-year contract which ends in December. The industrial customer has given notice that he does not intend to renew the contract, but Harrison is considering a bid to supply sheet metal parts to another heating equipment manufacturer under a fixed-price contract for an equivalent quantity of goods.

The new contract would enable Harrison Industries to maintain its current single shift production at Plant #2 at the same level as in the previous two years, assuming that the other customers continue to purchase the same quantities. Harrison, however, must be in a position to place a firm bid in the hands of the buyer before November 15, if he expects to have the bid considered.

In the preparation of the bid, Harrison must consider the following matters:

1. *The buyer has a reputation for accepting the lowest bid, since the products purchased tend to be standard sheet metal products. (The products of each manufacturer are essentially identical.)*
2. *Since the contract is for a fixed unit price, the cost of production must be determined with some degree of accuracy.*
3. *A large number of the competitors of Harrison Industries will likely be interested in the contract.*
4. *The contract will be for a two-year period.*
5. *The cost of materials will probably be the same for each manufacturer who bids on the contract.*
6. *Harrison's competitors in every case have updated their equip-*

ment within the last five years, and all maintain somewhat similar production facilities.

7. *The most important factor in a successful bid will be the labour cost component of the unit bid price.*

8. *Delivery of parts would be expected as soon as the contract is signed (i.e., November 15).*

9. *The buyer is known to insist on a clause in the contract that would permit termination unilaterally in the event of a strike or lock-out at a supplier's plant.*

10. *A failure on the part of Harrison Industries to obtain the contract would mean a staff reduction at Plant #2 of about 20 percent, effective January 1st.*

Production at Plant #1, the foundry operation, is expected to remain steady during the next year. The company has already received firm orders for the entire year's output. Some of the production equipment, however, is in need of replacement and the plant manager has suggested that new equipment be installed as soon as possible in the new year in order to handle the heavy demand for the company's products. The estimated cost of the new equipment would be in the $125,000–$150,000 range.

The total sales for the company year ending September 30th were $7,601,890. The profit (before tax) was $524,208. Total assets of the company at the year end (including an inventory of $135,000) were $2,625,543.

The production break-down for the year was as follows: Plant #1 $4,049,981, Plant #2 $3,551,909. Profit as a percentage of sales was approximately the same for each plant.

COLLECTIVE BARGAINING INFORMATION
The wage rates, working conditions, and benefits set out in Harrison Industries Case (D) represent the current wage rates and benefits for collective bargaining purposes. Assume that all given data (where appropriate) was in effect at the time that notice to bargain was given.

HARRISON INDUSTRIES CASE (E)
ADDITIONAL MANAGEMENT INFORMATION

Selected financial data: Plant #2 (for year end September 30, 1983)

Value of produced goods	$3,551,909
Material purchases	855,540
Fixed costs	189,963
Variable costs	160,147
Labour costs (nonsupervisory personnel)	1,682,546
Contribution to admin. expense	419,841
Contribution to R & D expense	8,509
Profit contribution from plant	235,363

Depreciation, Plant #1		$11,900
Plant #2		89,000

PART V
THE ADMINISTRATIVE PROCESS

CHAPTER NINE

THE ADMINISTRATIVE PROCESS

THE COLLECTIVE AGREEMENT

By definition, a collective agreement is a written agreement made between an employer and the bargaining representative or agent that is either certified by a labour relations board or voluntarily recognized in writing as the exclusive bargaining representative of a defined bargaining unit of the employees. The document sets out the terms and conditions of employment under which the employees will work for a specified period of time, and also sets out the rights and duties of both the employer and the bargaining representative. The agreement is signed by the authorized signing officers of the bargaining representative and the employer's organization, or the employer personally, and binds the employer, the bargaining representative, and all of the employees in the bargaining unit. Because the bargaining representative must meet the definition of a trade union under the labour legislation of most provinces, every employees' organization that engages in collective bargaining, whether it calls itself an "association," "syndicate" or "union," is essentially a trade union, and is generally referred to as such under Canadian labour relations statutes.

In its simplest form, the agreement is made between a single employer and a trade union that represents a bargaining unit of the employer's employees, but collective agreements need not always be of this type. In some industries, many employers are organized by a single union, and the employers may form an employers' association to bargain collectively with the union. In these instances, the agreement applies to a number of employers, even though only one collective agreement is negotiated. Similarly, a large employer may negotiate a collective agreement with a number of different unions, each representing different bargaining units of employees. In this case, the unions have banded together to bargain jointly with the employer and may negotiate a master agreement with, perhaps, special provisions which apply to each of the different bargaining units. A further type of agreement is one that may be negotiated by an employers' association and a group of unions (usually called a council of trade unions), covering not only a number of employers, but a number of trade unions as well. A collective agreement, therefore, may assume many forms, and may apply to many employees and organizations.

The contents of a collective agreement represent the product of the negotiation process and a number of statutory obligations. In most jurisdictions, the parties are free to include in their collective agreements whatever terms and conditions of employment they wish to be bound by, but some provinces require a number of provisions in every collective agreement. These clauses tend to be either essential to the relationship or the operation of the agreement itself, and are deemed to be included or represent statutory provisions which govern the application of the agreement. In Ontario, for example, every collective agreement must contain a clause which provides that no strike or lock-out may take place while the collective agreement is in effect,[1] a "recognition clause" whereby the employer recognizes the union as the exclusive bargaining representative of the employees,[2] and a compulsory arbitration procedure to settle any disputes that may arise out of the interpretation, violation, or application of the agreement.[3] Additionally, the term of the agreement must be for at least one year, otherwise the agreement is deemed to be a one-year agreement.[4] The purpose of the "required" clauses is to establish an administrative framework for the parties and to regulate activities that would interfere with the administration of the agreement. For example, strikes and lock-outs are prohibited in all jurisdictions while the collective agreement is in effect, and in an effort to establish a period of time that will be free from disruptive strikes or lock-outs, collective agreements are required to run for a period of at least a year. The parties may, of course negotiate agreements for longer periods of time, but agreements for shorter periods of time are only permitted under specific circumstances, or with the consent of the labour relations board.

The removal of the strike and lock-out as a means of resolving differences necessitates their replacement with some other means of settling disputes that may arise out of the collective agreement. All provinces and the federal government have essentially substituted arbitration of disputes for the strike or lock-out while an agreement is in effect, and if the parties fail to include an arbitration procedure in their collective agreement, most statutes provide for a procedure that is deemed to be included in the agreement. Collective agreements will usually provide for a grievance procedure as well, as a preliminary process for the resolution of differences in a less formal manner.

A final requirement which most provinces impose on the parties is a union recognition clause. This clause not only constitutes recognition of the union as the exclusive bargaining representative of the employees while the collective agreement is in effect, but enables the union to give notice to the employer to bargain for a new agreement as the existing agreement nears the end of its period of application. It also identifies the union as the bargaining representative entitled to the rights available to it under the collective agreement and the applicable labour legislation.

Apart from these basic requirements, the parties are free to deal with all aspects of the employment relationship and the rights of the union and employer in the agreement. A typical collective agreement, for example, may contain articles that deal with the following:

> **management rights**
> **union security**
> **seniority**
> **wages and benefits**
> **hours of work**
> **holidays and vacations**
> **promotion and demotion of employees**
> **layoff and recall of employees**
> **contracting out of work**
> **technological change**
> **grievance procedure and arbitration**
> **no strike – no lock-out clause**
> **recognition of the union**
> **description of the bargaining unit**
> **term**
> **renewal notice**

Most collective agreements are lengthy documents in order to deal with the many aspects of the employment relationship and the administration of the agreement itself. As a general rule, the larger and more complex the bargaining unit, the more detailed the collective agreement. Nonetheless, the agreement, even when it attempts to cover every conceivable aspect of the employment relationship, cannot anticipate every problem that might arise between the employees and the employer. As a result, most collective agreements tend to be viewed as policy documents rather than a detailed or specific body of rules governing the relationship.

THE THEORETICAL NATURE OF THE COLLECTIVE AGREEMENT

A number of theories have been developed concerning the nature of the collective agreement and the determination of the rights of the parties under a document that cannot possibly cover all contingencies. The rights and duties set out in the collective agreement obviously govern the actions of the parties where the document is clear and unambiguous, but where some ambiguity exists or where the agreement does not deal with a specific issue or situation, the question arises as to whether the matter falls within the ambit of collective bargaining. The most widely held theory associated with the notion of the collective agreement is the **residual rights theory**. This theory recognizes the historical development of bargaining rights and is based on the premise that originally the employer had all rights to manage the firm or organization, and was only restricted or limited by those limitations imposed by law or agreed upon between the employer and the employees. Applied to collective bargaining, the residual rights theory states that the employer retains all of the rights that he historically had, and only those terms and conditions of employment specifically included in the collective agreement fettered or limited the rights of the employer. By this theory, any right not covered by the collective agreement would be an exclusive right of the employer. Additionally, the employer would possess any other rights specifically retained in the collective agreement, or granted to him by the union as a result of the bargaining process.

In practice, under the residual rights theory, the rights of the union and the employees are limited to those established by the collective agreement, and the employer is free to operate the business or activity subject only to those limitations set out in the document. For example, if the collective agreement is silent on the right of the employer to contract out work, the employer would be entitled to do so, provided that it is done for sound management reasons, and not for the purpose of destroying the collective bargaining relationship. Similarly, if the collective agreement does not restrict the rights of the employer to establish additional work shifts, the employer would be entitled to do so.

An alternate theory (sometimes referred to as the **status quo theory** or fixed practice theory) states that the rights and duties of the parties are frozen at the time that collective bargaining is introduced to the employment relationship. The collective agreement not only alters the relationship specifically according to its terms, but all other rights of management not set out in the agreement must remain as they were when the agreement was made. In other words, the employer is obliged to follow all past practices not altered by the collective agreement, and changes in past practice may only be made through negotiation with the union. The employer is not entitled to make unilateral changes in working conditions or other practices not covered by the collective agreement, and must maintain the "status quo."

DISPUTE RESOLUTION IN THE ADMINISTRATIVE PROCESS

Differences of opinion that arise out of the interpretation, application, or administration of the collective agreement are generally resolved either through a relatively informal negotiation process known as the **grievance procedure**, or through a formal, third party process known as **arbitration**. In practice, the two processes are sequential. Most collective agreements require all disputes that arise out of the collective agreement to be framed in the form of a grievance, and processed through a series of steps or meetings whereby the problems are discussed by representatives of the union and the employer in an effort to resolve the issues. Only those disputes that are not resolved by the grievance process proceed to the more formal dispute resolution process where the decision is made by either a single arbitrator or an arbitration board.

Labour legislation in Canada does not require the parties to a collective agreement to include in the document a grievance procedure, but in all jurisdictions[5] strikes and lock-outs are prohibited while a collective agreement in effect; and any disputes arising out of the agreement must be resolved by binding arbitration. Very few collective agreements, however, do not contain a grievance procedure, since both parties realize that it represents an important mechanism for the resolution of disputes that will inevitably arise when the agreement is implemented. The complexity of the process, nevertheless, tends to vary according to the size and nature of the employer's firm and the size of the work force. In a small plant with few employees, the procedure may be a single step, where the employee, accompanied by a representative of the union, may present the grievance to the employer directly. In a larger, more complex plant, the process may involve as many as six steps, culminating in a meeting between senior executives of the employer's organization and their counterparts in the union.

A grievance procedure generally parallels the levels of management in the employer's firm with each successive step involving a more senior level of management, but in every case, it begins informally at the lowest level of supervision. A typical grievance procedure in a large firm might be described as follows:

Step 1.   *The employee verbally presents the grievance to his or her immediate supervisor, and may do so in the company of a shop steward or grievance steward.*

Step 2.   *If the grievance is not resolved by the employee's immediate supervisor, the grievance is reduced to writing and presented to the general foreman by the shop steward. The general foreman may meet with the steward with the grievor present, and discuss the grievance. The foreman must provide a written response within a specific number (e.g. five) days after receipt of the grievance.*

Step 3.   *If the answer to the grievance does not satisfy the union, the grievance may be submitted to the plant manager by the union. A meeting may be held with the union grievance committee to discuss the grievance and the plant manager must respond within a specific number of days.*

At the third step in the procedure, the meeting usually involves personnel from the firm's industrial relations department and perhaps members of the union executive if the step represents the final stage of the grievance procedure. Union policy grievances and employer grievances are usually presented at the final step, and in many cases, grievances concerning the discharge of employees may be presented at this step as well. In many large firms, a fourth step is also included in the procedure which would involve senior management (such as the Vice-President, Personnel and Industrial Relations) and the international union representative in a final attempt to resolve the dispute before the parties are faced with the decision to take the matter to arbitration.

The three- or four-step grievance procedure as outlined is often structured deliberately by the parties to encourage settlement at the lowest possible level in the procedure. Step 1 permits the employee to informally bring the grievance to the attention of the first line supervisor. Grievances are often simple misunderstandings, or minor errors on the part of supervision, and in most cases, the foreman is able to immediately satisfy legitimate grievances when they are brought to his or her attention. If the supervisor does so, the grievance is resolved at that step and proceeds no further. Where the supervisor rejects the grievance, the employee must then seek the assistance of the union to proceed to the second step.

Step 2 of the procedure in this example is a "screening" step in the process. The employee must reduce the grievance to writing for presentation by the union shop steward to the general foreman. The union shop steward, who is expected to be familiar with the collective agreement, will discuss the grievance with the employee and make certain that the grievance represents a legitimate concern of the employee before taking the grievance to management. In this way, the shop steward will sift out frivolous and imaginary wrongs from the genuine, and carry forward those that appear to merit further discussion. Step 2 in this case is the beginning of the formal grievance procedure, where the employer's representative at Step 2 is expected to meet with the union to discuss the grievance, then provide a written response to the grievance within a specified time-frame. Legitimate grievances are usually resolved at this stage, and only those which the parties cannot settle in a satisfactory manner move on to Step 3.

Step 3, in the example, represents a final attempt by the parties to resolve their differences. In this instance, the plant manager and the union grievance committee meet and discuss the grievance, and if agreement cannot be reached, the plant manager is expected to provide a formal response within a specified number of days. The written response usually represents the final answer of the employer to the union, and if the union is not satisfied, it must decide whether the grievance should be carried on to arbitration.

Grievances that are not settled by way of the grievance procedure do not necessarily proceed directly to arbitration. Union grievance committees will generally reassess the grievance before moving to arbitration in order to determine whether the particular dispute warrants the cost of having the matter determined by a third party. Serious matters, such as the failure of the employer to comply with agreed terms in the collective agreement concerning the layoff or recall of employees, or the unjust dismissal of an employee are generally carried forward, but some minor grievances, or those that appear to be doubtful in substance are sometimes abandoned by the union when the grievance procedure is exhausted.

The arbitration process provides for the final and binding resolution of disputes arising out of the collective agreement by a third party. This may be in the form of an award by either a single arbitrator or a tripartite board of arbitration. Most collective agreements will specifically provide for either a single arbitrator or board to hear and decide the disputes, but in some cases, the parties are permitted to select one or the other depending upon the type of dispute or problem. All jurisdictions[6] require grievances to be settled by some form of arbitration if the parties cannot resolve the problems in a satisfactory manner by way of their grievance procedure, and if the parties have failed to include an arbitration procedure in their collective agreement, most labour relations statutes provide a procedure which is either deemed to be included in their collective agreement, or which the parties must follow under the statute.

In Ontario, the *Labour Relations Act* provides for a three-person board to hear grievances. The make up of the board is representative in the sense that both the union and the employer each nominate one person to the board, and the two persons so chosen select a third person who becomes the chairman. Each party must nominate its representative within a relatively short period of time (within five days of the first nominee) and the two nominees must select the third party promptly (within a further five days). If either party should fail or refuse to nominate a representative to the board within the time specified, or if the nominees cannot agree on a chairman, the Minister of Labour may appoint a member in order to establish the board to hear the grievance.[7]

Arbitration boards are representative boards, and consequently, the respective nominees to the board tend to support the position of their nominators. The chairman is the neutral party, whose views on the grievance normally establish the final award. For this reason, many unions and employers will provide for a single arbitrator to hear any disputes arising out of their collective agreement rather than use an arbitration board. One of the advantages of the single arbitrator is reduced cost, and sometimes a reduced time-frame for the hearing of the grievance and the release of the award. Employers and unions who prefer the board method justify the added expense and time in terms of having a member on the board with sympathy for their point of view, and the ability to ensure that it is brought to the attention of the chairman in the executive sessions of the board which precede the preparation of the award.

THE ARBITRATION PROCESS

THE PROCEDURAL FRAMEWORK

Arbitration, as previously noted, is a process whereby disputes between the parties that arise out of the interpretation, application, administration or alleged violation of the collective agreement are referred to a third party neutral, either as a single arbitrator or board, for final determination. Arbitration is, in effect, the final step of the grievance procedure in the sense that the award of the arbitrator resolves the dispute. The process, however, is not a simple continuation of the grievance procedure but a separate procedure with its own rules and formalities.

The arbitration process is essentially a procedure established for the hearing of the grievance and all evidence and argument related to it. While the hearing is relatively informal, it must, nevertheless, be conducted in accordance with certain rules of procedure not unlike those of a court of law, since the arbitrator or board is acting in a quasi-judicial capacity in deciding the issues.

The process begins with a request for arbitration by either the employer or the union. In accordance with the collective agreement the parties then select a sole arbitrator or establish an arbitration board to hear the dispute. When the board is constituted or the sole arbitrator accepts the request to act as arbitrator, the sole arbitrator or chairman of the board proceeds to fix a convenient date and place for the hearing, usually at a hotel in the community where the firm is located. In preparation for the hearing, both parties will assemble their evidence and witnesses, and often engage legal counsel to act for them in the presentation of their respective sides of the case. If either party desires the presence of persons at the hearing who might be reluctant to attend, the party may request the arbitrator or chairman to issue a subpoena to ensure their attendance.

The hearing room is usually furnished with large board-room tables arranged in a "T" shape, with seating for the arbitrator or board at the head of the "T," and the counsel and interested parties facing each other on opposite sides of the base of the "T." The employer's side usually consists of legal counsel, the director of industrial relations (who sometimes acts in place of legal counsel), the supervisor of the plant or operation where the grievance arose, and the immediate supervisor of the grievor. Other members of the personnel department might also attend. In addition, witnesses that will give evidence in support of the employer's side of the case will also be present.

The union may engage counsel to present its case at the hearing, but often, international union representatives will perform the role of counsel and conduct the union's side of the argument. The remainder of the union team will usually include the president of the local union, the chief steward or chairman of the grievance committee, and perhaps the shop steward of the department where the grievor is employed. The grievor and witnesses that the union intends to call on to give evidence will also be present. A few minutes before the time fixed for the hearing to begin, the employer and union groups will assemble in the hearing room and take their places at the table, where they will await the arrival of the arbitrator or board. The board or the arbitrator will arrive at the hearing room at the appointed time and be seated at the head of the "T" shaped table arrangement. Counsel for the union and the employer will then introduce themselves and their group to the board, and after the brief introductions, the hearing will begin.

The arbitrator or chairman generally begins the hearing by asking both counsel if they agree that the grievance has been properly brought to arbitration, and that the board has jurisdiction to hear the matter. Any preliminary objections concerning the arbitrability of the grievance are then dealt with, since the arbitration board must determine that the grievance is valid and a proper matter for arbitration before it may be heard on its merits. If, after hearing the evidence and argument from both counsel on any preliminary objections, the board decides that the grievance is arbitrable, the hearing of the merits of the grievance will then proceed.

The hearing of the grievance on its merits generally follows a procedure whereby both counsel make an opening statement concerning their respective positions on the grievance, and advise the board of any facts or issues that relate to the grievance upon which the parties have agreed. The counsel who has the onus of proof usually leads his or her evidence by calling a first witness who will give evidence under oath on matters pertaining to the grievance. The evidence of the witness is presented in the form of responses to questions by the counsel, and is referred to as an **examination-in-chief**. When the counsel has finished questioning the witness, the opposing counsel is then entitled to ask the witness questions concerning the answers which the witness has given during the course of the examination-in-chief. In addition, the **cross-examination** may range beyond the statements given, and the counsel may ask questions that test the credibility or truthfulness of the witness if the counsel has any doubts about the statements made in evidence. Following the cross-examination, the witnesses' own counsel may **re-examine** the witness to clarify, explain, or correct any impressions that the opposing counsel may have created during the cross-examination. Counsel will then proceed to call additional witnesses and the procedure will be repeated until the counsel is satisfied that he or she has all of the evidence before the arbitration board.

On the completion of the evidence of the one party, counsel for the opposing party will then call evidence in an attempt to refute the evidence of the side with the onus of proof, or to establish the opposition case. This will proceed in the same manner for the examination of witnesses, and will continue until the evidence of the opposing party has been presented to the board. Documentary evidence is generally introduced by counsel through the various witnesses, who identify each document as being their own, or as received by them. Articles (such as stolen or damaged goods) are identified in a similar fashion.

When all of the evidence has been presented to the arbitrator or board, the counsel for each party in turn present their final arguments on the grievance. The **argument** constitutes a summary of the evidence and a commentary or assessment of it from the counsel's particular perspective. Legal argument or arbitral authorities are also cited at this stage to support the arguments presented to the board. As a general rule, the counsel with the onus of proof submits his or her argument first, and the opposing counsel follows. The counsel with the onus of proof then has a final right of **reply** to any matters raised in the argument of the opposing counsel, such as a response to a legal authority or other similar case raised in the argument. At this point, the hearing usually ends, and the arbitrator or board is left to consider the evidence and argument and prepare an award.

If the grievance was presented to a board of arbitration, the members of the board will usually hold an **executive session** to discuss the evidence and the grievance immediately after the hearing. If the grievance is extremely complex, with a great deal of evidence to consider, the executive session might be held at a later time, after the board members have had an opportunity to carefully examine and weigh the testimony and arguments. Following the executive session, the chairman will then prepare a draft award which will be submitted to the other board members for their comment or approval. As a general rule, the draft becomes the award if either or both of the other members concur with the chairman's decision. If either of the members does not agree with the award, the member will usually signify on the award itself that he or she **dissents**, and may prepare a dissenting opinion on the grievance. The majority award, nevertheless, is the award of the board, and is binding on the parties, even though one member does not agree with the award.

The award and any dissenting opinion is then submitted to the parties, and the parties are obliged to implement it. Enforcement methods vary from province to province, but generally an arbitration award may be enforced through the Supreme or Superior Court of the province if a party fails to comply with the decision. In Ontario, for example, the parties are obliged to comply with the award within a fourteen-day period after the date upon which the award is to be implemented. If either party fails to comply with the award within that period, the other party may file the award with the Registrar of the Supreme Court of Ontario, and the award may then be enforced as if it was a judgment of the court.[8]

THE NATURE AND LIMITS OF THE ARBITRATION PROCESS

Arbitrators, like all other persons, view situations on the basis of the information given to them, and consequently, their awards tend to reflect the impressions they acquire at the hearings from the witnesses and counsel in the course of the evidence and argument. Nevertheless, sole arbitrators and the chairmen of boards of arbitration are third party neutrals in disputes, and first and foremost, attempt to provide a fair and unbiased response to each grievance, fully aware that the decision may not satisfy both parties. This is inevitable in a dispute resolution system which requires the decision maker to act in a fashion not unlike that of a judge in a court of law.

Because the arbitration process has much in common with the judicial system, one theorist[9] who examined the arbitration process concluded that an arbitrator may be viewed as a **judge or chief interpreter of the collective agreement**; a person to whom the parties may turn when they cannot agree on the proper interpretation of a term or condition which they have included in their agreement. In this sense, an arbitrator acts in much the same fashion as a member of the judiciary, and in many respects is obliged to conduct a hearing in accordance with rules of procedure not unlike those of a court of law.

An alternate view of the role of the arbitrator is that an arbitrator is something more than a mere interpreter or judge of the agreement. This theory suggests that arbitrators in particular circumstances may interpret collective agreements not in accordance with the apparent meaning of the words alone, but in the light of broader, general labour relations goals. In these cases, the arbitrators become more than mere interpreters, and in a sense, policy makers who consider the public interest as well as the interests of the parties in performing their role.

Most Canadian arbitrators tend to consider themselves as "chief interpreters" or "judges" of the collective agreement rather than policy makers, and refrain from basing their decisions on broad overriding public policy goals, although in some instances they may feel obliged to consider certain types of grievances in the light of the public interest as well as the specific interests of the parties where the public interest represents an element of the grievance. These instances are not common, however, and arbitrators generally see their role as one which should be confined to the interests of the parties and their own collective agreement.

The attitude of the arbitrator to the impact of collective bargaining on the employment relationship, nevertheless, may have a profound effect on the decisions that an arbitrator might make with respect to management rights. Most arbitrators generally subscribe to the residual rights theory in so far as management rights are concerned, but some will interpret collective agreements as "living documents" that set out broad policy statements, rather than specific rights. Other arbitrators tend to look at the collective agreement in terms of the strict meaning of the words, rather than the intention of the parties in the interpretation of the various clauses in the document. While the approach of an arbitrator may vary depending upon the circumstances, an arbitrator who tends to read the clauses of a collective agreement in terms of the plain or ordinary meaning of the words sometimes acquires the reputation of being a **strict constructionist**. Others, who tend to look behind the particular words and at the behaviour of the parties in an effort to determine the intent of the parties when they negotiated the agreement tend to be labelled **liberal constructionists** as a reflection of the method that they use to interpret terms in a collective agreement. The attitudes of arbitrators, however, usually vary from case to case, and seldom does an arbitrator slavishly follow one approach or the other. In this regard, the reputations that some arbitrators occasionally acquire may very well be misleading.

The powers of arbitrators to decide grievances as they see fit are not unfettered. Both the process and the award are subject to specific legal limitations which are designed to ensure fairness and reasonableness on the part of the arbitrator. In most jurisdictions the authority of the arbitrator or board is founded in the collective agreement, the labour legislation, and the common law. Collective agreements (or in some cases the collective bargaining legislation, where the agreement does not include an arbitration clause) determine whether grievances will be decided by a single arbitrator or an arbitration board, and usually provide that the arbitrator may not add to or alter the terms of any clause in the agreement by an award. The collective agreement may also provide that a grievance will not be arbitrable unless the grievor has complied with the time limits and grievance procedure set out in the agreement before taking the grievance to arbitration. Ontario has attempted to provide some flexibility for arbitrators (and grievors) in these instances by permitting arbitrators to exercise discretion in dealing with cases where timeliness is raised as an objection to the arbitrator's jurisdiction to hear the grievance, but apart from this, arbitrators must generally abide by any restrictions which the parties have placed upon the arbitration process in their collective agreements.

The general practice followed by most arbitrators accordingly is to seek some assurance from the parties at the outset of the arbitration hearing that the grievance has been properly brought forward in accordance with the collective agreement. If one party or the other objects to the hearing of the grievance on its merits as a result of some procedural defect under the collective agreement, the arbitrator is obliged to determine the validity of the objection before proceeding further with the hearing. Since the validity of a grievance is determined by the collective agreement, the arbitrator must determine that the grievance has not only been brought in accordance with the procedure in the collective agreement, but that it also concerns the interpretation, application, administration or alleged violation of the collective agreement. A grievance concerning a matter outside the agreement, (for example, a complaint about the colour of paint used to paint the employer's delivery trucks), would not be arbitrable, since the colour of paint would not be covered by the collective agreement.

Preliminary objections to the arbitrator's jurisdiction to hear the grievance, then, may relate to either the substance of the grievance, or the manner in which it is brought to arbitration. Grievances that do not relate to the agreement are rarely brought forward to arbitration, as most union grievance stewards or international representatives realize that the validity of the grievance is determined by the collective agreement. Procedural defects are much more common, however, as a failure to comply with time limits in the filing or processing of grievances often occurs and may constitute grounds for complaint by the employer that the failure to properly process the grievance has rendered it unarbitrable.

In addition to compliance with the terms of the collective agreement, arbitration proceedings must conform to the common law rules of "natural justice." These rules place an obligation on the arbitrator to fix a hearing date and give the parties adequate notice in order to prepare their respective sides of the case, the opportunity to present evidence and call witnesses at the hearing, the right to cross-examine witnesses, and the right of each party to respond to the evidence of their opponent. Throughout the hearing, the arbitrator must treat the parties in a fair and unbiased manner and make no decision on the grievance until all of the evidence and argument has been presented. In some provinces, such as Ontario, the labour relations legislation permits arbitrators to establish their own rules of procedure and to accept certain kinds of evidence (such as hearsay evidence) which would not be acceptable in a court of law, but regardless of the legislative broadening of the power of the arbitrator in this regard, the arbitrator must take care not to offend the rules of natural justice in the conduct of a fair and impartial hearing.

The arbitration award itself is also subject to certain limitations. The authority of the arbitrator stems from the collective agreement and the law, but the award must fall within the jurisdictional limits of the arbitrator to be enforceable. In this regard, the award must address the issues brought before the arbitrator and must relate to the collective agreement. If the arbitrator makes an award that deals with something other than the issue brought to arbitration, the arbitrator will have exceeded his or her jurisdiction. Similarly, if the arbitrator makes an **error of law on the face of the award**, a party to the arbitration may apply to the courts to have the award quashed. For example, if the arbitrator gives a clause in the collective agreement an interpretation which it could not possibly bear, or if the interpretation is based upon erroneous and inadmissible evidence, the defect would constitute an error of law on the face of the award.

Arbitration awards, unlike the judgments of the courts, are not subject to appeal. However, where an arbitrator has exceeded his or her jurisdiction, or made an error of law on the face of the award, or failed to act in a fair and unbiased manner, a party to the proceedings may make an application to the Superior or Supreme Court of the province to have the award of the arbitrator quashed. The onus rests on the party who brings the action to prove to the satisfaction of the court at least one of four grounds in order to have the court act. These are:

1. *Bias or fraud on the part of the arbitrator.*
2. *A denial of natural justice by the arbitrator.*
3. *An error of law on the face of the award.*
4. *The arbitrator exceeded his or her jurisdiction.*

As a rule, bias or fraud on the part of an arbitrator is rare, as most arbitrators and the chairmen of arbitration boards are careful to maintain a neutral position in arbitration proceedings. The nominees to arbitration boards are recognized as having some bias or sympathy for the party who appoints them to the board, but they must, nevertheless, avoid acting as a vociferous advocate of their nominator's case during the hearing. The parties normally expect sympathy to be shown by their nominee to their own particular stance on a grievance, but the chairman is expected to remain neutral throughout the hearing. If the chairman shows bias, or acts in a fraudulent manner, the party who suffers as a result of the chairman's actions is entitled to apply to the courts to have the award quashed.

A denial of natural justice may be a result of a bias on the part of an arbitrator, or simply a failure on the part of an arbitrator to realize that an erroneous procedural ruling or an improper ruling on the admissibility of evidence may seriously affect the presentation of the case of a party at a hearing. In these instances, the arbitrator's bias or error may constitute a denial of natural justice. For example, if an arbitrator refuses to permit counsel for one party to cross-examine a witness of the opposing party, or if the arbitrator fails to notify all interested parties of the hearing date and place, the acts or omissions of the arbitrator would constitute a denial of natural justice. In the first instance, it would be a denial of a fair hearing, and in the second case, the failure to notify interested parties of the hearing would deny them the right to a hearing entirely.

As noted earlier, an error of law on the face of the award, and any instance where the arbitrator exceeded his or her jurisdiction would also constitute grounds for an action to have the award quashed. For an arbitrator to exceed or make an error as to jurisdiction, the arbitrator must not have been properly appointed (or in the case of a board, established) under the collective agreement, or the arbitrator or board must not have decided the issue put forward by the parties, or decided the issue on improper evidence. For example, if an arbitration board assumes jurisdiction to hear a grievance that did not arise out of the collective agreement, the board would have exceeded its jurisdiction.

Where grounds exist to challenge an award of an arbitrator, the procedure which the party must follow in most provinces is to make an application to the Supreme Court of the province for the issue of a writ of **certiorari, prohibition,** or **mandamus.** Boards of arbitration (or arbitrators) are established as **statutory tribunals,** and are governed by the labour legislation of the province which provides for their establishment under the collective agreement. The board's actions may therefore be subject to review. The three writs which the court may issue each have a different purpose, and depending upon the circumstances any one of the three may be requested. All three are known as **prerogative writs** and represent court orders directed to inferior tribunals or public officials. A **writ of certiorari** is an order which quashes a decision of a tribunal such as an arbitration board, rendering it a nullity. A **writ of prohibition** is, as the name implies, an order prohibiting the person to whom it is directed from doing something. In a collective bargaining context, it could be directed to an arbitrator to prohibit the arbitrator from holding a hearing if the arbitrator does not have jurisdiction. A **writ of mandamus** is essentially the reverse of an order of prohibition in the sense that it is an order directed to a tribunal or public official ordering the persons or tribunal to do something that they have a duty to do.

In Ontario, the application for the three writs has been replaced by an application for **judicial review,** a procedure whereby the courts examine the actions or award of an arbitrator or arbitration board for a lack of jurisdiction, bias, or the other deficiencies mentioned previously. The remedies which the court may issue and the legal principles which the court will apply are the same as those which would be applicable to prerogative writs in other provinces, and the remedial powers of the court would be much the same as well.

LEGAL PRINCIPLES AND DOCTRINES APPLICABLE TO THE ARBITRATION PROCESS

The role of the arbitrator in a rights dispute arising out of a collective agreement is similar in many respects to that of a judge hearing an ordinary contract dispute in a court of law. In both cases, the process is conducted to obtain an interpretation of the agreement, and to establish the rights or duties of the parties flowing from the interpretation. The process is also used in each instance to fashion an appropriate remedy for any violation of the agreement. Finally, the process itself is similar in that a judge and an arbitrator are obliged to act in a fair and impartial manner, and decide the issue placed before the forum only after a full and complete hearing has been held. Unlike the formal atmosphere of the courtroom, however, an arbitration is conducted with a somewhat greater degree of informality, and in less formal surroundings, but nevertheless, in accordance with much the same rules of procedure as those applicable to a court of law.

Labour legislation in each province has attempted to give labour arbitrators a considerable degree of flexibility in the conduct of arbitration hearings and the type of evidence that may be presented by the parties. This has contributed much to the informal atmosphere under which the hearings are conducted, but arbitrators are ever mindful of the fact that their hearings must be conducted in accordance with the rules of natural justice. The rules of natural justice are essentially universal in their application, and apply equally to courts and all other tribunals that act in a judicial or quasi-judicial manner. As a result, arbitrators have naturally looked to the procedures followed by the courts for guidance in the conduct of their hearings, and patterned their procedures after those models. In the conduct of arbitration cases, they have also turned to many legal doctrines and principles for assistance in the determination of the type and the propriety of the evidence and issues that they will hear.

In an effort to screen out or exclude grievances that represent the unfair assertion of rights under collective agreements, arbitrators generally apply a number of common law doctrines or principles which the courts have used to exclude similar claims. For example, where one party to a collective agreement is aware of a violation of the agreement by the other party and permits the violation to continue without objection for a long period of time, the party may lose the right to later enforce the right that has been violated, or obtain redress for the violation. If a long-standing violation is eventually brought to arbitration, the common law doctrine of **laches** may be raised to preclude the party from asserting the right to redress. The **doctrine of laches** states that a party who fails to enforce a right for a long period of time loses the right to bring the claim before the courts, provided that the court is satisfied that (1) the party was aware of the violation of the right by the other party, and did nothing for a long period of time to stop the violation, and (2) as a result of the failure to take action, the party who violated the right acted to his or her detriment to the extent that it would be unfair to permit the party claiming the violation to assert the right or claim redress.

Arbitrators have applied the doctrine of laches to grievances that the parties have failed to bring forward for long periods of time, where records relating to the matter have been destroyed in the interval,[10] or where key witnesses for one party are no longer available and cannot be found due to the lengthy delay.[11] It is important to note, however, that a long delay in itself would not necessarily invoke the doctrine of laches.[12] In order for the doctrine to apply, the party who committed the alleged violation must also establish that the delay had produced a change of position of the party to the extent that the assertion of the claim at the later time would be prejudicial. The party claiming prejudice, nevertheless, must not bear responsibility for any part of the delay, otherwise the arbitrator will permit the grievance to be heard.[13]

A somewhat similar situation arises where a party raises a grievance then fails to process the grievance either through inaction, or through some statement or conduct that would imply withdrawal. **Abandonment** is essentially the failure to actively process a grievance after it is lodged or formally presented to the employer. An employee, for example, may present a grievance verbally to his or her immediate supervisor if the collective agreement so provides. If the grievance is rejected, and the grievor does nothing thereafter to carry the grievance forward in accordance with the grievance procedure, the grievance may later be considered to have been abandoned by the employee, and cannot be brought forward for arbitration. Most collective agreements specifically provide that a failure to process a grievance within the time limits set out in the grievance procedure will constitute abandonment of the claim, but where the agreement is silent on the matter, or where time limits are not specified, the question of abandonment becomes a matter of fact to be decided by the arbitrator. As a general rule, where a grievance arises out of a single incident, if the grievor or union allows a lengthy period of time to elapse, the inaction may constitute abandonment, and prevent the grievor from later raising the same grievance.

Withdrawal differs from abandonment to the extent that withdrawal normally requires some statement or conduct by the party with carriage of the grievance that would indicate that the grievance will not be processed further. In contrast to abandonment, withdrawal requires some action as opposed to inaction. Withdrawal is essentially a unilateral act by the grieving party, and once made, precludes the same grievance from being raised again or submitted to arbitration.

The **settlement** of a grievance will also preclude the same grievance from being brought on for arbitration. Settlement must, however, be shown to be the final determination of the dispute, and not simply a conditional resolution of the matter which later proves to be unacceptable. Where the parties reach some understanding during the course of the grievance procedure, the agreement on the grievance is usually reduced to writing, and the minutes of settlement constitute the resolution of the grievance. If the written agreement represents the final determination of the dispute, the grievance at that point will vanish, and may not later be raised.

The rules concerning abandonment, withdrawal and settlement are designed to establish a point in time when a grievance right ends. Employers, in particular, are concerned with this issue, and it is important to them to know when a response to a grievance has been accepted as final by the grievor or the union. Unless some rule is applied to the presentation of grievances which determines how and when the rights of the grievor on a particular grievance are finalized, the system would be open to abuse by grievors who might wish to harass their employer by a multitude of complaints which may or may not have substance, but which are repeatedly raised. The rules relating to abandonment, withdrawal and settlement preclude the raising of subsequent grievances by a grievor where the initial grievance has been settled or dropped.

Promissory estoppel is a legal doctrine which the courts recognize as a defence in cases where parties are bound in a legal relationship and one party has given assurances or stated facts concerning an intended course of action or state of affairs which the other party relies upon to his or her detriment. The doctrine may be invoked where assurances or statements of fact are made which a defendant relies and acts upon, only to discover later that the party who gave the assurances or stated the facts is not prepared to stand by them, but instead, pursues a different course of action. For example, in a labour relations context, if an employer approaches the union with a proposed plan to reduce the work force on a temporary basis by the layoff of certain employees which the employer believes appropriate, and the union agrees that the layoff is proper, the union cannot later grieve the layoff, if the employer carries through the plan which had been agreed upon by the two parties. **Estoppel** is a legal term which means that a person may not later deny the truth of a statement if another party relied upon it to his or her detriment. In such circumstances, the party who relied upon the statement may raise estoppel as a defence if the party who made the statement attempts to enforce a right against the party which is contrary to the statement made.

As a defence, four elements of the doctrine must be established:

1. *a legal relationship must be shown to exist between the parties;*
2. *a statement or representation was made by a party which the party intended the other to act upon;*
3. *the statement or representation must affect or alter the legal relationship between the parties;*
4. *the other party must act or rely on the promise or statement to his detriment.*

If these elements are established, the party who made the statement will be "estopped" from denying the truth of the statements made, and will only be permitted to enforce the legal relationship between the parties in the form modified by the statement.

In a labour relations context, the doctrine is also limited to use as a defence, and may not be used to enforce a right or as a basis for grievance. Some arbitral authority would suggest that the doctrine may be limited by giving notice of an intention to revert to the existing position, say, when a new collective agreement comes into effect, or when the state of affairs to which the statement related comes to an end. However, where an employer in the course of settlement of a grievance does so on a particular basis or ground, he may be held to do so on the same basis if a similar grievance should arise at a later time.[14]

One caveat however, should be noted. Where the estoppel is based upon the conduct of the parties, some arbitrators believe that they may not possess the authority to apply the doctrine. While the courts have noted that the application of the doctrine may be appropriate in some cases, some arbitrators are of the view that an award based upon estoppel by conduct in the absence of authority to do so under the collective agreement would in some circumstances have the effect of changing the agreement itself, something which may well be beyond their authority.[15]

A final legal concept or doctrine which has some application to the unjust assertion of rights under a collective agreement is **double**

jeopardy. Double jeopardy is applicable to only a narrow range of arbitration matters which have some similarity to criminal cases, the area of the law where the principle or concept was developed. In arbitration, the cases most similar to criminal matters are those related to discharge and discipline. The principle of double jeopardy states that a person may not be tried and convicted for the same crime twice. In a collective bargaining context, the principle might be said to be that an employee may not be punished twice for the same transgression.

Double jeopardy is usually raised as a defence in an instance where an employee violates a rule, or engages in some activity in the work place that warrants some form of disciplinary action by the employer, and the employer punishes the employee twice for the same offence. For example, if an employee violates a strict no smoking rule by smoking in an extreme hazard area, the employee's supervisor may suspend the employee for a period of time for the violation. If, on the employee's return to work the plant manager discovers that the employee had violated the no smoking rule, and dismisses him in the belief that a short suspension was not an adequate penalty, the employee may grieve the dismissal on the basis of double jeopardy, since he had already served the suspension as punishment of the violation. To impose a second penalty would, in effect, punish the employee twice for the same violation.

In addition to the legal doctrines and principles which arbitrators have brought into the arbitration process to prevent the unjust assertion of rights under the collective agreement, a number of other rules have also been developed by arbitrators which have a similarity to, or basis in law. These rules or principles are generally used to identify or establish rights in a collective bargaining context. The legal principle of **res judicata** for example, has been adopted by arbitrators. The term means essentially that the matter has already been decided, and that the decision stands as conclusive until reversed by a higher authority. In an arbitration situation, the rule may be applied where an arbitrator has established a particular interpretation of a clause in a collective agreement, and is later called upon to decide an identical grievance related to the same clause in the agreement. In such an instance, where the arbitrator has already decided the matter in the previous arbitration, unless new circumstances are cited which would pursuade the arbitrator to decide differently, the arbitrator's decision would probably be the same. The matter would be **res judicata**, as the arbitrator had previously decided the issue. For example, a grievance arises out of a wage clause in a collective agreement which could be interpreted to mean that a wage increase is either discretionary (based on merit) or mandatory (based upon average performance) depending upon how the words "if the work of the employee is satisfactory" are interpreted. If the arbitrator decides that the words are to be interpreted to mean that the wage increase is mandatory if the employee's work is acceptable, a second grievance filed by another employee on the same issue may be treated as res judicata, since the arbitrator has already interpreted the clause in the previous arbitration case.

Res judicata is generally applicable only to those situations where the same arbitrator is faced with a second, identical grievance raised by the same party or another grievor on the same clause in the collective agreement.[16] Other arbitrators, however, are not bound by previous decisions, and where a grievance identical to a previously decided issue is brought before a different arbitrator, the previous award need not be followed, although it would undoubtedly have a strong persuasive effect. It might also be noted that even where the same arbitrator is called upon to decide a grievance concerning the same issue or clause dealt with in a prior award, the arbitrator is not necessarily bound by the previous award that he made, although the likelihood of an arbitrator reversing his own interpretation without good reason is remote.

Notwithstanding the rule that arbitrators are not bound by previous decisions of other arbitrators, and indeed, not even by their own awards, over time, a body of arbitral decisions or awards on a wide variety of arbitration issues has been developed which tend to have a persuasive effect on arbitrators in a very general way. The result of this has been the creation of a condition in the arbitration field not unlike that which exists in the courts of law. In the common law provinces, the courts are subject to the doctrine of **precedent** or **stare decisis** which requires inferior courts or courts of concurrent jurisdiction to abide by previous decisions in deciding similar issues which are brought before them. Under this doctrine, a court is bound to decide cases in accordance with previous decisions for reasons of certainty in law, since the common law consists of the recorded judgments of the courts, rather than a written code. While in theory the courts are bound by previous decisions, the law remains flexible, because minor differences permit judges to distinguish the case before them from previous decisions, and in this fashion the law may adapt to new circumstances and social changes in general. Unlike the courts, however, arbitrators are not duty bound to follow precedent, but may decide each case entirely on its own particular merits. The large body of arbitral authority, however, does have a substantial persuasive effect on arbitrators, if only because the reasoning or justification of these decisions by other arbitrators cannot be ignored, and for an arbitrator to decide to stray from what has developed as a particular **arbitral stance** on an issue would require very compelling reasons to support the departure from norm. Some authorities, nevertheless, have greater persuasive effect than others. Judicial decisions applicable to issues raised at arbitrations may be referred to by arbitrators, and while arbitrators are not bound to follow a judicial decision in the same manner as a common law court, most arbitrators will adhere to such decisions. Similarly, where a court has judicially reviewed an arbitration award and handed down a judgment, the judicial decision is essentially binding on arbitrators, for to ignore the decision in the arbitration process would fly in the face of all reason. Consequently, the prior awards, while clearly not binding on arbitrators, constitute a body of authorities similar in nature to the common law, and the attitude of arbitrators to the authority of these awards is not unlike that of the courts to the common law.

Arbitrators have also drawn on legal rules in order to formulate a number of other arbitral doctrines. An important doctrine of this nature is the doctrine of **past practice**, which arbitrators have developed as an aid in the interpretation of collective agreement clauses that are ambiguous. The doctrine permits arbitrators to look outside the collective agreement in order to arrive at an interpretation of clauses which are unclear as a result of either a poor choice of words by the parties or an obvious defect in the preparation of the clause itself.

Ambiguity in a collective agreement clause may arise in a number of different ways, but most often it is due to problems that arise from a failure to carefully proofread the text for errors, or from a choice of words which inadvertently (or sometimes deliberately) convey different meanings. An error in the preparation of the text, such as missing key words, gives rise to a **patent ambiguity**, where the clause itself does not make sense due to the error. For example, a collective agreement clause, due to an oversight, may state: "The work week shall consist of days and of eight hours work per day." The sentence should obviously have stated that the work week shall consist of some number of days and of eight hours work per day, but the parties failed to notice the missing key word for the sentence to make sense. In this instance the arbitrator may look at the past practice of the parties in order to determine what the work week has been previously. If the past practice indicates that the work week consists of five days, then this evidence may then be used to interpret the collective agreement.

A more common type of ambiguity is a **latent ambiguity** which arises when the parties each interpret a collective agreement clause in a different manner. Again, past practice may be used under these circumstances to determine the manner in which the clause was implemented by the parties or interpreted in the past.

The doctrine of past practice, nevertheless, may only be utilized to interpret clauses that are ambiguous, as another legal principle known as the **parol evidence rule** bars any evidence (such as evidence of past practice) where the wording of a collective agreement clause is clear and unambiguous. The parol evidence rule states that extrinsic evidence may only be introduced to explain the written words of an agreement, and may not be used to alter or add to the agreement. If the wording of the agreement is clear and unambiguous, the parol evidence rule would bar evidence which would differ from the clear meaning of the words, for the evidence could only conflict with the clear meaning, and to accept the extrinsic evidence would, in effect, change the meaning of the clause. As a consequence, the doctrine of past practice may only be followed by an arbitrator where some ambiguity exists in the wording of the collective agreement clause which the arbitrator is called upon to interpret.

A final "tool" of arbitrators which may be used to interpret the wording of a collective agreement is the **negotiating history** of the parties. In some cases, the parties over time may have altered the wording of clauses in a collective agreement, and occasionally, the changes in the wording may give rise to different interpretations of the revised words. Under these circumstances, an arbitrator may accept evidence concerning the negotiating history of the clause or changes as an aid in interpretation. The reasons for change are normally discussed during the negotiation of the agreement, and evidence of the reasons why a change was proposed often provides as well the intent of the parties in their revision of the clause. Prior arbitration awards or settled grievances that concerned the agreement clause may also be used in a similar fashion to assist in the interpretation of the wording, although grievances which were settled on the basis that they did not constitute a precedent would probably be excluded as evidence.

THE REMEDIAL AUTHORITY OF ARBITRATORS

The authority of an arbitrator stems from the collective agreement and applicable labour legislation. Consequently, where a determination is made concerning a violation of the agreement or where an improper interpretation of a clause by a party occurs, the authority of the arbitrator to fashion appropriate remedies is necessarily subject to the limitations imposed on the arbitrator by these two sources of authority. As noted previously, collective agreements frequently provide that the arbitrator may only interpret or apply the agreement, but may not change or add to the content. Even where the agreement is silent on the matter, the same restrictions would probably hold true, as the statutory provisions related to collective agreements normally provide arbitration for the settlement of disputes arising out of the interpretation, application, administration or alleged violation of the agreement, and do not expressly provide for alteration of the agreement itself. Apart from this limitation, arbitrators are usually permitted to formulate appropriate remedies for violations, although these again may be subject to specific limitations imposed by the collective agreement or general principles of law. For example, a collective agreement may acknowledge that an arbitrator may award compensation in cases of improper work assignments, but restrict the compensation from the point in time when the grievance was filed to the date of the implementation of the award. An arbitrator in such a case would be bound by the collective agreement to limit the award of compensation to the time-frame specified.

Unless restricted by the collective agreement, arbitrators in general have the authority to provide a number of remedies which naturally flow from a violation of the collective agreement. An arbitrator may, therefore, award compensation to an employee wrongfully discharged or improperly placed on layoff. Similarly, the arbitrator may compensate a union for lost union dues which an employer failed to deduct from the wages of employees contrary to the collective agreement, or where a union has called an unlawful strike, an arbitrator may award the employer compensation for any loss or damage caused by the unlawful strike.

Penalties imposed by employers as a part of a disciplinary system may also be varied by arbitrators if the collective agreement or the labour legislation of the province (such as that of Ontario)[17] so provides. However, unless this authority to vary is given, the arbitrator is limited to finding either that the employer was justified or not justified in imposing discipline, and compensation would only be possible where a finding of no justification for the discipline was made.

Some variation in the power of arbitrators to provide remedies occurs from province to province, due to the statutory authority granted to arbitrators under the legislation. Nevertheless, arbitrators generally have relatively broad powers, either under the statute or the collective agreement itself, to provide appropriate relief where a violation of the collective agreement is determined. The specific remedies available for each issue are examined under specific topic headings in Chapter 10 of the text.

IMPLICATIONS OF AN ARBITRATION AWARD

The written award of an arbitrator sets out the issue which the parties have presented to the arbitrator for determination, and the conclusion which the arbitrator has made, together with the reasons why or how the conclusion was reached. If the issue was found to be arbitrable (and this is a matter which falls within the jurisdiction of the arbitrator to decide) and if the arbitrator or board has acted properly and within its authority, the decision will be binding on the parties and the grievor. The parties are obliged to implement the award according to its terms, and as noted previously, if either party fails to do so within a specified period of time, in most jurisdictions the award may be lodged with the Superior or Supreme Court of the province, and enforced as if the award was a judgment of the court.

The issue of an award normally completes the arbitration process, and the authority of the arbitrator to deal further with the grievance ends when the award is placed in the hands of the parties. In some cases, such as where the arbitrator awards an employee lost wages in a wrongful discharge grievance matter, the arbitrator may be requested by the parties to remain seised of the case until the question of compensation is resolved. Arbitrators are generally prepared to retain jurisdiction under these circumstances because they seldom have the data concerning wage and benefit rates, etc., placed before them to calculate the compensation. Instead, they tend to award the successful grievor compensation, or determine that the grievor be "made whole," which requires the employer to place the grievor in the same position that he would have been in had the employer not violated the collective agreement. The time that the arbitrator agrees to retain jurisdiction, however, is generally specified in the award, and the parties must comply with the award within the time which the arbitrator specified, otherwise the arbitrator's authority to deal with the award ends. The doctrine of **functus officio** applies to arbitration awards, and according to this doctrine, the award or finding is final and acts as a termination of the arbitrator's authority unless the award clearly indicates that the findings are of an interim nature and do not represent a final determination of the matter. Except for rulings on preliminary objections, arbitration awards are seldom of an interim nature, and consequently, the doctrine generally applies to the award on its release to the parties.

EXPEDITED ARBITRATION

The arbitration process has been occasionally criticized for the delay which appears to be built into the system, and in some cases, the criticism is perhaps justified. The grievance procedure sometimes takes many weeks, and once the grievance is moved to arbitration, several additional weeks are often required to establish a board of arbitration. A suitable hearing date more often than not must be fitted into the busy schedules of the three persons on the board, the legal counsel for the employer and the union, and the schedules of the employer and union representatives. As a consequence, the earliest suitable hearing date is often many months away from the date that the board is constituted. The time required to prepare the award after the grievance is heard frequently requires from several weeks to several months. In all, the processing time for a grievance from the date it is lodged with the employer to the date of the award may run from a number of months to a year, or even longer. In an effort to reduce the time required for some types of grievances, some unions and employers have sought some form of expedited arbitration which will provide decisions in a much shorter time-frame than the ordinary arbitration process.

Most unions and employers are content with the conventional arbitration process to deal with most grievances, since in truth, the parties themselves are largely responsible for the speed at which the process moves. Urgent cases, of course, may be and are quickly dealt with if all parties are aware of the need for prompt action and are prepared to adjust their busy schedules accordingly. Less important cases, however, where an award in a relatively short time may be desirable but not essential, required a restructuring of the arbitration process itself. In response to this need, two forms of expedited arbitration have been developed.

The first type of expedited arbitration is statutory in nature and typified by the arbitration procedure provided in Ontario, where the Ministry of Labour through its Office of Arbitration plays a part in the process. Under the *Ontario Labour Relations Act*,[18] a request for arbitration may be made by either the union or the employer when the grievance procedure has failed to resolve a dispute, and the Ministry will promptly send out a field officer to investigate the dispute and attempt to resolve the differences. If the grievance cannot be resolved, the Office of Arbitration will appoint a sole arbitrator to hear the grievance and arrange a date when the hearing may be held. The arbitrator will then hear the grievance and render an award either at the end of the hearing or within a short time thereafter. The time may vary before an award is issued, but the proceedings to and including the hearing must be completed within a twenty-one day period.[19]

Other provinces have taken a slightly different approach to the problem, and in some cases, the provincial labour relations board members may perform the role of an arbitrator or arbitration board to hear grievances or disputes between the parties. For example, the labour relations boards in Saskatchewan,[20] and British Columbia,[21] are empowered to act in this manner. The Ontario Labour Relations Board also acts as an arbitration board in construction industry disputes if the parties to a dispute so desire.[22]

A second form of expedited arbitration has been established by a number of large firms that have found that they must deal with a relatively steady flow of grievances of a minor or largely disciplinary nature. To prevent a backlog of cases in the regular arbitration process, the unions and the employers have developed an expedited procedure whereby an arbitrator will deal with a succession of cases on a given day. As each case is completed, an award will be immediately made by the arbitrator, or handed down within a specific time period after the case is heard.

The expedited arbitration procedure may vary from firm to firm, but generally follows a pattern which calls for limited argument at the hearing, and a prompt award, usually without reasons or sometimes in a verbal form. For example, in one firm the union and management have agreed to set aside a hearing day each month, and a single arbitrator attends on that day to hear the cases that the parties wish to bring forward. The type of evidence is agreed upon by the parties, and on the basis of the evidence presented before the arbitrator, an award is made without reasons and without establishing a precedent. In this manner, a number of cases may be dealt with during the course of the day, leaving only those important cases that require collective agreement interpretation or which will establish a precedent for the conventional arbitration process.

Expedited arbitration has been in use in the United States by large firms for a decade or longer, and in most cases, both the unions and the employers are relatively satisfied with the procedure. Minor grievances such as job classification, bumping rights, minor discipline, and similar cases are usually satisfactorily resolved by this form of arbitration to the extent that two-track arbitration processes are no longer considered experimental in nature. Expedited arbitration, apart from the expedited processes under statute, has not been adopted in Canada to the same extent as in the United States, but this is due in part to the size of the Canadian business firms, rather than any defect or drawback with the process. The parties themselves are unlikely to see a need for expedited arbitration unless a large number of grievances arise on a regular basis, and this situation is unlikely to exist in most smaller firms. In any event, the expedited procedures which are now provided by provinces (such as Ontario) perhaps eliminate the need for the establishment of two-track arbitration procedures in the collective agreements.

REVIEW QUESTIONS

1. *The collective agreement sets out the agreement between the parties. What must it contain in terms of required clauses?*
2. *What theories have been developed to explain the nature of the collective agreement? Why has it been necessary to develop theories concerning management rights?*
3. *What is the purpose of a grievance procedure? Why does it usually consist of several "steps" or "stages"?*
4. *Determine the method of enforcement of a collective agreement, and explain why such a procedure is necessary. Why does it tend to be a "two-stage" process?*
5. *What are the advantages and disadvantages of a sole arbitrator over a three person board of arbitration?*
6. *Contrast the arbitration process with the judicial process. How do the two differ?*
7. *Explain the nature of judicial review of arbitration awards. Why is this a necessary review in some instances? On what grounds might judicial review take place?*
8. *Identify the legal principles used by arbitrators to prevent the unjust or improper assertion of rights by grievors. How does the application of each differ from their use by the courts?*
9. *Why do arbitrators generally consider themselves to be "interpreters" rather than policy makers?*
10. *Explain the following terms: examination-in-chief, status quo theory, error of law on the face of the award, strict constructionist, certiorari, prerogative writ, laches.*

NOTES

[1] *Labour Relations Act*, R.S.O. 1980 c. 228 s. 42.
[2] *Ibid.*, s. 41.
[3] *Ibid.*, s. 44.
[4] *Ibid.*, s. 52.
[5] Saskatchewan for many years did not require arbitration, but 1983 amendments to its labour legislation prohibited strikes and lock-outs, and introduced the arbitration process as a means of dealing with grievances, (although the Act does not make the process compulsory). See: the *Trade Union Act*, R.S.S. 1978 c.T-17 as amended by S.S. 1983 c. 81.
[6] Saskatchewan does not specifically impose compulsory arbitration, as disputes may also be taken to the labour relations board. The board in effect acts as a board of arbitration to deal with the matter brought before it.
[7] See *Ontario, Labour Relations Act*, R.S.O. 1980 c. 228, s. 44.
[8] See *Ontario, Labour Relations Act*, R.S.O. 1980 c. 228 s.44(11).
[9] See Weiler, P.C. "The Role of the Labour Arbitrator: Alternate Versions," Vol. 19, *University of Toronto Law Journal*, p.16 (1969).
[10] *Re Allied and Technical Workers, District 50 and Liquid Carbonic Canadian Corp. Ltd.* (1971) 23 L.A.C. 78.
[11] *Re Ottawa Newspaper Guild and The Ottawa Citizen* (1969) 20 L.A.C. 27.
[12] *Re Algoma Steel Co. Ltd. and United Steelworkers, Local 4509* (1973) 2 L.A.C. (2d) 230.
[13] *Re Yardley of London (Canada) Ltd. and International Chemical Workers' Union, Local 351* (1973) 4 L.A.C. (2d) 75.
[14] See, for example, *Re Carling O'Keefe Breweries of Canada Ltd. and United Brewery Workers, Local 325* (1982) 5 L.A.C. (3d) 302; *Barber-Ellis of Canada Ltd. and United Automobile Workers, Local 397* (1976) 11 L.A.C. (2d) 280.
[15] See for example, *Re Domglas Ltd. and United Ceramic Workers, Local 203* (1983) 8 L.A.C. (3d) 365. For the opinion of the court, see *Canadian National Railway Co. et al. v. Beatty et al.* (1981) 34 O.R. (2d) 385.
[16] See for example, *Re United Steelworkers, Local 2868, and International Harvester Co.* (1962) 12 L.A.C. 215.
[17] See *Ontario, Labour Relations Act*. R.S.O. 1980 c. 228 s. 44(9).
[18] See *Ontario, Labour Relations Act*. R.S.O. 1980 c. 228 s. 45.
[19] *Ibid.*, s. 45(7).
[20] *Trade Union Act*, R.S.S. 1978 c. T-17 s. 24.
[21] *Labour Code*, R.S.B.C. 1979 c. 212 s. 96.
[22] *Labour Relations Act*. R.S.O. 1980 c. 228 s. 124.

CHAPTER TEN

THE ARBITRATION OF RIGHTS DISPUTES

INTRODUCTION

The arbitration process where a collective agreement is in effect is concerned with a determination of the rights of the parties under the agreement. The award of the arbitrator in effect interprets the rights or deals with their enforcement or violation. Because both the employer and the union (and the employees which the union represents) have rights under a collective agreement, it is important to examine the extent of these rights, and to determine their extent in terms of collective bargaining theory and arbitral authority. While these rights are clearly dependent on the wording of the collective agreement, a number of very broad and general observations may be made about a number of rights which are commonly found in the agreements which the parties make. For simplicity, they may be classified as management rights, union security rights, and employee rights. From the exercise of these rights flow a number of disputes which frequently are placed before arbitrators to resolve. The nature of these rights and the attitudes of arbitrators towards the exercise of the rights is the subject matter of this chapter.

THE LIMITS OF MANAGEMENT AUTHORITY: MANAGEMENT RIGHTS

Employers are unlikely to rely on the residual rights theory as a source of authority to manage a firm or organization, and instead, insist that a clause be inserted in the collective agreement which will set out the rights of management. **Management rights clauses** may take on any number of different forms, and may include any number of rights, but the most common type of clause will specify in relatively broad, general terms the exclusive rights of management. Most unions are prepared to concede that management has the right to operate the business as it sees fit, provided that it does so in accordance with the terms of the collective agreement. Management rights clauses, as a result, usually contain some form of restriction that requires the employer to act fairly and subject to the agreement in the exercise of its authority. An example of a broad management rights clause may read as follows:

> The employer shall have the right to conduct the operation of the business and manage the firm and its employees as it sees fit, and without restricting the generality of the foregoing, the employer shall have the exclusive right and authority to:
>
> (a) Set hours of work, determine the number of shifts and the staffing of the same, schedule work and establish the production methods and procedures to be used;
>
> (b) Determine the number and type of products to be made, purchased, and sold, the type of equipment to be utilized, and the number of plants or production facilities;
>
> (c) Hire, promote, transfer, lay off, and generally determine and adjust the number of employees to be employed, subject only to the provisions of this agreement;
>
> (d) Make reasonable rules of conduct to be observed by all employees, and to discipline, suspend, or discharge employees for proper cause, subject to their right of grievance.

Where a dispute arises between an employee or the union and the employer concerning an act of management, the union is obliged to satisfy an arbitrator that the employer violated the collective agreement by the conduct of the particular act. Where the management rights clause is broadly written, such as the clause described above, the union must demonstrate that the management act was restricted in some manner by some other clause in the collective agreement in order to succeed, as an arbitrator will be expected to determine from the agreement the limits of management authority. For example, a supervisor might decide to perform bargaining unit work for short periods of time each day during busy production intervals, and the union may object to the practice on the basis that the supervisor's actions deprived bargaining unit employees of the opportunity to do overtime work. The union, however, must relate the grievance to the collective agreement, and demonstrate to the arbitrator that the supervisor's actions violated the collective agreement. Where the collective agreement does not provide a fetter on the right of management personnel to engage in bargaining unit work, the employer might point to the management rights clause as authority for the supervisor's right to do the work.

Arbitrators generally acknowledge the right of management to do bargaining unit work where it is not prohibited by the collective agreement, but consider the right subject to some overall limitations. For example, it must not be engaged in for the purpose of destroying the bargaining unit, nor must it be done to replace a member of the bargaining unit, otherwise the union may insist that the person doing the work be included in the bargaining unit.[1] However, where the work done constitutes only a small part of the management person's overall job, or where a supervisor has historically performed some bargaining unit work, arbitrators have generally held that the performance or assignment of the work falls within the rights of management.[2]

For some time, arbitrators have generally distinguished internal work assignment (such as the assignment of jobs within the organization to non-bargaining unit personnel), from the contracting out of work to other firms. The contracting out of work in the absence of a specific prohibition on the practice in the collective agreement has always been considered to be an inherent right of management, provided that it is done in good faith and for legitimate business reasons.[3] However, this differs from the internal assignment of work to non-bargaining unit personnel. In distinguishing the two forms of work assignment, arbitrators usually examine the relationship between the employer and the party to whom the work is assigned to make certain that the non-bargaining unit party is in fact an independent contractor or independent firm.

THE PRINCIPLE OF SENIORITY AND ITS IMPLICATIONS IN COLLECTIVE BARGAINING

Seniority as it relates to the work place is a principle whereby long-service employees acquire greater rights to employment and benefits over employees with less service. Seniority is based upon the premise that the reward for long and loyal service should be greater job security and more generous monetary benefits than those extended to employees with a shorter period of service with the employer. Seniority, therefore, represents an important basic component of all job security clauses found in collective agreements, except those in the construction industry.

Two general types of seniority may be found in collective agreements: **Benefit seniority** and **competitive status seniority**. Benefit seniority establishes entitlement to employee benefits that accrue to employees on the basis of their length of service with the employer. The most common types of benefit clauses are those which provide additional vacation time for long service, or pension benefits based upon years of service. For example, a collective agreement may provide for a three-week paid vacation for employees with five or more years of service, and a four-week paid vacation for employees with fifteen or more years of service. In this example, the number of years of service determines the eligibility of the employee for the benefit. Benefit seniority is usually plant-wide or employer-wide in its application, rather than job-related.

Competitive status seniority is a type of seniority which determines the rights of an employee to job-related benefits in relation to other employees. For example, the right of an employee to a particular position in relation to the rights of other employees in the firm may be based upon the seniority of the employees eligible for the position. Under a strict application of seniority, the employee with the longest service would be entitled to the position. Strict seniority of this type might also be followed in the event of a layoff of employees. In this case, the employees with the least seniority would be placed on layoff first, and the longest-service employee would be the last to be terminated. Seniority may also be applied to the recall of employees from a layoff, with the employee with the longest service recalled first, and the employee with the least seniority recalled last.

Strict competitive status seniority on a plant-wide basis is not commonly found in collective agreements, because most employers require employees with different skills for the efficient operation of a firm, and layoffs or changes in the work force seldom occur in such a way that the employee with the least seniority may be placed on layoff or displaced when a reduction of the work force is necessary. This would also be the case where a position becomes open that requires special skills to perform the work. Because of these limitations on the applicability of a strict seniority system, employers generally insist that some criteria in addition to seniority be considered in cases concerning job vacancies, promotions, transfers and layoffs. In most cases, employers require that the skill and ability to do the required work be considered, and only where the skill and ability are relatively equal would the seniority of the employees be the factor to govern the selection.

In large organizations, competitive status seniority is sometimes limited to only parts of the firm, and not infrequently, to particular jobs or clusters of jobs. Such seniority is frequently referred to as **departmental seniority** or **job seniority** to indicate the extent to which the competitive status seniority may be applied or considered.

Procedures related to work assignment, job vacancies, promotions, transfers, demotions, layoffs, and the recall of employees are often incorporated in complex collective agreement clauses which describe the application of seniority to each of these matters, and a failure on the part of management to comply with the collective agreement in this regard may give rise to grievances concerning the violation of employees rights.

In all cases, the rights of employees on the basis of seniority or skill and ability (as the case may be) to promotions, jobs, or recall from layoff are governed by the provisions of the collective agreement, and for an employee to successfully grieve, the union must establish that the employer had violated the particular provision in the collective agreement. Consequently, if the collective agreement is silent on the application of seniority, then the employer would be free to fill vacancies, lay off, promote, or transfer without regard to the length of service of the employees.

REDUCTION OF THE WORK FORCE
Job seniority is perhaps one of the most important benefits that collective bargaining has established for long-service employees. Except in the construction industry where the nature of the work renders ordinary job seniority meaningless, most collective agreements make some provision for the recognition of long service when employers are obliged to reduce their work force. While the application of seniority to any reduction in a work force may appear simple and straightforward, in reality this is not so. A reduction in the number of employees required to perform the work during periods of decreased demand for the employer's products or services seldom means that the reduction can take place uniformly throughout the entire operation. Some employees, regardless of their length of service must be retained because of their essential skills. In addition, the personnel needs in some departments may be substantially less than in others. Consequently, where a reduction in the number of employees takes place, it often has a disruptive effect throughout the organization if a job security system based upon plant-wide seniority has been included in the collective agreement by the parties.

One of the more common types of job security clauses found in collective agreements entitles a long-service employee whose position has been eliminated to request placement in an existing position occupied by a less senior employee. This process, which is referred to as **bumping**, usually permits the long-service employee to replace the less senior incumbent in the position, provided that the senior employee is able to perform the work required. A notice of layoff, where a staff reduction is proposed, as a result, may trigger a series of moves throughout the work force, as positions are eliminated (either on a short-term or permanent basis) and senior employees in those positions demand the right to jobs held by less senior employees. Under these circumstances, the employer must assess the suitability of each senior employee for the position described, based upon the criteria set out in the collective agreement and in accordance with procedure established for the moves.

"Bumping" criteria set out in a collective agreement is negotiated, and consequently, will constitute a set of requirements particular to each collective agreement. A common type of clause will permit a senior employee whose job is eliminated to replace a less senior employee, provided that the senior employee has the skill and ability to perform the work without further training. In some cases the clause may provide that the employee will have a short period of familiarization in order to become accustomed to the work, but normally the employee who wishes to displace an incumbent must be fully qualified, otherwise the move may be denied by the employer.[4] The more senior employee, if unable to do the work, would then be placed on layoff.

The recall of employees from layoff, under most collective agreements, is generally in reverse order of the layoff, that is to say, the last employee to be released becomes the first employee to be recalled. However, this may not always be the case. If the nature of the employer's business is such that employees who possess certain skills are required before others, the recall clause may provide that the recall will be made not only on the basis of seniority, but upon the employer's skill requirements as well. Where employees may be grouped by skills, the recall provisions in the agreement may provide for recall on a seniority basis within each skilled group.

PROMOTION AND TRANSFER

Promotions and transfers are separate and distinct matters in a collective bargaining setting. A promotion is considered to be a move into a position that carries with it greater skill requirements or job responsibilities. Occasionally, promotions may represent a move by an employee out of the bargaining unit or into a supervisory position. A useful indicator of a promotion is an upward change in wage or salary rate, since wage rates usually reflect the hierarchy of work positions in a firm, although this is not always the case.

The right to promote an employee, particularly if the promotion is to a position of a supervisory nature, is a right of management, but the provisions of a collective agreement may require the employer to take into consideration the seniority of employees when the selection process is instituted. Since employees are seldom already qualified for the position to which they will be promoted, training in the new position is usually provided by the employer. Nevertheless, employers usually reserve the right to select the most suitable employee for the promotion, and as a result, collective agreement clauses concerning promotion will often provide that the employer may select the most suitable employee, but where a number of employees are relatively equal in terms of skill, ability, experience and suitability, then seniority will be considered. A variation of this type of promotion clause would be one which requires the employer to give seniority the same weight as a number of other factors in the selection of the most suitable employee. For example, the clause may provide that the employer shall "... consider the education and experience, seniority, and suitability of the employee for the position." Here, seniority becomes one of the four factors which the employer must consider.

Transfers, unlike promotions, do not involve an upward move in the job hierarchy in the firm, but represent a form of lateral or even a voluntary downward move in the job matrix. Transfers most often arise where a vacancy exists in a particular position due to the retirement, promotion or resignation of the incumbent, or where a new position is created as a result of plant expansion, the addition of a new shift, or technological change. Once aware of the vacancy, an employee in some other similar position may wish to fill the vacancy, and request consideration for the position. Where more than one employee applies for the vacancy, the collective agreement once again may require the employer to give preference or consideration to the seniority of the employees in the selection process, if the competing employees are otherwise equally qualified for the work.

Notice to employees of vacant positions is an important part of the selection process for both transfers and promotions under most collective agreements. In order that all potential candidates for a position are made aware of the work opportunity, the procedure set out in most agreements requires the employer to post a notice of the job vacancy in some prominent place in the plant or office. **Job posting** as a result, has become the most common method of bringing job vacancies to the attention of all employees. The procedure which the employer follows after a job has been posted for a specified period of time is often dictated by the collective agreement in detail, but in most cases the employer is normally obliged to examine the qualifications of each applicant in terms of the criteria set out in the agreement, and select the appropriate candidate accordingly.

Regardless of the procedure set out in the collective agreement, certain basic obligations are placed on the employer in the performance of the selection function. As a general rule, arbitrators insist that the employer assess the qualifications of the candidates against some reasonable standard, and that the employer conduct the selection process in a fair and unbiased manner.

The concern of most employers during negotiations tends to focus on the retention of a highly qualified work force in those instances where a reduction of the employee complement in a plant or department becomes necessary. Regardless of the employer's desire, the reduction in the number of employees must be made in accordance with the collective agreement, and if the employer fails to comply with the appropriate provisions or the procedure set out, the failure on the employer's part will be cause for grievance. For example, if the collective agreement provides for a seven-day notice of layoff, and the employer proceeds to lay off employees without notice, or on less than seven-days' notice, a grievance complaining that an affected employee was entitled to seven-day's notice would probably be upheld, and the employee compensated for the equivalent of the notice period or seven-day's wages.

The reorganization of the work place as a result of a layoff is more often a cause of grievance. Seniority related clauses which permit senior employees to "bump" junior employees frequently give rise to grievances where the employer has a "skill and ability" or "best qualified" criterion to follow in the selection of employees to be retained. In many cases, the selection of the employees based upon the employees' "ability," "suitability" or "qualifications" may be subjective to a degree. Arbitral review of the employer's decision consequently tends to be concerned with the process that the employer followed as well as the criteria upon which the decision was based. As a general rule, arbitrators are concerned with the overall actions of the employer, and must be satisfied that the employer complied with the procedural requirements of the collective agreement, considered all of the employees' qualifications and records, judged the qualifications of each employee against the same standards, and acted fairly and without bias or discrimination in the selection of the employees entitled to "bump" or be retained. As in the case of promotions and transfers, where employees are competing for job vacancies, arbitrators tend to be reluctant to substitute their judgment for that of management in the selection of the proper employee for a position. However, an arbitrator must be satisfied that the employer acted in accordance with the collective agreement and made the selection fairly and reasonably on the basis of all of the information available, otherwise a finding that the employer failed to comply with the collective agreement would likely be the result. Where two or more persons applied for the same position, and the employer improperly selected one, the usual remedy of arbitrators would be to remit the matter back to the employer for a proper determination.[5] However, where only one employee has asserted the right to a position on the basis of seniority, such as in a bumping situation, where the arbitrator is satisfied that the right was improperly denied to an otherwise qualified grievor, an arbitrator may direct that employer to place the grievor in the position.[6]

Arbitral review of management decisions concerning promotions, transfers and job vacancies in general is characterized by a reluctance on the part of arbitrators to substitute their judgment for that of management.[7] Most arbitrators will readily concede that the employer is undoubtedly in the best position to select the most suitable applicant for a position, and as a consequence, the review of the employer's action tends to focus on employer compliance with the provisions set out in the collective agreement, and the reasonableness of the decision. The usual approach taken by arbitrators is to establish the requirements for the vacant job, then assess the reasonableness of the methods or criteria used by the employer in the assessment of the applicants. Additionally, the employer must satisfy the requirements of good faith and fairness in the selection process. For example, if an employer should manipulate job requirements or establish qualifications for a position which bear no relationship to the job or the work to be done, then an arbitrator may find that the employer acted unfairly, and for the purpose of defeating the just claims by otherwise suitable candidates for the position open.[8] A failure to comply with the procedure set out in the collective agreement, such as a failure to post a job vacancy, would of course, constitute a violation of the agreement on the part of the employer, and render the employer's decision invalid. Overall, most arbitrators view their duty in job vacancy cases to determine the reasonableness and correctness of the employer's decision as it relates to the collective agreement,[9] and management decisions will usually be disturbed only when the employer acted contrary to the provisions of the collective agreement, unfairly, or unreasonably. Where an arbitration finding is made that the employer made an unreasonable decision or acted contrary to the requirements of the collective agreement, the courts have held that an arbitrator must remit the matter to the employer for determination unless the collective agreement permits the arbitrator to substitute his or her judgment for that of the employer.[10]

UNION SECURITY RIGHTS

Most collective agreements will contain clauses that are designed to provide the union and its officers with a number of enforceable financial and security benefits. For the most part, these clauses are inserted in the collective agreement to require the employer to collect union dues from employees, or to encourage or maintain union membership, but some agreements permit union officers to conduct union business or process grievance matters during working hours without loss of wages. Occasionally, unions might also obtain the right to use a part of the employer's premises for union business or meetings, and in some cases the agreement may grant union officers and stewards "super seniority" for layoff purposes in order that some representatives of the union will be on the job to deal with employee problems during severe cutbacks in the work force.

Union security clauses that relate to employee membership in the union or to the collection of union dues are often negotiated to protect the incumbent union from raiding by other unions, and to prevent difficulties in the work place between employees who pay union dues to support the union, and those who do not, but reap the benefits which the union negotiates for them. Unions usually argue as justification for union security clauses that a secure union will be less likely to be unrealistic in its demands on the employer, particularly if it is not constantly faced with the threat of displacement by non-union employees or other unions. However, most employers are likely to assess the union's demand for security in terms of the support that exists for the union at the time the demand is made, rather than any future benefits which might accrue to the employer from a security clause. One exception to this rule, nevertheless, exists. In the construction industry, where employers rely on the union hiring hall for a skilled work force, employers in that industry are quite prepared to provide the union with security to gain access to the labour pool which the union provides. Consequently, in the commercial and industrial construction industry the type of union security clause most commonly found is the **closed shop clause** which restricts the employer to hiring only persons who are already members of the union, and who remain members in good standing during their employment. Employers who are concerned about the union's ability to provide the necessary work force, negotiate a variation of the closed shop which would allow the employer to hire non-union skilled employees when union members are not available, provided that the non-union employees obtain a work permit or ticket from the union.

In the industrial manufacturing and commercial sector, the type of union security clause that a union may negotiate tends to vary from a strong union security clause which requires all employees in the bargaining unit to join and remain members of the union as a term of their employment (a **union shop clause**) to a less secure **maintenance of membership** clause which only requires employees who are members of the union when the agreement is negotiated to remain members of the union during the life of the agreement. In between these two extremes, the parties may negotiate a variety of different clauses, again one of the most common being a **modified union shop clause** which requires all persons who were union members at the time that the collective agreement comes into effect remain members of the union, and all persons who join the firm after a specified date join the union and remain members as a term of their employment. This type of clause is designed to protect older, non-union employees, but over time, the clause will gradually develop into a full union shop clause as the exempted employees retire or resign from their employment, hence the common name of "grandfather shop clause" for this type of union security.

In some cases, either as a result of employer resistance or union strength, the union may not negotiate a membership clause, but instead, negotiate a clause that would require the employer to collect union dues on behalf of the union at regular intervals (usually monthly) and remit the amounts to the union. Again, these clauses may take many forms, and may range from a **Rand Formula clause** under which all employees in the bargaining unit (whether union members or not) must pay union dues by way of employer deduction from their wages, to a **voluntary check-off** of union dues whereby union members may, if they so desire, have the employer deduct the union dues payable from their wages until such time as they wish to have the procedure ended. A variation of the latter type of clause is a **compulsory membership check-off clause** which requires the employer to deduct the membership dues from the wages of all union members and turn over the deductions to the union.

In some provinces, the labour legislation has established the right of unions to demand that union dues be deducted from the wages of employees, and where the right to check-off of union dues is established, either by way of the statute or under the terms of the collective agreement, the employer must carry out the service as required. An employer who fails to do so would be subject to a union grievance if the clause was in the collective agreement, and the union would be entitled to have an arbitrator or arbitration board determine if the employer had violated the collective agreement by failing to deduct the union dues. A finding in favour of the union would require the employer to pay an amount equivalent to the uncollected union dues to the union for the number of employees and the period of time that the union dues were not collected.

EMPLOYEE BEHAVIOUR: DISCHARGE AND DISCIPLINE

The behaviour of employees in the work place is often a cause for discipline if the behaviour disrupts work, interferes with other employees, or constitutes a safety hazard. The employer is entitled to the undivided attention of the employees during working hours, and to expect that all reasonable orders or work directives issued by supervisors will be promptly carried out by employees, provided that the directives do not endanger the safety of the employees in question. When some doubt exists as to the propriety of a supervisor's direction, an employee is not expected to engage in a debate with the supervisor, nor refuse to promptly carry out the order unless it would endanger the employee or others. If the order is improper, the employee has the right to file a grievance, hence the general rule: "work now and grieve later."

One of the fundamental rights of the employer is the right to maintain an orderly and efficient work place, and concurrent with this right is the duty to maintain a safe working environment. In terms of employee behaviour, this includes in the employer's duty the obligation to protect all employees from behaviour that may constitute a physical danger. As a result, arbitrators generally agree that unless the collective agreement restricts the employer's right, the control of employees falls within the ambit of management responsibility.

In large plants or organizations, basic employee control is frequently set out in posted rules designed to delineate unacceptable behaviour on the employer's premises during working hours. These rules are usually posted on bulletin boards and in areas where employees normally congregate, such as lunch rooms or locker rooms. Plant rules tend to be specific in nature, and may include prohibitions against fighting, horseplay, shouting, foul language, smoking in certain designated areas, arrival and departure from work, careless workmanship, unauthorized absenteeism, and similar activities. In some firms, the rules will be divided into "serious" and "minor" matters, and specific penalties may be provided for the infraction of each type of rule. In other firms, the question of the penalty for the violation of a rule is left to the discretion of the supervisor.

Arbitration cases concerning discharge or disciplinary action by the employer require the employer to bear the burden of proving that the action taken was warranted, and that the employer had just cause to impose the penalty in question. Originally, the onus shifted to the employer only in discharge cases, but arbitrators to-day are generally of the view that the onus rests on the employer in disciplinary cases as well, since the employer is in possession of all of the information upon which the decision was based, and in fairness to the grievor, should be obliged to satisfy the arbitrator that the action taken was justified.

The standard of proof required of the employer in discipline cases is generally that of the civil courts, whereby the employer is required to establish **on the balance of probabilities** that the alleged violation of rules or the offence was committed by the grievor. In discharge cases, some arbitrators have suggested that a higher standard of proof is required, and while they have not insisted upon the criminal law standard of **"beyond a reasonable doubt"** they have required the employer to show a **reasonable probability** in order to prove its case.[11]

A common disciplinary system employed by firms that have posted rules of behaviour is the **progressive or constructive discipline** system. Under this system, the penalties imposed for violations of the rules becomes increasingly more severe if the offences are repeated, with discharge as the ultimate sanction. A typical progressive discipline system might include a verbal warning for the first violation, a written warning for the second, a short suspension for the third, a longer suspension for the fourth, and finally, discharge for the fifth violation. The theory behind progressive discipline is that some employees will only change their behaviour pattern when the discipline system makes them realize that some form of unpleasant punishment will follow improper behaviour. The theory is premised on the assumption that a verbal warning is the only penalty usually required to correct improper behaviour by most employees, while for some, a more severe penalty is necessary. For the less responsive, progressively more severe penalties may be imposed to bring the employee's behaviour in line with that expected in the work place, and only when the employee fails to respond to the message which the discipline imparts, is the employee discharged.

Where a progressive discipline system is used, and where it has failed to alter the behaviour of an employee, the incident which finally results in the discharge of the employee is often not serious enough in itself to warrant such a severe penalty. However, the overall behaviour of the employee may dictate a termination of the employment relationship. When this occurs, the employer will usually argue the **doctrine of culminating incident** if the employee grieves the discharge. The doctrine of culminating incident provides that the employer may be justified in discharging an employee on the basis of the history of the employee's behaviour, even though the incident which "triggers" the dismissal in itself would not warrant so severe a penalty.

A discharge based upon a culminating incident that is related to repeated violation of the employer's rules would also require the employer to satisfy a number of obligations with respect to those rules. Arbitrators in general are concerned that any rules related to employees that are unilaterally imposed by the employer are fair and uniformly enforced. Consequently, where the discharge (or discipline) is related to a violation of a rule or rules, the employer is obliged to prove that the rules were brought to the attention of the employee prior to the first violation, that the rules were reasonable and consistently enforced, that any penalty attached to a rule violation was appropriate as a penalty, and that the employee could reasonably expect some form of discipline if the rule was violated. In addition, the employer would be obliged to prove that the rule violation had taken place, and that the penalty imposed took into consideration the employee's past record and length of service.[12]

Rules that are agreed upon between the employer and union and inserted in a collective agreement are a different matter, as the violation of a rule would then be treated in the same manner as any other violation of the collective agreement. The establishment of rules on a unilateral basis by management is more common, however, and even where rules of behaviour are included in the collective agreement, new rules may be promulgated by the employer, provided that they do not conflict with the rules set out in the agreement.[13]

As an alternative to the use of punishment as a means of controlling employee behaviour in the work place, a variety of different approaches have been taken by employers and unions, either separately or in concert. Some years ago, a system of "discipline without punishment" was suggested as an alternative to the punitive methods presently employed.[14] Under this system, violations of rules of behaviour would result in counselling of the employee in order to bring about a behaviour change. Each violation would result in further counselling, but would change with repeated violations until it constituted a request that the employee seriously consider seeking employment elsewhere, if he or she could not conform to the behaviour norm expected of employees in the firm. If the behaviour did not change, the employee would perhaps be given some paid time at home to consider the future, and would eventually be terminated. A substantial time commitment on the part of supervisory staff or Personnel Department employees is required for this type of program, and few firms have adopted the approach to employee discipline. The need of documentation, in particular, would be substantial in the event that the employee was eventually terminated and a grievance filed, as the system does not involve a threat of punishment if the behaviour does not change. Only in the final stages of the counselling does the possibility of termination become apparent and the threat of dismissal become real. Consequently, most firms tend to follow the progressive discipline system as a means of behaviour control.

A recent departure from progressive discipline has taken place in some of the larger firms concerning absenteeism where the absence from work is alcohol- or drug-related. The United Automobile Workers' Union in particular has been concerned about employee alcohol and drug abuse for a number of years, and in conjunction with some of the larger employers, notably the General Motors Corporation, have developed a rehabilitation program whereby employees who have alcohol or drug problems may be retained as employees during a rehabilitation period. Unauthorized absence from work is generally the type of incident that puts the employer on notice, and instead of discipline, the union and the employer jointly investigate and counsel the employee. Where the employee is prepared to undertake a rehabilitative program, the employer continues to retain the employee on the payroll, and the employee attends a special rehabilitation program conducted by the employer and union. On the completion of the program, the employee is returned to his job on the condition that if he or she reverts to alcohol or drug use in the future, a discharge based upon absenteeism related to alcohol or drugs would not be challenged by grievance or carried to arbitration by the union. Similar programs have been established by other unions and employers who see alcohol and drug addiction as essentially an illness rather than a cause for discipline.

Arbitrators generally uphold management's right to discipline or discharge employees who are repeatedly absent from work without excuse, but recognize the fact that employees from time to time encounter circumstances that prevent their attendance. Employers are entitled to expect regular employee attendance at the work place, otherwise the scheduling and performance of work would become an impossibility. Repeated absence for periods of long or short duration may, as a result, raise questions in the employer's mind as to the reliability of the employee and the desirability of retaining the employee on the work force. To control absenteeism, and to provide a uniform policy as to notice, employers usually establish rules for absence which require absent employees to notify the employer and provide an excuse for the absence. Usually employers are prepared to accept reasonable excuses for absence, but in some cases where attendance is important, may require the employee to call in prior to the work shift if the employee will not be available for work to enable the employer to find a replacement for the period of the absence.

Absence from work may occur for many reasons. The employee may be ill, or have family responsibilities such as a child requiring medical attention, a transportation problem, or any number of other legitimate reasons. These absences are usually considered to be **innocent absenteeism** and seldom constitute grounds for disciplinary action unless the employee has deliberately ignored any required call-in notice obligations. On the other hand, where the employee is absent from work without a justifiable excuse, or where the employee without good reason fails to notify the employer of an absence in accordance with the rules set down for notice, the absence is considered **blameworthy absenteeism**. Under these circumstances the employer may impose disciplinary sanctions on the employee, and where repeated violations occur, may be justified in discharging the employee. Arbitrators seldom uphold grievances where the absence constitutes blameworthy absenteeism if the arbitrator is satisfied that the employer's rule concerning unauthorized absence without excuse or call-in notice is reasonable and has been consistently and fairly enforced.[15]

It should be noted, however, that in cases of innocent absenteeism, even though these may not be grounds for discipline, the employer may be justified in terminating the employee if the absence or repeated absences are such that the employee is unable to perform his or her duties with some degree of consistency. Grievances of this type are the most difficult to deal with because arbitrators are reluctant to dismiss the grievance where the disability is through no fault of the employee. However, arbitrators also recognize that the employer should be entitled to replace employees who are unable to perform their duties where the infirmity is likely to continue into the future and if their past record of absence is excessive. Such determinations generally turn on medical opinion evidence if the absence is a result of some physical illness, but in every case, the employer is expected to satisfy the arbitrator that the grievor's attendance record is much poorer than that of other employees and below some established standard.[16]

Other circumstances that might warrant disciplinary action or discharge by management would include theft of the employer's property, incompetence, careless workmanship, fighting, insubordination, wilful damage, falsification of time or employment records, criminal or improper behaviour away from the work place which would embarrass or injure the employer's business, violations of health and safety regulations, repeated lateness or unauthorized absences, and a variety of other activities such as sleeping or drinking alcoholic beverages on the job. The degree of seriousness of each of these incidents and the circumstances surrounding each will naturally determine whether the penalty imposed was justified.

Arbitrators generally uphold the dismissal of employees who deliberately steal the employer's property on the basis that the employer is entitled to trust his employees, and the theft would be a violation of that trust.[17] A more difficult matter arises where the employer discharges an employee for criminal activity away from the employer's premises. Normally, any activity which takes place away from the employer's premises would not be grounds for disciplinary action unless the act took place while the employee was engaged in the employer's business. However, where an employee engages in some act of violence or criminal pursuit on his or her own time, under certain circumstances the employer may take steps to terminate the employee. If the criminal act affects the employer's business, for example, where a person employed by a public utility as a meter reader is convicted on a morals charge, unprovoked assault, or theft from a dwelling house, the employer may be entitled to discharge the employee if homeowners or tenants are likely to be apprehensive or unwilling to allow such a person entry into their homes on the employer's business. The right to discharge might also exist where the continued employment of the person would pose a potential threat to the safety of other employees.[18]

Where the criminal activities of the employee result in a period of detention in a provincial institution or federal penitentiary, the employee is often terminated on the basis of an inability to perform his or her required employment responsibilities. However, in cases where the employee is given a suspended sentence or fine for the violation of the *Criminal Code*, the potential for grievance arises, and in such cases the employer would be obliged to show just cause for the discharge or any disciplinary action taken.

The falsification of production records has also been treated by arbitrators with much the same degree of seriousness as the theft of the employer's property, but as a general rule, mitigating circumstances such as a long and discipline-free employment record will be considered in the determination of the appropriate penalty. In the past, arbitrators would frequently confirm discharge penalties for the falsification of production records, but today, most arbitrators are likely to give greater weight to any mitigating factors, and where permitted, substitute a lesser penalty such as a suspension for the violation of trust.

The misrepresentation of information on employment application forms, if made deliberately and with the intention to deceive the employer, may also constitute grounds for discharge when the misrepresentation is discovered. Fraudulent misrepresentation, however, must be distinguished from innocent nondisclosure, and where the latter type of oversight occurs, arbitrators may reinstate a discharged employee if the circumstances surrounding the nondisclosure warrant.

Nondisclosure or deliberate misrepresentation may be made for many reasons, but the most common reasons are to hide a criminal record or a medical condition from the employer. Both of these matters would likely eliminate the employee as a candidate for a position if the position requires either "bonding," (in the case of a criminal record) or work of a heavy physical nature (where any medical or health problem would be affected). Consequently, persons with either a criminal background or a background of medical problems which would affect their employment may attempt to hide the information. Nevertheless, most arbitrators believe that the employment relationship rests on honesty and trust, and a violation of that trust by dishonesty on the employee's part may entitle the employer to terminate the relationship.[19]

REMEDIES IN DISCIPLINE AND DISCHARGE CASES

The burden of proof rests on the employer, and the employer must satisfy the arbitrator that proper cause or just cause existed for the disciplinary action taken. After hearing all of the evidence and assessing any mitigating factors brought forward by the union, an arbitrator may not necessarily agree with the penalty imposed by the employer for the infraction of the rule, misdemeanor, or failing of the grievor. Collective agreements frequently provide that an arbitrator has the authority to substitute a lesser penalty for the penalty imposed by the employer in discipline and discharge cases, and in some provinces, the right is established by statute.[20] However, where the collective agreement does not permit the arbitrator to alter the penalties, but provides instead a negotiated catalogue of offences with specific penalties for each, the arbitrator is probably bound by the penalty set out in the collective agreement if the employer satisfies the arbitrator that he had just cause to invoke the penalty. Apart from this restriction, arbitrators are normally free to vary the penalty where the statute or collective agreement permits. The arbitrator may, therefore, reduce a discharge to a suspension, reinstate a discharged employee with or without compensation, reduce a suspension, reinstate under specific conditions, or alter the seniority status of the employee under certain circumstances. The arbitrator may, of course, agree with the penalty imposed by the employer if just cause is proven, and if the penalty is deemed just and proper, dismiss the grievance.

WAGES

Wage rates are generally set out in a schedule attached to a collective agreement, and specify the wages applicable to specific jobs or classes of jobs. Employees whose jobs fall within each classification are entitled to payment at the rate set out in the schedule, and a failure on the part of the employer to pay the rate fixed (in the absence of a provision to the contrary) would constitute a violation of the collective agreement. Grievances rarely concern payment of specified rates, since wage schedules are usually clear and explicit in their application. However, where employer discretion is included, such as in merit pay or performance-related compensation, grievances sometimes arise where the employee believes that he or she is entitled to a merit rate, when the employer has decided otherwise.

Grievances concerning merit wages are usually dealt with by arbitrators in much the same manner as grievances concerning promotions, as employer discretion and assessment of the employees performance represent important ingredients of both types of decisions. Arbitrators will usually examine the reasonableness of criteria and standards which the employer has set for the determination of merit rates. While arbitrators expect the employees to be compared to a "standard," the standard may include a number of factors which are not directly related to the performance of work itself, such as punctuality, attendance record, and ability to work well with other employees. As a general rule, arbitrators will not disturb the judgment of the employer where the assessment of all of the employees has been made against a reasonable standard in a fair and unbiased manner, as arbitrators generally hold that the employees' supervisors are in the best position to make the determination. The concern of the arbitrator is that the decision was made fairly and honestly, and in accordance with the collective agreement.

The eligibility of employees for wages that are not work related, such as periodic wage increases specified in the collective agreement, or wage increases based upon the period of employment that an employee is engaged in a particular position, are determined from the wording of the collective agreement. Grievances related to this type of wage increase are interpretive in nature, and often arise out of ambiguous language in the agreement itself. The past practice of the employer is often used to arrive at a proper interpretation of the ambiguous provision, but apart from this, arbitrators may sometimes examine the conduct of the employer where unfairness or bias on the part of the grievor's supervisor is alleged in the grievance. The remedy in wage-related grievance cases where the employer is found to be in violation of the agreement is usually monetary compensation to the employee for the period of time that the wage increase was denied.

HOLIDAY AND VACATIONS

The collective agreement and statute law govern the entitlement of employees to vacations and holidays. Statutory holidays, as the name implies, are certain days designated by law as holidays in each year. The holidays may not necessarily be paid holidays in all provinces unless statutory requirements are met, but payment of a wage equivalent for a statutory holiday has long been considered an **earned benefit** by employees and trade union negotiators, and collective agreements as a result usually reflect this view in the form of a holiday-with-pay clause. The collective agreement fixes the holiday entitlement of the employees, and many collective agreements include a number of holidays in addition to those fixed by statute. Employees required to work on a prescribed holiday may be entitled to the wage rate fixed for holiday work in addition to the holiday pay equivalent, and in some cases may be entitled to a "lieu day" instead of extra compensation.

While employees and unions view holidays as earned benefits, employers recognize the potential problems that the extension of a holiday to an extra day or two may cause to the production process in a firm. To limit holidays to the days fixed by the collective agreement, employers will generally insist on a **surrounding day** provision which restricts entitlement to holiday pay to employees who work their last scheduled work day before, and first scheduled work day after the holiday. Surrounding day clauses, unfortunately, are occasionally worded in an ambiguous manner, and arbitrators may be called upon to interpret the clause in answer to a grievance. Each interpretation hinges on the specific wording of the qualification for payment, but arbitrators tend to view absences on either of the surrounding days that are legitimate in a different light from those that are holiday related, and have ruled that where the employee is ill, on layoff, or absent due to some action on the part of the employer, the surrounding day restriction would not apply to disentitle the employee to holiday pay. Only persons who are in a position to show that the employment relationship was in existence at the time would, of course, be entitled to claim holiday pay,[21] and persons who had severed the relationship would not be eligible, unless the collective agreement so provided.

The reasoning behind this view (which, it should be noted, is not universally held) is that holiday pay is a benefit that employees should be entitled to receive except in those circumstances where the absence on one or both of the surrounding days represents a refusal on the part of the employee to work, or a dereliction of the employee's duty. The wording of the collective agreement clause, nevertheless, must permit this form of interpretation, otherwise the arbitrator is limited as to the interpretation that may be given to the proviso. For example, if the surrounding day qualification specifically excludes pay entitlement to those employees who are absent from work on either of the surrounding days because they are on layoff, the arbitrator clearly could not uphold a grievance requesting holiday pay if the grievor was on layoff at the time. Similarly, if the agreement provided that the employee must work the full shift on each of the surrounding days, the arbitrator would be bound to reject a grievance for holiday pay if the grievor failed to complete both shifts.[22] The clear language of the surrounding day clause would limit the finding of the arbitrator regardless of his or her philosophical attitude towards the intent of surrounding day qualifications.

Vacations are also treated as earned benefits where eligibility is based upon length of service, and hence, are subject to benefit seniority, and contingent on the employment relationship subsisting at the time that the vacation entitlement arises. Where a collective agreement stipulates that an employee who has accumulated a specific period of time as an employee is entitled to a vacation of a fixed term, the employer is bound to provide the paid vacation, but usually not immediately. The time when an employee may take a vacation is usually not set out in the collective agreement, and under those circumstances the employer would normally be entitled to establish the time when the vacation might begin.[23] Where the agreement is silent on vacation times, the employer would also be free to schedule all vacations at a specified time, and shut down operations for the vacation period, as indeed many firms do. However, to fetter the right of unreasonable demands by employers, many unions have negotiated collective agreement clauses concerning vacations which require the employer to make reasonable efforts to accommodate the vacation times requested by employees, or require the employer to permit the vacation to be taken within a specific time-frame after the employee becomes eligible. In some cases, vacation time scheduling is determined on a seniority basis, with the most senior employee entitled to select a specific time, the next most senior employee the second opportunity, and so on down to the employee with the least seniority. Where scheduling is determined by seniority, the agreement may also provide that the employer must approve the schedule, and require any changes if the schedule would interfere with the efficient operation of the organization. In any event, vacation rights (except for statutory minimums) are negotiated, and governed by the collective agreement. The agreement, therefore, determines the entitlement and the conditions under which vacations may be taken. The role of the arbitrator in dealing with vacation benefits is largely restricted to a determination of eligibility and an interpretation of any provisions related to specific rights such as scheduling of vacation times. The remedies available to grievors who satisfy arbitrators that their employers have failed to give them the required number of weeks or days of vacation time usually consist of monetary payment or an equivalent vacation time to be taken by the employee. Most other grievance situations simply require an interpretation of the collective agreement provisions by the arbitrator, and do not involve redress.

REVIEW QUESTIONS

1. *Describe the limits on management rights. How are these limits determined?*
2. *Outline the nature and use of seniority clauses in a collective agreement. On what basis would the principle be justified?*
3. *Distinguish between "benefit seniority" and "competitive status seniority."*
4. *Why do employers frequently insist that a "skill and ability" qualifier be attached to seniority clauses concerning the layoff and recall of employees?*
5. *What is "super seniority"? On what basis do unions justify this type of seniority?*
6. *Distinguish a "closed shop" clause from a "union shop" clause. Why are closed shop clauses seldom found in industrial collective agreements?*
7. *Explain the importance of the right to make rules of behaviour and the right to discipline when the rules are violated. What must employers establish at arbitration if they wish to discharge their burden of proof in a discipline case?*
8. *Explain the nature of a progressive discipline system. Under what circumstances would an employer be obliged to ignore the system?*
9. *Explain the difference between "innocent absenteeism" and "blameworthy absenteeism".*
10. *Explain the following terms: surrounding day, earned benefit, Rand Formula, modified union shop clause, "bumping," job posting, job seniority.*

NOTES

[1]*Re United Steelworkers, Local 1817 and Fittings Ltd* (1960) 10 L.A.C. 294.
[2]*Re Retail Wholesale and Department Store Union, Local 414 and Versafood Services Ltd.* (1971) 23 L.A.C. 19.
[3]*International Brotherhood of Pulp, Sulphite and Paper Mill Workers Local 742 and Crown Zellerbach Canada Ltd.* (1972) 72 CLLC 14,144; (1971) 71 CLLC 14,086.
[4]*Re Domtar Packaging Ltd. and Canadian Paperworkers' Union, Local 1597* (1981) 3 L.A.C. (3d) 18.
[5]See for example, the direction to arbitrators in *Falconbridge Nickel Mines Ltd. and United Steelworkers of America. (1973) 1 O.R. 136 (C.A.)*.
[6]See for example, *Re Canadian Trailmobile Ltd. and United Automobile Workers, Local 397 (1975) 10 L.A.C. (2d) 92*.
[7]*Re Hydro-Electric Power Commission of Ontario and Office and Professional Employees' International Union* (1976) 11 L.A.C. (2d) 36.
[8]See for example, *Re Textile Workers' Union and Lady Galt Towels Ltd.* (1969) 20 L.A.C. 382.
[9]*Great Atlantic & Pacific Co. of Canada Ltd. and Canadian Food and Allied Workers, Local 175* (1976) 13 L.A.C. (2d) 211; See *Canadian Food and Allied Workers Union, Local 175 v. Great Atlantic and Pacific Company of Canada Limited et al.* (1976) 76 CLLC para 14,056.
[10]*Falconbridge Nickel Mines Ltd. and United Steelworkers of America* (1973) 1 O.R. 136. (Ont. C.A.).
[11]See for example, *Polymer Corp. Ltd. and Oil, Chemical and Atomic Workers Local 9-14* (1973) 4 L.A.C. (2d) 148; *Re United Automobile Workers and Massey-Ferguson Industries Ltd.* (1969) 20 L.A.C. 178.
[12]These comments represent a summary of the requirements set down for rule enforcement in the leading case of *Re Lumber & Sawmill Workers' Union, Local 2537 and K.V.P. Co. Ltd.* (1965) 16 L.A.C. 73 at pp. 85 *et seq.*
[13]*Ex-Cell-O Corp. of Canada Ltd. and International Molders' Union Local 49* (1975) 10 L.A.C. (2d) 44.
[14]See Huberman J. "Discipline Without Punishment," *Harvard Business Review*, July-August 1964, pp. 62–68.
[15]See for example, *Re Port Arthur Shipbuilding Co. v. Arthurs et al.* (1968) 70 D.L.R. (2d) 693; *United Packing House Workers, Local 489 and Robson Lang (London) Ltd.* (1965) 16 L.A.C. 145.
[16]See for example, *Re De Havilland Aircraft of Canada Ltd. and United Automobile Workers, Local 112* (1983) 9 L.A.C. (3d) 271; *Re Niagara Structural Steel (St. Catharines) Ltd. and United Steelworkers, Local 7012* (1978) 18 L.A.C. (2d) 385; *Atlas Steels Co. and Canadian Steelworkers' Union, Atlas Division* (1975) 8 L.A.C. (2d) 350; *Re United Automobile Workers and Massey-Ferguson Ltd.* (1969) 20 L.A.C. 370.
[17]See for example, *Ford Motor Co. of Canada Ltd. and United Plant Guard Workers, Local 1958* (1975) 8 L.A.C. (2d) 188.
[18]See *Re Bundy of Canada Ltd., Sinterings Div. and United Steelworkers, Local 6012* (1975) 9 L.A.C. (2d) 141.

[19]*Douglas Aircraft Co. of Canada Ltd. and United Automobile Workers, Local 1967 (1973) 2 L.A.C. (2d) 147.*
[20]See for example, Ontario, *Labour Relations Act*, R.S.O. 1980, c. 228, s. 44(9).
[21]See for example, *Re Sudbury General Workers, Local 101, and Dominion Stores Ltd.* (1970) 22 L.A.C. 72.
[22]See for example, *Re United Steelworkers of America, Local 1005, and Steel Co. of Canada Ltd.* (1967) 18 L.A.C. 432.
[23]See *Municipality of Metropolitan Toronto and Toronto Civil Employees' Union, Local 43 et al.* (1975) 62 D.L.R. (3d) 53.

RECOMMENDED REFERENCES AND SOURCE MATERIAL

Adell, B.L. *The Legal Status of Collective Agreements*. Kingston, Canada: Queen's University Industrial Relations Centre (1970).
Brown, D.J.M. and D.M. Beatty. *Canadian Labour Arbitration* (2 ed.). Toronto,Canada: Canada Law Book Limited, 1984.
Cox, A. "Reflections Upon Labor Arbitration." 72 *Harvard Law Review* 1482 (1959).
Curtis, C.H. *The Development and Enforcement of the Collective Agreement*. Kingston, Canada: Queen's University Industrial Relations Centre (1966).
Dunlop, J.T. and J.J. Healy. "The Grievance Procedure." *Canadian Labour and Industrial Relations* (H.C. Jain, ed.). Toronto, Canada: McGraw-Hill Ryerson (1975), p.199.
Kane, S.E. "Current Development in Expedited Arbitration." 24 *Labor Law Journal* 282 (April 1973).
Little, W. *The Role of Arbitration in Industrial Relations*. Kingston, Canada: Queen's University Industrial Relations Centre, 1974.
Muir, J.D. "Arbitration of the Collective Agreement." *Canadian Industrial Relations: A Book of Readings* (S.A. Hameed, ed.). Toronto, Canada: Butterworth and Co. (Canada) Ltd. (1975), p. 359.
Palmer, E.E. *Collective Agreement Arbitration in Canada* (2nd ed.). Toronto, Canada: Butterworth & Co. (Canada) Ltd. (1983).
Weiler, P.C. "The Arbitrator, the Collective Agreement and the Law." 10 *Osgoode Hall Law Journal* 141 (1972).
Weiler, P.C. "The Remedial Authority of the Labour Arbitrator: Revised Judicial Version." 52 *Canadian Bar Review* 29.
Weiler, P.C. "The Role of the Labour Arbitrator: Alternative Versions." 19 *University of Toronto Law Journal* 16 (1969).

CASE PROBLEMS FOR DISCUSSION
FIREPROOF FILE CABINET COMPANY CASE

The Fireproof File Cabinet Company was formed by Jones and Smith, two young entrepreneurs, after a serious fire in the building where they had operated a mail-order business destroyed their office and all of their records. The mail-order business had been totally incapacitated by the loss of all of their files, customer lists, and accounting records, and during the months that followed the fire the two men lamented on many occasions their failure to keep all of the business records in a fire secure cabinet of some sort. Finally their conversations turned to the lack of suitable fireproof storage cabinets on the market, and then consideration of the possibility of selling small fire resistant containers through their mail-order business.

Jones, who had an engineering background, immediately proceeded to sketch a plan for the construction of a small insulated metal container with a storage capacity of about one cubic foot. The design appealed to Smith, and they then proceeded to have a small quantity manufactured for them by a friend who operated a sheet metal firm. The fire resistant container was advertised in their first catalogue issued after their own fire, and proved to be an instant success. The small stock which they had on hand was immediately sold out, and they soon found that a large market existed for their product.

Over time, new and different models and sizes of cabinets were added to their line of fire resistant storage containers, and eventually they purchased the sheet metal plant from their friend as a part of a long-range plan to produce and market a full line of fire resistant storage cabinets for home and office use.

The name of the manufacturing firm was changed to the Fireproof File Cabinet Company in 1970, and gradually expanded over the next decade until it employed a work force of about forty-five employees. The production and maintenance employees had been originally organized by the Metal Equipment Workers Union before the plant was purchased, and the union continued to represent the plant employees. The office staff was not represented by a union. The union-management relationship was relatively informal and friendly, and successive collective agreements had been negotiated since 1970 without resort to strikes or lock-outs. The current collective agreement contains the following relevant clauses:

1.01   The parties agree that it is mutually beneficial and desirable to arrange and maintain fair and equitable earnings, labour standards, wage rates and working conditions to obtain efficient operations, to protect the safety and health of employees and to provide machinery for the adjustment of disputes which may arise between the parties hereto.

Article 4 – Management Rights

4.01 The Company shall be entitled to exercise all the usual rights of management which are not expressly modified by this Agreement and more particularly, and without limiting the generality of the foregoing, it is the exclusive right of the Company, subject to the provision of this agreement, to:

(a) direct its working forces;

(b) plan, direct and control its plant operations;

(c) determine the means, methods, processes and schedules of its operations;

(e) establish reasonable production and operating standards in order to maintain the efficiency of the employees;

(f) establish reasonable company rules and regulations;

(g) hire, transfer, or lay off employees and to relieve employees from duties and to suspend, demote, discharge and otherwise discipline employees for just cause;

(h) to determine the locations of its plants, the products to be manufactured, the scheduling of its production and its methods, processes and means of manufacturing.

15.03 Persons not in the Bargaining Unit with the exception of students or trainees, shall not perform the manufacturing of standard production runs.

Article 27 – Contracting out

The Company reserves the right to contract work out. However, during the duration of this agreement the Company will not contract out existing production work that will directly result in the layoff or discharge of employees with seniority and working as of the date of signing of this agreement. This contracting out clause does not apply to Company affiliates.

Plant production was governed to some extent by the equipment buying habits of its customers, which tended to take place during the spring, summer and fall of the year, and tapered off during the winter months. The firm historically operated at about 60 percent of its capacity during the months of December, January, and February, then moved back to full production for the remaining months of the year. Overtime work was not uncommon during May and June, and occasionally, if demand was particularly high, some of the fabrication of relatively standard parts was contracted out to another local firm. The plant was closed during the week between December 25 and January 1 in each year for inventory, which was taken by Jones and Brown with the assistance of a few office employees.

In late November, as a result of the seasonal decline in demand for the type of product that the company manufactured, the management gave layoff notice to fifteen employees in accordance with the layoff provisions in the collective agreement. The reduction in the work force tended to be uniform throughout the plant, and included a few employees (those with the least seniority) in each department. The layoff normally extended to February in each year, when production demands once again increased, and the plant returned to its full productive capacity.

Early in December the company was notified by its paint supplier that the type of paint which it had supplied in the past would be discontinued, and the paint line replaced by an improved product which had been developed for fire resistant products. The new paint was delivered to the company the following week, and the employees soon found that the difference in drying time and/or adhesion qualities of the two paints was causing problems for the Paint Department. The fabricated parts apparently had uneven paint adhesion and occasionally, "paint runs" left the painted surfaces with an uneven finish.

The Paint Department operation was in part an automated production line. Fabricated sheet metal products were hung on a moving overhead conveyor by material handling employees, then the parts moved through a cleaning tank which removed all surface rust, dirt, oil, and grease. Once clean, the conveyor carried the parts through a dryer, and on into a second dip tank where each was surface treated for painting. The parts went through a second drying process, then on into the paint application booth and finally through a paint "oven" where the paint was baked on the surface. The conveyor continued to carry the parts a distance to the parts storage area of the plant where they were removed from the conveyor by material handlers and placed in special racks or partitioned bins for movement to the assembly area.

The duties of the material handlers in the Paint Department included the inspection of all metal panels and parts for dents, deep scratches, or defects before the parts were placed on the conveyor, and an inspection of the painted products for visual paint imperfections when the products were finally removed. Inspection of the parts during the cleaning and painting process was the responsibility of the painters, who monitored the paint process and adjusted temperatures or conveyor speeds to achieve the proper paint finish on the product.

Defective parts were generally stored in salvage areas, where other production employees would inspect the defects and recycle those parts that could be repaired or refinished.

During the week of December 15 to December 20, Jones spent a great deal of time dealing with paint problems. In an effort to determine the cause of the problem he experimented with temperature settings, drying time, strength of cleaning solutions in the preparation processes, and inspection of the panels and parts as they proceeded through the process. By the Thursday of that week, the problems had been eliminated, but during the first part of the week, Jones believed that he had probably removed and inspected over half of the finished parts from the conveyor on each of the days, and perhaps filled as many of the parts racks as each of the two material handlers who were also working on the job. On the Friday of that week, however, he was surprised to be presented with a grievance from C. Marcos, a material handling employee on layoff, which stated in part, as follows:

Nature of Grievance: I grieve that the company has violated the collective agreement by management performing bargaining unit work on December 15, 16, 17, and 18 while I was on layoff.

Agreement Violation: Article 15.03 and all other pertinent articles of the collective agreement.

Settlement Requested: full redress.

(signed) C. Marcos.

During the same week, Smith had decided to prepare for the taking of inventory, and had spent part of the Monday of that week arranging the parts salvage areas for the count of parts to be made. With the aid of a material handling employee, he sorted the salvage areas in the Stamping Department into piles of parts which could be recycled, and those which could only be scrapped. Part of the time he used a small fork lift to move the bins of parts, and occasionally moved bins which had been sorted into the production area for repair and reprocessing. On the Tuesday morning he sorted the salvage areas in the Paint Department unaided, and moved a number of bins of reuseable parts which he had sorted back into the production area in the Stamping Department. On the Wednesday afternoon, Smith also worked for approximately an hour in the Receiving Department rearranging the raw stock for the inventory count. At the end of the day, he used the fork lift to move a new shipment of material to a separate area of the Receiving Department to permit access to the stock which he had previously arranged for the inventory count.

On the Friday of the week, a grievance signed by P. Daniels, a material handling employee, who was also on layoff, was delivered to Jones. The Daniels grievance was worded in terms identical to those of the Marcos grievance. Jones and Smith discussed the grievances with the plant foreman, then decided to reject both complaints.

The union was duly informed of the management decision, and the grievance processed through the grievance procedure as provided in the collective agreement. When the dispute could not be resolved, the union moved for arbitration.

CASE DISCUSSION QUESTIONS

1. *On what basis were the two grievances filed?*
2. *Where does the burden of proof lie in this case?*
3. *What defences are available to the employer? How should the employer prepare for arbitration?*
4. *Determine the arbitral authority available to assist (1) the employer, (2) the union. How would this be used?*
5. *What issue must the arbitrator decide? What principles would the arbitrator likely apply?*
6. *Render an award.*

METRO-CITY ARBITRATION CASE

Metro-City operated a ferry service from the lakefront area of the municipality to an island located some distance from the shore. The island was a part of the municipality and the ferry service was maintained by the city on a twelve month basis for the benefit of the residents and business firms located on the island. During the summer months, ferry traffic increased substantially and the municipality operated the ferry with greater frequency, putting into service a number of additional ferry boats.

The work force employed in the ferry service consisted of three full-time crews of permanent employees and a seasonal work force of temporary employees, hired for the summer months. Crew adjustments were made for each summer season, with the seasonal employees hired in late April or early May of each year for a period of approximately six months.

Temporary or seasonal employee requirements for the summer season were normally established in February of each year by the department head responsible for the ferry service. Once budget approval was obtained, the request for employees was forwarded to the Personnel Office.

The Personnel Office maintained a list of names of ex-employees who had worked the previous season and followed the practice of first calling back the temporary employees of the previous year before inviting applications from the general public. Temporary employees that had worked in excess of six months in the previous year would be notified of the available work in reverse order of their time of termination in the preceding year. Thus, the last employee terminated would be called first. All other temporary employees were generally called on a random basis. If an insufficient number accepted the call-in, the Personnel Office would then seek the necessary additional applicants by way of a newspaper advertisement or the local employment office.

Except for persons who had been employed in excess of six months during the previous year, the Personnel Office treated all seasonal employees as new applicants for the positions open. After preliminary screening and selection interviews, the Personnel Office sent prospective employees to the department concerned. This was usually done to confirm that the applicants possessed the necessary licenses or certificates required for the positions open. The final selection of seasonal employees was left with the department head, but where the individuals had worked for the municipality for a number of seasons in the past, the process was largely routine.

During the summer season, permanent employee crews were generally reassigned to different ferry boats and each ferry was normally manned by a mixed crew of permanent and seasonal employees. Changes were not uncommon, and often an employee might be employed upon a number of different boats over a variety of shifts during the course of the summer season.

The employees of the municipality were organized as Local 34 of the City Employees' Union and were employed under the terms of a collective agreement which covered both permanent and temporary (seasonal) employees. However, the rights of temporary employees under the collective agreement, subject to certain limited recall rights, applied only while they were in the employ of the municipality.

In September, 1982, an opening for a Marine Oiler occurred in the permanent service of the employer. The employer, in accordance with the provisions of the collective agreement, advertised the position to both permanent and temporary staff as Job Call #3214. The job requirements were as follows:

1. Minimum education of secondary school, with preference to a technical course graduate.

2. Possession of a Temporary Engineer's Certificate (issued by the Department of Transport).

3. Physically able to perform manual labour.

4. Some experience in a diesel-equipped marine engine room.

5. Capable of handling diesel equipment in an emergency.

Three applications were received by the personnel officer for the permanent position of Marine Oiler. On the closing date for applications, the Personnel Officer examined the employment records of the three applicants, and prepared an eligibility list which ranked the employees in the following order: (1) A. Brown, (2) C. Allard, and (3) R. Abercrombie.

The eligibility list was delivered to the department head who then proceeded to interview each candidate named on the list. Shortly after the completion of the third interview, Mr. Abercrombie informed the departmental head that he wished to withdraw his name as he had accepted a similar position with a shipping company and had submitted his resignation to the Personnel Office.

Of the two remaining applicants, both had experience as Marine Oilers on ocean-going and/or Great Lakes vessels. Both employees had been employed by the municipality in the ferry service as temporary employees for many summers in a number of different capacities, and both were in the employ of the municipality at the time that the permanent position was posted. Both applicants possessed the requisite Temporary Engineer's Certificate and both men had demonstrated that they were capable of doing the work of a Marine Oiler on the ferry boats.

The department head carefully reviewed the employment records of the two employees, then concluded that he must select Mr. Brown for the position as he was the applicant with the greatest seniority. When the selection of Mr. Brown for the permanent position of Marine Oiler was announced, Mr. Allard, the other applicant, filed a grievance claiming that he had been unjustly denied the position since he was the best qualified applicant.

The grievance was denied by the employer and when the matter could not be resolved by way of the grievance procedure, the union requested that an arbitration board be established to hear the dispute. The relevant provisions of the collective agreement in force at all material times provide as follows:

s. 4.01 Local 34 and the employees coming within the bargaining unit recognize and acknowledge that it is the exclusive function of the Employer to:

(i)   maintain order, discipline, and efficiency;
(ii)   hire, discharge, direct, classify, transfer, promote, demote, and suspend or otherwise discipline any employee within the bargaining unit, provided that a claim for discriminatory promotion, demotion or transfer, or a claim that an employee has been discharged or disciplined without just cause, may be the subject of a grievance and dealt with as hereinafter provided; and
(iii)   generally to manage the operation and undertakings of the municipality, and without restricting the generality of the foregoing, to select, instal and require the operation of any equipment, plant or machinery which the municipality in its uncontrolled discretion deems necessary for the efficient conduct of its operations.

s. 4.02   The Employer agrees that it will not exercise any of the functions set out in clause 4.01 in a manner inconsistent with the provisions of this agreement.

s. 9.01   Whenever appointments or promotions are to be made, the Department Head concerned shall notify the Personnel Officer accordingly, setting forth the duties of the position and specifying the qualifications thereof, and the Personnel Officer shall arrange for the position to be made known to all employees through the Job Call procedure hereinafter described. The Personnel Officer shall:

(i)   send copies of Job Call notices in accordance with Article 9.02 to all Departments to be prominently posted;
(ii)   where necessary, prepare and conduct competitive examinations to evaluate the fitness of applicants by education, experience, and ability to perform the work satisfactorily;
(iii)   establish eligibility lists of candidates, and send such lists to the appropriate Department Heads for selection or recommendation for promotion or appointment.

9.02   (a)   Each Job Call notice shall state:

(i)   the general duties of the position
(ii)   the Department and location where possible
(iii)   the Bargaining Unit in which the position is situated
(iv)   the salary range or wage rate
(v)   the qualifications required
(vi)   the procedure for making application
(vii)   the time limit for receiving applications

(viii)   the examination, if any, that candidates must successfully complete for the position.

9.03   (a)   An employee whose application has been rejected because he or she does not possess sufficient qualifications for the position shall be notified in writing at least seven days prior to the date of the examination.

(b)   Any applicant for an examination or candidate participating in an examination who deems he has a complaint regarding the procedure or any other matter may have his complaint placed before the Personnel Officer.

9.04   (a)   If the successful completion of an examination is required to qualify for a particular position, such examination shall be conducted in a manner that will provide a fair evaluation of the fitness of all applicants. All applicants shall be evaluated against the same set of standards.

(b)   Examinations may be written, oral, or by demonstration of skill, evaluation of training, experience, seniority, or any combination thereof, as the Personnel Officer may decide.

(c)   All applicants shall be notified in writing of the outcome of their examination and their standing on the list.

9.05   (a)   The list of suitable candidates established from each Job Call shall be either:

(i)   a Final Candidate List which shall be valid for the filling of the advertised position only, or
(ii)   an Eligibility List which shall be valid for a period of six months for the purpose of filling other vacancies that may occur in the same position classification if made in accordance with the Job Call notice.

9.06   (a)   The Personnel Officer shall establish for selection purposes the list of candidates resulting from each Job Call, ranked in order of standing.

(b)   The selection of the qualified candidate for the position available shall be made by the Department Head on the basis of ability, seniority, and suitability for the position.

(c)   Candidates ranked higher on the list than the candidate selected for the position shall be informed in writing by the Department Head, and the writing shall include an explanation of the reason or reasons why the individual was not selected for the particular position.

15.01   Where the services of persons in the temporary (seasonal) service of the Employer become surplus to its work requirements, their employment shall be terminated in order of least seniority within the position classification in the department involved, and when work becomes available, such persons, if not more than six (6) months have elapsed from the date of their termination, shall be referred for re-employment in the reverse order of their termination, provided that they possess the necessary qualifications for such work.

SCHEDULE A

Excerpts From The Employment Records of The Applicants For The
Position Of Marine Oiler.

A. Brown

Classification:
Temporary (seasonal) Employee.

Educational Background:
Secondary School Graduation Diploma.
Vocational School Diploma as a diesel mechanic.

Certificates/Licenses:
Temporary Engineer's Certificate (D.O.T.) first issued August, 1981.

Previous Employment:
Deck Hand, Lake Shipping Co. April 1, 1970 – November 30, 1971
Marine Oiler, Lake Shipping Co. December 1, 1971 – January 5, 1976

Employment with Municipality:

Dates	Positions	Wage Group
May 8, 1976 – October 3, 1976	Deck Hand	8
May 7, 1977 – September 30, 1977	Deck Hand	8
May 10, 1978 – October 7, 1978	Deck Hand	8
May 6, 1979 – October 1, 1979	Deck Hand	8
May 5, 1980 – October 4, 1980	Deck Hand	8
April 21, 1981 – December 28, 1981	Deck Hand	8
	(to May 18, 1981)	
	Marine Oiler	
	(May 18-Dec. 28/81)	9
April 6, 1982 –	Deck Hand	8

Foreman's Note
A. Brown appointed Marine Oiler May 18, 1981 to replace M. Smith on leave
of absence for education purposes until end of December, 1981.

C. Allard

Classification:
Temporary (seasonal) Employee.

Educational Background:
Secondary School graduation diploma.
Provincial Trades Institute course in welding.

Certificates/Licenses:
Certificate in welding.
Temporary Engineer's Certificate (D.O.T.) first issued September, 1977.

Previous Employment:
Deck Hand, Deep Sea Transport Lines, May 10, 1969 – August 31, 1972.
Marine Oiler, Deep Sea Transport Lines, September 1, 1972 – March 15,
1973.
Marine Oiler, Excelsior Lake Shipping Co. March 16, 1973 – December 22,
1974.

Employment with Municipality:

Dates	Positions	Wage Group
May 3, 1975 – September 30, 1975	Marine Oiler	9
May 7, 1976 – October 3, 1976	Marine Oiler	9
May 7, 1977 – September 30, 1977	Marine Oiler	9
May 10, 1978 – October 7, 1978	Deck Hand	8
May 6, 1979 – October 1, 1979	Deck Hand	8
May 5, 1980 – October 4, 1980	Deck Hand	8
May 5, 1981 – November 2, 1981	Deck Hand (to May 18, 1981) Assistant Engineer (May 18-Nov. 2/81)	12
May 11, 1982 –	Deck Hand	8

Foreman's Note

Mr. Allard appointed assistant engineer (wage group 12) on temporary basis for balance of season to replace D. Cook, the permanent assistant engineer absent from work on disability leave until the first week of November, 1981. Marine Oiler position not offered to Allard on May 18, 1981 as he accepted higher wage rate position of assistant engineer instead.

CASE DISCUSSION QUESTIONS

1. Determine the issue which the parties will place before the arbitrator.
2. Outline the nature of the union's case. What evidence will it introduce to support its position?
3. What defence does the employer have? On what basis does the employer justify its actions?
4. What principles of arbitral authority would the arbitrator likely consider applicable to this grievance?
5. How should the case be decided by the arbitrator? Render, with reasons, an award.

RADIO MANUFACTURING COMPANY CASE

Radio Manufacturing Company is an old, established manufacturer of specialized radio, telephone and communications equipment. Most of the products manufactured must meet specific government regulations as to quality and performance standards for use in critical commercial and government communication applications. Competition in the particular segment of the industry occupied by Radio Manufacturing has been intense for many years and profit margins have been under pressure almost continuously in order to keep prices more or less in line with those of foreign manufacturers. The most profitable lines at the present time consist of high quality, low volume specialized equipment used in aviation, and to a limited extent, marine service applications.

Manufacturing facilities are housed in a relatively modern (1975) single plant, situated in a small community located some ten miles distant from a large metropolitan city. The work force, which consists of approximately three hundred production and maintenance employees, is about evenly divided between male and female persons, most of whom reside in the immediate area. The employees are unionized and have been represented by an industrial union for almost two decades. The relationship between the company and the union has been excellent for many years, and apart from a brief strike in 1971, successive collective agreements have been negotiated on a businesslike but friendly basis each year.

Under the terms of the collective agreement all jobs in the plant are "rated" and assigned a classification number which carries with it a specific rate of pay. Jobs of equal complexity are generally grouped together in each classification, and employees are encouraged to learn as much as possible about job operations related to their own particular job in order that they might progress upward through the job classes to higher rated jobs. Employees are also encouraged to undertake training seminars and "in-house" courses which are offered for each product line as changes in product technology are introduced. Employer support is generally provided for employees who wish to undertake job-related courses at the local community college or nearby university. The support usually consists of payment of the tuition fees charged for the course when the employee submits proof of successful completion. However, the suitability of the program in each case must be first assessed by the personnel manager and approval granted if the employee wishes to later claim for payment of the fees paid. Employee performance in all outside courses is included in each employee's personnel file, and considered along with all other evidence for employee evaluation purposes.

Some months ago, the discontinuance of a particular product line due to obsolescence required a realignment of the work force, and the layoff of several employees. Seven of the employees who were working in Grade 12 and Grade 14 jobs were placed in equivalent grade positions for the test model production of a new product which the company had designed. Three employees, who had previously been engaged in relatively unskilled jobs (Grade 4), were placed on layoff pending the start-up of full-scale production of the new product. The remaining two employees, Delta Baker and Charles Fox, who worked in Grade 10 positions, were placed in Grade 9 jobs on a related product line. When informed of the job change, both employees requested the Grade 10 position of Parts Controller, ERMC Products, presently held by Romeo Sierra.

The job of Parts Controller, ERMC Products, involved the scheduling of parts for the production of a variety of complex electronic devices. Each device was based upon a standard core module to which different subassemblies were constructed from electronic parts and added to the core assembly. The wide variations of the product required different parts to be added at each employee work station depending upon the particular model manufactured, and while a production line was used, each model was essentially different, and seldom did an employee handle more than two or three of the same model in sequence as the products moved down the production line from work station to work station. The mode of construction was for equipment to be assembled on a mobile platform which resembled a small cart, and as each work station completed its part of the fabrication, the cart was moved down the line to the next location.

The job of the parts controller requires the operator to consult the schematic diagram for each job as it is received, then order the appropriate "package"of parts from the parts inventory located in the Material Storage Department for delivery to each work station. This would be timed in sequence in order that the proper parts would be available at each station to be added to the model when it reached that particular spot in the assembly line. Parts orders received by the Material Storage Department would be assembled for the various work stations and delivered to them in time and in the proper order for installation on the module when it arrived at that point in the production line.

A second aspect of the parts controller's job is to verify that the parts required to produce the particular model are on hand in inventory and to enter into the main computer the number of parts withdrawn from inventory for production purposes as each model is placed in production. A final part of the work involves a weekly balancing of inventories and the determination of the nature of shortages between the master inventory and the inventory of parts used in the production of products, then a reordering of parts in accordance with required lead times for the maintenance of minimum safe inventory levels.

The job analysis for Parts Controller, ERMC Products, includes the following requirements:

(1) Must possess the ability to read equipment schematic designs and to determine parts required for the production of each model.

(2) A knowledge of the identity and part numbers of all components used in the manufacture of ERMC units is essential.

(3) Must be familiar with the assembly process for all models produced and the installation sequence of all components.

(4) Ability to use a computer terminal, familiarity with computerized inventory control procedures and master parts lists required.

(5) Must be capable of trouble-shooting errors in parts inventories and determining proper stock balances and inventory levels for uninterrupted production.

(6) Must be familiar with parts reorder and order authorization procedures.

The education and experience requirements of the job were:

1. Minimum of Secondary School Graduation Diploma. Applicants who have completed a Community College Program in Production Management or related courses preferred.

2. Two to three years experience in the production of ERMC units (Dept. 50) with related experience in inventory control. Such related experience may be obtained in job analysis 63-10 (Parts Storeroom Senior Clerk).

3. Experience in the operation of a computer terminal and the retrieval and entry procedures related to the Master Production System and Inventory Module.

The relevant provisions of the collective agreement under which Delta Baker and Charles Fox requested the position of Parts Controller, ERMC Products read as follows:

ARTICLE III   MANAGEMENT'S RIGHTS

3.01   The union acknowledges that it is the exclusive right of the company to manage the enterprise and without limiting the generality of the foregoing, to determine the location of the plant or plants, the products to be produced and the methods of manufacture, production schedules, processes, the control of products made, produced or purchased, to maintain order, discipline and efficiency, and to hire, discharge, transfer, promote, demote or discipline employees, provided that a claim of discriminatory promotion, demotion or transfer or discharge or disciplinary action without just cause may be the subject of a grievance and dealt with as hereinafter provided.

ARTICLE V   REDUCTION OF WORK FORCE AND DISPLACEMENT OF PERSONNEL

5.03   Where an employee with seniority is employed on a production job which is no longer required due to technological change, the employee may move to a lower classification job which he or she is qualified to perform and displace the incumbent provided that the employee has greater plant-wide seniority than the incumbent.

5.04   An employee with seniority who is displaced may displace any employee with less seniority in the same job grade position provided that the employee with the greater seniority has the required skill, ability and experience to perform the work required.

5.05   Where two or more employees with seniority are displaced and wish to displace an employee in the same job grade position the employer shall select the employee with the greatest skill, ability, and experience to perform the work, and only where the qualifications of the competing employees are relatively equal, shall seniority govern.

5.06   A senior employee selected to displace an employee with less senior-ity shall be entitled to a familiarization period of five working days under normal supervision, but normal supervision shall not include training for the position. Where the senior employee so selected is unable to perform the requirements of the job, the employee shall be placed in a lower grade level position for which the employee is qualified, and the previous incum-bent returned to the position notwithstanding that the employee has less seniority.

Both Delta Baker and Charles Fox maintained that they were capable of performing the work of Romeo Sierra as Parts Controller, ERMC Products. Delta Baker maintained that her qualifications for the job were relatively equal to those of Charles Fox, and that her seniority, which was one day more than Charles Fox, required the company to place her in the position.

Charles Fox argued that his educational background and work experience gave him greater skill and ability to perform the work, and while he conceded that Delta had greater seniority by one day, his qualifications were superior to hers, and they were not "relatively equal" in terms of their qualifications to perform the work. He main-tained that he was entitled to displace Romeo Sierra under Article 5.05 of the collective agreement.

Mike Victor, the Personnel Manager, interviewed both Delta Baker and Charles Fox, after he reviewed their employment records (Schedules 'A' and 'B' attached). During her interview, Delta explained that she had worked for over three years on the ERMC assembly line as a production worker and tester and was familiar with the com-ponents used in the production of ERMC units. She was also familiar with the schematic diagrams for each, as she had used the diagrams in the course of assembly of components. She had taken a ten-hour "in-house" course on the inventory control system and after taking the course had spent her coffee break time for several weeks at Romeo Sierra's computer terminal where he had explained to her how the system worked, how he ordered parts, and how he balanced the inventories. She admitted that she had never actually performed the work on the job but had performed simulated work on the computer in the course she had taken because the instructor had used the parts ordering and inventory control procedures in ERMC production as examples in the course. Since she had passed the course, and had subsequently observed Romeo Sierra perform the same job functions on the terminal, she felt confident that she could perform the work.

Charles Fox, in his interview, pointed out that he had spent two years in Department 50, and two years in Job function 63-10. In the latter job he had worked at assembling the component "packages" for each job station from stock, and had also been responsible for maintaining an inventory check in the stockroom. He, in turn, would determine the actual count of stock on hand when Romeo Sierra found discrepancies between the computer records and the stock used in the production runs. It was also his job to enter into the computer inventory records the amount of each component taken into inventory when received from the firms that supplied materials to Radio Manufacturing. During the course of the interview he explained that his community college program in production management included courses in inventory control, and he was, as a result, quite familiar with the system used at Radio Manufacturing. Moreover, he understood how the job performed by Romeo Sierra fit into the overall materials management system. While he had never actually performed the work of Romeo, he had performed numerous exercises at the community college which involved doing the same job functions, and he was familiar with computer operations.

Following the interviews, the personnel manager discussed the two applicants with their respective supervisors to confirm their past experience and to obtain the supervisor's opinion as to the suitability of each applicant for the position. Delta Baker's supervisor expressed some concern that while Delta could perhaps perform the work at a basic or threshold level, she might not fully understand the system and how the inventory control functions of the job related to it. She pointed out that the ten-hour course which Delta had taken did not provide an in-depth examination of the system, but only of the inventory control system module.

Charles Fox's supervisor confirmed that Charles had a solid knowledge of the inventory control system and was familiar with the parts requirements for the various ERMC models, but expressed some doubt as to his ability to read the complicated schematic diagrams for a few of the more advanced ERMC models without some familiarization time on the job. He pointed out that Charles had not worked in Department 50 for over two years, and during that time new product designs had been introduced, and many of the models had become very complex in terms of component requirements.

The personnel manager returned to his office after his discussions with the two supervisors, and once again reviewed the employment records of the two employees. He then notified both of them that in his opinion they did not possess the necessary qualifications to "bump" Romeo Sierra from the position of Parts Controller.

The next day, union stewards presented the supervisors of Delta Baker and Charles Fox with written grievances from each employee, which stated in part:

> I claim that the employer violated Article V of the collective agreement when it denied my right to bump the junior employee in the job of Parts Controller ERMC Products, Job Grade 10.
>
> Redress Requested: That I be placed in the job of Parts Controller, ERMC Products with full compensation.

The employer denied both grievances on the basis that it had not violated the collective agreement, and when the dispute could not be resolved, the union requested arbitration.

PERSONNEL DEPARTMENT DATA
Employment Record of Delta Baker

Date of Hire: 16 May 1977.
Educational Background:
High School Graduation Diploma, 1976.
One year attendance at University–General Arts Program (1976–77).
Inventory control systems seminar (10 hr) completed 8/4/83.
Previous Experience:
Employment as a life guard during high school summer vacation months, 1972–75.
Work as a sales representative during summer months, June-August, 1976.
Employment at Radio Manufacturing Company:
Dept. 40 (HF Eq.)
16/5/77–1/12/77 Production line worker, general layout (Grade 4)
1/12/77–1/4/78   Machine operator (Grade 6)
1/4/78–1/8/78   Production line, advanced assembly (Grade 7)
1/12/78–1/3/79   Production line complex assembly (Grade 8)
1/3/79–1/12/79   Test and repair operator (Grade 9)

Dept. 50 (ERMC Eq.)
1/12/79–1/6/81   Production line assembly core module (Grade 9)
1/6/81–1/12/81   Production line, advanced assembly units (Grade 9)
1/12/81–   Production test and repair (Grade 10)

Employment Record of Charles Fox

Date of Hire: 17 May 1977.
Educational Background:
High School Graduation Diploma, 1974.
Community College, graduate Production Management Program, 1977.
Radio and TV Technician's Course (correspondence course 1974–75).
Previous Experience:
Employment as a farm worker during high school summer vacation months,
    1972–74.
Road construction worker, general labour, summer 1975.
TV repair shop employee, summer 1976, part-time during year 1975
    and 1976.
Employment at Radio Manufacturing Company:
Dept. 60 Parts and Material Storage
17/5/77–1/12/77 Inventory clerk (Grade 8)
1/12/77–1/12/78 Parts expediter (Grade 9)
Dept. 50
1/12/78–1/ 3/81 Production test and repair (Grade 10)
Dept. 63 Special Parts Inventory Store-room
1/3/81–   Senior clerk, parts storeroom (Grade 10)

CASE DISCUSSION QUESTIONS

1. *How should the union approach arbitration where two of its members have filed grievances concerning the same job?*
2. *Identify the issues that must be addressed by the union. How should these be framed for presentation to the arbitrator?*
3. *What defences are available to the employer?*
4. *Indicate the different lines of argument that might be raised by the employer and the union in this case.*
5. *Render, with reasons, a decision.*

THE CHAMBERLAIN ACADEMY CASE

Chamberlain Academy, a private academic institution, employed a substantial number of employees in nonacademic activities to maintain the campus buildings and provide necessary services for both students and staff. The nonacademic staff had been organized by the Independent Service Workers' Union in 1959 and the union was certified in 1960. The bargaining unit, as defined at the time of certification consisted of the following employee classifications:

Caretaker I, Caretaker II
Gardener I, Gardener II
Bus Driver I, Utility Driver
Pastry Cook, Cook, Assistant Cook
Maintenance Worker I, Maintenance Worker II
Cafeteria Worker I, Cafeteria Worker II
Kitchen worker
Housemaid
Laundry Worker I
Stores worker

The first collective agreement negotiated in 1960 recognized the union as the exclusive bargaining representative for the above-noted employee classifications, excluding foremen, persons above the rank of foreman, office employees, and persons employed less than twenty-four hours each week. The description of the unit remained the same in subsequent collective agreements except for a change in the 1978 collective agreement relating to the term "stores worker." The 1978 agreement changed this classification to "storekeeper."

The "stores worker" employee in the bargaining unit was responsible for the maintenance of supplies for the four building complex. The position involved two storerooms, one which housed materials and equipment for outside yard maintenance, and a second storeroom which contained building cleaning and "inside" supplies. Storeroom work did not require the full-time attention of the employee, and a substantial part of each day was devoted to general maintenance work related to the the replacement of used supplies. This included the cleaning of washrooms, the replacement of light bulbs, the replenishment of soap dispensers, paper towel holders, and similar duties. The stores worker was employed on a five-day, forty-hour week.

The collective agreements negotiated since 1960 each contained a union security and check-off clause that provided as follows:

8.01   All employees who are now or hereafter become members of the union shall maintain their membership in the union while this collective agreement is in effect.

8.02   It is agreed as a condition of employment each employee shall deliver to the Employer a properly authenticated membership application card signed by the employee in a form satisfactory to the Employer, but not otherwise. Upon receipt of which the Employer will deduct from the first pay of such employee earned by him following thirty (30) working days, an amount equal to the union initiation fee. The amount of such initiation fee shall be communicated to the Employer by the Secretary-Treasurer of the Union.

8.03   Employees covered by the terms of this agreement shall, as a condition of continuing employment, deliver to the Employer a properly authenticated dues check-off card, and the Employer shall deduct from the first pay due to the employee in each month the amount of the union dues, as determined by the union.

In 1981, the General Manager, Mr. Alex MacDonald, was contacted by Mr. Barker, the union Business Agent, and presented with a union policy grievance claiming that the Academy had failed to include in the bargaining unit of the union all employees classified as storekeeper.

The purpose of the grievance was apparently a move by the union to include in the storekeeper classification two employees who were working in a faculty supply room and shop.

MacDonald reviewed the past treatment of employees in the faculty supply room and met a second time with Barker. MacDonald took the position that the employees were not a part of the bargaining unit, and since Barker disagreed, the issue remained unresolved. MacDonald heard nothing more on the matter following the two brief meetings and presumed that the union had dropped the grievance.

The faculty supply room work was very similar to the work done in the "plant" storeroom, but in the past, the work had apparently not been considered by the parties to be work of the bargaining unit.

Historically, the employees had been treated in a different manner. According to the documentation relating to the certification application in 1960, the employee working in the faculty storeroom was not included on the voters' list for the representation vote. The union had not bargained for wages for the faculty storeroom employee in the number of collective agreement negotiations since 1960, and the employer had established a wage on an individual basis with the employee each year.

Faculty storeroom work involves the maintenance of teaching supplies, paper, books, and laboratory equipment, as well as the operation of a small shop in the student building where students could purchase packaged snacks, soft drinks, personal grooming and health products, and items of school clothing. The shop is currently open from 4 p.m. each afternoon until 10 p.m. in the evening on week-days.

Initially, one full-time employee maintained both the storeroom and the shop, but as the institution added new laboratory equipment, and a photocopier service in the storeroom, the employee was required to remain in the teaching building from 8 a.m. to 4 p.m. each day. To assist with the operation of the shop in the student building, it was necessary at first to employ additional help in order to keep the shop open from 4 p.m. to 8 p.m. each week day. In 1980, a second photocopier was purchased and made available for student use in the shop. At the same time, the shop hours were extended to 9 p.m. In 1983, the shop hours were further extended to 10 p.m. Except for the first hour (from 4-5 p.m.) each day, the shop is operated by a part-time employee who currently works twenty-five hours each week.

The second employee in the faculty supply room was first employed on a part-time basis in 1970 for ten hours each week. In 1974, the hours were increased to fifteen per week, and in 1980, to twenty hours per week. In 1983, several months before the meeting between MacDonald and Barker, the hours of work for the second employee had been raised to twenty-five hours per week, and the employee, in spite of the shorter hours, was treated as a full-time employee in so far as employee benefits were concerned.

In 1983, some two years after the first grievance had been filed, the union filed a second policy grievance claiming that the Academy was in breach of the collective agreement for failing to apply the union security and union dues check-off provisions of the collective agreement to the employees in the faculty supply room.

At the first grievance meeting (which was the last step of the grievance procedure prior to arbitration under the collective agreement), MacDonald brought to the attention of the union that the matter had been raised some two years before and fully discussed at that time. He could see no reason why the question should be raised again, and informed the union that he would not discuss the merits of the grievance since the matter was settled previously.

A few days later, the union notified the employer in writing of its intention to proceed to arbitration.

CASE DISCUSSION QUESTIONS

1. *On what basis should the union be permitted to bring the grievance at this point in time?*
2. *What arguments or legal doctrines could the Academy raise in defence of its position?*
3. *What issues raised in the case must be decided by the arbitration before it reaches a decision?*
4. *Render, with reasons, a decision.*

THE CENTRAL WAREHOUSE COMPANY CASE

The Central Warehouse company has a collective agreement with the Warehouse Worker's Union that bears the date November 10, 1982, and contains the following provisions:

4.01   The Union recognizes the Management's authority to manage the affairs of the Company, to direct its working forces, including the right to hire, transfer, promote, demote, suspend and discharge for proper cause any employee and to increase or decrease the working force of the Company from time to time as circumstances and necessity may require. Any such authority will be consistent with the clauses of this Agreement, Supplemental Agreement or memorandum that forms a part of this Agreement.

4.2   It is agreed that reasonable rules of conduct must be observed by employees while on Company premises, and the administration of such rules will be fair and reasonable. The parties agree that any minor infraction of rules issued by the Company shall only remain against the record of any employee for two calendar years from the date of the infraction; at the end of the time the record of the infraction will be removed from his file. Copies of any written infractions issued by the Company as a matter of record against the employee, will be given to the Union. The provisions of Clause 8.06 concerning the rights of an Arbitrator will apply including the question of warning notice.

5.04   *Step 3.*   If a satisfactory settlement of the grievance is not reached at Step 2 of the grievance procedure, or if the grievance involves the discharge or suspension of an employee, the grievance shall be presented in written form to the Plant Manager, who shall within three (3) working days arrange a special meeting with the Union Grievance Committee to discuss the grievance. If the dispute is not resolved by the parties at such a meeting, the Union may take the grievance to arbitration.

8.04   An employee may be discharged or suspended for cause by his foreman. Within three (3) working days following discharge or suspension the employee, union committee member and steward or substitute Union representative may interview the foreman, concerning the reasons leading to discharge or suspension. Within three (3) working days following the interview, the Union may submit their complaint as a third step grievance which will be dealt with at a special meeting provided for in Clause 5.04.

8.05   The parties shall adhere to all time limits set out in the grievance procedure, and a failure to carry a grievance to the next step in the procedure, or a failure to file a written grievance for any reason within six (6) days of occurrence shall constitute abandonment of the grievance.

8.06   An employee found to be wrongfully discharged or suspended will be reinstated without loss of seniority and with back pay calculated at day rate or average earnings, as applicable, times normal hours, less any monies earned; or by any other arrangement as to compensation that is just and equitable in the opinion of the conferring parties or in the opinion of the Arbitrator, if the matter is referred to arbitration.

Plant rules were posted on all bulletin boards in July of 1978. Rules 4 and 9 (b) are noted below:

4.   Employees must not engage in fighting or horseplay during working hours.
9.   (b)   Wilful damage of company property shall be cause for dismissal.

On May 16, 1983, Jason Brown, an employee, filed the following grievance:

I protest my discharge of May 15, 1983, as I feel that this penalty is too severe. I have never been warned or disciplined before. I have been employed by this company for three years, and I feel that my record should be considered. I request reinstatement without loss of seniority and with full back pay.

The next week, on May 23, 1983, Arthur Williams, an employee, filed a similar grievance stating in part:

I protest my discharge by the company. My breach of Company rules was provoked, and I feel that discharge is too severe a penalty. I request reinstatement with full back pay, and without loss of seniority.

Williams and Brown were employed by the Central Warehouse Company as general labourers. Both were discharged by the company following an incident that took place on the second floor of the warehouse building.

The union presented the grievance at the third (and last) step of the grievance procedure. When the company and the union could not resolve the dispute, the union decided to submit the matter to arbitration.

The facts relating to the discharges were revealed at the third step meeting, and were essentially as follows:

On May 15, 1983, Williams and Brown were directed by their foreman to open a large wooden packing case. Williams, using a 60 cm. steel pry bar, had difficulty removing the wooden top of the case. He managed to raise one corner about 5 cm. and asked Brown to "take hold of the top and lift" as he pried with the bar.

Brown placed his hands under the corner of the lid while Williams continued to lift the springy top with the pry bar. The bar, unfortunately, slipped from Williams' hands at this point and the lid snapped shut on Brown's hands, trapping him.

Smith, another employee of the company, arrived on the scene at that moment and watched Brown jump up and down in pain. Brown implored Smith and Williams to release him from the trap, but Smith made no effort to assist him; instead, he patted him on the shoulder and said: "Steady now old chap, just grin and bear it." Smith then left the area, laughing as he went through the door.

For some obscure reason Williams also found the situation amusing, and laughed as he pried up the lid to free Brown's fingers. Brown went to the first-aid room without comment following the incident.

A short time later, Brown returned to the work area where the packing case was located. The case was opened, and he noticed Williams bent over the side of the container removing the contents. Brown moved behind Williams, picked up a small plank, and applied it to the seat of Williams' coveralls. The blow knocked Williams into the packing case.

Williams crawled from the case, picked up the prybar he had been using previously, and threw it at Brown's head. Brown managed to avoid the flying prybar by diving behind a number of packing cases, but in doing so, dislodged a heavy box that fell against his leg. The box crushed his ankle and rendered him unfit for work for an estimated six weeks.

The flying prybar crashed through a window and smashed the windshield of a company truck parked in the parking area that was located outside and below the window.

The foreman arrived on the scene at the moment that Williams threw the pry bar, and immediately discharged both Williams and Brown.

Employment records relating to each employee revealed the following information:

Jason Brown
Hired July 5, 1980.
Granted leave of absence September 1, 1981 to October 20, 1981.

Failed to return on October 20, 1981.
Returned to work on October 22, 1981.
Verbal warning issued.

Arthur Williams
Hired March 17, 1973.
Struck fellow employee during argument December 10, 1975.
Suspended for 5 working days.
Absent April 27, 1980 w/o excuse.
Verbal warning issued 28/4/80. Absent May 2, 1980 w/o excuse.
Verbal warning issued 3/5/80.
Absent May 4, 1980 w/o excuse. Written warning issued 5/5/80.
Smoking in nonsmoking area of warehouse December 12, 1982.
Verbal warning issued 12/12/82.

CASE DISCUSSION QUESTIONS

1. *From the information given in the case, how would you describe management philosophy in the discipline area?*
2. *How should the union organize its case with respect to the Williams' grievance? Would the approach be different in the case of Brown?*
3. *What onus rests on management in this case? What evidence may be introduced to discharge this responsibility?*
4. *What evidence should be brought before the arbitrator to assist the arbitrator in reaching a decision?*
5. *What doctrines or principles used by arbitrators would you expect an arbitrator to consider in this case?*
6. *Render with reasons, a decision on each grievance.*

AUTOMATIC CASTING COMPANY CASE

The Automatic Casting Company operates a single plant in the industrial area of a large metropolitan city. The Company employs approximately 200 persons in its Production and Maintenance Departments. Since the casting process is, for the most part, an automatic machine operation, a great deal of the work is in the form of material handling, mould preparation, and machine maintenance. The automated equipment is designed to cast products using low-melting-point alloys and is referred to in the plant as an "automatic moulder," or a "die caster," depending upon the type of machine. Other semiautomatic casting techniques are also used in the production of the company's products. These involve the delivery of the moulds to the furnace area by way of a conveyor where the moulds are filled with molten metal, either by manual control of the crucibles (or pots), or by a machine control system.

Certain types of products, however, are produced using a process that requires the delivery of molten metal to the moulds by way of an "overhead pour." In this process, a crane operator picks up a large crucible of molten metal from the furnace and transports it to the moulds where the operator pours the hot, fluid metal into a "gate" (a funnel-shaped opening in the mould) until the mould is filled. The crucible usually contains a sufficient quantity of material to fill a number of moulds, and to facilitate the pour, the moulds are normally placed in a row. This enables the crane operator to move from mould to mould with a minimum of travel time.

Considerable skill is required on the part of the crane operator to perform the pouring operation as the molten metal must be carried quickly from the furnace and poured before the metal begins to solidify. It is also necessary for the crane operator to gauge the pour accurately to avoid overfilling the moulds and spilling the hot metal on the shop floor. For these reasons, new crane operators are usually trained on the job by more senior operators. Each trainee normally works as a spare operator for at least a year before filling a full-time crane operator vacancy.

The Automatic Casting Company plant is housed in a long, single storey building. It is divided roughly into two parts: the casting or furnace room, and the finishing room. In reality, however, the production area is essentially one large room with the furnace and moulding equipment at one end and the grinding and finishing equipment at the other. In essence, the plant is a long production line, with the raw material taken into the storage area adjacent to the furnace room, and the finished products leaving the plant from the shipping room at the finishing end.

The plant operates on a continuous three-shift basis that requires two crane operators and a spare to work each shift. The spare operator usually works at general maintenance for most of the shift, but he operates the equipment in the event of illness or absence on the part of a regular crane operator. For training purposes, the spare operator is usually expected to handle a few supervised pours during the course of a work shift.

The company employed Graham as a crane operator on the 12

p.m. – 8 a.m. shift. Graham was a comparatively young man (in his early thirties), who had worked for the company for a total of six years, the past four as a crane operator. He was classed as a good employee by management, and until May, 1982, had lost very little time by way of illness. During the period May to October, he was frequently absent from work and his pouring skill during that interval appeared to deteriorate to a marked degree. On a number of occasions he had overfilled moulds to such an extent that overhead pour production had to be halted temporarily to enable a maintenance crew to clean up the spills. Some spills were normal and expected on the job, but seldom involved more than a small quantity of metal falling to the floor. Graham's spills, on the other hand, involved substantial quantities of molten metal being poured over the mould with what appeared to be a complete lack of judgment. Graham attributed his errors to a lack of sleep, sore eyes, or some other affliction in each instance. While Graham's problems did not appear to be alcohol-related, on several occasions in October of 1982, the shift foreman noticed the smell of liquor on Graham's breath when he reported for work. On each occasion the foreman warned Graham that in the future he must not drink alcoholic beverages before his shift. On each warning Graham agreed to comply with his supervisor's wishes.

On November 12, 1982, Graham arrived for work in a drunken state and managed to reach the cab of the overhead crane without detection by the foreman. During the first few minutes of the shift, the foreman noticed the erractic operation of the crane, and when Graham missed the mould entirely with his first pour, the foreman cleared the area of employees and ordered Graham to come down from the crane cab. Graham, however, refused to listen to the foreman and continued to operate his crane back and forth along the track that ran the length of the building. The foreman finally shut down the electric power to the crane and sent the spare operator to fetch Graham and bring him to the plant office.

With a great deal of assistance from the spare operator, Graham eventually arrived at the foreman's office and staggered into a chair where he began to sob openly. Between sobs, Graham talked incoherently about the loss of his dog. The foreman concluded from Graham's actions that he was too intoxicated to discipline at that time and sent him home by taxi. The spare operator completed Graham's shift as crane operator.

When Graham had left the office, the foreman reviewed Graham's file and compiled the following information from his work records:

May '82.   Absent from work for two shifts. On both days the absence was for the first shift that followed Graham's week-end. In each case, Graham did not call in sick, but reported later, on his return to work, that he was ill on the days in question.

June '82.   Absent fom work on two occasions. In each case the absence was for the first shift following Graham's week-end. No call-in. Excuse later given that he was sick. Warned that he was required under company rules to have someone telephone the company (if possible) if he was too ill to report for work.

July '82.   On holidays for three weeks.

August '82.   Absent from work on one occasion. This was the last week of August, and the day of the absence was his first scheduled work shift after his week-end. A person (unknown) telephoned part way through the shift to advise that Graham was too ill to report in for work.

September '82.   Absent fom work on one occasion. Day following Graham's week-end. No call-in to advise of absence. Excuse was that he was out of town on the week-end and automobile trouble delayed his return. Maintenance employee reported to foreman that he found two empty beer bottles in the crane cab following Graham's shift on September 22. No action taken.

October '82.   Absent from work on one occasion. Missed shift was the day following Graham's week-end. No call-in. Later gave excuse that he was visiting a sick friend who did not have a telephone. Warned verbally that failure to call, in future, would result in discipline. Appeared at work on two occasions smelling of alcohol but appeared sober. Warned verbally that he must not drink just before reporting to work as he must be completely sober on the job.

The foreman discussed the situation with the plant manager, and both men agreed that the company could no longer tolerate Graham's absences or work performance.

Graham was dismissed by the company on November 13. The next day Graham filed a grievance requesting reinstatement. The grievance was rejected by the company, and the union, in accordance with the procedure set out in the collective agreement, took the matter to arbitration.

The collective agreement contains the following provision:

6.01   The company shall have the right to make reasonable rules of conduct, and where an employee fails or refuses to abide by such rules, the company shall have the right to discipline or dismiss the employee, subject to the right of grievance.

6.04   The company shall not dismiss an employee without just cause.

In 1976, the company had posted on all plant bulletin boards a set of rules of conduct that were divided into "serious" and "minor" violations. Employees who committed serious violations were subject to immediate discharge by the foreman. Minor violations invoked a disciplinary procedure that prescribed a verbal warning for the first infraction, a written warning for the second, a two-day suspension for the third violation, and finally, discharge upon the fourth violation. Included in the list of minor violations were: (1) attendance at work smelling of alcohol, (2) inability to perform required work due to the influence of alcohol or drugs, and (3) disobedience (failure to carry out a direct order of a supervisor). Major violations included theft, insubordination, and wilful destruction of company property.

CASE DISCUSSION QUESTIONS

1. *On what grounds other than the posted infractions might the company justifiably dismiss an employee?*
2. *Distinguish between insubordination and disobedience.*
3. *On what grounds might Graham file a grievance?*
4. *To what extent should the arbitrator consider Graham's actions during the month of October and his employment record in general?*
5. *Explain and identify the philosophy of the company with regard to discipline.*
6. *Render, with reasons, an award in this case.*

THE WHOLE GRAIN PET FOOD COMPANY CASE

The Whole Grain Pet Food Company manufactures a number of different brands of pet food under its own label and under a number of private brand names in a single plant which employs forty-nine production and maintenance employees.

The pet food is, for the most part, animal feed grain with the addition of bone meal and a number of other food supplements to provide a balanced, nutritional diet for animals. The production process involves grinding the various grains, and mixing the supplements with the grain formula to achieve an appropriate food balance for the different kinds of animals to be fed. The product is then formed into pellets, biscuits, or chunks, and weighed and packaged for shipment.

Much of the equipment is automatic, with material transfer from machine to machine effected by conveyor belts, chutes, or pipelines. As a result, most of the plant employees are engaged in either machine tending, maintenance, or material handling using mechanized equipment.

The production and maintenance employees were first organized by the Pet Food Workers' Union in 1976, a few months after the plant went into production, and currently work under a collective agreement which contains the following articles:

ARTICLE 4   MANAGEMENT RIGHTS

4.01   The Union recognizes Management's authority to manage the affairs of the Company, to direct its working forces, including the right to hire, transfer, promote, demote, suspend and discharge for proper cause any employee and to increase or decrease the working force of the Company from time to time as circumstances and necessity may require. Any such authority will be consistent with the clauses of this agreement.

4.02   It is agreed that reasonable rules of conduct must be observed by employees while on Company premises, and that such rules of conduct will be as uniform as possible and their administration fair and reasonable.

ARTICLE 8   GRIEVANCE PROCEDURE

8.01   A grievance under the provisions of this agreement is defined to be any difference between the parties or between the Company and employees covered by this agreement involving the interpretation, application, administration or alleged violation of any of the provisions of this agreement.

8.02   Grievances as defined above may be taken by the employee, the union steward or a union committee member directly to the employee's immediate supervisor for adjustment. No grievance shall be recognized unless this procedure is followed. The grievance shall be presented within fifteen (15) days. Any grievance submitted in writing to the foreman in accordance with this procedure will receive a written response from the foreman. Where a grievance has been submitted in writing, it will be dealt with in writing at all stages thereafter. Failing a satisfactory adjustment within five (5) working days, then,

STAGE 2 – The matter shall be taken up by the officers of the local union and/or their representative with the manager of the Company or his Representative. Failing a settlement within seven (7) working days, then,

STAGE 3 – Either party may, within the following fifteen (15) working days, refer the matter to arbitration.

8.06   A grievance arising from a claim by an employee that his discharge or suspension by the Company was unjust or contrary to the terms of this agreement, must be dealt with in writing by both parties, and must be presented to the Company not later than ten (10) days after the discharge or suspension becomes effective. In case of discharge or suspension by the

Company, the Company will immediately notify the employee and the steward in writing of the reason for such discharge or suspension. In the event that an employee is found by an Arbitration Board to have been unfairly discharged or suspended by the Company, the Company agrees that the employee will be reinstated on his job under terms and conditions decided by the Arbitration Board. A grievance hereunder shall be lodged at stage two of the grievance procedure.

Pursuant to Article 4.02, the Employer posted the following rule on all Plant bulletin boards on August 25, 1978:

RULE 4 *USE OF SAFETY EQUIPMENT* Employees must at all times carry out their job assignments in a safe and careful manner. Safety equipment must be worn where the possibility of injury exists, or where management directs such equipment be used. Failure to comply with this rule may result in disciplinary action, suspension, or discharge, as the case may warrant.

Due to the automated nature of the plant the risk of injury to employees was slight. Nevertheless, the work did involve material handling and exposure to a certain amount of dust. The dust hazard was normally very low and was effectively controlled by air exhaust and filtration equipment. Over time, however, dust would collect on the machines and conveyor equipment and it was necessary for the maintenance employees to regularly clear accumulated dust from the machinery and conveyors using high-pressure air hoses and brushes.

Dust removal and servicing of the upper conveyor system was the responsibility of Mack Hart who had been employed by the company since the plant first opened in 1976. Mack was a short, stocky, energetic person with a likeable personality but a quick temper. He was very much an individualist who preferred to work alone. He willingly accepted the servicing and maintenance of the upper conveyor system because few employees cared to climb amongst equipment twelve to twenty feet above the floor level.

On November 29, 1982, Hart was engaged in the cleaning of the overhead conveyor with a high-pressure air hose when a foreman noticed that he was not using his dust mask or dust goggles. Both hung by their straps around his neck. The foreman continued to watch Hart until he completed the cleaning, and when he descended to the floor level the foreman went over to him.

Initially, Hart did not notice the presence of the foreman as he was occupied with the coiling of the high-pressure air hose which he had used to blow the dust from the conveyor equipment, but as he raised the bulky roll to his shoulder, his eyes met those of the foreman. The foremen pointed to the dust mask and goggles hanging loosely around

Hart's neck and said: "I thought I told you before to wear that equipment when you airclean the conveyor!"

Hart stared at the foreman for an instant, his face gradually turning red with anger, then without a word, he slipped the coil of hose from his shoulder, threw it heavily to the floor at the feet of the foreman, and quickly walked away.

The foreman called to Hart to return, but Hart paid no attention to his call, and continued to walk in the direction of the plant lunch room. The foreman did not follow Hart but immediately proceeded to the general office where he prepared a discharge notice for the employee. Immediately thereafter, he informed the Chief Steward of the union of his action and gave his reasons.

On November 30, 1982, Mack Hart filed a written grievance through the union on the prescibed form which stated in part:

Statement of Grievance: Unjust discharge. I was discharged without reasonable cause.

Adjustment Requested: Reinstatement with full compensation for time lost and without loss of seniority.

A meeting between the company representatives and the union in accordance with the grievance procedure was held on December 2, 1982, at which time the following information concerning the grievor's employment record and the incident itself was presented.

1. The grievor had worked for the company without apparent conflict or difficulty from his date of hire in 1976 until October 4, 1979.
2. On October 4, 1979 he was involved in a fight with another employee in the plant lunch room. The incident resulted from what was alleged to be a practical joke. The other employee had welded Hart's lunch box closed, and Hart had not appreciated the humorous side of the prank. Both employees received two day suspensions for fighting.
3. On May 12, 1980, the grievor was given a one day suspension for failing to carry out a reasonable order given to him by his foreman. The suspension was later reversed on grievance when the evidence revealed that Hart had not heard the order due to machine noise.
4. On October 4, 1981, the grievor was given a one-day suspension for conduct and language that had indicated a lack of self-control, and had disrupted the work in the department where the incident took place. No grievance was filed.
5. All parties agreed that each incident, including the one at hand, was a result of the grievor's quick and uncontrolled temper. The grievor was otherwise a hard-working, loyal, and responsible employee.
6. The union contended that the grievor had thrown down the air hose and walked away because a senior manager of the company had told him (following the October 4, 1981, incident) to walk away from any

situation where he felt he might lose his temper. This "advice" was admitted by the Company manager in question.

7. The grievor was not wearing his dust goggles because fogging of the lens occurred in the high heat conditions of the building near the ceiling of the room.

8. Complaints had been received by management concerning the tendency of the dust goggles to fog in high heat areas. A different model of dust goggle which did not fog was tested, but no further action was taken when the employees complained that the headband was uncomfortable.

9. Dust goggles and dust masks were supplied by the company to all employees working in the plant who worked in areas where dust conditions existed. Employees were not required to use the equipment unless conditions warranted protection, or where instructed to do so by management.

The meeting failed to resolve the dispute, and the grievance was denied by the employer. The union then considered reference of the matter to arbitration.

CASE DISCUSSION QUESTIONS

1. *Should the union carry the grievance to arbitration? What factors should be considered before taking this step?*

2. *On whom does the onus lie to prove the case if the union should decide to refer the matter to arbitration? Why?*

3. *Outline the basis of the employer's case. What authorities might the employer refer to in support of its action?*

4. *What information should be brought before the arbitrator concerning the rules established by the employer?*

5. *What evidence should the union introduce?*

6. *Render an award.*

PLEASANTVILLE DAY-CARE CASE

The Municipality of Pleasantville employed Miss Dawson as a teacher in a day-care centre which the municipality operated. The teachers and assistant teachers were organized by the Municipal Employees' Union in 1977, and a first collective agreement was negotiated shortly thereafter. Miss Dawson was hired in February of 1979 as an assistant teacher and became a member of the union on the completion of her probation in March of the same year. Three months later, Miss

Dawson was promoted to the position of teacher, and continued to work in that capacity.

During the period from June, 1979, to May, 1983, Miss Dawson received regular salary increases in accordance with the collective agreement in force at the time. Wage increases were made under a clause in the collective agreement which had been negotiated in the first agreement, and included in each subsequent contract. The clause reads as follows:

> 6.02   An employee in a given range will receive, on the job anniversary date (or six months after, depending upon the range), an increment range increase, unless his or her work is shown to be unsatisfactory. In such an event the employee shall be advised in writing.

The collective agreement also contains a clause which sets out management rights which provides in part:

> 3.01   Management shall possess all of the rights ordinarily possessed by an employer except those rights that have been specifically limited or modified by the terms of this agreement, and without limiting the generality of the foregoing, the right to hire, transfer, classify, suspend, discipline, and discharge employees for cause.

In May, 1983, Miss Dawson was advised verbally by her supervisor that she would not receive an increment range increase on her job anniversary in June as provided by the collective agreement. This was subsequently confirmed in writing by the supervisor in a letter to Miss Dawson dated May 20, 1983.

The reasons given by the supervisor were:

1.   The supervisor had been informed by someone that Miss Dawson had taken more than her allotted fifteen minutes for coffee breaks on occasion.
2.   Miss Dawson had apparently left a student teacher alone in a classroom with three children for a few minutes while she (Miss Dawson) spoke to another teacher in the classroom across the hall.
3.   Miss Dawson did not "get along well" with two other (unspecified) teachers.

Miss Dawson filed a grievance in accordance with the grievance procedure set out in the collective agreement, and the grievance was carried through to arbitration.

In her evidence at the arbitration hearing, Miss Dawson admitted that she may have taken more than fifteen minutes for her coffee break on a few occasions but she added that this was something that most of the teachers did from time to time. She also admitted to a minor disagreement on two occasions with another teacher on staff but emphasized that they had remained good friends in spite of the disagreement. She admitted that she left a student teacher alone with three children for a few minutes but she could see nothing wrong in doing so, since she was only a few steps away, and the classroom door had been left open.

Miss Dawson also stated in her evidence that the only person with whom she had recently had a disagreement was her immediate supervisor. In February, 1983, her supervisor had requested her to sign an appraisal of another teacher which the supervisor had prepared, and which she (Miss Dawson) had refused to sign. The appraisal was, in her opinion, overly negative in its criticism of the other teacher, and she had felt that it was not her duty to appraise her colleagues. When she had indicated to the supervisor that she would not sign the appraisal, the supervisor snatched the paper from her hands and left the room. Since that time, the supervisor, had, in Miss Dawson's opinion spoken to her only on a formal basis concerning school matters.

The supervisor of the day-care facility testified at the hearing that on numerous occasions she had offered teaching suggestions to Miss Dawson, but Miss Dawson had not seen fit to adopt them, and this, coupled with the information which she had gathered concerning Miss Dawson's coffee breaks and her relationship with others at the centre, constituted the basis for her recommendation that the wage increase not be granted to the grievor.

Under cross-examination by the counsel for the union, the supervisor admitted that she had requested Miss Dawson to sign the appraisal of another teacher, but she insisted that Miss Dawson's refusal to do so had not affected her work relationship or attitude towards Miss Dawson.

CASE DISCUSSION QUESTIONS

1. *Identify the issue (or issues) in this case. How should the union address the issues?*
2. *Where does the onus lie in this grievance arbitration?*
3. *Describe the particular principles or doctrines used by arbitrators that might be used by the arbitrator as an aid in reaching a decision in this case. Explain how each would be used.*
4. *As an aribtrator, what additional information or evidence would*

*you consider valuable to assist you in reaching a decision? What
"tools" or outside assistance could you use in the preparation of
your award?*
5. *As an arbitrator, write an award in this case.*

POULTRY PACKING COMPANY CASE

The Poultry Packing Company operates a turkey processing plant in
a small municipality and employs approximately two hundred production and maintenance employees during its peak production
periods. The plant is divided into three parts: the Receiving and
Inspection area, the Processing area, and the Frozen Food Storage area.
The plant operates on a year-round basis, but tends to be seasonal in
the sense that a large volume of birds are processed during the late
summer and fall months in preparation for the consumer demand
which is highest during the Thanksgiving and Christmas/New Year
holiday times.

Staff reductions frequently occur during the spring and winter
months, but employees placed on layoff are normally rehired when
production increases in the late spring. Layoffs seldom affect more than
15 percent of the work force, since much of the plant's output is sold
to commercial food producers for use in institutions or for the production of soup and frozen meal types of consumer products.

The production and maintenance employees are represented by the
Poultry Workers' Union, and work under a collective agreement which
contains the following provisions:

ARTICLE 1   Definitions
(c)   "Regular employee" shall mean any person engaged in the bargaining unit on a full-time basis who has accumulated seniority. All employees
with less than 60 days service shall be deemed probationary employees.

ARTICLE 10.05   Public Holidays
(a)   The Company agrees to pay all regular full-time hourly-rated
employees for eight hours at their current hourly rate whether they work
or not, for each of the following public holidays:

(1)   New Year's Day   (6)   Labour Day
(2)   Good Friday   (7)   Thanksgiving Day
(3)   Victoria Day   (8)   Boxing Day
(4)   Canada Day   (9)   Christmas Day
(5)   Civic Holiday

(b)   Where any of the above designated holidays fall on a Saturday or

Sunday, the holiday shall be deemed to fall on the Monday immediately following.

(c)   An employee shall not be entitled to holiday pay if he or she did not work the last regular work day before and the first regular work day after a designated holiday, or was absent from work on both of the surrounding days. "Absent from work" shall be interpreted for the purpose of this article in the collective agreement to mean absent for any reason other than illness.

ARTICLE 15 Seniority

15.01   (b)   Employees who have acquired regular employee status shall retain their seniority rights, and shall continue to accrue seniority during layoff for the purpose of determining eligibility for vacation and pension benefits, but only actual time worked shall be considered in determining an employee's seniority for the purpose of layoff, recall, and eligibility for job posting, bumping rights, and promotion.

On January 13, 1984, Ann McCance filed a grievance in accordance with the collective agreement which reads:

I was hired by the Company on May 18, 1983, and worked a regular Monday to Friday work week until Friday, December 30, 1983. I was placed on layoff on the completion of my shift on that day, and told to report for work again on Monday, January 9, 1984. I returned to work on that day and worked my full shift. I did not receive holiday pay for New Year's Day as provided in Article 10.05 of the collective agreement.

Redress Requested: Holiday pay for New Year's Day.

On the same date, Albert LaChance also filed a grievance which stated:

I was hired on October 28, 1983, and worked full-time until December 30, 1983, when I was placed on layoff at the end of my shift. I was recalled to work on Monday, January 9, 1984, but I was not paid for New Year's Day.

Redress Requested: Payment for New Year's Day holiday as required in Article 10.05 of the collective agreement.

Another employee, Ethel Aldon, filed a grievance on January 13, 1984, which contained the following information:

I did not receive holiday pay for New Year's Day even though I worked on December 30, 1983, the last day before the holiday, and January 3, 1984, the first work day after the holiday. I have been employed by the company since April 5, 1981, as a full-time employee and I am entitled to the paid holiday.

Redress Required: Holiday pay for New Year's Day.

Beatrice Quan, an employee who had worked for the company for several years submitted the following grievance on January 16, 1984 which reads:

> I was ill on December 30, 1983 and unable to work. I submitted a medical certificate to the Personnel Office on January 4, 1984, the day that I returned to work. I was not paid for the New Year's Day holiday.
>
> *Redress Requested*: Payment for New Year's Day.

D. Bennett, the Personnel Manager, received the four grievances and investigated each in relation to the collective agreement and the employee's file. She determined that the facts as stated in the McCance and LaChance grievances were accurate, but in the Aldon grievance, the employee had left work at 12:30 p.m. and did not complete the remainder of the shift that day. Her excuse to the foreman was that she had a headache and decided to go home. Several of the employees who worked with her stated to the foreman later in the afternoon that Aldon had told them that she was leaving immediately after work for a ski holiday and had wished that she could leave early to have more time to pack her luggage.

The personnel manager also examined the medical certificate in the file of Beatrice Quan which read:

> "Beatrice Quan was examined by me at my office today, and I diagnosed her illness as a mild case of influenza. With prescribed medication Beatrice should be well enough to return to work within a day or two."

The certificate was signed by a qualified medical practitioner, and dated December 30, 1983.

On January 17, 1984, within the time required for a reply under the collective agreement, Miss Bennett prepared answers to each grievance. Her written responses maintained that the employer had not violated the collective agreement, and that in each case the employee was not entitled to holiday pay for New Year's Day.

The grievances were processed through the grievance procedure by the union, and when no settlement could be reached, the union decided to refer all four to arbitration.

CASE DISCUSSION QUESTIONS

1. *From the information available in this case on what basis did the personnel manager decide to reject each grievance?*

2. *How should the union prepare for arbitration on each grievance?*
3. *What theories or principles might be applicable?*
4. *How would an arbitrator likely decide each of the grievances? Render a decision on each, with reasons for your award.*

PART VI

PUBLIC SECTOR
LABOUR RELATIONS

CHAPTER ELEVEN

COLLECTIVE BARGAINING IN THE PUBLIC SECTOR

INTRODUCTION

The public sector, which consists of the various levels of government and their agencies and organizations, is largely supported by the tax revenues collected from the public-at-large. Employees engaged in public sector work would include the employees of the three levels of government: the federal, provincial, and municipal levels, and those employed by the various agencies, boards, commissions, and organizations that depend upon government financial support in order to operate. The many employee groups, in addition to those employed directly by a level of government, include teachers, hospital employees, some bridge and ferry boat employees, and the employees of many Crown agencies and boards, such as liquor store employees.

At the present time, the public sector represents about one-fifth of the nation's work force. These employees were not always represented by unions or associations, however, as collective bargaining in the public sector is a relatively recent phenomenon. Apart from Saskatchewan (a province that permitted collective bargaining by government employees under its *Trade Union Act* in 1944), broad, enabling legislation did not appear on the Canadian labour relations scene in other jurisdictions until the decade of the 1960s. Prior to that time, in some provinces, groups of employees in parts of the public sector were granted collective bargaining rights, but in general, the process of expanding collective bargaining to the public sector began with the Quebec *Labour Code* of 1964.[1] The major overhaul of the legislation in that year incorporated in the Code certain bargaining rights that had been previously granted in a limited way to a number of employee groups in the public sector. Outside of Quebec and Saskatchewan, the major change in public sector collective bargaining followed three years later when the federal government introduced the *Public Service Staff Relations Act*,[2] a statute that permitted the 165,000 employees of the federal government and its agencies to bargain collectively. In the years that followed, the remaining provinces made provision for public sector bargaining to varying degrees. At the present time, the rights of public sector employees may range from the right to bargain collectively over only a narrow range of issues without stoppage of work, to full collective bargaining rights including the right to engage in lawful strike activity. Even where employees have been granted broad bargaining rights and the right to take strike action, certain essential public service employees such as firefighters and hospital employees are usually limited in their right to strike. Under the federal legislation and that of several provinces, employees engaged in many safety-related activities (such as air traffic controllers) may also be "designated" and their right to strike denied.[3]

The reluctance to grant full collective bargaining rights to all public sector employees (apart from the safety and security reservations) is founded in part on the concept of Crown prerogative and the supremacy of Parliament. In theory, the Crown is not bound by any legislation that it may pass, since it has the power to repeal or amend such laws at its pleasure. For example, some time ago, just before the Post Office became a Crown corporation, postal employees engaged in a lawful strike. When attempts at resolving the dispute using ordinary collective bargaining methods appeared unlikely, Parliament passed legislation which ordered the striking employees to return to work. It did so as an exercise of its prerogative to override the collective bargaining legislation. Today, however, the right of government to exercise its rights (except in cases of security or safety with regard to the public interest) is to some extent fettered. In a number of cases, the courts have ruled that the Crown (and its agencies) may not extricate themselves from collective agreement rights on any whim or fancy, but must honour their duties and obligations in much the same fashion as any other employer.[4]

In recognition of the need to maintain certain essential public services without interruption, most provinces and the federal government have developed a number of different approaches to the resolution of collective bargaining differences and to balance the right of employees to bargain collectively with the duty of government to protect the public interest. Where a government has decided that specific employee groups are not engaged in essential, safety, or security-related activities, the right to strike is sometimes permitted by the legislation.

However, where the employees do work in safety- or security-related activities, the right to strike may be denied, and instead, interest arbitration substituted. Hospital employees in Ontario, for example,[5] are granted the right to bargain collectively, but if the employees cannot reach a collective agreement with their employer, unresolved issues are settled by a board of arbitration which decides the issues, and completes the agreement. Police and full-time firefighters in most jurisdictions are usually subject to compulsory arbitration of a similar nature in view of the essential service aspect of their employment.

Less essential public sector employees, where a withdrawal of their services would not affect the security or safety of the public, may be given optional collective bargaining tracks to follow rather than limit them to a strike or lock-out when negotiations break down. The methods range from the conciliation and mediation process familiar to employers and employees in the private sector, to fact finding, final offer selection, and forms of interest arbitration that tend to be found only in the public sector area.

The need for different approaches to dispute resolution in public sector bargaining is due, in part, to the nature of the bargaining itself. In the public sector, the employer is not constrained by the competitive forces that the market place imposes on the ability of the private sector employer to meet the wage demands of the employees. Since the employer in the public sector uses taxation as a means of producing the necessary revenues to operate the public service, the "ability to pay" argument of private sector employers (until the present time at least) has not been applicable. The power to tax, apart from political considerations, is unlimited, and the ability to meet the wage demands of the public service employee is theoretically possible regardless of the amount demanded. In practice, there are, of course, limits on what public sector employers are willing to pay, but this is quite a different matter, and largely dependent upon what the employer perceives as being a fair wage in the eyes of the electorate.

Apart from wage bargaining, collective bargaining in the public sector has been characterized by the negotiation of cost-related benefits and job security provisions not unlike those in the private sector. The collective agreements however, tend to reflect the realities of work in the public sector where the impact of economic recession is seldom as severe. The organization for collective bargaining and the negotiation process, nevertheless, does differ from private sector bargaining, and varies as well from province to province. Of the employees directly employed by these governments, the federal government public sector collective bargaining legislation is most important, and typical of the direction that this type of legislation may develop in the future. Since employees who work for the federal or provincial public service, together with teachers and hospital workers, represent the largest of the various groups of public sector employees, the public sector legislation under which each of these groups bargain may serve to illustrate the nature and policies that relate to the public sector bargaining in general.

THE FEDERAL PUBLIC SERVICE

Collective bargaining in the federal public service and in many of the federal Crown agencies is governed by the *Public Service Staff Relations Act*,[6] a statute which was passed in 1967, providing collective bargaining rights to the employees of the federal government throughout Canada. As is the case with collective bargaining legislation for the private sector, not all employees are entitled to bargain collectively under this Act, but unlike the legislation which pertains to the private sector, a great many employees who would normally be classified as management are entitled to collective bargaining rights under the *Public Service Staff Relations Act*.

The decision to examine collective bargaining rights for public service employees at the federal level was made in 1963, a year after the United States federal government granted collective bargaining on a limited basis to employees in its public service. In 1963, a committee under the chairmanship of Mr. A. D. Heeney, a former Canadian Ambassador to Washington, was set up to study the feasibility of granting collective bargaining rights to the public service, and in 1965, when the report was tabled by the government, the decision was made to prepare appropriate legislation.

Public service collective bargaining, unlike that of the private sector, represented a complex problem. In 1965, the federal public service consisted of over 165,000 persons employed in an enormous number of different occupations and job classifications. The 138,000 employees who fell under the *Civil Service Act* represented 1,700 different grades, and approximately 700 classes. In addition, some 27,000 employees covered by other legislation were employed under 1,385 other job titles. The committee also determined that the public servants in these various positions were paid according to hundreds of different pay scales, many of them unique, and based upon local factors.[7]

Such a diverse body of employees very clearly could not be organized according to the patterns established in the private sector, and the committee decided that an appropriate approach might be to divide the employees into broad groups with skills similar to those in the private sector, and in a sense, allow organization along the lines of something not unlike that of the private sector craft bargaining units. The result was the classification of employees into five general occupational categories under the *Public Service Staff Relations Act*. These five **occupational categories**, which were described as (1) operational, (2) administrative support, (3) administrative and foreign service, (4) technical, and (5) scientific and professional, were further subdivided into seventy-two **occupational groups** with twelve groups in the operational category, six in administrative support, thirteen in administrative and foreign service, thirteen in the technical, and twenty-eight in the scientific and professional category.[8]

Under the legislation, the Public Service Staff Relations Board was given the authority to define "appropriate" bargaining units, subject to the limitations imposed by the employee occupational groups. During an initial period it could certify as an appropriate unit all of the employees in an occupational group, but where a group included supervisory employees, the Board had the discretion to split the group into two separate units, one consisting of the nonsupervisory employees, and the other, the supervisory employees.[9]

In view of the fact that the introduction of collective bargaining powers to the public service was largely a move into the unknown, a two-year "initial certification period" was adopted, during which time the types of bargaining units were as noted. Thereafter, the Board would have somewhat greater latitude in the determination of the appropriate bargaining unit. The initial directive, then, generally restricted organization to occupational groups, rather than any other broader form of organization.

In determining the appropriate bargaining unit, the Board was obliged to take into account the occupational category of the employees as well. Under the Act, it was not permitted to include in a bargaining unit any employee whose duties or responsibilities did not relate exclusively to the occupational category to which the other employees belonged.[10] The employees, consequently, had to be appropriate in the sense that they belonged to not only the occupational group, but the occupational category in which the group fell in order to be eligible for collective bargaining. Employees who had responsibilities in other than the occupational category in question were not entitled to be included in the bargaining unit.

As with collective bargaining legislation relating to the private sector, the powers granted to the Public Service Staff Relations Board included the right to certify and to decertify bargaining representatives of the various employee units. Applications for certification under the Act, then as now, are permitted by either a single organization[11] or council of organizations.[12] The application may be made at any time where the employees are not already represented, or during an "open season" (the last two months) of the operation of any collective agreement if the agreement is for a term of less than two years. For longer-term agreements, and those with automatic renewal clauses, the open season for displacement of an incumbent organization would be the twenty-third and twenty-fourth months, and the last two months of each year that the agreement runs beyond the two years, and during its last two months of operation.[13]

Only certified organizations are permitted under the Act to represent bargaining units of employees, and the procedure for certification follows a procedure that resembles to some extent the process for the private sector. The organization makes an application for certification to the Board, which then determines the appropriate bargaining unit of employees. It then proceeds to satisfy itself that the organization has the support of the majority of the employees in the unit.[14] Majority support is determined by an examination of membership records of the organization, or by holding a representation vote. The constitution of the organization may also be examined to determine the "appropriateness" of the organization as well.[15] With regard to this last activity, the Board must be assured that the organization is not employer-dominated or influenced, and that it is not an organization that supports or is supported financially by any political party.[16] Certification would also be prohibited if there is evidence of discrimination against any employee on the basis of race, creed, colour, sex, religion, or national origin.[17]

An organization that is certified by the Public Service Staff Relations Board becomes the exclusive bargaining representative of the employees in the bargaining unit, and may bargain collectively on their behalf.

The negotiation of the collective agreement bears some similarity to the process followed in the private sector but with a number of notable differences. The subject matter of the collective bargaining in the federal public service is generally limited to hours of work, wage rates, leaves of absence, disciplinary rules and procedures, and other matters related to the terms and conditions of employment. However, a number of relatively important aspects of the employment relationship are excluded. Hiring or appointment practices and procedures, and the promotion, layoff, transfer, and discharge ("release") of employees are not open to negotiation, and represent rights that fall within the exclusive jurisdiction of the employer.

Another important difference relates to dispute resolution. In the negotiation process, under the *Public Service Staff Relations Act*, a bargaining agent must specify at the outset the manner by which it intends to resolve disputes,[18] and will be bound to follow the method chosen until such time as the Board, on application, changes the method.[19] Any change made becomes effective at the commencement of the negotiations for the next collective agreement.[20] The choice open is limited to two alternatives: compulsory arbitration of unresolved issues, or the conciliation/strike process. While the choice of methods is open to the bargaining representative, bargaining units which consist of large numbers of "designated employees" (employees who perform essential services of a safety or security nature) have very little choice but to opt for arbitration, since the strike vote would leave the unit with very little strength in the event that a withdrawal of services becomes necessary. Nevertheless, the choice is, in theory at least, open to all bargaining representatives.

Following certification and the selection of a dispute resolution procedure, the certified organization is in a position to give the employer (who in most cases is represented by the Treasury Board)[21] written notice to bargain. The employer is required to meet with the bargaining agent within twenty days after receipt of the notice, and must bargain in good faith with a view to making a collective agreement.[22] Negotiations then follow the typical bargaining pattern until either an agreement is concluded, or the negotiations reach an impasse. If the parties cannot reach an agreement, then the previously chosen dispute resolution process is requested.

Where the conciliation/strike route is selected by the bargaining agent, either party may apply for conciliation.[23] Provision is made under the Act for the appointment of a conciliation officer to assist the parties in their negotiations, and in this respect the process is similar to that of the private sector. The conciliation officer meets with the parties and assists them with their problems, but if he or she is unable to bring the parties together on an agreement the Board is so advised, and the conciliation board procedure then becomes operable.[24]

Where the Chairman of the Public Service Staff Relations Board agrees with the request for the appointment of a conciliation board, it is then appointed, but not until after a determination has been made concerning "designated employees" in the bargaining unit.

The designation process usually takes place at an early point in the negotiations. The employer is obliged to furnish the Board and the bargaining agent with a list of designated employees (or classes of employees) on receipt of the notice to bargain. If the list is unacceptable to the bargaining agent, an objection to the employer's selection may be lodged with the Board, which then holds a hearing to listen to the objections. After the hearing, it determines the designated employees and advises the parties in writing.[25] Thereafter, a conciliation board may be established.

Conciliation boards are comprised of three members, and on notice from the Public Service Staff Relations Board, each of the two parties must nominate a member within seven days. The two nominees then must select a chairman within a further five days. Any failure to appoint a member would result in the appointment of a person to fill the vacancy by the Chairman of the Public Service Staff Relations Board.[26] Once established, the conciliation board is free to establish its own procedure, but must hold a hearing to permit both sides of the dispute to present evidence and make representations concerning their position on the issues in dispute. A report must normally be made to the Public Service Staff Relations Board within fourteen days after the conciliation board is given the terms of reference concerning the dispute. The report need not be unanimous, but where the findings are not, the decision or recommendations of the majority constitute the report. As noted earlier, the report must not deal with any matter concerning the hiring, promotion, transfer, demotion, layoff or release of employees, as these matters lie outside the sphere of bargaining.[27]

An unusual variation of the process provides that the parties may agree in writing that they will be bound by the recommendations in the report on its release, and if they should do so, the report will in effect conclude their agreement. In most cases, however, the parties are unwilling to take such a risk, and await the report and its recommendations. In the latter case, if the recommendations fail to provide a common ground for settlement, the bargaining agent is free to proceed with strike action at any time after seven days.[28] Designated employees are not permitted to strike, however, and must remain at work regardless of the action taken by others in the bargaining unit.

The alternative to the conciliation/strike procedure is arbitration. Under the Act, the Public Service Staff Relations Board is required to establish two panels that contain at least three persons each, with one panel being representative of the interests of the employer, and the second panel being repesentative of the interests of the employees.[29]

Where a bargaining agent has indicated that it intends to follow the arbitration route, when the negotiations fail to produce an agreement, a request for arbitration may be made to the Board. The request must include a list of the matters to be dealt with by arbitration, and the applicant's position on each issue in dispute. The Board will then promptly notify the other party to the dispute, which is then expected to reply with its proposals concerning the award within seven days of receipt of the notice.[30] The arbitration board members are then selected from their respective panels, and these two persons, together with a member of the Public Service Staff Relations Board constitute the board of arbitration.

The board of arbitration must hold a hearing to allow the parties to present evidence and argument, and then render a decision that takes into consideration a number of "guidelines" or factors. For example, in making an award the board must consider the needs of the public service to retain qualified employees, the wages, benefits and working conditions of persons engaged in similar activities in the private sector, geographic and other differences, grade and occupational differences in the public service, and the need to maintain fair and reasonable conditions of employment.[31] It is also free to take into consideration any other relevant factors. Again, the award is limited to those matters which fall within the subject matter permitted.

The award must be in writing, and where the members are not unanimous in the findings and decision, the decision of the majority constitutes the award of the board. It is binding upon the employer, the bargaining agent, and the employees, and remains in effect for the term of any agreement reached previously or as the board deems relevant.[32] The award may deal with matters such as wage or salary rates on a retroactive basis, but may not refer back beyond the point where notice to bargain was given for the negotiation of a new agreement.

ADJUDICATION
The adjudication process in the public sector under the *Public Service Staff Relations Act* is the equivalent of the rights arbitration process in the private sector under provincial labour relations legislation. The

process is referred to as "adjudication" rather than "arbitration" in order to avoid confusion with the interest arbitration provided in the negotiation process. Consequently, it is important to note the distinction that the Act makes between the two processes, even though the process itself resembles the ordinary grievance resolution procedures found in private sector collective agreements. There are a number of differences, however, both in the procedure and the jurisdiction of the board of adjudication to deal with grievances.

Unlike the private sector, where the collective agreement sets out the arbitration procedure applicable to the parties and the bargaining unit, the *Public Service Staff Relations Act* provides that the board may specify the procedure which the parties must follow for the adjudication of grievances. The Act also permits the board to provide a grievance procedure which will apply in all cases where the parties have not provided a procedure in their collective agreement.[33] At the present time the Regulations under the Act specify that the grievance procedure shall consist of not more than four levels, and provides the documentation and time limits for each level in the process.[34] Where the parties are unable to resolve the grievance in the course of this process, the matter may then be referred to adjudication.

The Act provides for a hearing to be held before a single adjudicator or a board of adjudication. As an alternative, the parties may name an adjudicator in their collective agreement, in which case the person so named would hear the grievance. If no adjudicator is named, an application may be made to the Public Service Staff Relations Board to have a board of adjudication established. The board would consist of three persons, one from each party and a third member selected by the Public Service Staff Relations Board.[35] After the hearing of the grievance, the adjudicator or board of adjudication renders an award that is final and binding on the parties and the grievor.

SPECIAL DUTIES AND POWERS OF THE PUBLIC SERVICE STAFF RELATIONS BOARD

In addition to the authority to certify bargaining agents and generally administer the conciliation, arbitration, and adjudication processes applicable to public service collective bargaining, the Board also is empowered to perform many other duties not unlike those of a typical labour relations board. For example, it may deal with decertification proceedings, successor rights matters, unlawful strikes, and consent to prosecute where alleged violations of the Act occur. It is important to note, however, that due to the nature of the public service and the position of the employer, the Board is much more active in the bargaining and administrative process than the ordinary provincial labour relations board. This role may be typified by the control exercised over the selection of chairman on the various boards of conciliation, arbitration, and adjudication, as well as the authority to amend, alter, and vary arbitral awards,[36] and preside over the implementation of the decisions of adjudicators.[37] To this extent the Public Service Staff Relations Board plays a much greater part in the federal public service collective bargaining than do boards which are concerned primarily with the private sector. The Act, nevertheless, has worked reasonably well since its introduction in 1967, and apart from a major overhaul in 1974–75, has been subject to very little change in the period of time that has transpired since. Provinces which have used the *Public Service Staff Relations Act* as a model for their provincial public service collective bargaining legislation have also found the procedures and practices established at the federal level an effective method of regulating the process as well.

PROVINCIAL PUBLIC SERVICE COLLECTIVE BARGAINING

Public employees at the provincial level include employees of the provincial governments, provincial government Crown agencies and boards. Collective bargaining rights tend to vary substantially from province to province with regard to these employee groups, and it is difficult to establish any general pattern of organization under the circumstances. As noted earlier, the Province of Saskatchewan has included Crown employees under its *Trade Union Act* since 1944, and was the first province to permit collective bargaining by public sector employees. Since that time, collective bargaining rights have been granted to employees of the various provincial governments and Crown agencies, but often only to a limited degree.

The Province of Quebec permits collective bargaining by its public service under its *Labour Code*,[37] but excludes certain groups of public employees,[39] while other provinces such as Nova Scotia,[40] and Prince Edward Island[41] permit collective bargaining by employees of Crown agencies and boards under their general collective bargaining legislation, but exclude employees appointed by their Civil Service Commission. In the case of Prince Edward Island, the designation of the employee group remains discretionary, and permission may be withheld by the Lieutenant Governor in Council.[42] Alberta, Manitoba, Ontario, New Brunswick, and most other provinces have enacted special legislation applicable to collective bargaining by public service employees at the provincial government level, but did not do so until it became apparent that the federal government was preparing to move in that direction. The process, nevertheless, was not immediate, but something which took place over a number of years.

Many of the provincial statutes that were introduced set up special machinery to permit collective bargaining and to provide some means of dispute resolution, but the governments in most cases established their own unique legislative framework. Of all of the provinces, New Brunswick's legislation[43] most reflects the influence of the federal government's *Public Service Staff Relations Act*. Others were undoubtedly influenced by the federal legislation as well, and many of the features of the Act have been incorporated in modified form in the provincial statutes since its introduction in 1967. Surprisingly, provincial Crown employees were among the last to acquire collective bargaining rights, as many other public employee groups were granted the right to bargain collectively under either general or special legislation during the period before the federal government and the provinces passed enabling legislation. In many provinces, for example, municipal employees were granted collective bargaining rights long before the rights were available for exercise by the employees of the provincial governments.

At the provincial level, considerable variation exists with respect to the mechanism established to determine the appropriate bargaining units for collective bargaining, and for the determination of the "appropriate" union to represent them. In a number of provinces (Manitoba, Nova Scotia, Prince Edward Island, and Ontario), the bargaining agent is identified in the legislation, but in other provinces any organization that meets the qualifications of a bargaining agent could apply for certification. In Quebec for example, the public service employees are currently represented by six different unions, including several which are C.N.T.U. affiliates.

Much variation also exists with respect to the size and composition of the provincial bargaining units. The Province of New Brunswick adopted the federal government classification of categories and occupational groups, while other provinces established a less complex system of bargaining units. Alberta, for example, placed all of its public service in a single bargaining unit, while Ontario provided for seven major groups with separate units for a number of its boards and commissions. Nova Scotia divided its public service into eight separate units.

A number of provinces (for example, Newfoundland and British Columbia) use their provincial labour relations boards to certify public sector unions, but most use a special tribunal for this purpose. The criteria for certification which the legislation imposes also varies substantially, and only seven provinces[44] require the applicant to show initial membership support at the time of its application. Even here, it is subject to considerable variation, ranging from a low of 25 percent in Saskatchewan to over 50 percent in Alberta and Newfoundland. Voting procedures to determine majority support also vary, with the majority in some provinces determined on the basis of the bargaining unit (Alberta, New Brunswick and Newfoundland) and in others, on the basis of the votes cast (British Columbia, Quebec, Saskatchewan and Ontario).

Collective bargaining by provincial government employees also varies substantially from province to province. Saskatchewan has treated its public sector employees in the same manner as any private sector employee group, and permits the employees to strike if negotiations and third party assistance fails to produce a collective agreement. Newfoundland, British Columbia, New Brunswick and Quebec grant public sector employees (with certain exceptions) the right to strike, but either impose a number of restrictions on the right, or require certain procedures to be followed before the strike may take place. The remaining provinces do not permit strikes by employees in their public service, but impose compulsory arbitration as the method of collective agreement settlement. However, certain public employees in Nova Scotia who bargain under the general provincial collective bargaining legislation, do have the right to strike.

Dispute resolution while a collective agreement is in effect tends to follow the general pattern of the private sector with a few differences. Except for Saskatchewan and Manitoba,[45] the legislation provides some form of grievance procedure and settlement by binding arbitration, and in a number of provinces, special grievance settlement boards[46] may deal with employee grievances of a discharge or disciplinary nature notwithstanding any procedure set out in the collective agreement.

MUNICIPAL EMPLOYEE COLLECTIVE BARGAINING

Municipal employees, with the exception of full-time firefighters and police officers are permitted to bargain collectively under the same labour relations legislation that governs the private sector, and may strike if collective bargaining fails to produce an agreement. In most provinces, full-time firefighters, police officers and hospital workers are subject to special collective bargaining legislation which prohibits or limits the right to strike, but permits collective bargaining. For these employee groups, compulsory arbitration or some other method of dispute resolution is required when the bargaining fails. Ontario, for example, has separate legislation dealing with collective bargaining by full-time firefighters, members of police forces, and teachers. Hospital workers are permitted to bargain collectively under the general *Labour Relations Act* of the province, but are subject to special legislation which substitutes interest arbitration for the right to strike when the parties cannot reach an agreement.[47]

The general trend in collective bargaining in most provinces (with a few exceptions) has been to broaden the application of collective bargaining legislation to include all public employees at the municipal level, and to impose only minimal restrictions on those groups employed in public safety and security occupations. Even in these areas, the limitation has usually taken the form of a prohibition on the use of the strike, although surprisingly, police officers in some provinces have the right to do so if negotiations with their employer fail to produce an agreement.[48]

COLLECTIVE BARGAINING BY EMPLOYEES IN SAFETY- OR SECURITY-RELATED OCCUPATIONS

The right to bargain collectively is not available to members of Canada's armed forces, although some civilian employees of the government engaged in defence-related nonmilitary positions are entitled to do so.[49] The Royal Canadian Mounted Police also does not fall under the *Public Service Staff Relations Act*, but bargaining by this group takes place under separate legislation which prohibits strike action by members of the force.[50] The R.C.M.P. acts as a provincial police force in all provinces except Quebec and Ontario, and in these two provinces, police officers have collective bargaining rights but are subject to a special legislative exception which substitutes arbitration for the right to strike. At the municipal level, police officers are generally subject to a similar restriction, and in only a few provinces do they have the right to engage in strike activity if negotiations fail.

Full-time firefighters at all levels of government tend to be treated as employees who must always be available for duty, since their work by its very nature is concerned with "emergencies" and the public safety. At the federal and provincial levels they are found under the designated groups who are denied the right to strike, and at the local government level they may bargain collectively, but frequently under separate legislation which prohibits strikes. Volunteer firefighters who form the most common type of firefighting organizations in rural areas are not covered by collective bargaining legislation since their status as employees only arises while they are actively engaged in fighting fires, and usually then only to bring them under the municipal umbrella insurance or Worker's Compensation Act protection in the case of injury.

Hospital employees represent the remaining large group of employees whose work is of a public safety or security nature. The right of hospital employees to bargain collectively, and in particular, the right to strike, is subject to much variation across Canada. This is due for the most part to the fact that hospital "employers" may be governments, public or private boards, corporations, or religious organizations. Government-owned hospitals generally fall under the collective bargaining legislation applicable to government employees in general, subject perhaps to a restriction on the right of employees to strike either by "designation" or the substitution of special dispute resolution machinery. Municipally owned hospitals or publicly owned hospitals, operated under a board appointed at the local level are usually subject to the general collective bargaining legislation, but in some provinces, such as Ontario, control is exercised over the right to strike in all hospitals regardless of their nature or the type of employer.

The Ontario legislation[51] applies to all hospitals, nursing homes, homes for the aged, sanitaria and sanitoria, whether publicly or privately owned, and whether or not in receipt of public funds. The Act provides that where the parties are unable to make a collective agreement, the employees are not permitted to strike, and the employers are not permitted to lock-out their employees. Instead, the parties are obliged to follow the dispute resolution procedure provided in the statute.

Under the Act, if the parties are unable to resolve their differences with the assistance of a conciliation officer, and if any existing collective agreement has expired, they must notify the Minister of Labour, and the Minister will then implement the required interest arbitration procedure. The parties may either mutually select a single arbitrator, or the Minister will establish a three-person board to hear the issues in dispute. If the board approach is selected, then each party nominates a member of the board, (usually within seven days) and the two members so chosen must select a third person (who becomes the chairman) within a further ten days. Once established, the chairman then proceeds to arrange for a hearing of the issues upon which the parties have been unable to agree. At the hearing, the board is free to determine its own procedures, but it is obliged to give both parties a full opportunity to present their evidence and proposals to the board.

At the conclusion of the hearing, the board will discuss the submissions of the employer and the bargaining representative in an executive session, and formulate an award. The award will represent a decision on each of the matters brought before the board, and the decision of the board concludes the collective agreement for the parties. The parties will then be bound by the agreement for the term which either they have fixed, or which is determined by the Act.

Persons employed in education also represent a special case. Teachers at both the elementary and secondary school levels constitute a significant number of the employees who work in the public sector, and while their particular role may not be considered a safety- or security-related activity, without question they perform an essential public service function. As a consequence, collective bargaining by the teaching profession in a number of provinces has been viewed in a similar fashion to that of hospital workers or persons engaged in important public sector activity. In many cases, these groups are also brought under special legislation for collective bargaining purposes.

Education is a provincial matter, and as a result, labour relations as it relates to teachers falls within the exclusive jurisdiction of each individual province. The legislative response to collective bargaining by members of the profession consequently has varied from province to province to a remarkable degree. The province of Saskatchewan,[52] for example, permitted collective bargaining by teachers under its general collective bargaining legislation in 1944, while a few provinces did not respond until very recently to the need for a framework within which collective bargaining by teachers could take place. This is not to say that collective bargaining or something which resembled collective negotiations did not take place in most provinces before the enabling legislation was passed. Teachers in most provinces have engaged in informal negotiation with their employers for many years. Teachers in Ontario, for example, had a relatively long history of informal bargaining when the province finally enacted legislation to formalize many of the procedures which the parties had carried on informally for many years.

Fundamentally, collective bargaining rights for teachers are the same in all provinces, but the levels at which negotiations take place and the dispute resolution aspects of the legislation may differ substantially. Ontario, for example,[53] provides a different track for teachers to follow when compared to the typical private sector negotiations, and the right to strike, while available, may only be exercised after an elaborate third party intervention process has been exhausted. The Ontario legislation is unique as well in the variety of different forms of dispute resolution processes which may be selected if agreement cannot be reached in the normal course of negotiations.

The Ontario legislation applies to all teachers employed by school boards under the province's education legislation, and requires all negotiations to take place in accordance with the Act. Notice to bargain, therefore, is generally given in January of the year in which a collective agreement expires to allow approximately six full months for negotiation, as all collective agreements expire on August 31, and new agreements commence on the day following.[54]

Where notice to bargain has been given, the parties are obliged to meet and bargain in good faith with a view to making a new agreement, but if the bargaining representative of the teachers and the board are unsuccessful in reaching an agreement, the parties may request assistance from the provincial Education Relations Commission. This may take the form of a person appointed to assist the parties (using mediation or concilation techniques) or it may take the form of fact finding.[55] In the latter case, the person appointed as a fact finder meets with the parties and determines the issues which have been settled and the issues which remain unresolved. At the conclusion of the meeting, the fact finder then files a report with the commission in which recommendations for the settlement of the issues in dispute may be made. The parties are expected to consider the report and its recommendations, and continue their efforts to reach an agreement.[56]

As a means of resolving their differences and as alternatives to fact finding (and a strike route), the parties may request voluntary binding arbitration[57], or the appointment of a "selector" to choose between the final offers of the parties.[58] The arbitration process is similar to the interest arbitration process used under the province's *Hospital Labour Disputes Arbitration Act,* but the final offer selection process represents an innovative approach to dispute resolution. A third alternative is also available which combines mediation and arbitration in an informal "med-arb" process. While not expressly provided under the Act, the Commission (if the parties agree) may appoint a mediator to meet with the parties as a prelude to voluntary arbitration, and if the mediator cannot resolve all of the issues, only those which remain outstanding are then settled by arbitration.

The strike or lock-out remains as a weapon of last resort in teacher-board negotiations, and if the voluntary arbitration or final offer selection is not an acceptable alternative to the parties, a lawful strike or lock-out may take place after any existing agreement has expired, but not until the report of the fact finder has been released to the public and fifteen days have elapsed. In addition, the teachers may not strike until after a vote by secret ballot (conducted under the direction of the Education Relations Commission) has been held whereby the teachers may vote for or against the last offer of the board on all matters remaining in dispute, and the offer has been rejected. The Act also imposes a five-day notice period following the vote in favour of the strike, and to comply with the Act, this notice must be in writing and presented to the board by the branch affiliate which represents the teachers.[59] Only then may a lawful strike take place. Lawful lock-outs may not take place until after a strike has been called, and then only after the final offer of the branch affiliate of the teachers is discussed by the board in a public session.[60]

The Ontario legislation represents a response to the needs of the teachers and school boards to have a flexible system that incorporates a number of choices for interest dispute resolution as well as the traditional strike/lock-out remedy.[61] It is perhaps more elaborate in this regard than what applies in other provinces where only the strike or lock-out, and voluntary arbitration is available. It also stands in contrast to the compulsory arbitration approach used for the safety- and security-related essential public services where no choice is available to the parties.

Other provinces have taken a somewhat different approach to collective bargaining by teachers, and established a more centralized procedure for negotiations. In the provinces of Quebec[62] and Saskatchewan[63] for example, a two-tier system of negotiations is employed, with negotiations at the provincial level used to deal with the major issues, and local negotiations used to deal with issues particular to the individual school board and teacher groups. In these provinces, financial matters (such as salary levels and benefits) and the terms and conditions of employment are determined at the provincial level. The parties to the bargaining in the case of Saskatchewan are the Association of School Trustees and the teacher federations, while in Quebec the negotiations take place between the union and the Ministry. The particular advantage of this method of negotiation from the provincial government's point of view is that it is better able to monitor the costs of education by way of the centralized negotiations, an important factor, since it is responsible for a substantial part of the cost of education.

A CONCLUDING WORD

The constitutional make-up of Canada has foreclosed any possibility of establishing an overall labour policy for the country, and rendered impossible the formulation of uniform collective bargaining procedures for all types of employees. This is particularly true of the public sector, where the mix of legislation applicable to this diverse group of employees is reflected in a host of different procedures for each group in each province. Perhaps over time, some trend may develop toward uniform procedures or legislation for public sector collective bargaining in the provinces, but at present, no move in this direction has occurred. A 1983 decision of the Supreme Court of Ontario,[64] however, which has indicated that public sector employees may not be denied the right to strike may have far-reaching implications for governments at both the provincial and federal levels if on appeal to the Supreme Court of Canada the decision is upheld. Should this occur, a major overhaul of all public sector collective bargaining legislation will be necessary to conform with the court interpretation of the constitutional rights of employees. For the present, however, collective bargaining by public sector employees remains subject to a mix of very different procedures for many public sector groups.

REVIEW QUESTIONS

1. *Why was the establishment of bargaining units in the federal public service a difficult task?*
2. *Distinguish between an* **occupational group** *and an* **occupational category** *under the Public Service Staff Relations Act.*
3. *How would the size of the public sector bargaining units affect employer bargaining power?*
4. *Distinguish between an* **arbitrator** *and an* **adjudicator** *under the Public Service Staff Relations Act.*
5. *How does the Federal government differ from an ordinary employer on matters concerning collective bargaining?*
6. *Explain how a "designated employee" differs from an ordinary employee. How does a "designation" affect the collective bargaining rights of the employee?*
7. *Why is the right to strike often denied to employees in safety- or security-related positions in the public sector?*
8. *What role does a fact finder play in public sector collective bargaining?*
9. *Why is interest arbitration frequently compulsory in the public sector? Describe two situations where it represents the only dispute resolution procedure.*
10. *Describe briefly the different methods of collective bargaining by teachers.*

NOTES

---

[1]See *Labour Code*, S. Q. 1964, c. 141, (most public services, however, were still excluded from the *Labour Code*).
[2]*Public Service Staff Relations Act*, R.S.C., 1970 c.P-35.
[3]See for example, *Public Service Staff Relations Act*, R.S.C. 1970 c.P-35 s.79.
[4]See for example, *Nova Scotia Government Employees Association et al. v. Civil Service Commission of Nova Scotia et al.* (1981) 119 D.L.R. (3d) 1.
[5]See, *Hospital Labour Disputes Arbitration Act*, R.S.O. 1980 c. 205.
[6]*Public Service Staff Relations Act*, Stat. Can. 1967 c.72.
[7]Canada, *Report of the Preparatory Committee on Collective Bargaining in The Public Service.* Ottawa, Queen's Printer, 1965.
[8]See *Public Service Staff Relations Act*, R.S.C. 1970 c. P-35 s.2. The occupational "groups" were defined by the Public Service Commission as provided in s.26 of the Act.
[9]See Act, s. 26.
[10]See Act, s. 32.

[11]See Act, s. 27.

[12]*Ibid.*, s. 28.

[13]*Ibid.*, s. 30.

[14]*Ibid.*, s. 34.

[15]*Ibid.*, s. 35.

[16]*Ibid.*, s. 39.

[17]*Ibid.*, s.39(3).

[18]*Ibid.*, s. 36(1).

[19]*Ibid.*, s. 37(2); s. 38.

[20]*Ibid.*, s. 38(3).

[21]Some Crown agencies may be designated to act as the employer for collective bargaining purposes. In 1983, twelve agencies or boards did so. Some examples are: National Film Board, National Research Council of Canada, Atomic Energy Control Board, and the Public Service Staff Relations Board itself.

[22]*Public Service Staff Relations Act*, R.S.C. 1970 c.P-35 s. 50.

[23]*Ibid.*, s. 52, 77.

[24]*Ibid.*, s. 78.

[25]*Ibid.*, s. 79.

[26]*Ibid.*, s. 80.

[27]*Ibid.*, s. 86.

[28]*Ibid.*, s. 101.

[29]*Ibid.*, s. 60.

[30]*Ibid.*, s. 63, 64.

[31]*Ibid.*, s. 68.

[32]*Ibid.*, s. 73.

[33]*Ibid.*, s. 99.

[34]Public Service Staff Relations Act Regulations and Rules of Procedure s. 69-78.

[35]*Public Service Staff Relations Act*, R.S.C. 1970 c.P-35 s. 93.

[36]*Ibid.*, s. 76.

[37]*Ibid.*, s. 96.

[38]*Labour Code* R.S.Q. 1977 c.C-27 s. 1(k).

[39]*Ibid.*, s. 1(3), (4), (5), (6).

[40]*Trade Union Act*, S.N.S. 1972 V.2 P416 (C.S.N.S. c.T-17) s. 3(2).

[41]*Labour Act*, R.S.P.E.I. 1974 c.L-1 s.7(i).

[42]*Ibid.*

[43]*Public Service Labour Relations Act*, R.S.N.B. 1973 c.P-25.

[44]Ontario, British Columbia, Alberta, Saskatchewan, Quebec, New Brunswick, and Newfoundland.

[45]Public sector employees in Saskatchewan fall under the *Trade Union Act*, and disputes may be resolved by "arbitration or otherwise." The Manitoba Act does not mention a grievance procedure.

[46]Ontario, for example provides for a Grievance Settlement Board to hear employee disciplinary grievances. See *Crown Employees Collective Bargaining Act*, R.S.O. 1980 c. 108 s. 18, 19.

[47]*Hospital Labour Disputes Arbitration Act*, R.S.O. 1980, c. 205.

[48]See for example, *Nova Scotia Trade Union Act*, S.N.S. 1972 c. 19 s.1(l)(k)(i).

[49]For example, persons employed by the Defence Research Board.

⁵⁰*Public Service Staff Relations Act*, R.S.C. 1970 c.P-35 s.2(e).
⁵¹*Hospital Labour Disputes Arbitration Act*, R.S.O. 1980 c. 205.
⁵²Saskatchewan originally permitted collective bargaining by teachers under its *Trade Union Act*, in 1944. Special legislation now applies.
⁵³See, *School Boards and Teachers Collective Negotiations Act*, R.S.O. 1980 c. 464.
⁵⁴*Ibid.*, s. 10.
⁵⁵*Ibid.*, s. 12.
⁵⁶*Ibid.*, s. 14-27 (Part III of the Act).
⁵⁷*Ibid7.*, s. 28-36 (Part IV of the Act).
⁵⁸*Ibid.*, s. 37-49 (Part V of the Act).
⁵⁹*Ibid.*, s. 63.
⁶⁰*Ibid.*, s. 68.
⁶¹For a more detailed discussion of the collective bargaining in education, See Downie, B. M. *Collective Bargaining and Conflict Resolution in Education*. Kingston, Canada: Queen's University Industrial Relations Centre, 1978.
⁶²See Quebec, *An Act Respecting Management and Union Party Organization in Collective Bargaining in Sectors of Education, Social Affairs and Government Agencies*. R.S.Q. 1982, c.O-7.1 (Chapter II, Division 1).
⁶³See Saskatchewan, *Teachers' Collective Bargaining Act*, R.S.S. 1978 c.T-4, s. 3, 9.
⁶⁴See *Durham Board of Education v. Ontario Secondary School Teachers' Federation and Education Relations Commission*. (Supreme Court of Ontario, October 24, 1983.)

RECOMMENDED REFERENCES AND SOURCE MATERIAL

Barnes, L.W.C.S. and L.A. Kelly. *Interest Arbitration in the Federal Public Service of Canada*. Kingston, Canada: Queen's University Industrial Relations Centre (1976).

Downie, B.M. *Collective Bargaining and Conflict Resolution in Education*. Kingston, Canada: Queen's University Industrial Relations Centre 1978.

Finkelman, J. *The Rationale in Establishing Bargaining Units in the Federal Public Service of Canada*. Kingston, Canada: Queen's University Industrial Relations Centre (1974).

Goldenberg, S.B. *Public Service Bargaining: Implications for White-Collar Unionism*. Kingston, Canada: Queen's University Industrial Relations Centre (1973).

PART VII
THE FUTURE FOR LABOUR RELATIONS IN CANADA

CHAPTER TWELVE

THE FUTURE FOR LABOUR RELATIONS: CHALLENGES AND RESPONSES

INTRODUCTION

The format of the text to this point has been to examine the current state of labour relations in Canada in the light of its historical context. While the past often provides some guidance as to the direction that organizations such as labour unions might take in the future, a more important indicator of the future is represented by the difficulties and problems faced by the participants in labour relations at the present time. On this basis, a brief examination of the collective bargaining environment today is perhaps justified, in the sense that the problems and the possible solutions may well provide some clues as to the track that the participants in collective bargaining might choose to follow into the future.

THE ECONOMIC CHALLENGE

Both industry and organized labour have been seriously affected by the economic downturn since the beginning of the present decade. The combination of high interest rates, shrinking markets due to fierce foreign competition, and rapid technological changes in those industries which in the past have been the highly unionized sectors of the economy have had a significant impact on the labour relations scene, and in many cases on the participants themselves. The period 1981–83 has been characterized by plant closures, mass layoffs, declining union membership in many of the industrial unions, and a final realization of the fact that Canada as a country is a competitor, willing or not, in a world market.

The recession forcefully brought to the foreground the need for Canadian industry to be more productive either through the adoption of more efficient work practices, or through technological change. The union response to these changes has been, in general, an attempt to acquire a greater measure of job security for employees at a time when employers are unable or unwilling to offer any assurance that even the firm itself will survive the difficult times.

Foreign competition has forced many Canadian firms to examine closely their traditional work practices, particularly in the mass production sector of the country's secondary industry. For example, the automobile and agricultural machinery manufacturers in particular were especially hard hit by foreign competition in the period 1980–83 on two fronts: lower labour costs and the use of advanced technology. Immediate changes in production equipment and methods were required to enable the firms to remain viable. The result has been the installation of many new computer controlled "robots" to perform routine assembly line jobs, and optical laser gauging systems to inspect the work done for flaws. The changes, while far from complete, have already produced a dramatic improvement in the quality of the product and the productivity of the employees who have remained on the job, but the changes were not without a cost in terms of manpower. Many of the employees who were engaged in the production line functions and inspection work now performed by automated equipment will unlikely be rehired in the industry, for the jobs which they were capable of doing in the past will no longer be required in the future. This reduction in the work force for the automobile manufacturers was not insignificant, since it represented a reduction of approximately 15 percent in the number of employees required to perform the same amount of work. Similar changes in work practices and technology are already underway in other sectors of industry and commerce, which will result in a decrease in a demand for many of the skills possessed by employees today. On balance, however, the changes will create new demands for special skills compatible with the technology which must be adopted by Canadian industry if it wishes to survive and compete effectively in a world market.

Nor is the impact of change limited to the manufacturing sector. The rapid expansion of computer-based information systems, and the development of the micro processor have spawned an enormous change in work methods and information processing in white collar occupations. While the transition in the office will be equally as profound as in the plant, it will perhaps be less traumatic and devastating for the office worker. A computer, fortunately, bears some resemblance to its predecessor, the typewriter, but this similarity notwithstanding, the nature of the work and the numbers required to process it will likely change as the skill requirements change.

Office employment and persons engaged in commercial establishments that are information related will likely feel the full impact of the desk-top computer and computerized data banks before the end of the decade, with many of the traditional office roles disappearing long before that time. The decade will likely see a shift of many skills from clerical personnel to management, and perhaps a shrinking of the middle management level as well, as managers communicate directly with each other using their computerized information network and typing skills formerly possessed by only those in the secretarial pool. One of the major impacts which this change will have on the office clearly will be a reduced need for letter writing as it is known today, and much less work for employees engaged in stationery-related positions within firms.

While the advent of second generation automation will undoubtedly have a negative impact on employees who lack the skills required for the work place of the future and upon those who are not prepared to broaden their skills to meet the needs of the new technology, the new technology itself will probably create employment opportunities for those trained to manufacture, use and maintain it. The many new firms established to produce and service the new technology are ample evidence of the change already underway. The advent of the new technology and its effect on the work place is now beginning to be more readily understood, and both employers and unions must examine the implications of these changes in terms of their own existence and role, and the effect that it will have on the collective bargaining relationship. The responses of both the employers and the unions to these challenges will have a profound effect on the direction of labour relations in the decade ahead.

THE EMPLOYER AND UNION RESPONSES
The need for Canadian business organizations to embrace technological change and streamline production methods became painfully evident by 1980, and in some cases the survival of the firm was only possible through a massive reorganization of the entire production process at an enormously expensive cost in terms of both capital and employee sacrifice. At the bargaining table the need for change was reflected in employer demands for an end to automatic wage increases, and the elimination of unproductive practices for the

employees who managed to retain jobs after the crisis.

Apart from increased efforts by employers to remove unproductive practices and to limit increases in labour costs to increased productivity, employers have also recognized the need to maintain a work force with skills compatible with changing technology. Large firms, notably General Motors and Ford in the automotive field, have established joint programs with their unions for the retraining of employees who possess obsolete skills. These training programs have a twofold purpose: to provide employees retained on the job with the required skills to use or service new technology as it is introduced, and to train redundant employees for work elsewhere in industry. How successful these programs and others like them will be is unclear at the present time, but given the recognition by employers and unions that change will be a characteristic of this decade, the need for continuous retraining and upgrading of skills will probably find more widespread acceptance as an alternative to termination, and in itself become a form of job security. For those employees too old to retrain, early retirement with improved pension benefits may prove to be the route that employers might follow to provide job openings and opportunities for younger, more productive employees. The cost of early retirement, however, will undoubtedly represent a thorny issue at the bargaining table for some years to come.

For many employers, automated assembly lines and manufacturing processes will result in a smaller, more highly skilled work force. The nature of work, however, will perhaps increase the need for a more harmonious relationship between the employer and the employees in order to maintain an efficient operation, and this in turn might result in a greater effort on the part of the employer to remain sensitive to the needs of employees to insure uninterrupted production. How employers react to the highly competitive, constantly changing world market place, and how these competitive pressures affect each employer will undoubtedly be reflected in the collective bargaining itself.

The economic recession of 1980–83 also had an enormous, negative impact on the trade union movement, particularly in the primary industry and manufacturing sectors. Many firms failed to survive the recession, with a resultant loss of membership for the unions, and while these were predominantly blue collar bargaining units, white collar employees were also affected, and so too, were the unions that represented them. Among the firms that managed to survive the recession, reorganization of production methods and equipment in many cases substantially reduced the number of employees recalled to work, leaving the bargaining units much smaller than in the past. The overall effect of these changes has been reduced membership in those unions which had previously represented large segments of predominantly blue collar industry. While these losses have been offset by increased organization in the public sector and white collar areas of the private sector, the loss of blue collar membership by unions will undoubtedly have an effect on the union movement itself in the future.

Within the union movement the shift in membership may produce a shift in power within the federations, from private sector to public sector unions, and perhaps a change in direction at the policy-making level. A consequence of this shift may be a greater emphasis on policy matters of concern to the predominantly white collar public sector unions rather than those of the representatives of blue collar workers. This in turn might result in a further fragmentation of organized labour if private sector blue collar unions should feel a need for a federation of their own.

On the individual union level, membership losses may result in union mergers, as the weaker unions find themselves unable to provide adequate levels of service to their membership. However, mergers of unions are complex matters that are seldom achieved with any degree of success unless the leadership of each see genuine benefits flowing from such a change. For one thing, the political aspirations of the leaders of unions from the local level to the international level often prove an insurmountable obstacle unless all parties can be accommodated satisfactorily within the new organization. For another, the sentiments of the membership often dictate an independent path, no matter how rational the arguments for merger might be. Whether these obstacles can be overcome in those organizations where merger represents a viable solution for survival of the organizations as effective bargaining agents will depend in no small part on the ability of the leadership to adapt to the changing collective bargaining climate of the future.

In some cases, industrial unions are already faced with the problems that others have been spared for the present. The automobile industry, as noted earlier, experienced the painful transformation from a labour intensive production line operation to a more capital intensive, computer- and machine-oriented facility, characterized by the use of robotics and optical laser inspection systems. In the United States, the change not only substantially altered the skill requirements of the automobile companies in many work areas, but left about 115,000 of the 780,000 previously employed auto workers without employment.

Employee concern for job security not only in the automobile industry, but in primary industry, secondary manufacturing and many other parts of both the private and public sector will undoubtedly pose a problem for many unions at the bargaining table. Many of the old solutions for unemployment, such as shorter work weeks, longer vacations, restrictive work practices, and generous layoff benefits no longer represent viable bargaining positions for unions to take where employers are obliged to compete against foreign competition with lower wage costs, more efficient production equipment, and the resultant greater productivity. The challenge faced by the unions in the future will be to develop or suggest ways and means of improving productivity that will also provide job security or protection for the employees who perform the work.

Solutions have been suggested for some of the problems raised by technological change and unemployment, such as work sharing, flexible jobs, flexible work hours, profit sharing and greater employee participation in decision making in the production process. None of these are likely to prove viable in terms of job security unless they can be demonstrated to have a positive effect on productivity as well.

The collective bargaining process, being a resilient vehicle for the resolution of difficult problems will no doubt be tested throughout the decade of the 1980s as unions and employers seek to resolve the thorny problem of maintaining the firm as a competitive organization in a rapidly changing world market place, yet satisfying the security needs of the employees. The challenge will essentially be to develop an employment relationship that will provide greater flexibility for the employer in terms of manpower and technological change, stimulate productivity, and at the same time provide worker security and retraining, preferably within the firm itself. There are no easy solutions to these problems, and very clearly the solutions cannot simply be legislated by governments as they frequently have been in the past. What will be required is a realization on the part of employers, employees, and unions that all parties have a common interest in the well-being of the firm, and that perhaps the best method to satisfy the needs of all concerned is the negotiation process. How well the parties succeed in dealing with these issues will be determined by their ability as negotiators at the bargaining table to develop innovative solutions to their common problems. In due course, historians will assess their efforts, and that of the system itself.

GLOSSARY

arbitration: a procedure for the final and binding settlement of disputes arising out of the interpretation, application, or alleged violation of a collective agreement using the services of a third party neutral or board to hear the dispute and render a decision.

bargain in good faith: a statutory obligation imposed on unions and employers in some jurisdictions whereby each party must make a genuine or honest attempt to reach an agreement.

bargaining agent: a union that is either certified by a labour relations board or voluntarily recognized by an employer as the exclusive bargaining representative of a unit of employees for collective bargaining purposes.

bargaining unit: a unit of employees that a labour relations board determines to be appropriate for collective bargaining purposes.

benefit seniority: entitlement to benefits (such as vacation time, etc.) based upon the length of service of an employee.

black list: a practice conducted by employers in the past whereby union organizers and supporters were identified to other employers. The practice is now unlawful.

blameworthy absenteeism: unauthorized absence from work where the failure to report or attend at the work place was a decision that fell within the control of the employee.

blue sky bargaining: an unrealistic demand made during the course of collective bargaining negotiations.

bumping rights: the right of a more senior employee to displace another employee with less seniority in a particular job or position when the more senior employee's position is eliminated either temporarily as a result of lack of work, or on a permanent basis.

cease and desist order: a court order directed to specified individuals ordering them to cease doing certain specific acts.

certification: a procedure under labour legislation whereby a labour union may acquire the exclusive right to represent a defined unit of employees for the purpose of collective bargaining.

certiorari: a prerogative writ which a court may issue following a judicial review of an arbitration hearing. The writ quashes the award of the arbitrator or board, rendering it a nullity.

closed shop clause: a union security clause in a collective agreement which requires the employer to hire only persons who are members of the incumbent union.

collective agreement: a written agreement made between an employer and the bargaining representative of a unit of employees that sets out the terms and conditions of employment and the rights and duties of the employer, the union, and the employees.

company-dominated union: an independent union that is supported or dominated by the employer of the employees which the union represents or seeks to represent.

company union: a *bona fide* independent union that represents the employees of a single employer.

competitive status seniority: the entitlement of one employee over another to a job or benefit based upon the relative seniority of each employee.

compulsory membership check-off clause: a clause in a collective agreement that requires the employer to deduct union dues from the wages of all union members and forward the sums deducted to the union. A form of union security.

conciliation: see mediation and conciliation.

convention: a meeting of trade union delegates from local unions usually held bi-annually at the national or international level for the purpose of establishing union policy or dealing with union matters. Labour federations also hold conventions for a similar reason.

craft union: an association or union with membership based upon a particular craft or skill, and which organizes and represents employees who possess the particular skill.

craft unit: a bargaining unit of employees organized on the basis of the the craft or skill possessed by the employees.

departmental seniority: a seniority system used to determine the layoff or recall rights of employees based upon the employees' length of service in a particular department. Under this system the employee with the least seniority in the department would be first to be placed on layoff and the last recalled to work.

dependent contractor: an independent contractor, whose work is so closely controlled by the "employer" that the contractor is essentially an employee. In many jurisdictions dependent contractors are entitled to bargain collectively as a separate bargaining unit.

doctrine of culminating incident: a doctrine which states that the discharge of an employee may be justified on the basis of the employee's past unacceptable behaviour, even though the violation that precipitated the discharge was, in itself, not sufficient to warrant such a harsh penalty.

doctrine of past practice: a labour relations doctrine that suggests that a labour arbitrator or arbitration board is justified in examining the past actions of the parties as a means of determining an appropriate interpretation of a clause in a collective agreement that contains a latent or patent ambiguity.

executive session: a private meeting of a board of arbitration, held after a hearing of the issues in dispute for the purpose of discussion of the evidence and argument.

final offer selection: a dispute resolution procedure where a collective agreement is finalized by a third party who selects without modification either the final offer of the employer or the union to be the offer that will be inserted in the agreement.

functus officio: a legal doctrine which when applied to the arbitration process provides that an arbitrator's authority ends when the award is released.

grandfather shop clause: see modified union shop clause.

grievance procedure: a dispute resolution procedure set out in a collective agreement which the parties follow in an attempt to resolve disputes or grievances that arise out of the agreement. A grievance procedure precedes arbitration.

hot cargo: a derisive term coined by trade unionists for goods made in a struck plant or made by non-union employees. The term is used to identify the goods as material that other unionists should not handle.

industrial union: a labour union that organizes the employees of an employer whether unskilled or skilled, without concern for craft or occupation.

injunction: an order issued by a court that directs the persons named to cease the activity identified in the order.

innocent absenteeism: unauthorized absence from work due to circumstances beyond the control of the employee, such as illness or injury.

interest arbitration boards: a board of arbitration that hears the bargaining issues in dispute, then makes an award which finalizes the collective agreement between the union and the employer. A dispute resolution method used in place of the strike or lock-out in the public sector.

job posting: a method of filling job vacancies whereby the employer posts a notice of the job in a prominent location to bring the notice of the vacancy to the attention of all qualified employees who may wish to apply for the position.

job seniority: entitlement to a particular job based upon an employee's length of service in the job or group of similar jobs. Usually the greater the length of service, the greater the entitlement to the job.

labour relations board: a board established under the labour legislation of a jurisdiction to supervise or administer the legislation, and to carry out various duties assigned to it under the law.

latent ambiguity: ambiguous wording in a clause in a collective agreement which permits several different interpretations to be drawn from the words used.

lieu day: the entitlement to a paid holiday on a regular work day as a result of the employee working on a statutory holiday.

lock-out: a refusal by an employer to allow employees to work if agreement on the terms and conditions of employment cannot be reached by the employer and union.

maintenance of membership clause: a union security clause which may be included in a collective agreement which requires all employees who were members of the union at the time of execution of the agreement to remain members of the union until the collective agreement expires.

majority rule: in a labour relations context, the principle that the wishes of the majority should prevail in determining whether a group of employees should bargain collectively with their employer through a bargaining representative.

mandamus: a prerogative writ which a court may issue ordering the person named in the writ (usually a public servant) to perform those duties which he or she is required to perform.

mass picketing: a large number of persons who assemble at an employer's place of business to show support for a strike. See also **picket line**.

mediation or conciliation: a process whereby a neutral third party attempts to resolve a labour dispute by assisting the parties in their negotiations.

modified union shop clause: a union shop clause that exempts from union membership requirements all employees hired before a date specified in the collective agreement. The clause usually provides that any exempt employee who voluntarily joins the union must remain a member.

open season: a period of time during the term of operation of a collective agreement when a union may attempt to displace an incumbent union as the bargaining representative of the employees or when the employees may wish to cease collective bargaining. Usually a two-month period during the third year of operation of a long-term agreement.

package deal: a bargaining proposal whereby a lump sum of money and a number of unresolved money-related issues are included together in an offer made at the bargaining table, with the responsibility for the allocation of the money to each particular issue left in the hands of the recipient of the offer.

patent ambiguity: ambiguous wording in a collective agreement where the clause makes no sense due to missing words or terms.

picket line: a group of employees who assemble at the employer's place of business for the purpose of informing the public of the labour dispute that exists between the employer and the employees, and for the purpose of encouraging others to support the employees in their dispute.

progressive or constructive discipline: a discipline system based upon the premise that employees will eventually change unacceptable behaviour patterns if subjected to increasingly more severe discipline each time an offence is committed. The normal pattern consists of a verbal warning for the first violation, a written reprimand for the second, a suspension for the third, and finally, discharge for the fourth violation.

prohibition: a prerogative writ that may be issued by a court prohibiting the person named therein from doing any act set out in the writ.

proposal: an offer made at the bargaining table as a solution to a problem.

Rand formula clause: a form of compulsory check off of union dues whereby the employer agrees to deduct from the wages of all employees in the bargaining unit (whether union members or not) union dues, and to pay the money to the union.

recall rights: the right of an employee under the terms of a collective agreement to be called back to work following a layoff (either temporary or permanent).

recognition clause: a clause in a collective agreement whereby the employer recognizes the union as the exclusive bargaining representative of a defined unit of employees covered by the agreement.

residual rights theory: a theory of management rights which states that an employer retains all rights of management except those expressly limited or altered by the collective agreement. Also known as the "reserved rights theory."

secondary picketing: the picketing of the premises of a person or business not directly related to a labour dispute.

selector: a person appointed to decide between the final offers of the employer and union, and to select only one of the two for the purpose of making a collective agreement. See also **final offer selection.**

shop steward: a union official who is usually selected by the employees in a particular department of the work place to carry out specific union duties on their behalf.

status quo theory: a theory of management's rights which states that an employer's rights to manage are limited to those set out in the collective agreement and the practices conducted at the time the agreement is entered into. Any change in work practices must therefore be negotiated if the right to change is not set out in the agreement.

strike: a cessation or refusal to work by employees. In some jurisdictions a strike would also include any concerted effort to restrict output.

successor union: a union that obtains the right to represent a unit of employees following a merger of unions.

super seniority: special status granted to union officers or officials which permits them to be retained on the job and not subject to layoff on the basis of their actual length of service. Persons with super seniority are usually the last employees terminated in the event of a contraction of the work force.

surrounding day clause: a clause in a collective agreement that requires an employee to work on specified days preceding and following a holiday in order to receive pay for the holiday in question.

tag end unit: a small group of employees not represented by a union in a plant or office where most of the other employees are part of bargaining units represented by unions.

trading horse: a demand made at the bargaining table by either the union or the employer for the purpose of trade at a later time of some other demand.

union shop clause: a union security clause in a collective agreement which permits the employer to freely hire new employees, but which requires all employees to join and remain members of the union during the term of their employment.

union: a voluntary association of employees organized for the purpose of improving their working conditions, wages, and benefits through collective bargaining with their employer.

voluntary check-off: a clause in a collective agreement which permits employees on a voluntary basis to authorize their employer to deduct their union dues from their wages and submit the money to the union.

watching and besetting: a criminal offence. In a labour relations context it would include activity by strikers designed to intimidate or injure persons who attempt to cross a picket line.

wildcat strike: a spontaneous cessation or stoppage of work by employees which is not authorized by the union. A wildcat strike which takes place while a collective agreement is in effect is an unlawful strike.

yellow dog contract: an employment contract which contains a promise by the employee not to join a union or engage in any strike activity against the employer. The practice is now unlawful under labour legislation.

INDEX